RUSSIA IN REVOLUTION

S. A. Smith is a historian of modern Russia and China and was educated at both Moscow State University and at Peking University. He has published on the Russian and Chinese revolutions, including *Red Petrograd: Revolution in the Factories, 1917–18* (1983), and *Revolution and the People in Russia and China: A Comparative History* (2008), and is editor of *The Oxford Handbook of the History of Communism* (OUP, 2014). He taught for many years at the University of Essex, where he is a Honorary Professor, and then at the European University Institute in Florence, before being elected to a senior research fellowship at All Souls College, Oxford, in 2012.

PRAISE FOR *RUSSIA IN REVOLUTION*

'In what is the most assured general history yet to appear, Smith uses his deep knowledge of twentieth-century Russia to place the upheavals in their larger social and historical contexts.'

Tony Barber, *Financial Times*

'S. A. Smith's majestic book sets the overthrow of Tsar Nicholas and the Bolshevik revolution in context [. . . and] skilfully reconstructs the cultural and socio-economic context of 1917.'

Geoffrey Roberts, *The Irish Times*

'This is a sweeping, dazzling, and incisive new look at the Russian Revolution by a master historian. Readable and probing, comprehensive in its scope, informed by the most recent scholarship, and with an eye on the big questions, this will surely become the new standard by which histories of the revolution are judged.'

Diana P. Koenker, University of Illinois at Urbana-Champaign

'Easily digestible . . . It is one of *Russia in Revolution's* merits that the author lays out the scope of contending interpretations and leaves it to his readers to make up their own minds.'

Robert Service, *Times Literary Supplement*

'Fluently written and convincingly argued.'

Saul David, *Evening Standard*

'S. A. Smith's authoritative *Russia in Revolution* treats Russia's revolutionary crisis in a "longish time frame". It is an excellent decision. . . . Historians of Russia, as well as anyone interested in twentieth-century history, will benefit from this excellent book.'

Peter Holquist, University of Pennsylvania

'Among the best one-volume introductions to not only the history of the revolution, but also of late tsarism, the Civil War (1918–21), and the years of the New Economic Policy.'

Mark Edele, *Australian Book Review*

'A well-proportioned and skilfully condensed panorama of the revolutionary situation in the Russian empire and its aftermath, covering nearly 40 years.'

Roland Elliot-Brown, *The Spectator*

'A master historian of the Russian Revolution, S. A. Smith has wrestled the events and personalities, policies, and mass politics of the years 1890 to 1928 into a coherent and compelling story of the entrance of ordinary people onto the stage of history and the brutal, violent descent of Russia into dictatorship. . . . Smith explains better than anyone else how a revolution marked by radical democracy and hope for social justice sacrificed many of its ideals to win and hold power and inspire an international movement against capitalism and imperialism.'

Ronald Grigor Suny, Distinguished University Professor of History and Political Science, University of Michigan

'Smith's *Russia in Revolution* is an authoritative view of a seismic event, but also much more. By covering nearly thirty years from 1890, he illuminates what Franco Venturi called the roots of revolution, profiling the creation of a revolutionary generation as well as the fall-out . . . it far transcends the limitations of a 'general history.' Above all it shows, impartially and decisively, both why the revolution failed to deliver its promises, and why it happened in the first place.'

Roy Foster, University of Oxford

S. A. SMITH

RUSSIA IN REVOLUTION

An Empire in Crisis, 1890 to 1928

OXFORD
UNIVERSITY PRESS

OXFORD
UNIVERSITY PRESS

Great Clarendon Street, Oxford, OX2 6DP,
United Kingdom

Oxford University Press is a department of the University of Oxford. It furthers the University's objective of excellence in research, scholarship, and education by publishing worldwide. Oxford is a registered trade mark of Oxford University Press in the UK and in certain other countries

First published 2017
First published in paperback 2018

Published in the United States of America by Oxford University Press
198 Madison Avenue, New York, NY 10016, United States of America

British Library Cataloguing in Publication Data
Data available

Library of Congress Cataloging in Publication Data
Data available

ISBN 978–0–19–873482–6 (Hbk.)
ISBN 978–0–19–873483–3 (Pbk.)

Printed and bound by CPI Group (UK) Ltd,
Croydon, CR0 4YY

ACKNOWLEDGEMENTS

The book has been much improved as a result of detailed comments by Nicholas Stargardt and Chris Ward, both of whom read the whole manuscript, and by David Priestland and Ian Thatcher who read crucial sections. I also benefited from conversation with Erik Landis. I thank all of them warmly. None bears any responsibility for any errors that remain. I would like to thank the Warden and Fellows of All Souls College, Oxford, for the senior research fellowship that allowed me to write the book.

As ever, the book is dedicated to Phil Jakes.

S.A.S.

CONTENTS

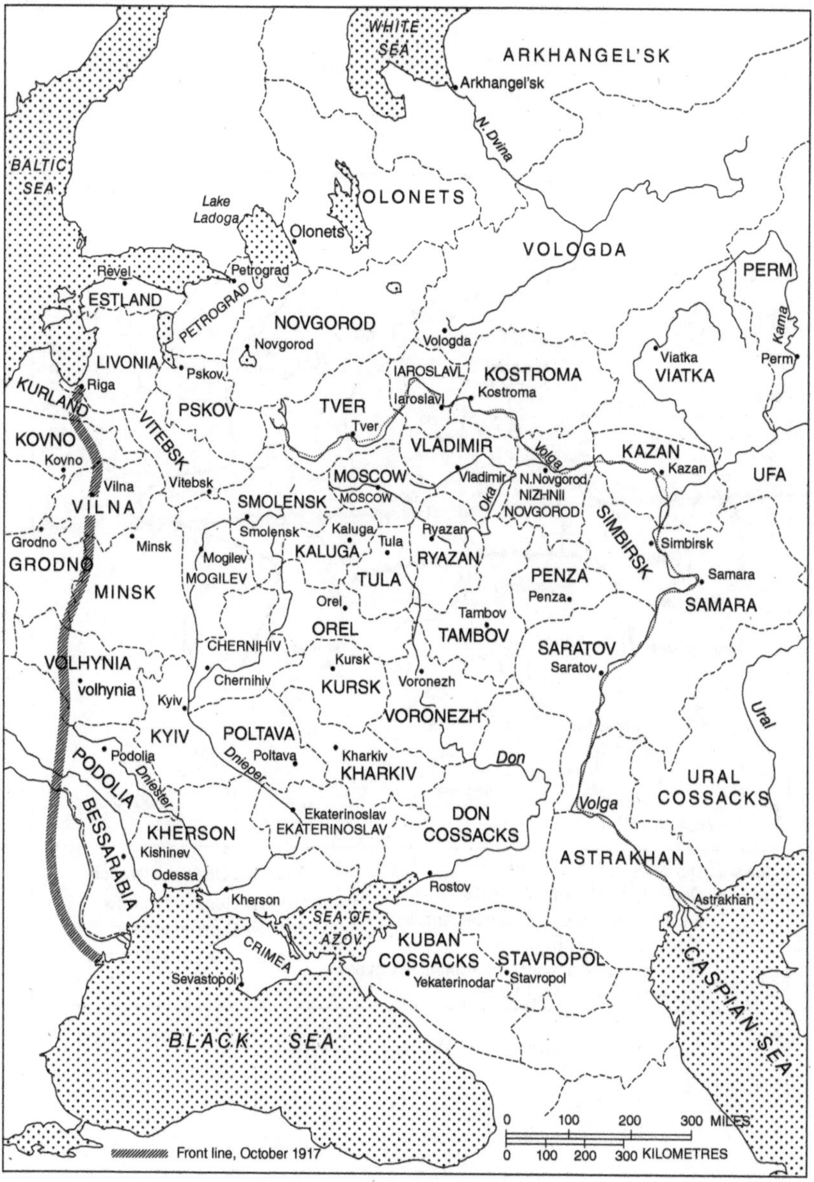

Map 1 European Russia in 1917–18

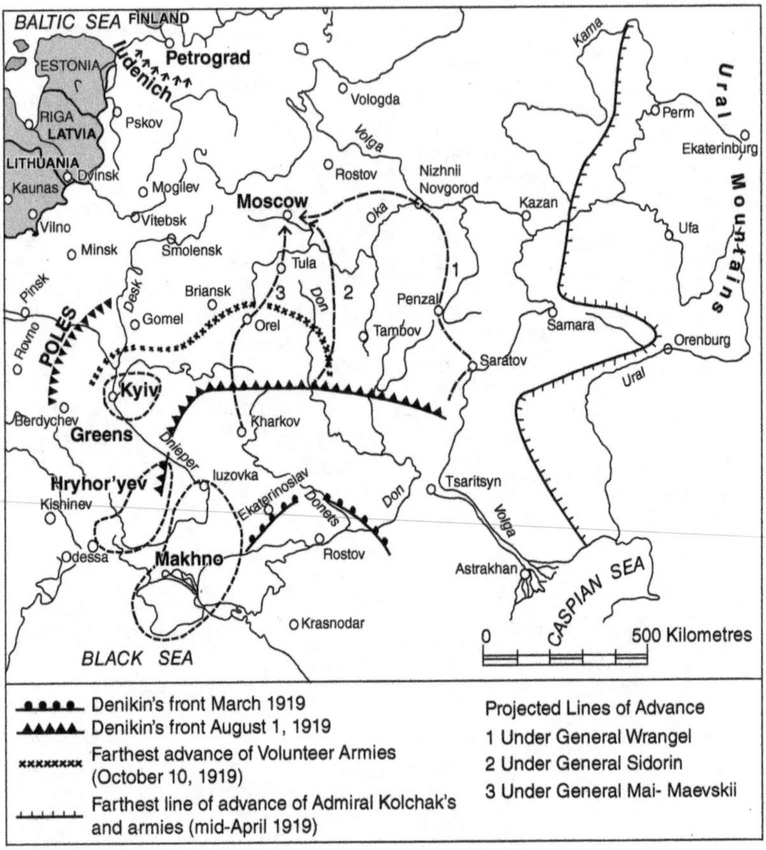

BALTIC SEA
FINLAND
ESTONIA
Iudenich
Petrograd
RIGA
LATVIA
Pskov
LITHUANIA
Dvinsk
Kaunas
Vilno
Mogilev
Vitebsk
Minsk
Smolensk
Vologda
Volga
Rostov
Moscow
Nizhnii Novgorod
Oka
Kazan
Kama
Perm
Ekaterinburg
Ural Mountains
Ufa
Tula
1
2
3
Don
Penza
Briansk
Desk
Pinsk
POLES
Gomel
Orel
Tambov
Samara
Orenburg
Rovno
Saratov
Ural
Kyiv
Berdychev
Kharkov
Greens
Dnieper
Iuzovka
Hryhor'yev
Kishinev
Ekaterinoslav
Donets
Don
Tsaritsyn
Volga
Odessa
Makhno
Rostov
Astrakhan
CASPIAN SEA
Krasnodar
BLACK SEA
0
500 Kilometres
Denikin's front March 1919
Denikin's front August 1, 1919
Farthest advance of Volunteer Armies (October 10, 1919)
Farthest line of advance of Admiral Kolchak's and armies (mid-April 1919)
Projected Lines of Advance
1 Under General Wrangel
2 Under General Sidorin
3 Under General Mai- Maevskii

Map 2 The White Armies in 1919

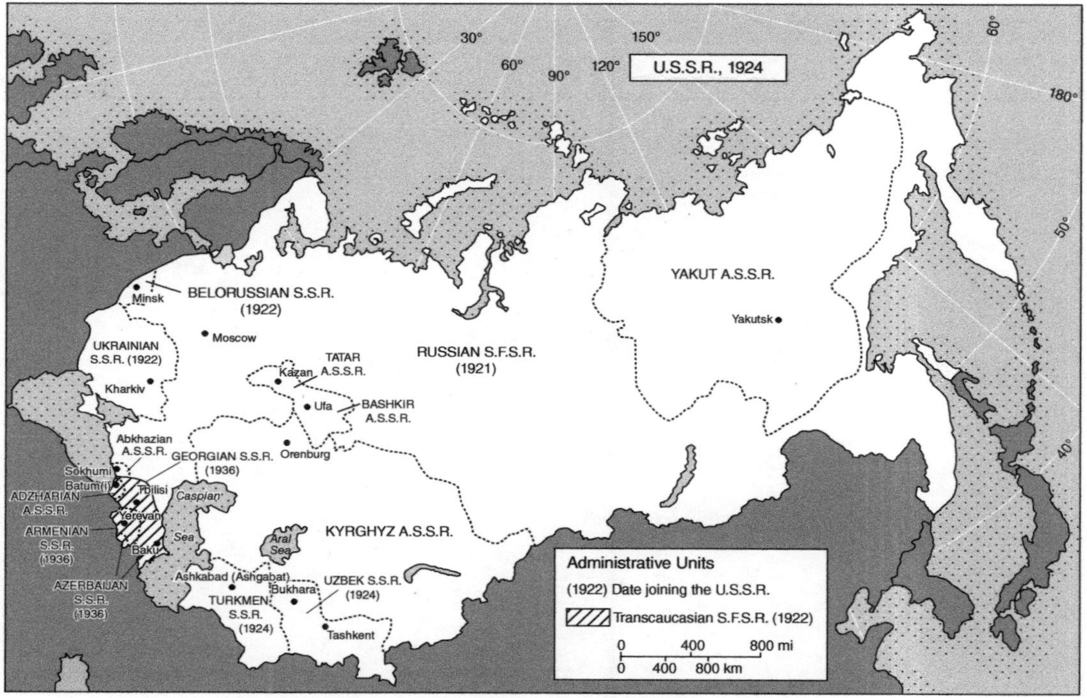

Map 3 The Soviet Union in 1924

INTRODUCTION

> 'The Revolution was a grand thing!' continued Monsieur Pierre, betraying by this desperate and provocative proposition his extreme youth.
> 'What? Revolution and regicide a grand thing?'
> 'I am not speaking of regicide, I am speaking about ideas.'
> 'Yes: ideas of robbery, murder, and regicide', again interjected an ironical voice.
> 'Those were extremes, no doubt, but they are not what is most important. What is important are the rights of man, emancipation from prejudices, and equality of citizenship.'
>
> — Tolstoy, *War and Peace*

As Tolstoy wonderfully captures in the opening scene of his masterpiece *War and Peace,* the historical significance of the French Revolution was bitterly contested throughout the nineteenth century and indeed for most of the twentieth. In 1978 the French historian François Furet boldly declared that the 'French Revolution is Over', a judgement which is questionable, but which made the point that a historical event that once excited lethal passion had ceased to divide contemporary politics or be the object of deep psychological investments. It is doubtful that one can say the same of the Russian Revolution in its centenary anniversary year, even though the regime that it brought into existence has been defunct for more than a quarter of a century. The challenge that the Bolshevik seizure of power in October 1917 posed to global capitalism still reverberates (albeit faintly) and, more pertinently, so does its challenge to the contemporary western conception of politics as a field bounded by ideas of free markets, human rights, and democratic government. Furet observed that writing the history of the French Revolution was not like writing the history of the Frankish invasions of the fifth century: 'What the historian writes about the French

Revolution is assigned a meaning and a label even before he starts working: the writing is taken as his *opinion*, a form of judgement that is not required when dealing with the Merovingians... As soon as the historian states that opinion, the matter is settled; he is labelled a royalist, a liberal or a Jacobin.'[1] Of course, there is no such thing as history writing that is devoid of political resonance: historical interpretation always entails commitments, and history writing is itself part of history and so subject to constant revision. While few today would evaluate the Russian Revolution in the same spirit as Pierre Bezukhov evaluated the French Revolution in *War and Peace*, it is worth reminding ourselves that in 1945 many would have defended the October Revolution in an analogous way, seeing it as giving rise to a state which, despite its faults, had made a massive contribution to the defeat of fascism. So Furet is right to suggest that there are certain historical events and personages that evoke particular passion, where the writing of their history is a peculiarly political enterprise. And the Russian Revolution, one hundred years on, is still such an event. Because of that, I have tried in this book to write as dispassionately as possible about the crisis of the tsarist autocracy, the failure of parliamentary democracy in 1917, and about the Bolshevik rise to power. I have sought to avoid moralizing and to write with sympathy about those to whom I feel some aversion and, conversely, to write critically of those to whom I am more positively disposed. But for the reader who would like to pin a label on me at the outset—and a reader certainly has the right to know where an author stands—I suggest they start with the conclusion.

This book is written primarily for the reader coming new to the subject, although I hope that, as a synthesis of recent research by Russian and western scholars, and as an attempt to question some familiar interpretations, it will have something of interest to say to my academic colleagues. The book offers a comprehensive account of the main events, developments, and personalities in the former Russian empire from the late nineteenth century through to the onset of the First Five-Year Plan and forced collectivization in 1928/9, when Stalin unleashed a 'revolution from above' on the Soviet people. It seeks to answer the big questions that interest school students, undergraduates, and the general reader who enjoys learning about the past. Why did the tsarist autocracy fail? Why did the attempt to establish parliamentary democracy after the February Revolution of 1917 also fail? How did a small extreme socialist party manage to seize power and to sustain itself through a ferocious civil war (1918–21)? How did Stalin rise to power? Why did he unleash brutal collectivization and crash industrialization on the Soviet people at the end of the 1920s? At the most fundamental level the book aims to offer some insight into the nature of power: how the determination to continue to rule in the old way can lead to the collapse of an entire social order or how those seeking to create a better society become corrupted by their determination to hold on to power at any price. These are all hoary issues, but since the fall of the Soviet Union in 1991 a mass of new source-material has become available that sheds much fresh light on the political and social history of this period. Over the past quarter of a century historians in Russia and the West have begun to use this material to reexamine old questions, to raise new ones, and to rethink some entrenched categories. The book seeks to reflect this archivally based scholarship and to give the general reader a sense of how scholarly understanding of the Russian Revolution has changed over recent decades. At the same time, it reflects the fact that the Russian Revolution continues to be a subject on which historians' interpretations differ greatly. Its main purpose, however, is to offer the general reader a wide-ranging account of the collapse of the tsarist autocracy and the rise of a Bolshevik party, but one that pays more attention than was possible prior to 1991 to such matters as the imperial and national dimensions of the Revolution, to the complexity of forces involved in the civil war, to the attempts by moderate socialist and anarchist parties to resist the Bolshevik monopolization of power, to peasant and worker resistance to the Bolshevik regime, to the massive economic privation and suffering wrought by the Revolution, to the conflict between Church and state, and to the economic and social contradictions of the Soviet Union under the New Economic Policy of the 1920s.

Revolutions are about the breakdown of states, the competition between rival contenders for power, and the ultimate reconstitution of a new state power. For that reason, the backbone of the narrative is political, and it ranges back to the time of the Great Reforms of Alexander II in the 1860s and forward into the high Stalinism of the 1930s. The choice of a longish time-frame is motivated by the fact that the book seeks to emphasize some important continuities across the revolutionary divide of 1917. Fundamentally, developments are analysed in terms of the interplay between external pressures (geopolitics and rivalry within the international state system) and internal pressures that derived from the undermining of social hierarchies by rapid economic modernization. Revolutions are not created by revolutionaries, who at most help to erode the legitimacy of the existing regime by suggesting that a better world is possible. So less attention is devoted to the political activities and arguments of revolutionaries prior to 1917 than in some standard histories. As Lenin himself well knew, it is only when the existing order is in deep crisis that revolutionaries can break out of political isolation and seek to mobilize popular forces to bring the old order to its knees. For virtually all the socialist revolutions of the twentieth century, it was not a crisis of the capitalist system, but imperialist war that pushed old orders into crisis, so war figures large in my account.

For shorthand I have referred to 'Russia' up to now, but the book follows recent research in looking at the Revolution in a Eurasian perspective, paying much more attention to Central Asia, the Caucasus, Siberia, and the Far East than would once have been the case. Empire and the rise of nationalism are key themes of the recent historiography of the Revolution that are integrated in this account. The history of the Revolution is set squarely in the context of the disintegration and ultimate reintegration of empire. Fighting for their survival, the Bolsheviks lost control of most areas outside the Russian heartland between 1918 and 1920, including Ukraine, the Caucasus, the Baltic regions, and Central Asia. Eventually, by appealing to nationalism and anti-colonialism, they managed to put the empire back together again—with some exceptions (Poland, Finland, the Baltic littoral, the western parts of Ukraine and Belorussia, and Bessarabia). Although power in Russia was always highly centralized in the capitals—all the major events recounted in this text took place in St Petersburg or in Moscow after the capital moved there in 1918—but recent research on the Russian provinces has brought out how the Revolution was shaped by local ecological, socio-economic, and ethnic structures, and how conflicts in the countryside and provincial towns influenced its outcome. I have tried to give a sense of the diversity of the Revolution by choosing examples from the remote provinces in order to challenge an understanding of the Revolution that is circumscribed by too great a concentration on the events in the capitals. Finally, since the 1970s much of the most innovative work on the history of late-imperial and revolutionary Russia has been done by social and, more recently, cultural historians and this is incorporated into the present account.

Revolutions aspire not only to create a new state but also to overturn and transform social and economic relations. They differ from military coups or seizures of power by dictators and political cabals because the breakdown of state authority is total, and this breakdown opens up a space for mass mobilization. Politics, in other words, is taken out of the hands of elites and functioning institutions and brought into the streets and the fields. The activities and aspirations of peasants, workers, soldiers, non-Russian ethnic groups, women, and young people in toppling the old order and in seeking to make a new one are central to the story this book tells. Millions in 1905 and 1917 organized to oppose oppression and to achieve justice, equality, political rights, and an end to war. A history of revolution must, then, be a history of a whole society in turmoil. So while political events form the backbone of this account, it pays much attention to the economic, social, and cultural changes that shaped political developments and to the ways in which different social groups were activated by and responded to those developments. The peasantry, the great majority of the population, is still too often marginalized in accounts of the Revolution, yet they were its primary agents and victims. They suffered under tsarism, they rose up against the old rural order in 1905 and 1917, they appeared to realize their age-old dream in 1917–18, only to find themselves bearing the main cost of socio-economic modernization. Yet they also displayed a striking capacity to thwart the schemes of governments until Stalin unleashed violent collectivization at the end of the 1920s. A social-historical perspective on the Revolution sets a benchmark against which the actions of reformers and revolutionaries can be judged, allowing us to assess the extent to which they responded to pressing economic and social problems and the adequacy and effectiveness of their responses. Ultimately, it is only by looking at how far the social and economic order was transformed that we can measure the scale of the Revolution, which was highly uneven in its effects.

Finally, in the past quarter of a century there has been an efflorescence of cultural history, and this book seeks to incorporate some of its findings, showing the impact of economic change on ingrained cultural patterns, the critical importance of generational conflict within the Revolution, and the efforts of the Bolsheviks to carry through what they called 'cultural revolution'. As bastard children of the Enlightenment, they understood the Revolution through the lens of civilizational progress, believing in the capacity of science to bring about freedom from scarcity and in the capacity of rational forms of thought and social organization to liberate the 'backward masses' from religion and superstition. The Bolshevik state was the first in history to seek to create an atheist society and their assault on the Church is a project about which we now know much more. The book, therefore, pays attention to the ways radical cultural innovation clashed with the inherited beliefs and dispositions of different groups of the population, especially in the sphere of religion. Paradoxically, the regime would consolidate itself only by compromising with, and even appropriating, beliefs and practices that it initially excoriated.

The centenary of the two revolutions of 1917 occurs at a time when there is little sympathy for revolution in the advanced capitalist or even in the developing world. Talk of 'revolution' has not entirely disappeared, but it is, in the words of Arno Mayer, 'the celebration of essentially bloodless revolutions for human rights, private property, and market capitalism'.[2] One might now add that even revolutions of this kind—the 'colour' revolutions in Ukraine, Eastern Europe, and the Caucasus, or the revolutions of the Arab Spring—have hardly been good copy for those who would effect radical political and social change through mass mobilization and violent means. This has affected the way that historians write about revolutions in the past.[3] In the West historians are more likely to see 1917 as the initiation of a cycle of violence that led to the horrors of Stalinism than as a flawed attempt to create a better world. They are more likely to see the mobilization of peasants, soldiers, and workers as motivated by irrationality and aggression than by outrage at injustice or a yearning to be free. Looked at across the massive growth of capitalism that has taken place in the last hundred years, the October Revolution seems as though it led Russia up a historical cul-de-sac: from capitalism to socialism and back to capitalism again. Looked at from the vantage point of Vladimir Putin's Russia, it may seem as though the Russian Revolution barely made a dent on Russia's political culture. So why study the Russian Revolution a century on? First, because it offered by far the most radical challenge to the existing order up to that time, with the Bolsheviks committed to replacing what they saw as a society based on exploitation, inequality, and war with a classless and stateless society they called communism. If Bolshevik-style communism has little appeal in the twenty-first century, it is too early to conclude that its implications for the future are entirely exhausted. Just as the English Revolution put paid to the principle of divine right of kings and the French Revolution to the idea of an aristocracy of birth, the Russian Revolution's challenge to the idea that there is something natural or inevitable about social hierarchy and socio-economic inequality may yet prove to be its legacy. Capitalism may have seen off state socialism, but it has yet to adapt to that challenge. Secondly, Russia remains a considerable power today and if we are to understand the combination of anxiety and ambition that motivates much Russian foreign policy we need to know its history. The era of state socialism proved to be short if judged in a long-term historical perspective, but the impact of the Soviet Union on the turbulent history of the twentieth century was immense, most obviously in respect of the Second World War and the Cold War. Finally, we *can* learn lessons from history, and there is a great deal to learn from the history of the Russian Revolution about how the thirst for power, the enthusiasm for violence, and contempt for law and ethics can corrupt projects that begin with the finest ideals.

* * *

This is a book intended mainly for the general reader so I have tried to keep endnotes to a minimum, signalling the sources of quotations and statistics, but otherwise lightly referencing the key texts on a particular theme. The endnotes mainly indicate the works on which I have relied, and from which I have benefited, and indicate some of the more specialist literature to the interested reader.

In referring to domestic events, old-style dates are used up to 31 January 1918, when the Bolsheviks introduced the Gregorian calendar. Dates then jumped forward thirteen days to 14 February 1918, bringing the Russian calendar into line with that of the modern world. However, international events are dated according to the Gregorian calendar (mainly in relation to the First World War). Most Russian names have been transliterated according to the revised Library of Congress system, except for well-known names such as Witte, Zinoviev, or Trotsky. All Russian measurements have been converted into metric units.

1

ROOTS OF REVOLUTION, 1880s–1905

The collapse of the tsarist regime in February 1917 was ultimately rooted in a systemic crisis brought about by economic and social modernization, a crisis that was massively exacerbated by the First World War.[1] From the 1860s, and especially from the 1890s, the autocracy strove to keep its place among the major European powers by industrializing the country and by modernizing its armed forces, even though it knew that economic change would release social forces that threatened political stability. Time, however, was not on its side. From the late nineteenth century the major industrial powers—Germany, the USA, Britain, and France—were rapidly expanding their geopolitical and economic might, threatening to reduce Russia to second-rate status. As Russia's extremely backward society underwent brisk economic, social, and cultural change, new social and political forces were unleashed that eroded the social base of the autocracy. Industrialization, urbanization, and rural to urban migration gave rise to new social classes, notably industrial workers, commercial and industrial capitalists, and the professional middle classes, which did not fit into the traditional system of social estates that was dominated by the landed nobility. These emerging social classes demanded that the autocracy treat them as citizens, not as subjects, by granting them civil and political rights. It was these demands, raised in the context of a war with Japan, that led to the outbreak of a massive social and political revolution in 1905. In that year a liberal movement based in the middle classes, a militant labour movement, and a colossal peasant movement against the landed gentry, built up such momentum that Nicholas II was compelled to concede significant political reform in the October Manifesto. Once order was restored, however, the tsar reneged on his promise of a constitutional monarchy.

Anticipating the next chapter, we may note that the years between 1907 and 1914, sometimes called the 'Years of Reaction', were characterized by a stalemate between the new parliament, known as the duma, and the government, and a retreat from political reform. At the same time, the regime came under fire from groups that had traditionally been its social support, namely, the nobility and the Orthodox Church. However, these same years also saw the growth of a civil society, evident in the expansion of the press, the proliferation of voluntary societies, and in a new consumer culture. So despite the dampening of hopes for political reform, there were reasons to think that in the years up to 1914 Russia might be moving away from revolution, as the countryside quietened, as industry revived after 1910, and as Russia's armed forces were strengthened. The international environment, however, was menacing, and the problems of managing a multinational empire were becoming increasingly acute. If the First World War had not broken out in July 1914, it is possible that the gulf between the common people and the privileged classes, and between the duma and the government, might gradually have been bridged. But the war put paid to any such hopes. The demands of 'total war' strained the industrial and agrarian economies and widened the gap between the common people and the privileged classes. It was the combination of utter frustration with the tsar on the part of political elites together with mounting dissatisfaction with food shortages and the burdens of war on the part of the common people that would trigger the February Revolution and bring about the overthrow of the 300-year-old Romanov dynasty.

The great nineteenth-century historian Vasilii Kliuchevskii once remarked that the fundamental characteristic of Russia's history was colonization on a boundless and inhospitable plain.[2] Lacking natural frontiers, Russia's landlocked plains, backward economy, and poverty-stricken peasantry made it vulnerable to invasion, as the Poles demonstrated in the seventeenth century, the Swedes in the eighteenth, and the French in the nineteenth. Each invasion was repelled, but at ever greater cost in terms of mobilizing human and material resources, with the result that an ever more powerful and imperial autocratic state was forged. While Russian colonists moved through the steppe and tundra as far as the Pacific, the dynastic-autocratic state steadily expanded south into Ukraine and the Caucasus, while to the north victory over Sweden led to the incorporation of the Baltic territories. In the course of the nineteenth century Poland and Central Asia were also swallowed up. Into the middle of the nineteenth century, with few resources, the autocracy managed to rule its unwieldy continental empire largely by co-opting non-Russian elites, but the imperial ambition of the rising European powers during the last quarter of the nineteenth century, impelled by the grab for territory, raw material, and markets, and underpinned by heavy industry, railways, steamships, and telegraphs, threatened Russia's borderlands and put immense strain on traditional techniques of imperial rule. Britain, Germany, France, Austria-Hungary, and Russia strove through alliances to maintain the fiction of a balance of power, but great-power relations in the decade up to 1914 became 'an inherently risky game that included significant elements of bluff and gambling and…that largely revolved around calculations about the power of rivals and their willingness and ability to back up their claims with force'.[3]

After defeating Napoleon in 1812, Russia had enjoyed international pre-eminence in Europe, but this was shattered by the Crimean War (1853–6) when France and Britain intervened on the side of the Ottoman empire to thwart Russia's expansion into the Mediterranean. Following the Treaty of Paris, which denied Russia the right to a navy or land fortifications on the Black Sea, Grand Duke Konstantin Nikolaevich, second son of Nicholas I, reflected: 'We cannot deceive ourselves any longer. We are both weaker and poorer than the first-class powers, and furthermore poorer not only in material resources but also in mental resources, especially in matters of administration.'[4] Defeat, however, precipitated the launch of a far-reaching programme of reforms under Alexander II (1855–81), the most significant of which was the abolition of serfdom in 1861. This was supplemented by judicial reforms, which included establishing justices of the peace and limited trial by jury, along with military reforms, which included the introduction of universal conscription, the overhaul of military administration, and the setting up of cadet—*junker*—schools. Crucially important was the establishment of local government institutions known as 'zemstvos' and municipal dumas in the towns. Had these reforms been carried forward, the chances of revolution in 1905 would have been much diminished. But in 1881 Alexander was assassinated by a member of the terrorist People's Will organization, and his son, Alexander III, reversed the liberalizing drive of his father.

The reforms of Alexander II had done little to stem Russia's declining fortunes in the international arena. Following the severe defeat of Turkey in the war of 1877–8, Russia's gains in the Black Sea and on the Bulgarian and Caucasus fronts were whittled down by the Congress of Berlin in 1878 when Chancellor Otto von Bismarck reduced the territory of independent Bulgaria, created with Russian help, and granted Austria-Hungary, Russia's chief rival for influence in the Balkans, the right to administer the Ottoman provinces of Bosnia and Herzegovina. These concessions enraged pan-Slav opinion in Russia, which clamoured to seize Constantinople, former bastion of Orthodox Christianity, and control of the straits between the Black Sea and the Dardanelles. Bismarck's orchestration of the Congress underlined the threat now posed to Russian expansion by a recently unified and economically powerful Germany. Russia's continuing concern about the threat posed by Germany led in 1894 to the alliance with France, which stipulated that if one of the parties in the rival Triple Alliance (comprising Germany, Austria-Hungary, and Italy) should attack France or Russia, the other would go its defence. France would remain Russia's principal ally down to 1917, providing her with extensive financial and military assistance in the interim.

When war came, however, it came not from the west but from the east. On 8 February 1904 the Japanese navy launched a surprise attack on the Russian fleet moored outside Port Arthur in Manchuria. From the 1850s Russia had been steadily encroaching on the territory of China, as the Qing dynasty declined; the founding of Vladivostok in 1860 was a sign of Russia's intention to establish its hegemony in the Far East, something that the British viewed with alarm. Japan, which had embarked on its own course of modernization at roughly the same time as Russia under Alexander II, had made great strides in industrialization and in creating a national conscript army and a centralized bureaucracy, and increasingly it looked for raw materials, markets, and prestige to Korea and Manchuria. In 1891 Finance Minister Sergei Witte, with the backing of the future tsar, Nicholas II, inaugurated the construction of the Trans-Siberian railway, partly as a means to encourage resettlement of peasants from the overcrowded black-earth provinces of central Russia and partly to consolidate Russian control of the Far East. Following China's defeat by Japan in the war of 1894–5, Russia pressured the Qing government to allow it to build the Chinese Eastern railway as a shortcut for the Trans-Siberian railway through northern inner Manchuria via Harbin to Vladivostok. In 1898, Russia began to build a southern spur of the railway from Harbin through the Liaodong peninsula to the warm-water naval base that it had begun to create at Lüshun, known as Port Arthur. Russia's expansion into Manchuria coincided with Japan's seizure of Korea, following its victory in the Sino-Japanese war, and brought the two imperial powers into conflict. In 1898 the Naval Ministry demanded 200 million rubles on top of its annual budget of almost 60 million (the budget of the Ministry of Agriculture was just 40.7 million rubles in 1900) in order to ensure the superiority of its Pacific Fleet over the Japanese navy.[5] But the Japanese did not intend idly to stand by. In February 1904 they attacked Port Arthur, eventually forcing the Russians to send another fleet to China which, after an epic 18,000-mile voyage, was obliterated at the Battle of Tsushima in May 1905. Public disgust at the humiliating series of defeats served to harden opposition to the regime at a time when there was mounting clamour for political and social reform.

Like all empires, the Russian empire was a vast conglomeration of different ethnicities—well over one hundred—and religious confessions. The 1897 census showed that although Russians considered themselves the dominant political, religious, and cultural force in the empire, they were in fact a minority demographically (if one excludes Ukrainians and Belorussians), making up only 44 per cent of the population of 122.6 million inhabitants.[6] The empire was ruled on the principle of difference, with the Russian as well as non-Russian peoples defined in terms of social estate (*soslovie*), religion, and—for non-Russians—the hard-to-translate category of *inorodtsy*, 'persons of other origin', a category originally applied only to the nomadic and semi-nomadic tribes of Siberia but gradually extended to all non-Slav peoples.[7] The heterogeneity of the empire was evident too, in the complex criss-crossing of ethnic, religious, and social divisions. Ukrainians, for example, were divided between Ukrainian and Russian speakers, between the Uniate (Greek Catholic) and Orthodox faiths, and between those under Russian rule and those under Austrian rule in Galicia (where they were known as Ruthenes).[8] In addition, in the nine majority-Ukrainian provinces there were Jewish, Polish, German, and Tatar minorities.

Historically, as this dynastic-aristocratic empire expanded across Kliuchevskii's 'boundless and inhospitable plain', it ensured domestic stability by incorporating non-Russian elites as co-rulers of the borderlands, by tolerating a panoply of administrative and judicial forms, and by respecting religious diversity (notably with respect to Islam).[9] As the borderlands of the empire came under pressure from rival powers—Ukraine literally means 'borderland'—concerns about security intensified. Increasingly, the existence of different modes of internal governance was perceived as a problem. From the 1880s especially, this spurred the state into undertaking greater centralization and uniformization of administration. One dimension of this policy of homogenization was the policy (or, more accurately, the policies) of Russification. After putting down the Polish uprising of 1863, a drive to impose Russian language and culture got under way, which was especially vigorous in the western borderlands and the Baltic littoral. In 1881 the use of Ukrainian was banned in schools and in 1888 in all official institutions. Enforcement of the Russian language and of the Orthodox faith was designed to integrate Ukrainians, Belorussians, Lithuanians, and others into the dominant Russian culture. Poles and Jews, however, were seen as the groups most antipathetic to Russian values, and were most subject to discriminatory legislation, right down to 1917. At the same time, there was recognition in parts of government that if Russification were pushed too hard in areas such as education or employment, it might produce a backlash.

In other regions, Russification took a less aggressive form: in the Volga–Urals region, for example, it entailed fragmenting a pan-Muslim identity by increasing the prestige of Russian language, culture and institutions yet fell far short of cultural assimilation.[10] In Central Asia, however, the mode of rule remained unambiguously colonial. A series of harsh military campaigns between the mid-1860s and the mid-1880s swallowed up lands as far south as Fergana, although the khanates of Bukhara and Khiva were allowed to preserve a modicum of independence as Russian protectorates. In the Caucasus, too, brutal wars of conquest of the mountain peoples and growing official hostility to Islam also produced a classically colonial form of rule, with officials stressing the need for the 'Russian element' to spearhead the colonization of peoples perceived to be less 'civilized'.[11]

Despite such conquest, because of the variation in forms of rule over the non-Russian peoples, historians are no longer inclined to see the tsarist empire as a 'prison house of nations', as Vladimir Il'ich Lenin, future leader of the October Revolution, styled it. They tend instead to emphasize modes of accommodation with non-Russians, as well as modes of repression.[12] This principle of differentiation allowed the tsarist government considerable flexibility in its mode of rule, assigning different groups different privileges and obligations. However, towards the end of the nineteenth century, there was a perceptible shift towards seeing empire in national rather than dynastic terms, with ethnic categories tending to squeeze out estate and confessional categories. Indeed the 1897 census for the first time tentatively deployed the politically sensitive category of 'nationality'.[13] The official preference was still to use the legal category of *inorodtsy*, but that term had come to resonate with a sentiment of cultural otherness and also, at least in the eye of the self-defined 'Russian element', with a sense of threat to the integrity of the state. By the twentieth century, therefore, the empire had become an unstable compound of a dynastic-aristocratic empire (what Kappeler calls a 'Hausmacht'), a nationalizing state, and a colonial regime (the last most evident in Central Asia and the Northern Caucasus).[14] Nevertheless down to 1917 it continued to define itself as *rossiiskaia*, as a state containing all the peoples of the Russian lands, rather than as *russkaia*, that is, as ethnically Russian.[15]

Nationalism was on the rise in Russia's borderlands, and would emerge in the course of the 1905 Revolution as another destabilizing factor threatening the continuance of autocracy. The nationalist challenge was in part a response to policies of Russification—especially in Ukraine and Poland. More fundamentally, it was a response to modernization, a highly mediated expression of the emergence in the non-Russian areas of urbanized, educated elites responding to modern communications and the expansion of the market and political constraints. At root it expressed the growing conviction of urban (and some rural) intellectuals and of elements of the middle classes that non-Russian peoples possessed the right, by virtue of common history, language, cultural practices, or religion, to separate from their alien rulers and create a state having its own autonomy and territory that represented their ethnic community. Nevertheless non-Russian nationalisms were not a prime factor weakening the Russian empire until the First World War.[16]

Autocracy and Orthodoxy

Nicholas II came to the throne in 1894 (see Figure 1.1). He was an aloof, quiet man whose world centred on his wife and family. His diaries contain little about affairs of state, mainly comprising laconic remarks on family life, his physical fitness, hunting, or the weather.[17] Nicholas believed that autocratic power had been bestowed upon him by God and he was resolute in resisting efforts to circumscribe that power by law or constitution. Even after the October Manifesto, which appeared to establish a constitutional monarchy, had been promulgated, Article One of the Fundamental Laws of 1906 declared, 'The Emperor of All Russia is an autocratic and unrestricted monarch. To obey his supreme authority, not only out of fear but out of conscience, God Himself commands.'[18] Nicholas looked on himself as a father whose duty it was to protect his people. Hostile to educated society, he looked to resacralize the monarchy, imagining himself as bound in a mystical union with the Russian people through faith and a common history.

Figure 1.1 Nicholas II, Alexandra, and their family.

Increasingly he looked for spiritual guidance to holy men, such as Grigorii Rasputin, a faith healer revered by the common people, who from 1906 exercised extraordinary influence in court circles. He was hostile to bureaucracy as a principle of government, and his ministers, who no longer came primarily from the higher nobility or army backgrounds, found it hard to gain his attention. The entire system depended on having a strong leader to coordinate its operations, yet Nicholas did not even have a personal secretariat that could prioritize the issues with which he had to deal.

Despite its panoply of military and administrative power, the tsarist state was essentially weak, although certainly not ineffective. Central government had limited material and human resources at its disposal, its tax base was narrow, its administration was understaffed, and it was impaired by overlapping jurisdictions, vaguely defined areas of competence, corruption, and rank inefficiency. Through the course of the nineteenth century, but especially under Alexander II in the 1860s, there was recognition that if the autocracy were to compete successfully with rival powers and cope with the ever growing demands on government, the reform and strengthening of administrative structures was vital. Special commissions were set up to discuss administrative incapacity, lack of coordination between ministries, and corruption, and these generated mountains of paperwork. But projects and laws were drafted, only to be shelved. Nicholas II's two most outstanding ministers, Sergei Witte, Minister of Finance, and Pëtr Stolypin, Minister of the Interior, both recognized that administrative reform was necessary. Witte believed that an autocracy governed by the rule of law and by formal administrative procedure could achieve economic modernization and maintain social stability. And after the 1905 Revolution, Stolypin hoped to see the monarch retain his authority while working with the new duma, confidently declaring that it had parted from the 'old police order of things'.[19]

Some have likened the autocracy to a police state.[20] Certainly, the police worked vigorously to suppress organized political opposition and public dissent. Anyone deemed 'seditious' could expect imprisonment or administrative exile to Siberia. The Okhrana, or secret police, intercepted mail and placed agents in public institutions and factories, and they were required to write regular reports on any unusual activities or deviant opinions. The secret activities of the revolutionary parties were fairly well known to the Okhrana, as they were riddled with agents; and janitors, cabmen, and others spied on the comings and goings of ordinary citizens. A strict system of censorship functioned, although it was eroded after the 1905 Revolution, and there was a deliberate if not especially effective effort to prevent the circulation of radical literature. Perhaps the most telling evidence for seeing the autocracy as a police state is that it ruled huge areas of the empire by emergency decree. In the wake of the 1905–6 Revolution, 70 per cent of the empire was under a state of emergency, and though this was scaled back during the Years of Reaction, there were still 2.3 million people under martial law and 63.3 million subject to some form of 'reinforced protection' by 1912.[21] Emergency powers allowed provincial governors to take whatever steps they liked to secure order; but, as the historian Peter Waldron observes, the delegation of such extensive powers to provincial governors sits oddly with the centralism one would normally associate with a police state.[22] Indeed what is striking is just how few police there actually were: until the 1890s, they were the only representatives of government beneath the county level, yet in 1900 an individual constable in the countryside, assisted by a few low-ranking officers, might find himself responsible for up to 4,700 square kilometres and anywhere between 50,000 and 100,000 inhabitants.[23] Since policemen were far more expensive than soldiers, the regime turned to the army to suppress any serious challenge to its authority. In key respects, then, tsarist Russia was 'under-governed' and the bureaucracy too ramshackle to qualify as a police state in the way that Stalin's Russia would become.[24]

The penetration of the central state into the countryside was limited. A quarter of the expenditure of government went on administration (compared with more than a third on the military), but the power of the centre effectively stopped at the eighty-nine provincial capitals where the governors had their offices. The latter were personal representatives of the tsar, subject to the Ministry of the Interior, and enjoyed wide powers.[25] Following the emancipation of the serfs in 1861, the nobility was expected to maintain order in the localities through the new zemstvo institutions, but central government had few means of ensuring they exercised leadership in a way the government approved. Though the zemstvos were elected by curia representing the different social estates, they were dominated by the nobility (74 per cent of zemstvo members were nobles, though nobles constituted only 1.3 per cent of the population).[26] They took on a wide range of local government functions, including education, health care, agriculture, veterinary services, roads, and so on, yet they existed only at provincial and county level and not at the lowest level of the township. Their political heyday came in the years up to the 1905 Revolution, when they pressed for political reform, but they continued to expand and professionalize their functions down to 1918, with their budgets doubling and their employees increasing by 150 per cent between 1905 and 1914. Beneath the level of the county, townships and villages were subject to 'self-government'. At village level the assembly of heads of household, known as the *skhod*, was responsible for ensuring villagers paid taxes and contributed to the upkeep of local infrastructure. Elders were chosen to elect a head and assistants to run township affairs, such as taxation, education, or charity, and to act as judges to the township court, which handled the bulk of peasant litigation, according to customary law. In 1889 Alexander III instituted the land captain to oversee the activities of the township and village assemblies, and this official had the authority to act as judge in certain civil and lesser criminal cases that had formerly come before the elected representatives of the peasants. As the personification of autocracy in the localities, he was widely reviled.[27]

An indispensable pillar of the tsarist state was the Russian Orthodox Church. Subordinated to the state under Peter the Great, it was administered by the Holy Synod, a branch of the bureaucracy, which provided it with an annual budget. Konstantin Pobedonostsev, a notorious reactionary, was Procurator of the Holy Synod from 1880 to 1905. Seventy per cent of the empire's population were assumed to be Orthodox and in 1914 there were 40,437 parish churches in the predominantly Russian dioceses, and 50,105 deans and priests, 21,330 monks and novices, and 73,299 nuns and novices within the empire as a whole.[28] The Church owned 3 million hectares of land and one-third of all primary schools. In addition, there were sizeable religious minorities, including Roman Catholics in Poland and Lithuania, Lutherans in Latvia and Estonia, Muslims in the Caucasus and Central Asia, and Jews in the western provinces. In Ukraine most of the people were Orthodox, but there was a sizeable Uniate community that accepted the authority of the pope while practising Orthodox rites. Only the Orthodox Church was allowed to proselytize and any individual seeking to convert to another faith could be punished under criminal law for apostasy.

That said, the Orthodox Church was never simply an arm of state; nor was it as rigid and immutable as is sometimes supposed.[29] The theological education of the clergy improved during the nineteenth century, monasticism was reinvigorated, and the institution of spiritual eldership revived. In the expanding cities efforts were made to set up missions for the working class, though the attempt to create strong parishes proved difficult. The promotion of a temperance movement among city folk was one of the Church's notable successes in the fin-de-siècle, and a few younger clergy who undertook pastoral work among the poor became increasingly vocal in their criticisms of the status quo.[30] Nevertheless, the secularism of the intelligentsia, the growing movement for civil rights, the rise of socialism, and the ecclesiastical perception that rural life was being corrupted by migrant workers returning to their villages all served to create a sense of beleaguerment on the part of the Church. The 1905 Revolution would bring tensions within the Church to a head and relations between Church and state would come under great strain.

Popular Religion

Peasant culture was permeated by the Orthodox faith, which was rooted in mainstream ritual and dogma but which had many local saints, feast days, and rituals, along with an admixture of folkloric beliefs and practices that the hierarchy sometimes condemned as 'superstitious' or even pagan. At the centre of popular faith were Mary, the Mother of God, and national and local saints, such as St Nicholas, whose veneration was mediated through icons and relics.[31] An icon did not merely depict a person or an event in sacred history, but was a medium that conveyed the numinous presence of that which it depicted. Unlike the eucharist, which only priests could administer, icons offered communion with the sacred in which anyone could participate. Saints looked after the well-being of the family and village, the health of animals, and the fertility of the fields. They righted wrongs, cured illness, and offered general protection against the depredations of nature. The main feast days of the liturgical calendar structured community life and farming. The determination of local communities to promote local saints or miracle-working icons could lead to tension with the hierarchy, although there is evidence that after 1905 the ecclesiastical authorities were more willing to tolerate what once they might have regarded as semi-pagan. The critical stages of the life cycle—birth, marriage, death—were marked by the rituals of faith. A newborn baby for example, still considered only partly human, was particularly vulnerable to demonic force. The birth was followed by the ritual burial of the placenta and consultation between midwife and priest on the child's name. Eight days after birth baptism would take place, after which family and friends would celebrate with a meal in which buckwheat would be eaten (swollen grain symbolizing new birth), and at which the midwife would say a special grace to ask God's blessing on the child.[32] At the heart of peasant religion was demonic evil—the 'unclean force'—which over the centuries had become centred on the Christian devil but which still extended to the spirits of the fields, forests, and rivers. In V. I. Dal's dictionary of 1864 there were over forty names for devils and sprites.

One should not infer that religious culture was unchanging. The forces of modernization brought changes: railways encouraged the faithful to go on pilgrimage; increasing literacy allowed them to read newspaper stories and pamphlets about miraculous healings or the activities of charismatic spiritual elders; lithography allowed them to buy cheap mass-produced icons. Between 1861 and 1914, rural communities, especially in the north, almost doubled the number of chapels, these being separate administratively from the parish church, often out of a desire to commemorate events that linked the community to the Russian nation.[33] Migration and schooling encouraged a more distanced, more individualistic orientation to religious belief, yet it would be misleading to suggest that 'secularization' was taking place, since the indices of religiosity do not obviously signal a decline in religious observance. In Voronezh province, for example, church attendance did fall slightly between 1860 and 1914 but the annual obligation to take the sacraments continued to be maintained.[34] In other words, this was still a robustly religious society into which a regime bent on promoting state-backed atheism would erupt in 1917.

The 1905 Revolution fostered a more critical attitude towards the Church on the part of many ordinary people. Anti-clericalism had always been deep-rooted in popular culture and this fed into a more sustained criticism of the institutional Church. This was very much in response to the hierarchy's resolute condemnation of social disorder and its demand that the people respect the rights of property and submit to divinely ordained authority. In particular, peasants cast hungry eyes on the 3 million hectares of land that belonged to the Church—insufficient, in fact, to maintain all parishes at the legal norm of 47.8 hectares a parish—while some demanded that parishioners have the right to elect their clergy.[35] Among workers mistrust of the institutional Church was more marked although, as in the countryside, this did not necessarily mean that 'irreligion' was on the increase, as many contemporary churchmen claimed. Down to 1917, for example, it was common for workers to contribute their kopecks to buy oil for the icon lamps that were to be found in most workplaces.

Over the centuries, Russia had developed a strong tradition of apocalyptic thought at both elite and popular levels and in the last years of the *ancien régime* there was a surge of apocalyptic sentiment among religious thinkers, literary figures, and in the populace at large.[36] According to the American historian James Billington, 'nowhere else in Europe was the volume and intensity of apocalyptic literature comparable to that found in Russia during the reign of Nicholas II. The stunning defeat by Japan in 1904–05 and the ensuing revolution left an extraordinarily large number of Russians with the feeling that life as they had known it was coming to an end'.[37] In some ways this was odd, since there was no tradition of Bible reading in Russia except among the Protestant denominations, which had begun to grow in the latter part of the nineteenth century, and among the Old Believers, who had split from the Church in the 1660s in protest at reforms of Patriarch Nikon. Works attributed to Serafim of Sarov (1754–1833), who was canonized in 1903 at the behest of the tsar, predicted that before the Russian people could receive God's mercy, they must suffer under men who would kill the tsar and trample on God's law. The writings of John of Kronstadt—and the preaching of his followers—were crucial in promoting a message that Russia was sliding towards the abyss, a message propagated through stories such as the one in which John had refused to bless children brought to him, predicting that they would grow into 'live devils'.[38] The dominant strain of apocalypticism was politically reactionary: passionately Orthodox, strongly committed to autocracy, antisemitic, anti-democratic, anti-socialist, and anti-western.[39] Popular apocalypticism was permeated by a sense that God's presence could no longer be discerned in the secular world and that this was the prelude to the last times. It manifested itself, for example, in a wave of discoveries of icons whose image and colour had been miraculously renewed, a phenomenon that would take on a mass form in the 1920s.

Agriculture and Peasantry

Late-imperial Russia was an overwhelmingly agrarian society in which three-quarters of the population sustained themselves through farming (see Figure 1.2).[40] There was huge environmental variation across the empire, crucially between the fertile black-earth zone, which encompassed Ukraine, the central agricultural region (the provinces of Kursk, Orel, Tula, Riazan', Tambov, and Voronezh), the middle Volga, south-west Urals, and south-western Siberia, and the less fertile non-black-earth zone which included

Figure 1.2 Bringing in the harvest c.1910.

the central industrial region and the forested provinces of the north and west. Grain was the predominant agricultural crop, accounting for more than 90 per cent of total sown area as late as 1913. Agriculture was still technically backward: the three-field system and strip farming were widespread; there was little mechanization (the wooden plough and hand-held sickle were still the norm) and little use of fertilizers. Grain yields were well below those of other countries. An unusually fierce winter and a couple of bad harvests in a row could spell disaster, as happened in 1891–2, when a terrible famine saw up to 400,000 people in the Volga and central agricultural provinces starve to death (though the government was also at fault for not halting grain exports soon enough).[41] In the second half of the nineteenth century the population of the empire grew faster than in the preceding two-and-a-half centuries, rising from 74 million to 167.5 million between 1860 and 1914.[42] This put considerable pressure on the land, causing rents to rise: if the average amount of arable land was 13 hectares per household in 1877, it had fallen to 10 hectares by 1905.[43] This was still a large area compared with the average size of farms in Western Europe, but because yields were so much lower, the average peasant, especially in the central black-earth provinces and the western provinces, lived a precarious existence. One telling index of the backwardness of European Russia (i.e. the empire west of the Ural mountains) is that in 1905 fewer than half of babies—particularly boys—reached the age of 5. Endemic diseases, such as measles and diphtheria, overwhelmed the countryside, where dirt, overcrowding, poor ventilation, and, of course, miserable provision of public health prevailed.[44] That said, a direct cause of the high level of infant mortality—273 per 1,000 births in 1914—is that mothers working in the fields left their babies in the care of the elderly or young children who fed them with chewed bread covered by a rag which quickly putrefied in hot weather. Among Tatar women, who did no field work, infant mortality was much lower.[45]

Village society was highly conservative in its values and practices, these having evolved over the centuries as means to ensure as much collective control over the vagaries of climate and the arbitrariness of the authorities as possible. The community took precedence over the individual, and the village presented a 'common front against the outside', resenting the intervention of outsiders, such as tax collectors or military recruiters.[46] The commune was the institution that most embodied the collectivism of rural society. At the turn of the twentieth century about three-quarters of peasant land, including nearly half of all arable land, was subject to a unique form of management in which the heads of households periodically repartitioned the arable land belonging to the commune among its constituent households. In addition, this village assembly decided when households should plough, sow, reap, or make hay. Such collective control of farming was designed to minimize risk in an uncertain environment and to ensure that the poor did not become a drain on the community's resources. The village assembly was also responsible for ensuring that households paid their taxes and for law and order. In 1905 in forty-six provinces of European Russia 8.68 million households held land that was formally subject to the communal repartition, while 2.3 million held land in hereditary tenure, that is, passed from father to son. The total number of peasant households in European Russia was around 12 million. In the Baltic the commune was completely absent and in western provinces and Ukraine hereditary tenure was predominant.[47] The commune was seen by contemporaries as discouraging entrepreneurship and innovation, since there was little incentive to improve one's farm if there was a likelihood it would be subject to repartition at some point in the future (although in practice, by 1917 about two-fifths of communes in European Russia, including some in the overcrowded central agricultural provinces, had not undergone a repartition since the 1880s).[48]

Peasant society was patriarchal in that men held power over women and the elder generation held power over the younger generation. Only men had rights of property in the household and its land, and the assets of the household were divided equally between sons on the death of the head of the household. Even as the patriarchal order privileged males by granting them access to land and the labour of women, it subordinated sons to fathers almost as thoroughly as it subordinated women to men.[49] A young wife who moved into her husband's family was subordinate to her mother-in-law, although her status would rise once she bore children; and after her husband became a head of household, she might wield considerable power over her own daughters-in-law.[50] There was, however, increasing reluctance on the part of young couples to live under the roof of the patriarch and his wife and a trend for them to separate from the parental household and set up their own farms. This was reflected in a decline in average household size. In 1897 the average family comprised 5.8 people, although there was variation in household size, especially between the black-earth and non-black-earth zone.[51] Down to 1917, the law dictated that a wife owed complete obedience to her husband, and compelled her to live with him, to take his name, and to assume his social estate. It was her duty to take care of the household and to help her husband on the farm; in return, her husband was required 'to live with her in harmony, to respect and protect her, forgive her insufficiencies and ease her infirmities'. A wife was unable to take a job, get an education, receive a passport for work or residence, or execute a bill of exchange without her husband's consent. In 1914 limited reforms permitted her to separate from her husband and obtain her own passport.[52] Customary law protected the inalienability of a woman's personal property, which included, in addition to her dowry, revenues she might earn from selling vegetables, chickens, or woven and knitted items. And if her husband left her, a woman could expect some backing from the township court, although the courts were not sympathetic to complaints about physical abuse by menfolk.[53] Within the household women enjoyed considerable latitude in running domestic affairs. In addition to childcare, cooking, cleaning, washing, and making and repairing clothes, they spun yarn and wove cloth, looked after livestock, cultivated flax, and assisted with the harvest. By dint of their involvement in arranging marriages, presiding at childbirth and christenings, and generally upholding community standards and norms, married women enjoyed a certain informal authority in village life.[54] In regions where men migrated for wage work, women took on heavy farming tasks that had once been considered men's work, such as ploughing, sowing, haymaking, carting fuel, and feeding cattle.[55]

If agriculture remained backward and predominantly oriented towards subsistence, commercial farming nevertheless made rather rapid strides.

By 1914 Russia was the world's leading exporter of grain and in the last decade of the old regime grain production grew faster than population. Most commercial grain production was done by big estates, with wage labour, but by the turn of the century peasants were selling about a quarter of their harvest (if only because they had to pay their taxes).[56] The development of non-grain arable crops and of livestock was much more weakly developed, but in right-bank Ukraine (the provinces on the west bank of the Dnieper River, i.e. the 'right' bank as seen from Moscow) industrial sugar beet production grew substantially. And in the Baltic provinces, in the north-west, and the central industrial region (the provinces of Moscow, Vladimir, Iaroslavl', Kostroma, Tula, Kaluga, and Riazan') peasants began to specialize in market gardening, commercial dairy farming for growing urban markets, and industrial crops such as flax.[57] In Siberia, which had never experienced landlordism and serfdom to any great extent, there was even a slow adoption of binders, and threshing and mowing machines. In other words, where they had access to markets, such as on the steppes of southern Ukraine or south-eastern Russia, where there was access to railways, the Volga River, or the Black Sea, peasants did take advantage of new opportunities to farm more commercially. In the heartlands of European Russia, however, commercial agriculture remained weakly developed and fully-fledged capitalism—as measured by capital investment, technical innovation, and use of hired labour—was rare.

Contemporaries seeing endemic poverty in the countryside, noting that the size of the average farm was shrinking in size, and believing that the burden of redemption payments continued to be heavy (these had been imposed in 1861 to remunerate the landowners for the land they assigned to their former serfs), were convinced that the standard of living of the rural population was deteriorating. Certainly, peasant lives remained poor and insecure, but it is likely that the overall standard of living was slowly rising, for per capita growth of agricultural output exceeded the growth in population, and the amount of grain and other foodstuffs retained by the peasant household also increased.[58] The increasing height of army conscripts suggests that nutrition was improving.[59] There is also some evidence that the burden of taxation, rents, and interest rates was falling in real terms, to an average of around one-fifth of household income, although this is not uncontentious.[60] Finally, deposits in rural saving banks were healthy. This slow improvement reflected the fact that peasants were finding new sources of income in trade and handicrafts, such as brewing, making butter, spinning yarn, or tanning leather, and in wage work in agriculture, domestic service, forestry, transportation, and factory industry, usually by leaving the village on a seasonal basis. The picture of slow improvement of peasant life, however, varied by region. Almost one-third of peasants in European Russia lived in the central black-earth and Volga provinces and there the amount of grain produced per head actually declined from the 1880s. Moreover, livestock farming was in long-term decline and the wages of rural labourers were also falling.[61] Even so the evidence for a slow improvement in the standard of living of the rural population looks strong.

The most far-reaching of the reforms instituted in the wake of the 1905 Revolution—certainly the one that affected most people—was the edict of Prime Minister Pëtr Stolypin in November 1906, followed by the laws of June 1910 and May 1911, which made it possible for peasants to consolidate the strips of land they farmed within the commune and set up separate enclosed farms. Stolypin intended the reform as a 'wager on the strong', an attempt to promote a layer of vigorous yeoman farmers who would spearhead the modernization of farming. The hope was that they would become a pillar of conservative peasant support for the autocracy after the agrarian upheaval of 1905. Between 1906 and 1915 about 3 million households were granted title to the land they held within the commune, or were affected by a commune decision to participate in a group land settlement, or opted to separate from the commune. A further 3 million petitioned to be allowed to consolidate their land holdings and either had their applications turned down or were awaiting a decision when war broke out.[62] In the central black-earth region, the central industrial region, and the north there was very little take-up, the greatest concentrations of enclosed farms being in the north-west and west and in the south and south-east.[63] In general poorer families did not have the wherewithal to separate from the commune, though not all those who petitioned to separate were wealthy; indeed many wealthier households were averse to taking risks and chose to stay within the commune. It has been estimated that 15.9 per cent of communal land (not including Cossack land) had been privatized by 1914, and that between 27 per cent and 33 per cent of all households held their land in some form of hereditary tenure: the divergence between these two figures being due to the fact that only arable land could be enclosed, with the commune keeping control of pasture, forest, wasteland, ponds, cattle drives, roads, and so on.[64] It is difficult to come to a definitive judgement about the success of the Stolypin reforms, since the period of implementation was cut short by the war and because the focus of the reform gradually shifted from enclosure towards land improvement. There is reason to think that had war not intervened, privatization would have gathered pace, but the enormous upheaval brought to the rural economy by war and revolution served to reinforce the commune, as an institution that minimized collective risk.

Some contemporaries were convinced that as capitalism developed in the countryside, the peasants were stratifying along class lines. Social inequality was a fact of village life. At the turn of the century, statistical surveys suggest that 17 per cent to 18 per cent of households (perhaps as many as 25 per cent by 1908) could be classified as well-to-do, in that they had sufficient land, some livestock and machinery, and money in a savings bank; while at the other end of the scale, 11 per cent of the peasantry were without any arable land or livestock.[65] Those the peasants called kulaks—'fists'—were not usually defined by the amount of land they farmed, but by the fact that they lent money, rented out equipment or draft animals, or owned shops and mills. Some historians argue that such statistical surveys freeze in time what was in fact a very dynamic process in which the fortunes of individual households rose and fell over time. They contend that it was labour not land that was crucial in determining the wealth of a household, with wealthier households simply being those that had plenty of working members. Once adult sons split to form their own households, however, the wealth of the parental household declined. According to this view, any trend towards differentiation was offset by households' division and by periodic redistribution of land by the commune.[66] Another problem in determining whether there was a trend towards greater social differentiation is that it is hard to know how to measure it: it may be calculated according to the amount of land a household sowed, the number of horses or livestock it owned, whether it used hired labour or not (though most of this was seasonal or day labour), and whether it owned agricultural machinery. Moreover, social differentiation was less if measured in per capita terms than if measured by household. In European Russia the proportion of households without horses rose from 61.9 per cent in 1888–91 to 68 per cent in 1899–1900 to 74 per cent in 1912. This suggests that class divisions were deepening in the countryside until one remembers that households with large numbers of horses were concentrated in less commercially developed regions.[67] If differentiation was indeed increasing it was probably less connected to the development of commercial farming than to off-farm earnings. A study of eight provinces in the central industrial region shows that differentiation in the rural population was less in counties where the population was still largely involved in farming and greater in areas where cash crop production, handicrafts, and trade were developed, where wage labour was increasing, and where literacy levels were high.[68]

If there was slow improvement in the condition of the peasantry, why then was there so much unrest? To understand this one needs to go back to 1861 when serfs were finally emancipated. Peasants felt that they had been cheated by the land settlement. Not only were they required to pay for the land they received over a period of forty-nine years, in so-called redemption payments, but they also received less land than they had farmed as serfs. Moreover, their former masters kept roughly one-sixth of the area that had been under serf cultivation, often the land that was of best quality and most conveniently situated. In addition, the redemption payments on the land they received were set in excess of its market value. In 1917 there were still grandparents who had been born serfs and the memory of serfdom galvanized much of the militancy of 1905 and 1917. Even more fundamental was that, according to the moral economy of the Russian peasantry, only those who worked the land, who made it productive, had a right to possess it.

In one of Tolstoy's fables peasants decide whether or not to take in strangers according to the state of their hands: if their palms are calloused they will take them in. As one peasant explained:

> The land we share is our mother; she feeds us; she gives us shelter; she makes us happy and lovingly warms us... And now people are talking about selling her, and truly, in our corrupt, venal age land is put on the market for appraisal and so-called sale... The principal error lies in the crude and monstrous assertion that the land, which God gave to all people so that they could feed themselves could be anyone's private property... Land is the common and equal legacy of all people and so cannot be the object of private ownership.[69]

Notwithstanding the fact that the nobility got a good deal with the emancipation settlement of 1861, their fortunes went into steep decline over the next fifty years. By 1917 there were about 100,000 landowner families, of whom about 61,000 belonged to the noble estate.[70] These landowners had lost roughly half the land they owned at the time of emancipation, although they still owned more than half of all privately owned land (even if much of it was mortgaged to the Nobles' Land Bank).[71] Gentry estates varied greatly in size: there were some vast domains, but over 60,000 families had fewer than 145 hectares (100 *desiatina* in the measure used at the time). Moreover, notwithstanding the transformation of certain large landowners into capitalist farmers, the average noble estate was as undercapitalized as the average peasant farm. Significantly, by 1903 peasants were already leasing almost half the land belonging to the landowning class and some had taken out loans from the Peasant Land Bank to buy noble land.[72] We have seen that the liberal elements of the gentry became very active in the zemstvos through the 1890s and into 1905, but the increasing urban lifestyle of a large proportion and their declining interest in estate management undermined their standing in rural society. In any case, for the peasant, the nobleman, whether rich or poor, conservative or liberal, symbolized 'them', the privileged society from which they felt entirely excluded.

The tsarist state began to invest in primary education in the late nineteenth century, recognizing the need for literate, trained, and well-disciplined workers, soldiers, and sailors. Enrolment in rural schools increased fourfold between 1885 and 1914, while the number of teachers from peasant families grew from 7,369 to 44,607 between 1880 and 1911.[73] The census of 1897 found that 21.1 per cent of the population of European Russia was literate, but the gender gap was significant, with only 13.1 per cent of women being able to read and write compared with 29.3 per cent of men. Urban literacy stood at 45.3 per cent while rural literacy stood at 17.4 per cent, though both rose steadily in the years up to 1914.[74] In that year only one-fifth of children of school age were actually in school.[75] Doubtless this was because many peasants considered that schooling was not needed beyond the point when sons became functionally literate. As far as daughters were concerned, a widespread attitude was articulated by a villager in 1893: 'If you send her to school, she costs money; if you keep her at home, she makes money.'[76] Nevertheless by 1911 girls comprised just under a third of primary school pupils and the spread of schooling meant that by 1920 42 per cent of men and 25.5 per cent of women were literate.[77]

Evaluations of the record of the tsarist government in the sphere of schooling tend to be fairly positive.[78] Peasant communities paid for nearly one-third of teachers' salaries and assumed much of the responsibility for village schools.[79] But the proportion of the regular state budget spent on education rose from 2.69 per cent in 1881 to 7.21 per cent in 1914, a figure that includes spending by the Ministry of Education, the zemstvos, and municipalities.[80] Another figure suggests a less positive picture: after 1907, the proportion of the Ministry of Education's spending devoted to primary education rose from 20 per cent to 40 per cent, but it still meant that the lion's share went to secondary and higher education.[81] The government recognized the need to devote more resources to primary education, in order to improve technical skills and work habits of the working population, yet it shuddered at the thought that schools might encourage free thinking. It had some reason to do so, for the Revolution witnessed school strikes and student demonstrations on a mass scale—at least 50 secondary school students were killed and 262 wounded—and some 20,000 teachers were fired as order was restored.[82] Consequently, the regime monitored popular education, clamping down on anything that smacked of sedition. A decree on primary education of 1911 explained: 'Primary schools have the aim of giving students a religious and moral education, developing in them a love of Russia, communicating to them basic knowledge and enabling their mental development.'[83]

Industrial Capitalism

The origins of Russia's industrial development go back into the eighteenth century, when the state-owned mines and metal works of the Urals had been world leaders. But it was the perception of Russia's relative decline within the international system that prompted the state to embark on a programme of rapid industrialization.[84] Ivan Vyshnegradskii, Minister of Finance 1887–92, promoted railway building as a way of stimulating domestic mining and the iron and steel industries; he stabilized the ruble and stepped up exports of grain to enable the government to borrow on world financial markets; and he placed high tariffs on the import of coal and oil to protect Russia's infant industries. It was, however, his successor as Finance Minister, Sergei Witte (1892–1903), who threw himself into an ambitious programme of state-backed industrialization. Between 1890 and 1901 the length of railway track grew from 30,600 to 56,500 kilometres, the most notable achievement being the Trans-Siberian railway (this, of course, had key strategic importance, though any economic benefit was scarcely felt by 1914). In turn, railway construction stimulated the mining and metallurgical industries of the Donbass, which became a major area of foreign capital investment. In 1897 Russia followed other countries in adopting the gold standard, in the belief that this would facilitate the government and private borrowers obtaining funds on the capital markets. The alliance with France in 1894 accelerated French (and Belgian) private investment, mainly in mining, metallurgy, and engineering, though much also went into banking, insurance, and commercial firms. British private investment was critical for the development of the new oil industry in Baku, Batumi, and Groznyi and in gold mining.

German investment, too, was significant, despite the perception that Germany threatened Russia's strategic interests. By 1913 foreign capital accounted for around 41 per cent of total investment in industry and banking. A potential source of anxiety was Russia's reliance on trade with Germany, which amounted to some 40 per cent of total foreign trade by value.[85] State-backed industrialization was underpinned financially by the export of grain, the value of the turnover in foreign trade growing eightfold between the 1860s and 1909–13.

Too great an emphasis on the role of the state risks overshadowing the fact that Russian industry had a robust private sector. Consumer goods dominated industrial production, with textiles and foodstuffs accounting for about half of gross output by 1914. The estimable growth rates achieved in the 1890s segued into a downturn in 1900 that lasted into 1908. Thereafter the armaments programme gave a new boost to industrial growth, with total output growing by 5 per cent a year between 1909 and 1913, compared with an average of 3.4 per cent a year between 1885 and 1913 as a whole.[86] By 1913, the Russian empire ranked fifth in the league table of industrial nations (after the USA, Germany, Britain, and France)—a significant achievement. Yet in terms of output per head, Russia was closer to Bulgaria and Romania, US output being six times that of Russia on this measure. Moreover Russia remained overwhelmingly an exporter of foodstuffs and an importer of finished and semi-finished goods.

The connection between industrialization and urbanization was not as close as in many countries, since textile entrepreneurs, in particular, took advantage of the supply of cheap labour by locating their factories in the countryside. Yet industry and especially trade were a crucial spur to the rapid growth of Russia's towns: the urban population doubled to 25.8 million between 1897 and 1917 (although this still did not quite constitute a fifth of the empire's population). By 1913 there were a hundred towns of over 50,000 inhabitants and more than twenty of over 100,000.[87] By 1914 St Petersburg had a population of more than 2.2 million, making it the world's eighth largest city, and Moscow had a population of over 1.6 million. Recent historians have challenged the Chekhov-inspired image of provincial cities as cultural deserts from which the educated longed to escape. Many provincial capitals boasted an intelligentsia that proudly mapped the natural history and ethnography of its region, building schools, museums, libraries, and theatres and developing a local press.[88]

The rise in the urban population was largely the result of peasant migration, though much of this was seasonal in character, with peasants returning to the countryside to help with the harvest. In 1900 the proportion of inhabitants of St Petersburg who had not been born in the city was 69 per cent. The rapid growth of the urban population led to severe overcrowding and appalling living conditions. An average of 3.2 persons lived in a single-room apartment and 3.4 persons in a cellar, twice the average for Berlin, Vienna, or Paris.[89] St Petersburg enjoyed the dubious distinction of being the most unsanitary capital in Europe: in 1910 more than 100,000 people died in a cholera epidemic. In 1920, 42 per cent of homes were found to have no water supply or sewage disposal.[90] The rapidity of urban growth compelled municipal authorities to take responsibility for water supply, street lighting, transport, schools, and hospitals, but the quality of such services on average was extremely poor. This was partly because tax revenues were paltry, and partly because municipal authorities were often spectacularly incompetent. Moscow was something of an exception: by the First World War the city duma had overseen the installation of 20 kilometres of streets with electric lighting, a reasonable system of water supply and sewage, a tram network, and extensive free health facilities. In general it fell to philanthropic organizations to provide basic medical and other social services to the urban poor.

The emerging class of industrialists and financiers was divided by region and by industrial sector and these divisions translated into different orientations towards the autocracy. Although some industrialists emerged out of the traditional estate of merchants (*kupechestvo*) and, to a lesser extent, the estate of townspeople (*meshchane*), those who took up the opportunities offered by economic growth tended to go into commerce rather than industry. The textile manufacturers in the Moscow industrial region were the most influential sector of home-grown capitalists: they tended to be socially conservative and paternalistic in their style of management, many coming from Old Believer backgrounds. Unlike their counterparts in iron and steel, they did not depend on state orders, and after 1905 they were supportive of political reform, even forming a noisy Progressist Party.[91] By contrast, the textile manufacturers in the region around Łódź, known as the Polish Manchester, were largely German and they adhered to an autocratic form of industrial relations. The critical sectors of heavy industry and transportation depended on the government for orders, subsidies, and preferential tariffs, so entrepreneurs in these sectors—many of whom were foreign—did little more than gripe at bureaucratic control. In St Petersburg the owners of metalworking and engineering works, together with the big bankers of the city, were fairly well organized, but primarily concerned with ensuring their influence within government circles rather than supporting reform in politics or the modernization of industrial relations. In the Donbass owners of mines and iron foundries were often foreign—the Welshman John Hughes founded the iron works that grew into the city of Donetsk today—and it fell to the engineer-managers, themselves ethnically mixed, to support modest reform of industrial relations, largely to minimize the turnover of workers. In general, industrialists of South Russia (as they called themselves) were happy to tolerate industrial relations that were paternalistic at best, iron-fisted at worst, and were no champions of political reform.[92]

Government policy was generally favourable to commerce and industry.[93] Taxes on urban buildings, business licences, corporate capital and profits, income from securities, bank accounts, and inheritances were all very modest, and income tax was not introduced until 1916. Nevertheless the government cannot be said to have pursued a course that consistently favoured the interests of industrial capital. Many officials, for example, still associated private enterprise with personal greed and with exploitation of the 'people'. This group was significant in the Ministry of the Interior which, with an eye to social stability, urged employers to practise a policy of 'guardianship' towards their employees. The Ministry of Finance advocated a more modern style of industrial relations, supporting a modest degree of protective legislation, including a factory inspectorate set up as early as 1882.

Yet since the autocracy never failed to take the side of employers in the event of open conflict, the power of employers within the enterprise was barely limited by law.

Working conditions were wretched. According to Witte, the worker 'raised on the frugal habits of rural life' was 'much more easily satisfied' than his counterpart in the West, so that 'low wages appeared as a fortunate gift to Russian enterprise'.[94] A ten- or eleven-hour working day was commonplace. Workers sometimes slept at their machines or in filthy dormitories. Industrial accidents happened all the time, yet most workers were not covered by social insurance and were lucky to receive a few rubles' compensation if they were injured. The two most important factory laws were one in 1885 prohibiting the night-time employment of women and children, and the other in 1897 restricting the working day to eleven and a half hours. Small workshops were excluded from the legislation, although they probably employed the majority of the country's workforce, and certainly most of its women workers. Needless to add, strikes and trade unions were illegal. However, there were some employers, especially among the textile manufacturers of the Moscow industrial region, who sought to improve the lot of their employees. In 1900 the Trekhgornaia mill in Moscow won a gold medal at the World Fair in Paris for 'sanitary conditions and care for the daily life of workers'. This mill belonged to the Prokhorov merchant dynasty and after October 1917 Ivan N. Prokhorov would stay on as adviser to the now nationalized enterprise.[95]

Industrialization and urbanization had the effect of unsettling the system of social estates, whereby the state had historically sought to administer society by creating different legal-administrative categories, each vested with different privileges and obligations. In particular, it served as a means of ensuring recruits to the army and taxes to the state. Historically, the crucial distinction had been between those who were obliged to pay the poll tax, which was abolished in the 1880s—the mass of peasants—and those who were exempt. Whether one belonged to the nobility, the clergy, the merchants, the townspeople, or the peasantry, one's estate status determined the kind of taxes one paid, the duties one owed to the state, one's access to law, and the economic and educational opportunities open to one. After the peasant estate, the second largest was that of townspeople (*meshchane*), which comprised artisans, petty traders, and householders, and which in 1897 numbered 13.4 million.[96] The reforms of Alexander II had pointed towards the gradual elimination of estate categories, but under his successors the government opted to preserve the system in an effort to increase social control. Internal passports for peasants were maintained, separate land banks for peasants and nobility were established, elections to the zemstvos were by curia based on social estate, and noble status for recruitment to high bureaucratic or military office continued to be important. The system was not completely unresponsive to economic and social change.[97] Peasants petitioned to become townspeople, townspeople petitioned to become merchants (their number reached 600,000 by 1917), and wealthy merchants petitioned to become nobility. Nevertheless , the estates of merchants and, in particular, of townspeople maintained a corporatist and patriarchal character that was increasingly at odds with social and cultural change, and from the end of the nineteenth century the local boards that managed the affairs of each estate were increasingly strapped for cash, more concerned with dispensing charity towards their needy members than with carrying out administrative functions.[98]

Industrialization and urbanization created a working class that did not fit into the traditional system of social estates (most workers continued to be classed officially as members of the peasant estate). In 1900, 2.81 million workers were employed in factories, mines, railways, and steamships. If one includes construction workers, artisans, labourers, forestry, and agricultural wage workers then the total comes to 14 million.[99] The number employed in factories and mines grew to around 3.6 million in 1917 by which time the wage-earning workforce was approaching 20 million.[100] In 1913 92 per cent of the industrial workforce was concentrated in European Russia: the proportion of the workforce in the oldest industrial centre, the Urals, had fallen from 15.2 per cent in the 1870s to 10.2 per cent in 1913, while the share of the workforce in the Donbass had risen rapidly to 15.3 per cent.[101] Workers were recruited overwhelmingly from the peasantry, 'snatched from the plough and hurled into the factory furnace', in the memorable phrase of Trotsky.[102] There was undoubtedly a process of proletarianization taking place, whereby workers cut their ties with the land, one that was principally evident in St Petersburg. There in 1910 it is reckoned that about 60 per cent of the city's workforce had been born in the city. In 1908 the average length of service of the city's metalworkers was five years three months; and 53 per cent of married metalworkers had no ties with the land, compared with 35 per cent of single workers. Workers in the capital came from rather distant provinces so it was harder for them to maintain a vital connection with the land than it was elsewhere.[103] In regions such as the central industrial region, a centre of textile production, and in the Urals, the centuries-old centre of mining and metallurgy, a more symbiotic relationship existed between field and factory in which some family members worked for wages while others tended the farm. According to the 1918 Industrial Census, 30 per cent of workers had access to a family plot and 20 per cent worked the land with the help of family members.[104] Gradually, everywhere the average length of service of industrial workers increased and the proportion of those whose parents had also been workers grew. As this happened, more and more employees began to think of themselves as workers. This process was facilitated by the fact that the concentration of workers was high. About 58 per cent of industrial workers in European Russia were employed in enterprises of more than 500 workers, a much higher level of concentration than in Western Europe, and this is a key to understanding why it proved relatively easy to mobilize these workers in strikes and demonstrations. In a few cities, too, working-class districts began to emerge, such as the Vyborg district in St Petersburg and the Zamoskvorech'e district in Moscow. For young workers, in particular, the city offered cultural opportunities—evening classes, schools, clubs, libraries, theatres, not to speak of the commercial forms of leisure (discussed in Chapter 2), and this increased their sense of distance from the rural world in which their parents and grandparents had grown up. Already in 1897, for example, over half of all male urban workers and two-thirds of metalworkers were literate.[105] Nevertheless the emergence of a self-identified working class should not be read as suggesting social homogeneity. The differing strengths of the ties with the land, the gender divide, big differences in levels of skill and education, and wide variations in conditions of employment across different industrial and commercial sectors all served to divide workers. It would require political activity and ideological contestation if a heterogeneous labour force were to be transformed into a working class.

Political Challenges to the Old Order

Joseph Conrad once wrote that 'it is the peculiarity of Russian natures that however sharply engaged in the drama of action, they are still turning their ear to the murmur of abstract ideas'.[106] The Russian intelligentsia was famed for its fierce ideological skirmishes, but united by its opposition to autocracy and its commitment to the ideal of the autonomous individual. It was defined by its secular values and its belief that science held the key to overcoming Russia's economic and social backwardness, and by its commitment to raise the cultural level of the people through education and social improvement. The term 'intelligentsia' acquired broad circulation from the 1860s, referring to a narrow stratum defined primarily by its possession of cultural capital, that is, the status it enjoyed by virtue of education and talent rather than of the possession of material assets. Many of the intelligentsia did in fact come from privileged backgrounds, although an increasing number hailed from more humble origins. An example of a rather humble member of the intelligentsia was Lenin's father, Il'ia Ul'ianov. The son of a Chuvash tailor, he studied at Kazan' University and became a teacher of mathematics and physics, writing a couple of works on meteorology. In 1869 he was appointed inspector of schools in Simbirsk province and in 1882 was awarded hereditary noble status for his work in education. Among other achievements, he set up a training college for Chuvash teachers and national schools for Mordvins and Tatars. Ul'ianov typified the liberal intelligentsia in his concern to improve society through practical reforms in areas such as education, public health, women's rights, and the expansion of civil and political freedom. By the late nineteenth century this educated, civic-minded public, referred to by contemporaries as the *obshchestvo*, literally the 'society' or 'public', included lawyers, teachers, doctors, businessmen, the employees of the zemstvos and municipal dumas, and even elements of the government bureaucracy.[107] Through journalism and books, through participation in public organizations and voluntary societies, they disseminated the ideas and values appropriate to what the late-nineteenth-century Populist Pëtr Lavrov called the 'critically thinking individual'.

Revolutionaries such as Lavrov were a minority among the intelligentsia, albeit one that could count on the sympathy of the majority. The revolutionary tradition can be traced back to the Decembrist revolt against Nicholas I in 1825 , but a more useful starting point for understanding the revolutionary movement of the twentieth century is the summer of 1874 when hundreds of 'critically thinking individuals' 'went to the people' to awaken the peasantry to the moral imperative to revolt, only to find themselves turned over to the police. These middle-class Populists, or Narodniki, as they were known in Russian, believed that the peasant commune incarnated values of collectivism, cooperation, and egalitarianism on which a socialist society could be created, thus allowing Russia to avoid the evils of industrial capitalism. One reaction to the suppression of this essentially peaceful movement was the formation in 1879 of the People's Will, a conspiratorial organization that looked to acts of terror as the means to provoke popular insurgency, convinced that if those who personified the tyranny of autocracy were struck down, this would spark a revolutionary conflagration among the people. Between 1879 and 1881 they launched a wave of killings that culminated on 1 March 1881 in the assassination of Alexander II (after several failed previous attempts). Far from precipitating popular revolt, however, it led to the decimation of the movement, as leaders were hanged or sent to Siberia.[108] The debacle led some, notably Georgii Plekhanov, to turn to Marxism as offering a more scientific, less morally inspired theory of revolution. Plekhanov, who earned the epithet 'father of Russian Marxism', argued that rural society, far from representing an embryonic form of socialism, was undergoing capitalist development and that the peasantry was beginning to split along class lines. The proletariat, not the peasantry, would be the agent of revolution, and in 1883, he helped establish the Emancipation of Labour group which began to form propaganda circles among the educated workers of the cities. In Paris in 1889 at the founding congress of international socialist parties, known as the Second International, Plekhanov made the bold prediction that the Russian Revolution 'will triumph as a proletarian revolution or it will not triumph at all'.[109]

In 1887 a group of the terrorists was hanged for seeking to kill the new tsar, Alexander III, among them A. I. Ul'ianov, son of Il'ia and brother of the 17-year-old Vladimir Il'ich, who after 1901 would be known to the world as Lenin. Vladimir was devastated by the loss of his brother and threw himself into student protests at Kazan' University. Within months he had been expelled. Initially, Vladimir was attracted, like his brother, to the terrorism of the People's Will, though he moved rather quickly towards Marxism over the next two years.[110] Marxism entailed the rejection of terror as an instrument of revolution, yet Lenin's Marxism would always bear some of the élan of the Russian terrorist tradition with its commitment to the violent overthrow of the state. In other ways, too, his Marxism was marked by the Russian revolutionary tradition represented by thinkers such as Nikolai Chernyshevskii, Sergei Nechaev, or Pëtr Tkachëv, with its emphasis on the need for a disciplined revolutionary vanguard, its belief that willed action (the 'subjective factor') could speed up the 'objectively' determined course of history, its defence of Jacobin methods of dictatorship, and its contempt for liberalism and democracy (and indeed for socialists who valued those things). The revolutionary vanguard and 'barracks communism' espoused by Tkachëv, for example, was denounced by Marx and Engels, yet Lenin credited him with having a 'special talent as an organizer, a conspirator as well as the ability to enrobe his thoughts in astonishing formulations'.[111] In some ways Lenin was a more perfect Marxist than Marx himself, since despite deep theoretical reflection, he lived a life of more unremitting activism than his mentor.[112]

Returning from his first trip abroad in 1895, and by now a highly effective polemicist against the Populists, Lenin helped set up the Union of Struggle for the Emancipation of the Working Class in St Petersburg, together with Iulii Martov. This concentrated not on propaganda but on 'agitation', a tactic pioneered among Jewish workers in the Pale of Settlement in the western provinces, which focused on seeking to politicize workers' concrete economic struggles.[113] The new tactic seemed to pay off when 30,000 textile workers came out on strike in the capital in May 1896. By this time, Lenin and Martov were under arrest, and in January 1897 Lenin and his newly-wed wife, Nadezhda Krupskaia, herself an activist of some standing, were exiled to Siberia where they would spend three years. During his exile the new Russian Social-Democratic Labour Party (RSDLP) was formed, which held its first congress in 1898 in Minsk. Its manifesto was written by Pëtr Struve, who would soon move on to the liberal constitutionalist movement. A key issue in these years was the stance that Marxists should take towards the liberal opposition. According to Marxist theory, the forthcoming revolution would be 'bourgeois-democratic' in character, since the socio-economic preconditions for a socialist revolution did not yet exist in Russia. This was the issue at the heart of the split that would occur in the RSDLP at its Second Congress in 1903 between the Bolshevik and Menshevik factions. Those who emerged as the Menshevik faction, including Lenin's close friend and comrade Martov, saw liberals as the allies of the working class in the bourgeois-democratic revolution, whereas the Bolsheviks, led by Lenin, had only contempt for liberals and predicted that the bourgeois-democratic revolution would be made by the proletariat in alliance with the poorer layers of the peasantry. Lenin used his time in exile to write a major theoretical work, *The Development of Capitalism in Russia*, published in 1898, which marshalled a large amount of empirical data to demonstrate that capitalism was developing in the countryside and that class differentiation was taking place among the peasantry. This allowed him to appreciate the political potential of the peasantry, above all, the 'rural poor', to become allies of the industrial working class in bringing about a bourgeois revolution.[114]

In December 1900 the RSDLP published the first issue of *Iskra* (Spark), an illegal newspaper that over the next couple of years would help draw thousands of workers into the new party. In general, workers welcomed the services that intellectuals provided—writing leaflets, making speeches, raising funds, ensuring continuity and efficiency in what of necessity had to be a secret, conspiratorial organization. But the issue of the domination of local party branches by the intelligentsia led to worker disaffection.[115] In a pamphlet of 1902, *What is to be done?*, which became more influential than it perhaps warrants, Lenin argued that the overthrow of the autocracy required an underground organization of 'professional revolutionaries', steeped in Marxist theory and adept in the rules of conspiracy. Much has been made of the fact that he argued that workers by their own efforts could only achieve 'trade-union consciousness' and that it fell to intellectuals to inject political consciousness into their struggles. However, it does appear that he expected that a cadre of professional revolutionaries drawn from the working class would gradually emerge, and when the 1905 Revolution erupted he hailed the 'spontaneity' of the working class. What Lenin certainly did believe was that workers' struggles by themselves could not make a revolution, and that to maximize their revolutionary potential, leadership by an organizationally disciplined and ideologically unified political party was necessary. The Mensheviks objected to what they saw as the tendency inherent in his model of the vanguard party for professional revolutionaries to substitute themselves for the working class, as well as to Lenin's restrictive criteria for party membership, and at the Second Congress of the RSDLP, which ended up in London, this precipitated the split in the young party into Bolshevik and Menshevik factions.

Repression had by no means vanquished the indigenous tradition of Populism, and in the mid-1890s veteran Populists began to revive their organizational activities in several regions, and from 1900 they published an influential journal, *Revolutionary Russia*. It was Viktor Chernov, son of a former serf, who recast Populist ideology in the light of Marxist class analysis, recognizing the development of capitalism in Russia's cities. He argued that the 'toiling people', that is, industrial workers and peasants together, must unite to obstruct the advance of capitalism in the countryside by expropriating the landowners; this 'socialization of the land' would have the secondary effect, he maintained, of limiting the expansion of industrial capitalism. In 1902 the Socialist Revolutionary (SR) Party was formed, essentially a conspiratorial organization without a programme, but now oriented firmly towards mass agitation, although the early results, a few peasant brotherhoods, were meagre. The notoriety of the new party sprang from the fact that it revived the tradition of terrorism, its Combat Organization carrying out a series of spectacular assassinations of hated officials. Nevertheless, as with the RSDLP, until the 1905 Revolution the influence of the SRs was limited to a few thousand people.[116]

The prelude to revolution was created not by revolutionaries but by the liberal opposition. In response to the famine of 1891 and the attempt by Alexander III to clip their wings, the zemstvos moved into the political arena. In 1895 zemstvo leaders, most of whom still emanated from the gentry, petitioned the new tsar to allow them a national representative body, but Nicholas II dismissed their demand as a 'senseless dream'. In 1899 students at St Petersburg University went on strike after clashing with police, in protest at the latter's sweeping powers of arrest, detention, search, and interception of mail. In November 1904 zemstvo leaders went a step further and convened a semi-legal congress that called for civil liberties and a popular representative assembly. It was, however, the disastrous course of the war against Japan in 1904 that catalysed the educated public into demanding political reform. The poor leadership, equipment, and training of the Russian army and navy were brutally exposed and seemed to exemplify the rottenness of the political system. In January 1904, the now liberal Struve helped bring into being the underground Union of Liberation, a loose-knit coalition that pressed for a constitutional monarchy, universal suffrage, and self-determination for the non-Russian ethnic groups. Liberal groups organized a series of banquets across the country, most of which endorsed the resolution of the zemstvo congress, and some of which demanded a constituent assembly to determine the future form of government.[117] Despite the efforts of the moderate Minister of the Interior, Prince P. D. Sviatopolk-Mirskii, who had just replaced Vyacheslav von Plehve following his assassination by the Socialist Revolutionary Combat Organization, Nicholas made only vague promises and refused to give ground on the critical issue of political representation. With government greatly underestimating the strength of the opposition, the stage was set for revolution.

The 1905 Revolution

On 9 January 1905 Father Georgii Gapon, head of the Assembly of Russian Factory and Mill Workers, a semi-trade union set up with the approval of the Ministry of the Interior, led a procession of 150,000 workers and their families to the Winter Palace to present a petition to the tsar.[118] They were protesting against the sacking of delegates elected to the Assembly by the workers of the Putilov plant, the largest factory in Russia with over 12,000 workers. The city was paralysed by a general strike, and the authorities were jittery. The petition they bore was framed in the traditional language of supplication to the 'little father', but its demands, which had been formulated in consultation with the Union of Liberation, were far-reaching, and included inviolability of the person, freedom of speech, the press, and association, freedom of conscience, separation of Church and state, equality before the law, an end to redemption payments, freedom to form trade unions, the right to strike, an eight-hour working day, insurance benefits, and improved wages. Singing hymns and bearing religious banners, the procession wended its way towards the city centre. The tsar was not actually in the capital at the time, but ministers ordered that squadrons of cavalry prevent the demonstrators from getting close to Palace Square. As contingents continued to make their way towards the centre, armed infantry opened fire: 200 were killed outright and another 800 wounded. 'Bloody Sunday', as this massacre became known, had a traumatic impact on the country, setting off months of strikes, rebellions, demonstrations, and political organizing. The nascent labour movement now joined forces with the educated middle-class and gentry opposition in an 'all-nation struggle' for a constitution and civil rights and for an end to the Russo-Japanese war (Figure 1.3).[119]

Figure 1.3 Troops fire on demonstrators, Bloody Sunday 1905.

Strikes spilled across the empire in spring and summer, initially in outrage at the events in the capital, giving birth to a more organized labour movement. Most strikes were conflicts with employers, often very bitter, over wages and working hours, but the intervention of the authorities gave them a strongly political character. In some places strikers came out onto the streets, bearing banners proclaiming 'Down with autocracy' and 'Down with the war', but revolutionaries were not always welcomed by strikers. Railway workers in Saratov, who struck successfully in January for a nine-hour day, an end to compulsory overtime, and wage rises, prevented socialists from intervening in their strike. Yet it was their success that inspired employees of the Southern Railway Company to go on strike in February and they, too, achieved an eight-hour day, elected worker delegates, and a promise of freedom of assembly. When the government imposed martial law on the railways in an attempt to prevent the stoppages spreading, it precipitated the formation of the non-partisan All-Russian Union of Railway Workers.[120]

Some of the most tempestuous labour unrest occurred in Łódź in Poland, where conflicts with the Russian authorities took on a nationalist coloration.

The war with Japan had produced a downturn in the Polish economy, with 100,000 having lost their jobs, so Bloody Sunday provoked a furious response. On 5 June troops opened fire on a demonstration, killing about ten workers. The next day angry workers began setting up barricades and killed some members of police and military patrols. An insurrection followed which was eventually put down by six infantry and several cavalry regiments especially brought into Łódź. Polish nationalists came out in support of the insurgents, although clashes between the supporters of the Polish Socialist Party of Józef Piłsudski and supporters of the more right-wing militias of Roman Dmowski broke out. Russian troops crushed the uprising mercilessly, and the number of killed and injured exceeded the casualties of Bloody Sunday by some way.[121] The wave of strikes across the empire took on increasing momentum, drawing in all types of wage earners, from skilled male metalworkers to unskilled female textile workers, from artisans to white-collar employees. Central to the strike movement was a drive to establish trade unions and cooperatives and this was spearheaded by skilled, urbanized male workers, including artisans, white-collar workers, and workers in retail, who had come under the influence of socialist agitators. Printers, in particular, played a combative role, their strike in September for better wages and conditions being the prelude to the general strike the following month.[122] According to far from complete data, there were some 14,000 strikes in 1905 in which 2.86 million workers took part: it made a huge impression on the socialist movement internationally.[123]

The general strike that began in the oilfields of Baku in December 1904 was in many ways typical of the strikes of 1905, in that it was characterized by an urgent desire for concrete gains, the intermeshing of economic and political grievances, explosions of destructive fury, tension between workers and revolutionary parties, and bitter rivalry within the revolutionary camp. In summer 1904 the three Shendrikov brothers, who hailed from a Semirech'e Cossack background, arrived in Baku from Tashkent and formed the Organization of Balakhanski and Bibi-Eibat Workers. Although the local Social Democrats, mainly Mensheviks, supported this initiative, they were soon thrust aside by the Cossack incomers. The latter also attacked the small group of Bolsheviks for supposedly being contemptuous of workers' economic demands and hostile to democratic control of the RSDLP by workers. The three brothers were immensely energetic and powerful orators, especially Il'ia, and their influence grew fast. By December the Organization had 4,000 members—compared with about 300 in the Baku RSDLP—and in November it began to prepare a general strike to demand sizeable wage increases, a three-shift system, payment of wages during holidays and illness, the firing of those administrators the workers did not like, together with political demands for civil rights and the overthrow of the autocracy. The Bolsheviks argued that a strike in winter was folly because the movement of oil through the Caspian Sea was restricted, and they called for a political demonstration that might lead to an uprising. When the Organization went ahead with the stoppage on 13 December, however, some 50,000 workers joined it enthusiastically. By drawing in the Gnchak, the Armenian socialist party, and the Hummet, a mainly Azeri party, the Bolsheviks managed to seize leadership of the strike committee, which entered into negotiations with the employers and appeared to get a good deal. The committee advised the strikers to return to work on 28 December, but the Organization accused them of strike-breaking, and proceeded to unleash arson attacks on 265 oil derricks, doing lasting damage to the oil industry. In the face of this, the Union of Oil Industrialists caved in to most of the Organization's demands and signed the first collective contract in Russia. During spring 1905, as the labour movement surged across the empire, the Organization, now renamed the Union of Baku Workers, grew, organizing strikes in a number of large oil companies. Its basic demand was for the creation of elected commissions of workers that had the right to negotiate with the employers. In November these commissions played a key part in establishing a soviet in Baku, which was dominated by the members of the Union and by Mensheviks. During the preceding months the local Bolsheviks had grown in strength, however, and on 13 December 1905 they persuaded the soviet to call a general strike. Nothing came of this, in part because the brothers Shendrikov now seemed less keen to take on the employers. Meanwhile, their Menshevik allies were losing confidence in the Union, as evidence began to mount that the brothers were receiving payments from the Union of Oil Industrialists. It is possible that there was substance to the Bolshevik charge that from the first the Union had been an attempt to create a pro-government union, such as had been created by police chief Sergei Zubatov. But if the brothers did receive funds from the industrialists or the police, they certainly did nothing to curb labour militancy; quite the contrary. The exposé in 1906 of their closeness to the employers, however, did do lasting damage and the Union went into terminal decline. In an ironic postscript, after the October Revolution, the most charismatic of the brothers, Il'ia, became a representative of the Semirech'e Cossack Host under Admiral Kolchak and in 1925 founded a Cossack Union in Shanghai.[124]

Meanwhile during summer 1905 the liberal opposition grew apace and exercised a not insignificant influence on the labour movement. Student protests led to the closure of universities for several months, and the Union of Unions, which campaigned for universal male suffrage, helped professionals, white-collar workers, and a few blue-collar groups to form unions. By October 100,000 were affiliated to the Union. On 6 August Tsar Nicholas agreed to the formation of a consultative assembly, a concession that if made in February might well have satisfied the liberal opposition. Now it came too late. What shifted the balance of power in favour of the opposition movements was the general strike that was sparked when the Union of Railway Workers launched a strike on 4 October, thereby bringing activity in the country to a halt. Over the next weeks hundreds of thousands of workers walked off their jobs demanding an eight-hour day and an end to autocracy. The strike was supported by students and professional groups, and in Moscow between 12 and 18 October intellectuals and professionals met to form the Constitutional Democratic Party, known as the Kadets. This liberal party demanded universal suffrage, a Constituent Assembly, land reform, and many radical social reforms.

During the October general strike a novel form of organization came into existence—one that was to have far-reaching significance for the future revolutionary movement. On 13 October a soviet was formed in St Petersburg by

Menshevik labour leaders. It soon acquired the appurtenances of a revolutionary government, forming a militia, distributing food supplies, and publishing a newspaper that was read nationally. Significantly, however, it rejected the RSDLP political platform, declaring that 'there are no parties now'. Soviets sprang up in some fifty cities, not only leading strikes but also setting up militias, controlling railways and postal services, and printing newspapers. In Novorossiisk on the Black Sea the mayor and town duma agreed to accept the authority of the soviet after the local garrison mutinied.[125] The formation of soviets may have been what finally persuaded the tsar to listen to Witte's advice and make some serious political concessions. For on 17 October, he issued the October Manifesto, which granted civil rights and a legislative assembly, or duma, based on a broad but unequal franchise, and a legislative upper chamber, called the State Council. For moderate members of the liberal opposition, alarmed by the escalation of violence in the countryside and by labour unrest in the cities, this represented a victory. For the left, it was not enough.

By early November, the general strike in the capital was losing momentum and employers were preparing a lockout. In Moscow, however, a soviet had not yet been formed, it being late November before the Mensheviks took the initiative, this time with the support of Bolsheviks and SRs. On 2 December the soviet movement nationally received a body blow, when 260 deputies to the St Petersburg Soviet were arrested, including Lev D. Trotsky who, as a chair of the Soviet, had played an outstanding role in the turbulent events. With some reluctance the Moscow Soviet agreed to call a general strike, and was surprised and cheered when 80,000 workers responded to its call. This spurred the Bolsheviks to press ahead with what they had been calling for all year: namely, an armed insurrection. On 9 December, following bitter clashes between troops and strikers, workers' militias set up barricades in the Presnia district of the city. In the street battles that followed over the next week government troops fired artillery barrages, crushing the insurgents with appalling brutality. In all some 700 insurgents were killed and 2,000 wounded, compared with 70 police and troops (see Figure 1.4).[126]

Figure 1.4 The armed uprising in Moscow, December 1905.

The repressive organs of the state remained largely intact. From January to October the army was used no fewer than 2,700 times to put down peasant uprisings.[127] Yet most soldiers were peasants, who resented being used against their own people, so their reliability was always doubtful. Even among the infantry, however, the branch of the army most seriously affected by disorder, two-thirds of units did not engage in unrest, and the vast majority of officers remained loyal. So the government proved able to use relatively small, well-armed detachments to great effect against poorly armed and poorly trained bands of peasants and workers. Unrest ran deepest in the navy, where the reverberations of defeat by Japan were most acutely felt. On 14 June 1905 on the battleship *Potemkin* sailors of the Black Sea Fleet rebelled against their officers, the immediate cause being rotten meat and the squalid conditions on board ship. Sailors were mainly literate and had plenty of time to connect their grievances to wider political issues. The signing of the Treaty of Portsmouth in September, which ended the war with Japan, did nothing to quell the mounting unrest. Following the October general strike, the bonds of discipline snapped. There were more than 200 episodes in November and December, and 130 more between January and June

1906.[128] In late 1905 the government deemed it wise to activate 100,000 Cossacks whose privileges it confirmed with special charters. Even the Cossacks, however—the only social estate to be defined by their military obligations to the state—could not always be relied upon. In June 1906 the Cossacks of the Ust'-Medveditskii district in the Don revolted, declaring that 'police service is incompatible with the title of Cossack as a warrior and defender of the fatherland'.[129] Among soldiers and peasants the opening of the first duma in late April 1906 spurred a new round of turbulence in expectation of major land reform. By this date, however, the labour movement was in decline and this enabled the government gradually to reassert its authority.

From spring 1905 a colossal wave of peasant rebellion had swept across the central black-earth region, the middle Volga provinces (Penza, Samara, Saratov, and Simbirsk), and Ukraine. Rising up in spring and early summer 1905, it fell back in late summer, but soared again in the wake of the October Manifesto. It then subsided to resume in May to August 1906.[130] Peasants seized on the fact that the repressive organs of the state were overstretched in order to settle scores with the landowners, to 'smoke them out of their gentry nests'. In Voronezh, one of the most disorderly provinces in the central black-earth region, rebellion was heavily concentrated in the one-third of counties that were dominated by landlords.[131] Here peasants engaged in unprecedented assaults on landlord property, burning and destroying estates and outbuildings, illegally cutting wood, seizing meadows, pasture, and arable land, raiding barns and granaries, and engaging in rent and labour strikes. In the Baltic provinces and the Caucasus there was an admixture of national sentiment, with peasant disorders directed at the institutions and symbols of Russian authority.[132] The regions of high peasant militancy tended to be those where social differentiation within the rural population was less developed, with the majority of participants coming from the largest swathe of the rural populace, the middle peasants, although wealthier peasants also took part.[133] In right-bank Ukraine, in the provinces of Kyiv, Podillia, and Volyn', where agricultural capitalism was well developed, poor peasants instigated many of the riots.[134] Young men led the way, with women playing a prominent part in collective seizures of food and fodder.[135] Notwithstanding the land hunger of the peasantry, it is doubtful that economic distress as such was the direct cause of the revolt. In parts of the central black-earth and middle Volga province there were crop failures in 1905, but this followed a bumper harvest the previous year; and in Ukraine the harvest was normal. The key factor seems to have been the paralysis of the organs of authority and the impact of the Revolution itself, which led to a rapid politicization of sections of rural society. The Socialist Revolutionaries were active on the ground, creating peasant brotherhoods and expanding aspirations in a socialist direction. By contrast the All-Russian Peasant Union, created in July 1905, was based more in the zemstvos, and sought to steer the peasantry away from violence towards forming a mass party that would join the 'all-nation struggle' for a constitution and full civil and political rights and, in due course, achieve the abolition of private landholding.[136]

The October Manifesto said nothing about the land question, yet there was a wide presumption that the duma would enact a transfer of landlords' lands to the peasants. Yet peasant aspirations went beyond the land question to embrace demands for the nationalization of land, an elected Constituent Assembly, civil rights, and a political amnesty.[137] It was, above all, the convocation of the duma in April 1906 that significantly raised the level of political consciousness. Peasant petitions to the duma—which the rural intelligentsia and political activists helped to draw up—presented an abject picture of poverty, ruin, ignorance, and absence of rights. Major demands were for the abolition of private property in land and its redistribution to those who would work it. Even in a non-black-earth province such as Vladimir, about 190 km north-east of Moscow, more than a quarter of petitions demanded the return of 'cut-off' lands, that is, those lands once worked by serfs that the nobility had retained in 1861.[138] Present, too, were demands for the abolition of redemption payments and indirect taxes, and for the partition of forests and hay meadows. These petitions show that the political isolation of the countryside was breaking down. By the time the Revolution was quelled in 1907, the empire had endured the most intense wave of agrarian upheaval since the Pugachëv rebellion of 1773–5, and the centuries-long faith in the tsar as 'little father' had plummeted.[139]

In the non-Russian borderlands the impact of the 1905 Revolution was substantial, boosting the emergence of separatist nationalism. In Ukraine as early as 1900 a congress of student societies in Kharkiv had formed a Revolutionary Ukrainian Party, committed to socialism and self-determination for Ukraine. In December 1905, it transformed itself into the Ukrainian Social-Democratic Workers' Party, but despite increasing support for some form of autonomy, many socialists, who were active in organizing mass strikes and land seizures, worked within the framework of the All-Russian parties, notably the RSDLP, the SRs, and the Jewish Bund.[140] The Revolution was spectacularly violent in the southern Caucasus, where mass strikes, armed clashes, and assassinations of officials were legion. In Guria in Georgia, Mensheviks, teachers, and priests organized local peasants to throw out the tsarist administration and a revolutionary administration took over the running of the community.[141] In Armenia the head of the empire's police deplored the fact that the socialist Dashnaktsutyun movement, which rallied a broad swathe of popular support, had created a quasi-independent state with its own militia, courts, and administration. In the Baltic provinces, too, revolutionary turbulence ran high. In Latvia strikers protesting Bloody Sunday on 13 January were fired on by Russian troops, killing 73 and injuring 200. Through the summer agricultural and industrial workers went on strike, peasants refused to pay rents and sacked the estates of German landowners, and the public boycotted courts and administrative institutions run by Russians.[142] On 16 October in Revel' (Tallinn) troops killed 94 and injured 200 dispersing a demonstration at which the Estonian flag was raised for the first time. The first Estonian party, the National Progress Party, also emerged.

A major non-Russian population that was much less affected by the Revolution were the almost 20 million Muslims in the empire, who were roughly divided between the different ethnicities of Central Asia, the Azeri Turks and mountain peoples of Transcaucasia, and the Tatars of the middle Volga, Urals, and Crimea.[143] The latter were something of an exception, since incipient nationalism was already evident. The Tatars, who were scattered and interspersed with Russians, were the most socio-economically advanced of the Muslim peoples: a bourgeoisie existed in the Volga region, although in Crimea a landed nobility still preserved its privileges. Among the Tatars reformist intellectuals known as jadids—their name deriving from the 'new method' that they promoted in education—had from the last decades of the nineteenth century begun to reconfigure Muslim culture according to ideas of progress and enlightenment, in the teeth of opposition from the *ulama,* Islamic scholars. In 1905 merchants, clerics, teachers, lawyers, mainly from Kazan', Ufa, and other cities in the Volga and Urals regions, founded the Ittifak al-Mülimin, or Union of Russian Muslims, which called for a representative organ for all Muslims, for mullahs to have the same rights as priests, and for the easing of restrictions on education and the press. Nevertheless there was no sign that Muslims in this region were looking for independent statehood.[144]

The largest concentration of Muslims was in Turkestan, which had been incorporated into the empire in 1867 but whose conquest dragged on until 1889. Turkestan, including the ancient cities of Samarkand and Bukhara in Transoxiana, was a vast area of oasis and river agriculture, bordered to the north by the desert steppe (modern Kazakhstan) and to the south-west by desert (modern Turkmenistan). The sedentary peoples of the oasis, who under the Bolsheviks would develop identities as Uzbeks and Tadzhiks (the latter close to Iranian rather than to Turkic culture), combined agriculture with commerce and handicrafts. A majority of the Kazakhs of the northern steppes, the Kyrghyz of the eastern plateaux (both lumped together by contemporaries as 'Kirghiz'), and the Turkmen in the south-west tended to combine nomadic stock-breeding with marginal agriculture and the caravan trade. In Central Asia as a whole, identities were defined primarily at the level of clans, villages, or oases, or at the macro-level in terms of membership of the commonwealth of Islam. Ethno-national identities would only emerge after 1917 (and class identities barely at all). In this region, however, the issue of Russian colonization was stoking up conflict for the future, especially in the Kazakh steppes, which had been under Russian control longer than Turkestan, and where 1.5 million Russians would settle between 1906 and 1912, helped by the opening of the Orenburg to Tashkent railway. Tashkent, the largest city in Turkestan, already had a sizeable Russian population. The conflict to come would be between natives and settlers over land and water rights, as intensive cotton extraction was developed in the Fergana Valley.[145]

The 1905 Revolution put relations between Church and state under great strain. An edict of 17 April 1905 granted freedom of conscience to the subjects of the empire, in effect allowing those registered as Orthodox to convert to another (Christian) denomination. Churchmen were furious, alarmed at the edict's implications for the rapidly growing Protestant denominations, such as Baptists and Evangelicals, and for Uniates in Ukraine, interpreting the measure as a body blow to Russian identity. By supporting nationalists in the duma—and turning a blind eye to proto-fascists on the street—churchmen successfully blocked the attempt to enact the edict into law. Nicholas further embittered relations with the Church by refusing to allow a church council to convene (the last had met in 1681–2). The Revolution also deepened tensions within the Church: radical clergy called for root-and-branch reform, while forty-three seminaries were shut in November because of student protests. The occasional bishop such as Antonin Granovskii came out against the autocracy, but the majority of the hierarchy looked askance at the revolutionary movement, and a sizeable minority loudly denounced any concessions to a constitution or civil rights. Nevertheless the Church would never again be close to Nicholas II and would abandon him without demur in February 1917.

That the autocracy came out of the Revolution relatively unscathed had little to do with clever political tactics. Throughout 1905, it proved unable to deal effectively with a vast, socially diverse movement that clamoured for political and social change. Timely concessions early in the year—two official commissions recommended workers' representative commissions, trade unions, and the right to strike—might have prevented the escalation of political ambitions and the upsurge in violence that swept the country, but the recommendations were initially shelved. Working in favour of the autocracy was the fact that neither the liberal Union of Unions, nor the labour movement, nor the peasant movement, nor the nationalist movements were particularly well organized. Each arose out of the chaos of events and it took time for leadership to emerge, for structures to be set in place, and for aims to be clarified. Until the October Manifesto, there was loose unity around the goal of gaining civil rights and some form of democratic polity, but no unified national leadership, and the Manifesto drove a wedge between those whose aim was political reform and those who wanted social revolution. Moreover, the tempo of each movement varied, especially as between the cities and the countryside, and between the peasantry and labour movement, and this lack of synchronization also worked to the government's advantage. Significant concessions were made in the October Manifesto, yet they failed to still the social turbulence and, seeing the radicalization of the 'Days of Freedom', the government opted for repression as the principal means of restoring order. It was fortunate for them that the armed forces, although shaky in their loyalty, remained basically reliable. As the social movements lost dynamism, spectacular repression would ensue.

2

FROM REFORM TO WAR, 1906–1917

The proclamation of the October Manifesto seemed to augur major reform of the political system, a resumption of the course that had been started by Alexander II in the 1860s but aborted after his assassination. Yet it was evident that Nicholas had granted a parliament under duress. The Fundamental Laws of April 1906, though instituting a form of constitutional monarchy, a duma, civil rights, limited rights for trade unions, and a reduction in censorship, reaffirmed the tsar's role as autocrat, giving him complete control of the executive, foreign policy, the Church, and the armed forces. On 3 June 1907 final proof that the balance of power had swung back towards the establishment came when the second duma was dissolved and some of its members arrested. Pëtr Stolypin, who had replaced Witte as Prime Minister in July 1906, instituted a dramatic change in the electoral base of the duma, drastically cutting the representation of the lower classes and increasing that of the propertied, and thereby considerably reducing the number of liberal and socialist deputies in the third duma, which convened in November 1907.[1]

Following the October Manifesto, new political parties quickly emerged to contest the duma elections. The Kadets, or Constitutional Democrats, were a liberal party whose main demands were for a constituent assembly and universal suffrage, and this was supplemented by a relatively radical social programme, including a solution to the land question that would involve compulsory purchase of landowners' estates. At this stage, the Kadets tended to favour working with the more moderate Social Democrats, rather than with conservative deputies. The Octobrists, as their name suggests, supported the settlement established by the October Manifesto, and were altogether more conservative on the land question and anxious to see an end to revolutionary turbulence. Following the issuance of the Manifesto, socialist leaders such as Lenin and the Mensheviks Iulii Martov and Fëdor Dan returned from exile (Trotsky had returned in secret as early as February). The Bolsheviks opted not to participate in the election to the first duma, but the Mensheviks and SRs did, albeit with modest results. It was the Kadets, in alliance with the left-leaning Trudovik faction, which represented peasants, who won a majority in the elections, and the first duma proceeded to draft a substantial body of progressive legislation. Yet after only ten weeks the duma was dissolved when negotiations with the Council of Ministers, appointed by and accountable to the tsar, ended in rancour.[2] Elections to the second duma were carefully orchestrated by Stolypin, who banned meetings, removed voters from the electoral lists, and gave financial support to right-wing candidates. Although the radical right made significant strides in this second election, the clear winners were still the left, with socialists doubling their seats (the Bolsheviks participating this time). The influence of the Kadets, however, was much reduced, and they gradually turned away from the radical stance they had adopted in the first duma, opting to try to work with the government. The second duma also proved short-lived, becoming deadlocked over land reform and the use of repression by the government. When Stolypin's demand to expel Social Democratic deputies and deprive some of their parliamentary immunity was rejected, it was dissolved on 3 June 1906.[3] Finally, we should note a new development —one that reacted against the radicalism of the first two dumas—in the form of radical-right street politics, evinced in the rise of the Union of the Russian People and other organizations that mobilized a heavily lower-class membership around a rabidly nationalist, anti-democratic, and anti-revolutionary platform.[4]

Nicholas's determination to maintain his divinely ordained position as all-powerful autocrat hardened in the face of the radicalism displayed by the first and second dumas, puncturing any hope he might have entertained of restoring the sacred bond between tsar and people. At the same time, the ebbing of the mass movements from summer 1906 encouraged him to unleash the full might of state repression in order to suppress the insurgency. Already in late 1905 punitive expeditions had begun to pacify the countryside and insurrections in the Baltic and Caucasus. Following the bombing of his villa by Socialist Revolutionary 'Maximalists' in which twenty-eight were killed, including his daughter, Stolypin set up field courts-martial that summarily tried and hanged up to 3,000 insurgents between 1906 and 1909 ('Stolypin's necktie').[5] For its part, the Union of the Russian People, with the backing of Nicholas, together with paramilitary groups known as Black Hundreds, fought revolutionaries on the streets and carried out pogroms against Jews. They aimed to restore 'true' autocracy and eliminate everything pertaining to the hated innovations of October 1905, yet they did so through modern methods of mass mobilization. Alongside this, thousands of acts of terror were carried out by revolutionaries, mainly by SRs and nationalists, and were no longer aimed primarily at high-profile members of the political elite but at low-ranking officials and police. Stolypin himself was eventually killed by a Jewish anarchist in Kyiv in 1911, possibly with the connivance of the far right.[6] The Bolsheviks eschewed terrorist tactics, but did engage in 'exes', that is, armed expropriations of banks and government offices.

Prospects for Reform

The dominant discourse of 1905 was one of citizenship, rather than of socialism. The citizen was conceived as one who, regardless of the obligations and rights accorded them by virtue of the social estate into which they were born, insisted on their equality before the law and claimed the right to be represented and to participate in the polity on an equal basis with their co-nationals. Women were invisible when it came to the political rights of citizenship, although groups of middle-class women—inspired by the example of the Duchy of Finland—formed the All-Russian Union for Women's Equality in January 1905. Their campaign to be given the vote, however, came to naught, political leaders such as the Kadet leader, Pavel Miliukov, disdaining to support them.[7] For peasants and workers, this essentially liberal conception of citizenship mattered: but for them civil and political rights were inseparable from social rights. Individual rights, moreover, were inseparable from the collective rights of self-defence and subsistence. Whereas for educated society private property was the bedrock of citizenship, for working people citizenship, construed as an integrated package of civil, political, and social rights, could not be realized without a drastic restructuring of the social order, above all, around the land question.[8] Notwithstanding this crucial difference, the concept of citizenship was rooted in a new idea of national identity. As a result of the 'all-nation' struggle for citizenship in 1905–6, Russian national identity was no longer tied to the Orthodoxy, Autocracy, and Nationality formula of Nicholas I, except among conservatives, and had come to be associated with membership of a bounded political community that should be governed in the interests of its members.[9] This entailed the extension of civil and political rights to non-Russians in the empire even though the conception of national identity that underpinned it was still implicitly imperial, with Russians assumed to have a civilizing mission to lead non-Russians towards progress. The Russianness of this conception was most starkly in evidence when it came to dealing with the challenge of rising nationalism, not least among Muslims, where liberal and even socialist opinion tended to dismiss moderate Muslim demands for representation as a symptom of fanaticism and ignorance.

The period between 1907 and 1914 was referred to by contemporaries as the 'Years of Reaction', but historians today are more likely to emphasize the positive developments of this period, usually summed up as a strengthening of 'civil society'. By this they mean a sphere of civic life in which the 'public' expanded its activities in ways that were autonomous from the state. The origins of this sphere go back to the reign of Catherine the Great (1762–96), but after 1905 it expanded on an unprecedented scale, with the proliferation of voluntary societies and political parties, the growth of the press and a new reading public, and the development of new forms of commercial entertainment.[10] The interest in these developments shown by historians in the last two decades has reopened a long-standing debate between those who see Russia as moving away from revolution in the period after 1905, its more evolutionary path of development obstructed by the outbreak of the First World War, and those who see reformist energies as having exhausted themselves by 1914 and who point to the signs of a revolutionary crisis on the eve of war. Although this debate cannot be altogether avoided, it is perhaps more illuminating to resist its either/or character and to put emphasis on the contradictoriness and complexity of developments in the post-1905 period. These developments were not only tied to the political reforms instituted by the October Manifesto and to the advance of civil society but also to rapid economic, social, and cultural changes that did not move in tandem with high politics, and are not best understood by simply asking if Russia was moving away from revolution or heading towards the abyss.[11]

For many decades the debate between optimists and pessimists focused on the third duma and the prospects for cooperation between the new parliament and the monarchy in setting the empire on a road to peaceful modernization. Unlike its predecessors, the third duma lasted its full course, its reliability secured by the simple expedient of reducing the representation of non-Russians, peasants, and workers and increasing that of landowners and businessmen. The 1905 Revolution had profoundly shaken the confidence of the nobility who, in the face of popular insurgency and non-Russian nationalism, moved from a woolly liberalism towards an intransigent conservatism. In 1906, paying their own tribute to the idea of civil society, members of the nobility formed a pressure group, the United Nobility, which campaigned successfully to reduce the representation of the lower classes in the third duma. The nobility dominated the State Council, which had been transformed into an upper chamber of the duma in October 1905, and they used this dominance to block legislation, emanating from the lower chamber, to extend the zemstvos to the western provinces, to democratize the law courts and education system, and to provide legal guarantees for non-Orthodox faiths. One consequence of the failure to reform local government was that provincial governors, police, and administration carried on much as they had done for half a century. The failure of the duma, however, cannot be laid at the door of the State Council, since it managed to jeopardize the prospects for political reform by its own internal wrangling. Stolypin began his premiership keen to cooperate with the duma in implementing reforms that would buttress social stability, and his agrarian reforms were gradually passed into legislation. The Octobrists constituted the linchpin of Stolypin's support in the duma, but they increasingly divided between those who leaned towards the Kadets and those who leaned towards the Nationalists (a party that emerged in October 1909). More generally, Stolypin's ability to secure cooperation between duma and government was weakened by his own forceful character, by rightist intrigues, and by the withdrawal of the tsar's support. His successor as Prime Minister, V. N. Kokovtsov, lacking his energy and vision, was unable to cobble together a working bloc of support in the duma, and relations between Octobrists and Nationalists became deadlocked. Overall, the legislative record of the duma was not impressive, and as a mechanism designed to transform the political system it was a clear failure.[12]

If we look at relations between duma and government from a less institutional standpoint, however, their inability to cooperate becomes harder to explain. The expansion of a modern version of Russian national identity might have been expected to cement an alliance between a significant part of the educated public and government, if only because of loose consensus around foreign policy. The Revolution strengthened a conception of the vital forces of the nation that was no longer tied closely to the state, yet the liberal opposition never doubted that the Russian state must be defended against foreign threat (and against the exigent clamour of her non-Russian peoples).[13] So far as foreign policy was concerned, a broad swathe of elite opinion backed the government's determination to slow, and, with hope, to reverse Russia's decline as a great power, manifest in her defeat by Japan, in Austria's annexation of Bosnia, and soon in her impotence during the Balkan wars. The main threat, of course, came from an expansionist Germany, notably in south-eastern Europe, where for strategic and economic reasons Germany was cooperating with the Ottoman government, particularly in the plan to construct the Berlin–Baghdad railway (1903), in aggressive arms sales by the Krupp and Mauser companies, and in various Prussian military missions. Germany's clear desire to expand its power aroused anxiety across Russia's elites, to which the press gave political shape. The conservative newspaper *New Times (Novoe Vremia)* advocated a firm alliance with France and Britain to counter German expansionism, while the more widely read liberal newspaper *The Russian Word (Russkoe Slovo)* took the same position, although decrying jingoism. This made diplomatic efforts to mitigate tensions with Germany difficult.[14] Certainly, there were differences among the elites, notably between a vocal lobby advocating Slavic unity and cooler heads, such as Stolypin and Miliukov, who warned of the danger of war. Yet all agreed that it was Russia's historic destiny to maintain its status as a great power and supported the government's efforts to advance Russia's interests in the deeply unstable Balkans, even if this ran the risk of war. Kadets, Octobrists, and Nationalists all backed the massive rearmament drive of the government, which led to roughly one-third of the budget going towards the expansion of the navy and army between 1909 and 1913. Russia's military expenditure came to exceed that of Britain, which had a far-flung empire to protect.[15] Her naval expenditure, in fact, lagged well behind that of Britain and Germany, but expenditure on land warfare was much greater.[16]

So far as domestic policy was concerned, the symbol of Russia One and Indivisible was one around which a broad swathe of the elite could adhere, even if some, like Miliukov, favoured a less chauvinist policy towards the non-Russians than did the United Nobility.[17] This was evident in widely shared fears of pan-Turkism and pan-Islamism. It was evident, too, in the duma's response to a number of conservative measures to restrict the rise of non-Russian nationalism: it agreed to reduce the power of Finnish institutions; to support settlers in Central Asia who seized nomadic grazing land; to increase restriction on Jews; and to detach the region of Chelm (Kholm) from the Kingdom of Poland and to incorporate it as a 'true Russian' province. This last action in September 1913 incensed Polish nationalists such as Roman Dmowski. The duma also supported Stolypin's proposal to extend zemstvos to the western provinces—in reality, despite his plan to base electoral assemblies on nationality not social estate, a ploy to safeguard Russian interests. Indeed the duma showed only lukewarm support for increasing Polish representation and none at all for instituting Jewish representation.[18] As with foreign policy, then, despite entrenched divisions between the duma, State Council, and ministers, a broad swathe of the elite subscribed to an imperial version of Russian national identity. It was the tsar himself who prevented this shared sense of national identity cementing a bloc between government and the duma, for he was not prepared to tolerate the duma encroaching on matters of defence and foreign policy—areas that remained his prerogative under the Fundamental Laws.[19]

If we turn attention away from the Tauride Palace, seat of the new parliament, the prospects for Russia look less bleak, since this was a period of activism in the public sphere and of rapid cultural and social change. Many now see the years after 1905 as the time when people of all walks of life tried to realize the liberties of conscience, speech, assembly, association, and religion that had been granted by the October Manifesto. Professional associations of doctors, lawyers, and others grew more active, universities expanded, political parties were established. Most of these professionals rejected old-style family life, female subordination, and police rule, and sought to enlist education and social reform in the battle against communal control and the tyranny of custom. Yet though these professionals adopted the liberal ideal of the autonomous individual, they generally rejected western bourgeois regard for self-interest and self-fulfilment.[20] By 1900 Russia already had some 10,000 voluntary associations and these now mushroomed, in areas as diverse as science and education, agriculture, charity, sports, or local history. This represented a strengthening of civil society and may, correspondingly, have represented a diminution of the power of the state, although most of these societies existed legally and thus were ratified by the state. Moreover, their initiatives in such areas as improving public health, popularizing science, expanding education, or promoting patriotism coincided with the government's own projects.[21]

Another manifestation of the development of a public sphere lay in the rapid expansion of the press and of publishing more generally, which was aided by the easing of censorship. By 1913 Russia was the second largest producer of books in the world, ranking close to Germany in the number of titles.[22] Newspapers sought actively to shape public opinion and ministers were forced to justify their policies through them. The press expanded vigorously, as a result of a rapidly growing reading public, advertising revenue, new technologies that made illustration relatively cheap, and because there was a taste among new mass readers for content of a sensational nature. Newly literate readers consumed adventure stories, detective fiction, romantic fiction, all of which tended to promote more secular, rational, and cosmopolitan attitudes and encouraged individuals to feel they could take some responsibility for their lives.[23] The *Gazeta Kopeika* (*Penny Newpaper*) was a tabloid produced in St Petersburg, aimed at a lower-class readership, which by 1909 had achieved a circulation of 250,000, big by the standards of the time. By 1911 there were twenty-nine penny dailies in circulation.[24] To grab their readers' attention, these newspapers relied on news and sensational crime stories, sometimes accompanied by woodcut illustrations, along with advertisements for all kinds of consumer goods. At the same time, journalists on these newspapers sought to draw the lower classes into the public sphere, promoting values of honest work, individual choice, and social aspiration.[25]

The appearance of tabloids aimed at a lower-class readership was part of the growth of a consumer culture aimed at the urban classes with a small amount of disposable income. New patterns of leisure emerged in the city, with commercial entertainments, such as pleasure gardens, music hall, popular theatre, silent movies, and detective fiction, all offered to the lower classes at relatively affordable prices. These new cultural products exposed peasant migrants to the city to new kinds of characters and story lines, as the historian Louise McReynolds has argued. 'Rude resistance to authority, the predatory sexuality of gold-diggers, even the sharpened ethnic awareness of cityfolk were all new experience that gave characters motives unknown in the recent past. Personality became the focus and driving engine of narrative.'[26] Her larger argument—and the point at issue in this section—is that mass culture tended to depoliticize visions of the social order, to downplay class conflict, and to extol middle-class values that fostered social cohesion. This was almost certainly one effect of consumer culture, but we should be careful of assuming that it precluded the formation of more exclusive identities.

In the cities the structure of retailing was still traditional, in that the vast majority of urban consumers bought their goods in markets and fairs. Yet the appearance of the department store captured the imagination of urbanites, with its bright lights and advertisements, luxurious interiors, fancy display windows, and the variety of merchandise. The department store was the symbol par excellence of consumer culture, using goods and promotional images to educate consumers—mainly female—in fashion and good taste and to promote desire and to construct fantasies of affluence. The department store was principally a place where the bourgeoisie learned how to dress, furnish its homes, and spend its leisure time, but the lower classes, too, learned about the fashions of the day, standards of comfort, and ideals of respectability, mainly through window shopping. These things even percolated to the countryside, or at least to those regions from which there was extensive migration. Mikhail Isakovskii, whose sister migrated to Moscow from Smolensk to work in a textile mill, recalls how proud she was of the fashionable *sak*—a loose-fitting coat which draped from the shoulders:

> Women saved because you could not live without a sak. Those who did not have a sak felt they were deprived of their full rights, not fully valued, on the slide. There were endless conversations among the women workers about buying a sak. And if they bought one, they wrote to the village at once, to tell everyone that the long-desired sak had been purchased.[27]

Peasant migrants took back to the village newly acquired tastes in dress, home decorating, and diet, as well as cheap consumer durables. The acquisition of fashionable manufactured clothing, samovars, or lamps helped to shape notions of respectability, although intellectuals and churchmen were quick to deprecate 'tasteless and useless dandyism'. The crucial point for the argument about where Russia was going, however, is that values of consumer culture were shared across classes, shared between the lower middle classes and the 'respectable' strata of the lower classes and thus potentially capable of fostering an individualism that was antipathetic to class consciousness.

The historian Wayne Dowler argues that the 'culture, values, and goals of the majority of workers owed little to marxist intellectuals. The dynamics of urban life afforded industrial workers opportunities to interact in a complex environment with other social groups... Growing literacy among workers and exposure to the penny press, film and other commercialized forms of culture encouraged workers to assimilate to the culture and values of the larger society'.[28] There is no doubt that working people were eager to engage with consumer culture, quickly coming to appreciate style over utility in matters of dress, for example. Single women workers spent about one-fifth of their income on clothing, with many paying seamstresses to copy the latest styles from fashion magazines. Young men, too, learned that dressing well was an assertion of self-respect and was likely to command the respect of one's peers. The young Semën Kanatchikov, newly arrived in the city and soon to become a Bolshevik, bought himself a holiday outfit, a watch, and for the summer a wide belt, grey trousers, a straw hat, and some fancy shoes. 'In a word, I dressed in the manner of those young urban metalworkers who earned an independent living and didn't ruin themselves with vodka.'[29] Stylish dress, of course, helped to attract potential sexual partners. In Soligalich and Chukhlomskii counties in the province of Kostroma local women preferred men who had lived in St Petersburg. They were 'much more sophisticated than local men; their conversation was often indistinguishable from that of an urban-dweller, though adorned with fanciful expressions; their manner was copied from that of the metropolitan petty-bourgeois; they could dance, they wore dandified suits'.[30] Yet, as the example of Kanatchikov suggests, some caution is warranted before we assume that the attractions of consumer culture were necessarily at odds with the simultaneous development of class consciousness. Photographs of trade-union leaders invariably show them in urban, not peasant, attire: three-piece suits, straw boaters, canes, and leather shoes.[31] The pleasures associated with the purchase of enticing new goods and with new forms of commercialized leisure may have had the potential to promote social cohesion, but any such potential was provisional, and easily blocked by countervailing forces. The pressures of work and daily life were an ever present reminder to working people of their subordinate place in the social order; the pleasure of reading an adventure story or dressing respectably on a Sunday afternoon offered an escape, but only a fleeting one.

If we look more closely at labour we begin to appreciate that although a potential for reformism did exist after 1905, it was thwarted by the regime itself. In June 1906 a law permitting labour unions was enacted and strikes were partially legalized. By early 1907, as many as 300,000 had joined unions, more than half the workforce in some trades.[32] In Western Europe and the USA trade unions served both to extend the influence of workers in industry and politics and to incorporate them into the capitalist order. In Russia, trade unions served not to promote the interests of workers through the existing system but to articulate a radical challenge to it. The law on trade unions was vague and administered by the police—the perfect formula for official abuse—and following Stolypin's coup of 3 June police repression, combined with economic recession, rapidly undermined the union movement. Between 1906 and 1909, 350 trade unions were shut down and about 500 were refused registration. Nevertheless workers made some gains from the Revolution: working hours in large-scale factory industry were reduced by 8 per cent by 1913 and by that date the average annual wage in nominal terms was 36 per cent higher than in 1904.[33] Employers played their part in suppressing trade unions and in resisting any modernization of industrial relations. In St Petersburg, in particular, the Society of Factory and Works Owners made a sustained attempt to rationalize the labour process yet maintain an autocratic system of industrial relations.[34] Efforts to extend labour protection were resisted by the industrialists' lobby (they succeeded in reducing employers' contributions to social insurance), but finally in January 1912 the duma did pass legislation granting insurance against accidents and illness. Following the Lena Massacre (discussed in the section 'On the Eve of War'), the State Council confirmed this. It was precisely the closeness of government to the employers that prevented the separation of economic and political conflict that generally held in the West, and which facilitated the incorporation of labour into the capitalist system. In Russia, by contrast, state and capital appeared to constitute a *single* mechanism of exploitation and domination. One consequence was that worker resistance often focused not on capital in the abstract but on the person of the foreman, who lorded it over the workers, or on the police and Cossacks. What has been called 'autocratic capitalism' fused all the resentments of modern capitalism—conflict over the distribution of wages and profit and resentment at the intensity and boredom of mechanized work—with more 'traditional' resentments and memories of the village.[35] The subordination of the factory, for example, might be perceived through the lens of 'serfdom', so that aspects of work relations, such as not being addressed by foremen with the polite form of 'you', resonated with the despotism of the political system as a whole. Resistance to both the state and capital became condensed in notions of 'arbitrariness', 'rightlessness', and the denial of 'dignity'. Conversely, however, there were still workers who expected employers and government to act as paternalist protectors and when they failed to do so felt a sense of betrayal. It would be misleading to suggest that autocratic capitalism made workers 'revolutionary'—recall the endless complaints about the servility of the 'backward' masses—but the combination of the elemental energy of the peasant 'bunt'—the explosion of violent anger—with the constantly frustrated routines of collective organization was highly combustive. Moreover, the increasing articulation of economic and political grievances in the language of class and socialism helped to produce very high levels of labour militancy. Nowhere else in Europe was the level of strikes so high: in 1905–6 and again in 1912–14, the peaks of strike activism, the average number of strikers each year was equivalent to almost three-quarters of the factory workforce.[36] And these strikes, as we have seen, easily took on a political complexion.

Finally, we may note how a theme that was to come to prominence in 1917 was already adumbrated in 1905–6, namely, that of 'control' by workers over management. In the print industry especially, the idea of 'worker autonomy' became very popular, but elsewhere too, workers' representative organs at the level of the enterprise began to encroach on the rights of the management, demanding oversight of hiring and firing, the appointment of administrative personnel, or the imposition of fines. Such claims for control within the workplace would in 1917 be extended to social and political life as a whole. These were class-based demands and posed a more frontal challenge to capitalism than did demands for citizenship. Yet in these years, socialist ideas of class did not yet pull against liberal ideas of citizenship in the way they would come to do under the Provisional Government.

The revolutionary socialist opposition grew rapidly between 1905 and 1907. The Bolsheviks pushed for an armed insurrection to overthrow the regime but during 1905 had less impact on the burgeoning labour movement than the Mensheviks, who threw themselves into organizing strikes, trade unions, and soviets. The factional split was by no means as deep at the grassroots as is often supposed, but it would be broadly true to say that Bolsheviks were tougher, bolder, more disciplined, more intolerant, more self-confident, more amoral, and less squeamish about using violence and undemocratic means than their rivals, who were more cautious, more circumspect, more inclined to waver, more committed to democracy, more intolerant of primitive sloganizing. The growth of the RSDLP came between 1906 and 1907, when the Bolsheviks grew rather fast, having about 58,000 members by spring 1907 compared with the Mensheviks' 45,000. In the European part of the empire the RSDLP was strongest in Ukraine, especially in the Donbass, in the central industrial region around Moscow, in St Petersburg, and in the Urals. In non-Slav areas of the empire Russian speakers tended to form the core of SDs except in the Caucasus. Nevertheless the Polish and Lithuanian Social Democrats, the Latvian Social Democrats, and the Jewish Bund all affiliated to the RSDLP at the Fourth Congress in 1906, the party claiming a membership of 150,000 to 170,000 by spring 1907.[37] This looks impressive until one remembers that the Union of the Russian People and other radical right organizations claimed a membership of 410,000 in the same year (although whole families were sometimes claimed as members), they, too, being strong in Ukraine and Bessarabia.[38] The figures for the number of Bolsheviks and Mensheviks, in particular, should be taken with a pinch of salt. The differences between the two factions of the

RSDLP were apparent in the big cities, but in most provincial centres the two factions barely existed or were content to tolerate one another in a single organization. In much of Siberia, the Urals, and parts of Ukraine, most Social Democratic organizations remained 'unified'. And many of the abstruse but lethal disputes that split the party leadership had little resonance among rank-and-file Social Democrats, with the possible exception of Liquidationism, that is, the view that the RSDLP (and the SRs) should liquidate their underground organs and work exclusively in the legal organs. Arguably, the most stable Social Democratic organizations were the Bund, the Latvian Social Democrats, and the Georgian Social Democrats, where nationalist resentments reinforced socialism, and these seem to have been much less exercised by the ideological issues that obsessed Lenin. What is clear is that state repression—not least, via police infiltration—was highly effective from 1908 in destroying SD organizations, with leaders arrested or forced into exile and activists compelled to lie low, and with tens of thousands of members dropping out of party activity. By 1908 there were 260 SD organizations and this fell to 109 by 1911.[39]

The Socialist Revolutionaries grew during the Revolution to become the largest left party, with a membership drawn from all classes. By 1907 the SRs had 287 organizations with 60,000 to 65,000 members and a penumbra of sympathizers totalling around 300,000.[40] They enjoyed success especially in the countryside but also among factory workers, soldiers and sailors, teachers, paramedics, agronomists, and many others. The SRs held their First Congress in December 1905 and this refused to back a call for the immediate seizure of landed estates, but committed the party to political revolution via armed insurrection. However, the Central Committee had only loose control over the provincial committees, and the SRs, at the best of times a very loose political coalition, were soon weakened by deepening ideological splits. On the far right, the Popular Socialists, close to the Kadets, split from the party in 1906. On the far left, SR Maximalists, no more than a couple of thousand workers, students, and employees with an average age of 25, were barely distinguishable from anarchists, exulting in carrying out 'exes' and calling for mass terror and the immediate creation of a 'toiler's republic'. And in 1909, on the right of the party emerged a group of veteran Populists, notably E. K. Breshko-Breshkovskaia, the 'grandmother of the revolution', who called for the abandonment of all underground organization in favour of work in the legal labour organizations, cooperatives, and zemstvos. From late 1907, having restored a semblance of order in society, the regime set about destroying the mass organizations of the SRs, such as the Peasant Union, the railway and teachers' unions, and most of its combat units. The Okhrana had a major asset in the shape of Evno Azef, head of the Combat Organization from 1904 to 1908, who worked as an informer. In fact, only about twelve of the acts of terror carried out between 1902 and 1914 were the work of the Combat Organization; the rest, over 230 in number, were carried out by armed detachments or flying squads loosely attached to local and provincial organizations of the party.[41] Nevertheless the Combat Organization enjoyed an aura of heroism and martyrdom, receiving donations from liberal businessmen, Jewish émigrés, and others. Between 1908 and 1913 the number of SR organizations fell from 350 to 102, and these were mainly at provincial level.[42]

Despite the swingeing setback suffered by the revolutionary left it is easy to overlook the fact that, through speeches, leaflets, illegal publications, trade unions, medical funds, and evening classes, activists managed to put into circulation a discourse of socialism. In the major factories there was now a layer of 'conscious' workers, many of them members or supporters of the SDs or SRs, who were able to give some political direction to workers' struggles. They were mainly young men, concentrated especially in the metalworking industry, men who sought through self-education, self-discipline, and struggle to improve themselves and the lot of their fellow workers. Marxism, with its assignment to the working class of a pivotal historical role, was particularly attractive to them, though some believed in the mission of the entire 'toiling people' and a few were products of the temperance movement or disciples of Lev Tolstoy. This 'conscious' minority often looked down on the 'grey' workers around them, who seemed to look forward only to getting drunk, or to returning to their plot of land in the countryside, or who acquiesced in suffering in this world in the hope that this would bring them salvation in the next. Yet they were regularly surprised when the sullen quiescence of these 'grey' workers exploded into violent rioting.[43] For their part, the 'grey' workers looked ambivalently on the conscious worker, whose disquieting impact is vividly described by Buzinov, a worker-memoirist: 'His appearance was fierce, his gaze terrifying. It seemed he hated all the workers and so there was always an empty space around his bench, as though it had been infected by the plague.'[44] Nevertheless they stood in awe of these 'students', admiring their knowledge, their indomitable courage, and their spirit of self-sacrifice, and in times of crisis they turned to them for leadership.

On the Eve of War

The Lena Gold Mining Company, about 30 per cent of whose shares were in British ownership, was situated to the north-east of Lake Baikal in Siberia. Complaints by miners about working conditions were legion and one complaint about the poor quality of food escalated into a strike in March 1912. The strikers' demands apparently included an eight-hour day, a 30 per cent wage rise, the elimination of fines, and improvement in food supply. These were put to the company, which had the members of the strike committee arrested. On 4 April miners demanding the release of their comrades were mown down by soldiers, with as many as 200 being killed and 400 seriously injured.[45] The massacre provoked a storm of outrage, comparable to that provoked by Bloody Sunday. Strikes and demonstrations, involving a broad swathe of the public, swept across the empire, strikes being intense in major cities, such as the capital, Moscow, and Riga. The economy was booming once again, and this made strikers more willing to walk off their jobs. According to Factory Inspectorate statistics, which covered around two-thirds of the total number of industrial workers, in 1912 there were 2,032 strikes with 725,491 participants, in 1913, 2,404 with 887,096, and in the first half of 1914, 3,534 with 1,337,458 participants; by the latter year, moreover, the majority were political, with metalworkers in the capital hugely over-represented.[46] The radicalization of the labour movement reached its peak on 3 July 1914, when government troops fired on Putilov workers, killing two. This triggered a general strike that even saw the erection of barricades on the streets of the capital. The Petersburg Society of Factory and Works Owners, 'the most militant, anti-labour association of businessmen in the empire', responded with a lockout.[47] The secret police reported that 'the strike has taken extremely acute and disturbing forms'. Yet for all their trepidation, they remained well informed about the activities of all the revolutionary left and were able to decapitate underground committees when they so chose.[48]

In view of this, the recovery of the SDs and SRs during the years 1912 to 1914 was relatively modest, subject as they were to constant police arrest and infiltration. In January 1912 eighteen Bolsheviks met in Prague and set up their own Central Committee (one of whose members, Roman Malinovskii, kept the Okhrana fully informed of its proceedings) and this event is conventionally seen as the initiation of a separate Bolshevik 'party'. In May 1912 Bolsheviks in Russia began to publish *Pravda*, which was rather successful in attracting working-class readers. In the trade-union movement there was a shift to the left in the political leadership, with Bolshevik firebrands ousting more cautious Mensheviks in the metalworkers' and tailors' unions in St Petersburg and in the tailors' union in Moscow.[49] But factional strife within the socialist left alienated many workers and a sizeable section were hostile to political parties of all kinds. Despite the revival, K. K. Iuren'ëv, leader of the Inter-district Organization founded in November 1913 to bring about unity among Social Democrats, offered a very bleak retrospective of the state of Social Democracy in St Petersburg at this time: 'These were the most dismal days in the history of the RSDLP; they were years when liquidationism and hostility to political parties flourished, years of most appalling factional and intra-factional squabbling. The squabbling between Bolsheviks and Mensheviks reached its apogee, the conflict going on in clubs and educational organizations.'[50] It does seem that the Bolsheviks capitalized better than their opponents on the new mood of worker militancy, and they seem to have seized leadership at this time of the Latvian Social

Democrats.[51] Yet the revival of the revolutionary left should not be exaggerated. The number of SD organizations, which had reached its nadir in 1911 at 109, rose to 132 in 1913, but then fell spectacularly following the outbreak of war, so that by February 1917 only 39 organizations were functioning, mainly at provincial level. The number of SR organizations did not increase at all in this period: it stood at 102 in 1913 and had collapsed to 18 by 1917.[52]

Meanwhile high politics blundered along its myopic course, with the duma, the court, and the Council of Ministers unable to work with each other. A telling example came with the decision in 1913 to ban the production of alcohol, sale of which provided approximately 28 per cent of government revenue.[53] From the last years of the nineteenth century clergy and health professionals had waged a sustained temperance campaign, and more than 100,000 people were members of temperance societies by 1907. The decision to substitute complete prohibition for the state monopoly on the sale of vodka, which Nicholas II had introduced in 1896, seems to have originated in nothing more than a spat between Prince Meshcherskii, editor of *The Citizen* newspaper, and V. N. Kokovtsov, the Prime Minister and a former Minister of Finance. In 1912 Kokovtsov made himself unpopular by calling for Rasputin to withdraw from the court, a call that angered the tsar. Meshcherskii accused Kokovtsov of 'hysteria' and 'limitless spite' and, in turn, was accused of 'indulgence of Jews to the detriment of the state'. At the end of 1913, Meshcherskii successfully mobilized the duma against Kokovtsov by inveighing against the latter's raising of the alcohol tax while he was Minister of Finance. With no regard for the fiscal implications, Meshcherskii's circle persuaded Nicholas that it was his 'sacred duty' to ban alcohol in order to improve the health of the Russian people. In the event, prohibition was introduced by Nicholas as a wartime measure in August 1914. The result was an enormous fall in revenue, the revenue from the sale of alcohol falling from 26.5 per cent of the state budget in 1913 to a mere 1.5 per cent in 1916.[54]

So to return to the question with which this chapter started: was Russia moving away from Revolution on the eve of the war?[55] In a thought-provoking book, Wayne Dowler concludes that despite 'severe stresses and tensions...the clear trend before the war was towards cooperation and integration'.[56] One can certainly adduce evidence in support of this optimistic conclusion. It is clear that the revolutionary parties of the left, battered during the Years of Reaction, had not managed to re-establish themselves on anything like the footing they had enjoyed in 1906. The radical right organizations, too, had gone into serious decline, propped up only by government subventions.[57] Above all, the countryside was quiet.[58] It thus seems unpersuasive to speak of a revolutionary situation, even taking into account the barricades that had been erected on the streets of the capital; for with the important exception of areas such as the Caucasus and, to a lesser extent, the Baltic, the police and the Minister of the Interior seem to have felt confident that they could handle domestic disorder without the intervention of the army.[59] Dowler's book usefully captures the contradictoriness of trends in the post-1905 period, but his optimistic conclusion—'the passage of time in peaceful circumstances would likely have strengthened the middle-class liberal discourse'—was not one shared by contemporaries. At the beginning of 1913 the magazine *Ogonëk* (*Flame*) asked some leading public figures to offer toasts for the New Year. Many commented on the 'heavy depression of the social mood', while a New Year's Day essay in *Gazeta Kopeika* noted that the previous year's wishes for 'new happiness' had produced not only no 'new' happiness but 'no happiness at all', just 'bitterness and disillusionment'.[60] Certainly, civil society was more entrenched than it had been in 1905 but the existence of a civil society is no guarantee of social cohesion. Crucially, the momentum for peaceful reform had stalled mightily, and there was something close to paralysis in government. This mattered not primarily because of internal social conflict, increasingly dangerous though that was, but because there was now an immediate threat of war for which the government was ill prepared. Militarily Russia was better prepared for war than in 1904. It had acquired a navy with modern battleships, a large army that was reasonably well equipped, and an officer corps that had much improved in quality.[61] Yet in making Russia militarily stronger, rearmament had also served to increase tension between the great powers and increase the likelihood of war. Voices such as that of P. N. Durnovo, former

Minister of the Interior, would warn in February 1914 of the appalling consequences of a war with Germany on domestic stability, yet most of the elite preferred to ignore the risk rather than back down in the face of Austrian aggression and thus forfeit great-power status.[62] Optimists often present their case by implying that war came out of the blue, blowing the ship of reform off course. It did not. The tsarist government had pursued a policy of rearmament and a foreign policy that made war more likely, and the outbreak of war would massively exacerbate the deep-seated social tensions that had beset Russia since the government entered on a path of economic modernization.

First World War

On 28 June 1914 the assassination in Sarajevo of Franz Ferdinand, heir to the Austro-Hungarian throne, by a Bosnian Serb set light to the tinder box that was the Balkans.[63] Fearful of the danger it faced from Slav nationalism, Austria saw the assassination as the moment to crush Serbian pretensions once and for all. With its relative position in decline, it calculated that so long as it could rely on Germany, the risk of a general war was worth taking. For their part the Germans reckoned that not to support Austria would be to allow Russia time to continue its military build-up and to thwart their aspiration to expand into Eastern Europe. When Russia threatened to mobilize against Austria, Germany warned that it would deem this sufficient grounds for war. On 26 July the tsar ordered military districts in European Russia to move onto a partial war footing, and this accelerated two days later when Austria-Hungary declared war on Serbia. Russia's mobilization prompted Germany to declare war on 1 August. Fearing encirclement, and with a war plan that envisaged taking out France before turning on Russia, the German government sent an ultimatum to Belgium on the same day, demanding passage through the country in order to attack France, Russia's great ally. Hanging back, in spite of a secret commitment to France, Britain declared war on 4 August, as German troops crossed into Belgium, violating its neutrality. All the belligerents claimed to be acting defensively. In reality all were bent on exploiting the war to further imperial ends. Following the entry of the Ottoman empire into the war, Russia committed to securing the Bosphorus as the fruit of victory, and in 1915 the Kadets and Octobrists in the duma added to this claims on Austrian-ruled Galicia and a chunk of Anatolia.

These manoeuvres proved to be the prelude to warfare on a scale never seen before, in which the capacity of states to mass-mobilize material and human resources was as critical as success on the battlefield. The war unleashed extermination too on a hitherto unprecedented scale, legitimizing mass slaughter, and destroying nineteenth-century confidence in progress and civilization. Between 8 and 10 million soldiers died out of a total of roughly 65 million combatants, 21 million were wounded, and between 5 and 6 million civilians lost their lives.[64] Russia bore an enormous share of the military burden. By the end of the war her armed forces were 8.5 times larger than before the war (Germany's had grown ninefold, Austria-Hungary's eightfold, and France's fivefold). By June 1917, 288 out of 531 Allied divisions were Russian.[65]

Despite the barricades in the streets of St Petersburg the declaration of war brought working-class insurgency to a shuddering halt, unleashing a surge of patriotism across Russian society. On 20 July a vast crowd gathered along the banks of the Neva River in St Petersburg to await the arrival by yacht of Nicholas, Alexandra, and their daughters (the tsarevich was ill). The two dreadnoughts *Gangut* and *Sevastopol*, anchored at the mouth of the river, fired salvoes as the royal yacht appeared. The imperial family disembarked into a steam launch that took them to the Winter Palace as cannon were fired from the Peter Paul Fortress across the river. The crowd was in raptures, many of them on their knees, shouting 'Hurrah' and singing the national anthem, 'God Save the Tsar'. In the Malachite Hall of the Winter Palace, the tsar signed the declaration of war, which proclaimed: 'In this fearsome hour of trial let internal dissension be forgotten. May the unity between tsar and people become ever stronger, and may Russia, risen up as one, repel the impudent onslaught of the enemy.'[66] The scene encapsulated a moment of intense but short-lived patriotism.

In the third week of August 1914, the First and Second Armies advanced into East Prussia. They were poorly organized and hampered by lack of support services and poor communication with the front headquarters, known as 'Stavka'. The Germans scored victories at Tannenberg on 26–30 August and the Masurian Lakes on 7–14 September, capturing more than 250,000 Russian troops. For the rest of 1914, Russian casualties continued to mount in a series of bloody battles in Poland, but the inability of the German armies to extend too far beyond railheads was also exposed.[67] On the south-western front the war against Austria-Hungary, which began with the invasion of Galicia on 20 August, went rather better. Initially, hostilities went in Austria's favour but the Russians soon captured Lemberg (L'viv), the Galician capital, and invested the major fortress at Przemyśl. Austrian efforts to relieve the latter in January and February failed, with the loss of 800,000 men, most of them to disease. On 22 March the garrison of 120,000 surrendered to the Russian army. The latter quickly created an administration in Galicia which embarked on a violent programme of Russification and antisemitism. N. A. Bazili, director of the diplomatic staff at Stavka, opined that 'Russian farmers' would welcome 'emancipation from Jewish oppression'.[68]

On every front, military zones, together with vast swathes of territory behind front lines, were put under martial law. Commanders at different levels issued edicts to enforce security, fix prices, forbid trade in goods, and requisition labour, and stir up pogroms against Jews whom they saw as shirking their military duty and as having non-Russian values.[69] In early May, however, Austria and Germany combined forces to retake Galicia. In just six days 140,000 Russian prisoners were captured, forcing Stavka to order the abandonment of the region on 20 June. The Central Powers then launched a three-pronged attack towards the Narew River in north-east Poland and towards Courland in western Latvia. A relentless offensive continued into September, in the course of which Germany came to occupy Poland, Lithuania, and large parts of Belorussia. The retreat of the Russian army turned into a rout. Front commanders ordered the burning of crops and property in the hundreds of square miles they evacuated, along with the forcible expulsion of at least a million civilians to prevent them from being conscripted by the Germans. About 67 million people found themselves under enemy occupation. As the Baltic fell under German occupation, almost a million civilians were displaced from Lithuania and Latvia into central Russia, and about 300,000 Lithuanians, Latvians, and Estonians were drafted into the Russian army.[70] By 1917 there were perhaps 6 million refugees, including half a million Jews who had been expelled from front-line areas.[71] As many as a million men were taken prisoner and another million were killed or wounded. Yet the defensive capacity of the Russian army was not broken.

On 1 November 1914, Russia declared war on the Ottoman empire after the Black Sea fleet was attacked in Odessa. For Russia the Caucasus Front was always secondary to the Eastern Front, and the gruelling campaign to overpower Ottoman forces proved less than decisive. İsmail Enver Paşa was intent on recapturing Batum and Kars, which had been taken by Russia in the war of 1877–8, on seizing Georgia, and on occupying north-western Persia and the oilfields. The Russians and Ottomans, who played the pan-Islamic card, fought bitterly in the Caucasus and in Persia, where the Russians struggled to link up with British forces. During the perishing winter of 1914–15, Enver Paşa's forces were overstretched, and were resoundingly crushed at the Battle of Sarıkamış. The defeated Turks blamed their setback on the treachery of Armenians, for the Russians had encouraged Armenian volunteer units to carry out sabotage against the Turkish army in early 1915, and their resistance escalated into a full-scale uprising at Van in April 1915. The Committee of Union and Progress reacted by ordering the mass deportation of the entire, scattered Armenian population. As many as a million may have been killed outright or expired as they made the trek towards Syria and Iraq.[72] In the later stage of the war, most of the fighting took place in a wide area around Lake Van in eastern Anatolia. There General N. N. Iudenich, later the leader of anti-Bolshevik forces in north-west Russia, proved an able commander. Hostilities gradually swung in Russia's favour, with Ottoman forces fighting fiercely but suffering appalling losses, especially in the winter of 1916–17; but they were not defeated. As late as November 1918 the Ottoman army was still 'on its feet and fighting'.[73]

The number of men in the Russian armed forces in July 1914 is uncertain, but was probably around 1.4 million, and the mobilization of reserves soon increased this to around 3 million. By 1917, if one includes reserves, garrisons in the rear, and administrative staff, the number had soared to around 9 million (only 27 per cent of whom were combat troops).[74] In all, about 16 million Russians were mobilized into the armed forces. Military regulations prevented women from joining, but perhaps some 5,000 women disguised themselves as men and took up combat duties—women such as A. A. Krasil'nikova, a 20-year-old miner's daughter who was awarded the George Cross for bravery. Women, however, were far more likely to serve at the front as nurses and medical orderlies. In the rear the Red Cross, zemstvos, and doctors' organizations all put on training courses for nurses and nursing salaries proved relatively attractive. The tsar's daughters served as trustees of military hospitals and were prominently depicted in nurses' uniforms in the press. A total of 2,255 Russian Red Cross Society institutions operated at the fronts, including 149 hospitals with 46,000 beds served by 2,450 doctors and 20,000 nurses. Behind the front lines there were 736 local committees, 112 nursing societies, and 80 hospitals—but this was hardly a large number for the size of the army in the field.[75]

Half the wartime casualties were suffered in the first year of the war. How far this was due to poor leadership and how far to the inability of the government to mobilize the economy to support the war effort is disputed. Certainly during the German offensive of summer 1915, Russian troops were dogged by a crippling shell shortage and at times soldiers even lacked rifles and uniforms. The generals blamed shortages on the incompetence of the civilian administration, but there were similar shortages in other countries, which had also gravely underestimated the likely length of the war. Poor military leadership and incompetence on the part of the Ministry of War were certainly causes of the hideous losses of the first year, especially when compared with the superior leadership and administration of the German armed forces. Stavka was hamstrung by overlapping jurisdictions, and the

Supreme Commander-in-Chief, Grand Duke Nikolai Nikolaevich, a 58-year-old cavalry general and distant cousin of Nicholas II, though admired for his past military record, proved a less than brilliant strategist. He was removed in August 1915 and the tsar himself took command. General Mikhail Alekseev was effectively in charge. Nevertheless one should not exaggerate the disastrous performance of the army in the first year of the war. Certainly, it was no match for the Germans operationally and tactically, but it fought with valour against the Ottomans and Austrians.[76]

By 1916 the shell shortage had been overcome and on 4 June General Aleksei Brusilov launched a brilliant offensive in the south-west, along a 300-mile front. This was part of a coordinated Allied strategy and proof that Russia was still a valued ally. In striking contrast to the disasters of the Somme and Verdun, the offensive inflicted terrible losses on the Austro-Hungarian army, which lost a third of its forces, almost bringing it to the point of collapse. As Galicia came under occupation for a second time, Russian officials were warned not to ban the Ukrainian language or denigrate the Uniate Church, as they had done in the first occupation. It was not long, however, before German reinforcements halted Brusilov's advance, leaving the Russians with little to show for their immense and costly efforts. Brusilov's success had persuaded Romania to join the Allies in late August, but its army collapsed rapidly, allowing the Central Powers to occupy most of the country. This merely added to the scale of the problems facing the Russian army, opening up a new Romanian Front, forcing it to divert forty-seven divisions to the south in November and December. With losses of more than half a million men, morale plummeted.[77]

The critical need to replace dead, wounded, and captured men was the trigger that led to an immense revolt in Central Asia. The settlement of Russians under Witte and Stolypin had led to mounting conflict with the native population over land and water rights, as intensive cotton extraction was developed in the Fergana Valley. In 1914 the native population of Turkestan was spared the draft, but on 25 June 1916 the government announced that 390,000 Kazakh and Kyrghyz males would be conscripted to build defensive fortifications in front-line areas. Muslim clerics were furious and warned that the conscripts would be sent to fight against their brother Muslims on the Caucasus Front, and that whilst they were far from their homes their land would be confiscated and given to Russian settlers. The native population cut railways and telegraph lines, annihilated garrisons, and raided government offices. Colonel P. P. Ivanov, later a commander of the anti-Bolshevik forces in Siberia, ordered a ruthless pacification which saw Russian troops and settlers massacre and rape the native population. At least 88,000 rebels were slain while 250,000 fled from Semirech'e into China.[78]

By late 1916 the resolve of the armed forces was deteriorating. In the course of the war soldiers sent millions of letters to their loved ones, which censors used in order to draw up reports on morale on the different fronts and within different divisions. These generally reported that the soldiers' mood was 'cheerful', even in the second half of 1916 when the Brusilov offensive had stalled.[79] Over 80 per cent of soldiers were peasants, but it is reckoned that around 70 per cent could read or write to some degree.[80] An examination of their letters suggests that their patriotism—focused on love for their 'green and happy' village—was heartfelt, but that it was certainly not associated with the tsar or even with a sense that Russia was fighting for a just cause. The contradictory elements in soldiers' patriotism are illustrated in a letter of 25 August 1915 sent by a soldier who belonged to the 210th Infantry regiment that hailed from Bronnitsy in Moscow province.

> [The Germans] have created a cloud of gun fire, let loose a hellish volley, and reduced the trenches to dust. On the ground there's nowhere to stand. They've hit us all. But we fulfilled our duty and did not let them pass through to Vil'na. I think if all troops stood as we did, i.e. as our division did, then none of the fortresses would be given up, and this would become a real test for the enemy. But our reinforcements have almost given up without a fight. What else can we do? Take off our hats and say to the Kaiser, please come this way?...We captured one officer, ten Germans and two machine guns and they told us: 'We feel sorry for you Russians. Why are you laying your heads on the line, when you're already ours?' That's what the prisoners said, straight to our face. 'You were sold out long ago. We bought Russia with the money that is in the German banks'. The morale of our forces has fallen and whole battalions along with their officers have surrendered to the Germans. They

> throw away their rifles, stick their hands in the air and go over to the Germans to drink coffee.[81]

Such sentiment was probably widespread: pride in seeing one's regiment acquit itself with honour, disgust at the cowardliness (real or imagined) of some on one's own side, a grudging admiration for the Germans, and a suspicion that Russia's rulers were in hock to German bankers. Such complex attitudes, with their mix of hardnosed realism and a dash of class consciousness, did not equate to an absence of national identity.[82] But patriotism was focused on family, home, and the farm, which constituted a microcosm of the nation that soldiers felt they were defending against the foreign foe.[83]

It was commonplace to contrast the fighting qualities of Russian and German soldiers, always to the detriment of the former. L. N. Voitolovskii, a Social Democratic psychiatrist and editor of the literary section of the liberal newspaper *Kievan Thought* before entering military service, articulated a common view when he wrote:

> Among the Germans there is military firmness, discipline, bivouacs; among us there is carelessness, bonfires and the indolence of a Chumak camping ground [Chumaks were long-distance traders in southern Ukraine]. Among them there is a firm desire to fight, among us there is daydreaming, singing and yearning.[84]

Such a view should be treated with caution. It was the standard reason given for why more than 3.3 million Russians ended up in German and Austrian prisoner-of-war camps: one in every five soldiers, which represented a proportion considerably higher than in other armed forces.[85] Yet there were many battles in which Russian soldiers fought with valour, and during the initial campaign of 1914 and again in 1916 when the Battles of the Somme and Verdun were raging on the Western Front Russian successes forced Germany to move much needed forces to the Eastern Front. The great loss of life and the great number of prisoners captured were more probably due to the fact that although there were periods of positional warfare, when trenches were built and military headquarters set up, warfare was far more mobile than on the Western Front, the generals relying on costly campaigns, cavalry charges, and all-out assaults.[86]

By winter 1916, there was growing war weariness in the army and navy, and an overwhelming desire to see the war come to an end. The number of complaints in soldiers' letters about inadequate supplies of food, poor footwear, and at not getting leave rose steeply. Noteworthy, too, were denunciations of the horrors of war—of artillery attack ('it freezes the body and kills the soul'), gas attack, and the scandalous treatment of the wounded. There was also increasing criticism of the civilian population—especially although not exclusively of the privileged classes: anger at what was felt to be the inability of the civilian population to imagine the horrors that soldiers were suffering.[87] There is no doubt that the sacrifices of the armed forces were colossal. Figures for the number of casualties vary considerably, but a well-researched estimate is of 1.89 million combat-related deaths, which rises to a staggering 2.25 million if one includes deaths in captivity, from disease, and from accidents.[88] It has been suggested that relative to the number of mobilized soldiers, to the size of the male working population, and to the population as a whole, the Russian armed forces may actually have suffered less than other belligerent countries.[89] However, the total of combat-related deaths, the numbers of injured, ill, and gassed, and the numbers who were captured by the enemy comprises 60.3 per cent of the total numbers in the army, compared with 59.3 per cent for Germany, 55.9 per cent for France, 54.2 per cent for Austria-Hungary, and 53.3 per cent for Turkey.[90] Leaving these appalling figures to one side, what is crucial to grasp is that the end of tsarism came about not because of the breakdown in morale in the armed forces—discipline held up remarkably well through the winter of 1916–17, despite growing war weariness—but because of acute disaffection on the home front.

Politics and the Economy

Politics was relatively calm until summer 1915, as the mood of national unity persisted. Government was not slow to realize that it must act to support civilian morale and entrepreneurs were not slow to spot an opportunity to make a profit. The result was an explosion of patriotic propaganda that seized on traditional and new cultural forms, including postcards, posters, magazines, woodcuts (*lubki*), and cinema newsreels. The focus of patriotic identification was on Russia's military heroes and cultural figures, on her history and imperial geography. Significantly, there was little evidence of popular enthusiasm for the tsar himself.[91] Characteristic motifs were lampoons of the Kaiser, photographs of modern weaponry, heroic images of battle, and allegorical depictions of Mother Russia, and these were shared across class lines. The Supreme Commander-in-Chief, Grand Duke Nikolai Nikolaevich, about whom the public knew little, was presented in the press as someone alien to the artificiality of high society by virtue of his known severity and religious fervour (the press carried photographs of him entering the church at the army's General Headquarters).[92] One of the more repugnant expressions of popular chauvinism came in the form of violent attacks on the persons and property of 'enemy aliens', mainly Germans, and there was a surge in hatred of Jews. The main drivers of this were groups of rightists, now much less organized than in 1906. It was they who led the clamour for Poles and Jews to be deported, but not without support from the press and from across the social spectrum. The historian Eric Lohr suggests that the demand that government and economy be purged of foreign influence was part of a campaign to project the state as a national rather than imperial entity.[93] The mood of national unity, however, did not endure. By 1916, patriotic propaganda was fast losing its capacity to cement identification with the nation among soldiers at the front and among the urban and rural lower classes, who became convinced that they were being made to bear the costs of war.[94]

Many in the elite hoped that the war might revitalize the constitutional settlement promised in the October Manifesto. It was not long, however, before tension between government and Stavka began to mount as the munitions shortage became apparent and as the Galicia campaign began to stall. Even ministers were appalled by the Russification policy imposed by Grand Duke Nikolai Nikolaevich. As the Minister of Agriculture,

A. V. Krivoshein, observed: 'One cannot fight a war against Germany and against the Jews at the same time.' Krivoshein, one of the tsar's most able ministers, would soon find himself dismissed for advising Nicholas not to take on the position of Commander-in-Chief. In June 1915 duma circles (the duma was not in session at this time) forced the resignation of the Minister of War, V. A. Sukhomlinov, who was made to carry the can for the munitions crisis. On 19 July the duma was allowed to reconvene but the tsar ignored its calls for a government 'enjoying the confidence of the people'. This now became the rallying cry of a Progressive Bloc, which was formed by a duma majority comprising the Kadets, Octobrists, and Progressists. The Bloc campaigned for a political and religious amnesty and for the abolition of restrictions on nationalities, religious confessions, and trade unions. These demands provoked an angry tsar into suspending the duma on 3 September, in effect creating a constitutional crisis. The Prime Minister, I. L. Goremykin deliberately scuppered talks between the Progressive Bloc and the Council of Ministers, but his unbending attitude merely soured relations further. In February 1916, he was replaced by B. V. Stürmer, who prevailed upon Nicholas to seek greater cooperation from the duma. But when the duma was reconvened on 9 February, Stürmer disappointed the deputies by harping on the impossibility of pursuing constitutional reform at a time of war. He, too, did not last long in his post, a casualty of what became known as the game of 'ministerial leapfrog'.

From July 1914 to February 1917 there were no fewer than four Prime Ministers, six Ministers of the Interior, four Ministers each of Justice, War, and Agriculture, and four Procurators of the Holy Synod. This was due to the compulsive interference in government of the German-born Empress Alexandra Feodorovna, whom many of the populace believed to be working for German victory. There seems little doubt that she was under the mesmeric influence of Grigorii Rasputin, the peasant holy man, who, she believed, had the mystical power to cure the haemophilia of her son Alexei. He did not scruple to use his influence to interfere in court politics, all of which set off rumours of sexual shenanigans and treason by 'dark forces' at court. Rasputin's significance was more symbolic than real: but for people at all levels of society, not least for high military and political officials, he became an emblem of political corruption, lust, and debauchery. Rumours of 'dark forces' at court were hugely potent, corroding the mythic unity with the people that the tsar and tsarina had so desperately desired. By February 1917 the vast population that in 1900 had seen the tsar as the divinely appointed 'little father' of his people had dwindled to a handful.

Meanwhile civil society seized the opportunity of patriotic war work to expand its political influence. The government welcomed the work of the Red Cross, the organizations that offered assistance to the flood of refugees, the women's organizations that engaged in charity work, collected money, and knitted scarves and socks for soldiers at the front. More politically challenging was the formation in June 1915 of a union of zemstvos and urban municipalities, known as Zemgor, without the tsar's permission. Its chairman, Prince G. E. L'vov, would become the first head of the Provisional Government after the February Revolution. Zemgor took on a wide range of war-related tasks, including care for the wounded and the organization of supplies to the army. To this end, it purchased materials and subcontracted orders for equipment, munitions, uniforms, and foodstuff to private firms.[95] By the winter of 1916 Zemgor was criticizing the government openly, saying that it had become an obstacle to victory.[96] In the same month as Zemgor was created, a Central War Industries Committee was established on the initiative of a group of Moscow-based industrialists and merchants who were aggrieved that the Ministry of War was funnelling orders to the big metalworking and engineering plants of St Petersburg and southern Russia, to the exclusion of medium and small industry. The Central War Industries Committee was headed by the Octobrist A. I. Guchkov, who had been chairman of the third duma. It established a network of branches to distribute war-related orders to local firms. One innovation of the War Industries Committees was its formation of elected Workers' Groups: by February 1917 58 of these had come into existence, by which time there were 240 War Industry Committees.[97] Boycotted by the anti-war socialists, the political stance of the Workers' Groups seems to have been popular among workers. They called for the end of autocracy, but saw their main task as being to ensure that workers' interests were properly represented in the war effort. They emphasized the class character of the war and called for a democratic peace, while insisting that the working class must not allow Russia to be defeated.[98]

The struggle of the public organizations to wrest control of military supplies from the hands of official agencies did not lead to any substantial improvement in supply to the armed forces.[99] The War Industries Committee received no more than 5 per cent of all defence orders and they were hamstrung for credit and access to raw materials. In January 1917 they were told they would receive no new orders from government because they were too slow in fulfilling the ones they already had.[100] Nevertheless the fact that public organizations intervened in this crucial sphere in the middle of a war was a strong sign of how weakened the authority of the tsar had become. That said, the government was not unsuccessful in mobilizing the economy for total war: by 1916, production for defence accounted for 30 per cent of total production, a rise of 5 per cent over 1913.[101] Powerful procurement agencies for grain, meat, oil, and fodder had been quickly put in place, and in May 1915 a Special Defence Council was formed with the power to force state-owned and private enterprises to fulfil government orders and, if necessary, to remove directors and close private firms. As the War Industries Committee complained, however, this led to a cosy relationship between the War Ministry and big industrial and financial concerns, which made immense profits at government expense. Under pressure from the duma, the tsar replaced the Special Defence Council in August 1915 with four special councils for defence, food supply, fuel, and transport. These incorporated representatives of public organizations but kept the reins firmly in the hands of ministers.[102] Positive results were evident in the fact that by 1917 the output of shells had grown by 2,000 per cent, of artillery by 1,000 per cent, and of rifles by 1,100 per cent.[103] Yet the situation was by no means encouraging: there were critical bottlenecks due to shortages of fuel and problems of transportation, and by 1916 supplies of coal, iron, and steel were running out.[104] More significantly, satisfying the voracious appetite of the war machine was hugely costly. Peter Gatrell estimates that by 1916 the war was costing around 40 million rubles a day in contemporary prices.[105] This was both a reflection and a cause of soaring inflation, with prices tripling between 1914 and 1916 and wages doubling.

The costs of the war were met by internal and foreign loans, by direct and indirect taxation, by prohibiting exchanges in gold, and by pumping out paper money (the money in circulation rose from 1.53 million rubles on 1 July 1914 to 17,175 million rubles on 1 October 1917).[106] By 1916 the budget deficit stood at 78 per cent.[107] After decades of discussion, income tax was finally introduced (which meant that no one could any longer claim exemption by virtue of belonging to a privileged estate).[108] Enemy blockades in the Baltic and Black Sea cut exports by three-quarters by 1915 yet imports of military equipment soared. The French provided 1.5 billion rubles in loans and the British 5.4 billion, although the British demanded 2 billion rubles in gold bullion as collateral and insisted that the Russian government buy 1.8 billion rubles in British treasury bonds. The result was that Russia's debt doubled between 1914 and 1917, increasing by a total of 8 million gold rubles.[109] The efforts to encourage public subscription to war bonds were only partially successful: peasants preferred to save cash and workers objected when a contribution to the war loan was automatically docked from their wages. Problems were being stoked up for the future, with the boom in the war economy fuelled by inflation: currency emissions were five to six times the pre-war level, compared with a doubling in France, a tripling in Germany, and no change in Britain.

If the economy managed to satisfy the needs of the armed forces, this entailed the diversion of valuable resources away from consumption and investment. By 1916, with industry concentrating on production for the army and navy, the gross value of consumer goods production was 15 per cent lower than in 1913, and by late 1916 there were alarming shortages of consumer goods across the country, with grain in short supply in the major cities. Prices soared, and by February 1917 the purchasing power of the ruble had declined to about 30 per cent of its pre-war level.[110] Not least of the causes of shortages was a serious crisis in transportation, which would become disastrous in the course of 1917, with the railways having neither the network nor the rolling stock to bring much-needed supplies to the civilian population. The railway system had been designed in part to move grain from Russia's southern steppe and southern Ukraine to the Black Sea for export, whereas grain now had to be moved north and east to the main fronts. It is astonishing that grain supply should have proved to be the Achilles heel of the Russian economy, given that in 1913 exports from Russia constituted 30 per cent of the world's grain trade. The blockade of the Black Sea and Baltic ports by the Central Powers put an end to exports, and this ought to have meant that there was plenty of grain to feed the civilian population as well as the army. Harvests were no worse than usual: indeed that of 1915 was good and that of 1916 average.[111] The government's priority was to feed the armed forces but the different authorities had little confidence in the capacity of the free market to feed the armed forces and civilian population. This gave rise to conflicts between Stavka, the ministries, and the zemstvos over procurement and pricing. In August 1915 the newly founded Special Council for Food Supply introduced fixed prices for military procurements, stating that this was the best way to 'protect the consumer from extortionate prices'. Army procurement distorted the market, increasing demand, creating artificial shortages, and fuelling price rises. An embargo on the movement of grain out of provinces close to the front heightened the power of local governments in those areas and, together with local rationing, further fragmented what was intended to be a centralized system of procurement and supply. As early as February 1915 the government permitted the requisition of goods 'in cases where these are in short supply on the market', a phenomenon it blamed on merchants withholding stocks in the expectation of higher prices. Yet the special commissioners empowered to buy grain, having initially purchased direct from the producers, by July 1916 came to rely on these same middlemen, from whom they purchased 50 per cent of the army's grain requirement (compared with 18 per cent from landowners, 15 per cent from peasants, and 17 per cent from cooperatives).[112] The parallel existence of grain bought at fixed prices and grain bought on the open market was in fact an incitement to hoarding, and in September 1916 fixed prices for grain and flour were introduced for the population as a whole. By December 1916 a fully-fledged system of grain requisitioning had emerged—one that adumbrated the food monopoly instituted by the Bolsheviks in late 1918—with provinces assigned quotas of grain that they were expected to fulfil. In practice, the system was debilitated by the dismal state of transport and by the unwillingness of local zemstvos to cooperate. Following the February Revolution, the Provisional Government took the next logical step and declared a state monopoly on grain.

The impact of the war on agricultural production varied by region. The conscription of men and the removal of draught horses adversely affected regions where commercial production of grain was intensive, such as southern Ukraine, the lower Volga, and the North Caucasus. Inevitably, big commercial estates were more adversely affected by the labour shortage than peasant holdings.[113] Areas where subsistence agriculture was the norm, such as the central black-earth region and northern parts of Ukraine, maintained normal levels of production mainly by substituting the labour of women and youth for that of adult males. In any case, these were overpopulated areas where labour had been under-utilized. In western Siberia, by contrast, in spite of the constrained supply of labour and equipment, yeomen farmers actually increased the area under cultivation along with yield from crops and livestock, as well as increasing handicraft production.[114] After the first year of war, procurement of agricultural produce was concentrated on Siberia, which put a further strain on transportation. The crucial problem was that the fixed prices on grain left peasants with little incentive to market their produce, so they chose to eat better, feed more grain to livestock, or distil it into alcohol. Moreover, they were increasingly unable to use the money they made from grain sales to buy manufactured goods , such as textiles, kerosene, matches, salt, meat, or sugar. Peasants made substantial deposits in savings banks, although the fear that inflation would eat away their value soon set in. By winter 1916 food shortages had become acute and contemporaries were quick to blame the government. Doubtless it could have done better: but the problems were fundamentally structural and neither the Provisional Government nor the Bolsheviks would prove any more effective in dealing with them.

If one ignores vital regional differences, the standard of living of the rural population increased in comparison with its pre-war level, incomes on average rising 18 per cent. Yet even in a very wealthy region such as the Altai, the war saw the proportion of households without sown land increase from 3.2 per cent to 10.6 per cent; and in western Siberia as a whole some 5 to 6 per cent of households had no livestock by 1917.[115] In other words, inequalities within the rural population were increasing even where the average standard of living rose. In Khar'kiv province, by contrast, the average standard of living appears to have deteriorated—to judge from landholding and handicraft income. There the number of households not farming any land rose from 14 per cent to 22 per cent and the number of households farming 4.4 hectares (three *desiatina*) or less rose by more than 50 per cent.[116] In Khar'kiv—as in many other areas—it was women, now in charge of the family farm, who were in the forefront of protest. They clashed with the authorities over requisitioning of livestock and fodder for the army, over taxes, over land surveying (efforts to continue the Stolypin reforms were still going on) and, not least, on the rising cost of living.[117] Wives and widows of soldiers were particularly militant: they qualified for allowances from the government but these did not keep pace with inflation. In 1916 around 300 rural disturbances took place, nearly a third of which were put down by troops. This was nothing like the level of militancy of 1905, but it marked a break with the quiescence of the countryside that had set in during the Years of Reaction.[118]

In all, about 20 per cent of the industrial workforce was conscripted into the army.[119] Initially skilled workers were conscripted indiscriminately into the army, and the revolutionary activists who had been involved in the disorders in the capital in July 1914 were deliberately targeted. However, a shortage of skilled labour soon arose in the defence sector, with the result that wages were pushed up. Soon some of the skilled workers who had been enlisted were sent back to work in the armaments factories under military discipline. Mass production of armaments led to a rise in the proportion of unskilled female and peasant workers, the percentage of workers with ties to the land increasing to 60 per cent of the total labour force.[120] Women not only entered factory jobs on a significantly greater scale than before the war, but also entered male preserves in the job market for the first time, as they did in all belligerent countries. On the railways, for example, women took up jobs as conductors, stokers, and cleaners, and the increased visibility of women in such jobs sparked public debate about conventional gender roles and stirred fears of female sexuality.

If wages tended to rise in real terms initially, by 1916 rapid price inflation was eating away at their value. In the capital, which had been renamed Petrograd so that it sounded less German, there was a high proportion of skilled engineering and metalworkers, and by this time their average wages had fallen in real terms to 70–75 per cent of their pre-war level. In Moscow—where women textile workers predominated—real wages fell to about 60–65 per cent of their pre-war level by February 1917; and in the Urals, the third major centre of war production, average real wages fell by about a half.[121]

By winter 1916 all the towns, the industrial regions, and the consumer provinces were reeling from a severe grain shortage. Although this had structural causes, it was commonly blamed on the profiteering that was encouraged by government requisitioning. Even the Kadets, who were the most sympathetic of the political parties to the free market, declared on 3 March 1917: 'Let every trader open his warehouses, confident that there will be no more of the venality and extortion that has left some unpunished and others burdened with intolerable taxes.'[122] One of the more ugly features of popular protest was attacks on shopkeepers, traders, and suspected hoarders, often coloured by antisemitism, which could sometimes end in killings. As early as 12 April 1915, the Ministry of Internal Affairs warned provincial governors that disorders among the 'poorest layers of the population' were taking place because the supply situation was critical in certain areas.[123] In 1915, 23 'food or marketplace disorders' occurred, in a couple of dozen towns and industrial settlements, but this rose to 288 in 1916. In police reports soldiers' wives and youths were singled out as being at the forefront of these protests.[124] The women insisted that pensions, fair prices, and measures to put an end to speculation were entitlements due to them as the wives of men fighting for the fatherland.[125] And all their riots were driven by outrage that the burdens of war were not being borne fairly. Increasingly, some took on an anti-war tone: 'They are slaughtering our husbands and our sons in the war and at home they want to starve us to death.'[126]

The outbreak of war had seen labour militancy collapse. However, in the course of 1915 and, above all, in 1916 Russia saw a level of strike activity that was unprecedented in any other belligerent power, much of it having a strong political complexion. In 1915 there were 1,928 strikes; in 1916, 2,417, involving 1,558,400 workers; and in January–February 1917, there were 718 strikes involving 548,300 workers.[127] Still, this did not remotely match the level of 1905: in particular, railway workers showed none of the militancy they had done in that year. Strikes, moreover, were concentrated in Petrograd and Moscow, whereas the Baltic, Belorussia, and Caucasus were less militant than they had been a decade earlier (and Poland, of course, was under German occupation). Stoppages tended to be rarer in state-owned defence enterprises than in private enterprises, although this was not the case in Petrograd. Very worrying for the authorities was that the number of political strikes began to increase in 1916, especially following the prorogation of the duma in August 1915. Around a quarter of workers who went on strike in 1916 did so for political reasons.[128] The proportion was particularly high in the capital, where the Okhrana deplored the 'sharply negative attitude towards the government and...the further continuance of the war'.[129] At the Putilov armaments works in the capital, the workforce had grown to 29,300 by 1917. In a strike in February 1916 the workforce was locked out and 100 were arrested and 2,000 conscripted. The same occurred after a strike in November, when 5,000 soldiers from the Tarutinskii regiment were drafted in.[130] For the urban population more generally, the steep decline in supplies of fuel and food caused great anger and this was a driver behind the political strikes and demonstrations that occurred after the duma was again prorogued on 16 December, and again on 9 January 1917, the anniversary of Bloody Sunday. The Workers' Group of the War Industries Committee played a central role in these strikes, although anti-war militants were increasingly important in mobilizing workers on the ground.[131]

The war had split all the socialist parties into opponents of the war, known as internationalists, and (reluctant) supporters of the war, known as defencists. The Bolsheviks were less seriously damaged by this split than were the SRs and Mensheviks, though on the ground few Bolsheviks adhered to Lenin's call to turn the imperialist war into a civil war. The second half of 1914 saw the Bolsheviks decimated by arrests and by conscription. From 1916 their fortunes revived, but on the eve of the February Revolution there were probably no more than 12,000 Bolsheviks in the country at large.[132] In the course of 1915–16, other internationalist groupings, including SRs, the Inter-district group in the capital, and Menshevik Internationalists, also revived and were increasingly influential in agitating against the war.[133] The steep rise in labour militancy suggests that the mood of millions of workers was revolutionary; but as the internationalists conceded, the mood was more accurately described as 'revolutionary defencist': 'revolutionary' in that large swathes of workers were vehemently hostile to the autocracy and to those who were profiting from the war; yet 'defencist' in that there was no desire to see the Russian army go under at the hands of Germany, even as there was a desperation to see an end to the war. This was broadly the position articulated by the Workers' Group of the War Industries Committee, which comprised mainly defencist Mensheviks. The latter were broadly supportive of the war, but when Guchkov asked the Workers' Group to endeavour to preserve 'social peace', they retorted: 'it is difficult to talk of preserving something that does not exist and never has'.[134] It was the Workers' Group, along with the medical funds and trade unions it sustained, that would provide the main element of leadership as the country slid into revolution.

On 1 November 1916 the duma heard Pavel Miliukov, the leader of the Kadets, deliver a sensational attack on the government in which he denounced 'dark forces' and, listing a series of government failures, asked: 'Is this stupidity or treason?' The shameless intervention of Rasputin in politics had become the lightning rod for the frustration of the political elite with the incompetence of the government. On the night of 16–17 December Prince Felix Iusupov, scion of one of Russia's most ancient families, hatched a plot with Grand Duke Dmitrii and with Vladimir Purishkevich, one of the initiators of the Black Hundreds, to assassinate Rasputin. Later he wrote a florid account of their bid to dispose of Rasputin in an attempt to save the old order.

> The poison continued to have no effect and the starets [holy man] went on walking calmly about the room... I aimed at his heart and pulled the trigger, Rasputin gave a wild scream and crumpled on the bearskin... There was no possibility of doubt: Rasputin was dead. Dmitrii and Purishkevich lifted him from the bearskin and laid him on the flagstones. We turned off the light and went up to my room, after locking the basement door... We talked of the future of our country now that it was freed once and for all from its evil genius... As we talked I was suddenly filled with a vague misgiving: an irresistible impulse forced me to go down to the basement. Rasputin lay exactly where we had left him. I felt his pulse: not a beat, he was dead... All of a sudden, I saw his left eye open. A few seconds later his right eyelid began to quiver, then opened. I saw the green eyes of a viper staring at me with an expression of diabolical hatred... Then a terrible thing happened: with a sudden violent effort Rasputin leapt to his feet, foaming at the mouth... He rushed at me, trying to get at my throat, and sank his fingers into my shoulder like steel claws.[135]

The murder of Rasputin by members of his court circle seems to have done little to ruffle the tsar's equanimity. Asked in January 1917 by the British ambassador, Sir George Buchanan, how he proposed to regain his subjects' confidence, Nicholas retorted: 'Do you mean that I am to regain the confidence of my people, or that they are to regain mine?'

3

FROM FEBRUARY TO OCTOBER 1917

On 23 February 1917, International Women's Day, thousands of women textile workers and housewives took to the streets of Petrograd, the Russian capital, to protest at the bread shortage.[1] The demonstration occurred a day after workers at the giant Putilov works had been locked out; it quickly drew in workers, especially in the Vyborg district of the capital, notorious for its militancy. The demonstration had a largely spontaneous character, although the Vyborg committee of the Bolshevik party had called a protest. None of the revolutionary parties expected that it would prove to be the start of a process that would rapidly lead to the abdication of the tsar. The crowd, many of whose members had experience of strikes and demonstrations, threw up its own leaders in the form of local socialist activists. By the following day, more than 200,000 strikers took symbolic control of the capital by marching from the outlying districts across the bridges into the city centre, throwing rocks and lumps of ice at the police on their way. On 25 February students and members of the middle classes joined the crowds, bearing red flags and singing the 'Marseillaise'. Among the banners were many emblazoned with the words 'Down with the war' and 'Down with the tsarist government'. Soldiers from the garrison were ordered to clear demonstrators from the city centre but proved reluctant to do so. On Sunday, 26 February, soldiers were ordered to fire on the crowds, and by the end of that day hundreds had been killed. The following day, however, the die was cast when the Volynskii regiment mutinied, inspiring other military units to follow its example. By 1 March, 170,000 soldiers had joined the insurgents, taking part in attacks on prisons and police stations, arresting tsarist officials, and destroying 'emblems of slavery', notably the crowned two-headed eagle, symbol of the Romanov dynasty. A revolution was in progress, but, as one revolutionary put it, 'it found us, the party members, fast asleep, just like the foolish virgins in the Gospel'.[2] This needs some qualification since militants from the different socialist parties and groups at factory and district level did inject a political element into the demonstrations, even if party leaders were wrong-footed by the sheer speed of events. On 27 February, however, activists in the Workers' Group of the Central War Industries Committee, in coordination with socialist deputies in the duma, decided to reconvene the Soviet of 1905, as a temporary organ to give leadership to the movement. Immediately, factories and military units began to send delegates to the Tauride Palace, the seat of the duma, to form the Petrograd Soviet of Workers' and Soldiers' Deputies.

Also on 27 February liberal members of the duma created a committee, chaired by the Octobrist Mikhail Rodzianko, which proceeded to play an autonomous role in determining the course of events. It set about arresting ministers, generals, and police chiefs, and used personal contacts to persuade regimental commanders to side with the Revolution. Crucially, Rodzianko used his influence to get Stavka to persuade the tsar to abdicate. It was out of this committee that the Provisional Government would be formed on 2 March, after consultation with the Executive Committee of the Soviet.[3] Initially, Nicholas was minded to abdicate in favour of his brother, but Grand Duke Mikhail Aleksandrovich would agree to this only if ratified by an elected assembly. So on 3 March 1917, the 300-year-old Romanov dynasty came to an inglorious end. Whereas in 1905 the autocracy had withstood the revolutionary movement for twelve months, backed by an army that had remained uncertainly loyal, in 1917 it succumbed within less than twelve days, not least because the duma committee was able to bring the generals on side. Notwithstanding the enthusiasm of some members of the duma committee for revolution, others were alarmed from the first. V. V. Shul'gin, a deputy of reactionary views who nevertheless was instrumental in bringing about the tsar's abdication, later recalled the events of 2 March:

> The 'revolutionary people' again overflowed the Duma... The radicals talked of 'dark forces of reaction, tsarism, the old regime, revolution, democracy, power of the people, dictatorship of the proletariat, socialist republic, land to the toilers, and *svoboda* ('freedom'), *svoboda, svoboda*' until one felt sick to one's stomach... To all these speeches the mob belched 'hurrah!'[4]

The February Revolution gave rise to a short-lived mood of euphoria and national unity (see Figure 3.1). Liberty and democracy were its watchwords. Overnight everyone became a citizen—although there was some hesitancy initially about whether women would have the vote. Almost everyone, including bishops of the Orthodox Church, claimed to be on the side of revolution. Clerics of all kinds were subject to election until the autumn when the mood of the hierarchy became more sombre.[5] The public agreed that in order to realize democracy, they must organize. 'Organize!' screamed placards and orators on the streets. The exhilarating tenor of public life was noted by Lenin's wife Nadezhda Krupskaia, upon her return

Figure 3.1 Soldiers' wives demonstrate for an increased ration. Their banners read: 'An increased ration to the families of soldiers, the defenders of freedom and of a people's peace'; and 'Feed the children of the defenders of the motherland'.

to Russia in early April: 'The streets in those days presented a curious spectacle: everywhere people stood about in knots, arguing heatedly and discussing the latest events. Discussion that nothing could interrupt!'[6] Red, which had once been a colour that caused consternation in the propertied classes, was now embraced by all as a symbol of revolution. A joke did the rounds: His Excellency to his batman: 'You dunderhead! I asked you to get me a camouflage uniform and you have brought me one in green. Don't you know that red is the only protective colouring these days?'[7]

Yet from the first the scope of the Revolution was in dispute. Was this a political revolution in which autocracy had finally given way to democracy but which would continue the war in unity with the Allies? Or was it a revolution that was destined to bring about far-reaching transformation in Russia's social and economic structure? Many generals and duma politicians had supported the overthrow of the autocracy only because they believed that it would revitalize the war effort. For the lower classes, however, liberty and democracy were seen not only as principles for restructuring government but also as principles that must be applied in building a new type of society. Ordinary folk in town and countryside not only showed a surprising familiarity with ideas of a constitution, a democratic republic, and of civil and political rights, but moreover saw these as means to achieve peace, solve the economic crisis, and remedy deep social injustice.

Dual Power

The two forces that had together brought about the downfall of the monarchy—the duma opposition and the mass movement—became institutionalized in the political set-up that emerged out of the February Revolution, which became known as 'dual power'.[8] The new Provisional Government in its manifesto of 2 March pledged to implement a far-reaching programme of civil and political rights, and promised to convene a Constituent Assembly to determine the future polity, but it said nothing about the burning issues of war and land. This fitted with the Kadet view that the February events constituted a political not a social revolution. The new government emerged from the ranks of the duma deputies (nine out of twelve members had been deputies), although the remnants of the fourth duma, led by its sidelined chairman, Rodzianko, challenged its claim to be a legitimate government.[9] The head of the new government was Prince G. E. L'vov, scion of a princely family with a long record of service to the zemstvos. In its social composition the government was broadly representative of professional and business interests. The Minister of War, Guchkov, formerly the Octobrist chair of the third duma, was a man of substantial means derived from his interests in textiles, banking, and insurance. He had devoted his career to politics, shifting support to the Kadets in 1912, in protest at the imperial family's support for Rasputin (despite having challenged Miliukov, the new Minister of Foreign Affairs, to a duel in 1908). In a government of moneyed men, however, M. I. Tereshchenko, the Minister of Finance, stood out, by virtue of the 70 million ruble fortune he inherited from his family's sugar-making business. The only organized political party in the new government were the Kadets, who held six out of twelve ministerial portofolios, although there were significant political differences within their ranks. Over the next months, as the populace became more clamorous in its demands for radical social reform, the Kadets would evolve into the principal conservative party, adopting a 'state-minded' and 'above class' posture.[10] In spring, however, the new government instituted far-reaching democratic reforms, including an amnesty for political prisoners, the abolition of the Okhrana, repeal of the death penalty and discriminatory legislation against religious and ethnic minorities, and a declaration of freedom of association and the press—all of this, incidentally, legislation drafted by the first duma.[11]

Within a week 1,200 deputies were elected to the Petrograd Soviet from meetings in factories and barracks and the number soon rose to 3,000. For workers and soldiers, the Soviet was their political representative, the body that would ensure that their hopes for bread, peace, and land were realized. In view of this popular mandate, a few odd Bolsheviks, anarchists, and others pressed for the Soviet to become the sole organ of government, but the

Mensheviks and SRs who dominated its Executive Committee dismissed this as unfeasible and chose to work closely with the Provisional Government. The initial chairmen of the Soviet Executive Committee were: the Menshevik Nikolai Ckheidze, who had been born into a noble Georgian family, had been an active Social Democrat since 1892, and a duma deputy since 1907; Matvei Skobelev, who had led oilworkers' strikes in 1905 and 1914, and had been elected to the fourth duma in 1912 to represent the Russian population of the Caucasus; and Aleksandr Kerensky, a respected defence lawyer who had also been elected to the fourth duma as a Trudovik.[12] These men shared the view that the February Revolution was a 'bourgeois' revolution, that is, a revolution destined to bring democracy and capitalist development to Russia rather than socialism, and they feared that to press for too radical a programme would be to provoke 'counter-revolution' from the military leadership. Their policy was to give critical support to the Provisional Government so long as it did not act contrary to the interests of the people. For its part, the Provisional Government, uncomfortably aware of the narrowness of its social support and of the fact that it had no democratic mandate, endeavoured to induce representatives of the socialist parties to join the government. Only Kerensky agreed. Thus was born 'dual power', an institutional arrangement under which the Provisional Government enjoyed formal authority, but where the Soviet Executive Committee had real power, since it had the support of the garrison, control of transport and communications through its influence among railway workers, and general support among the urban population. There was some overlap of interest between the moderate socialists and the liberals, but essentially dual power expressed the division between 'us', the 'democracy', and 'them', 'propertied society'.[13]

The February Revolution produced a surge of patriotism and a renewed determination across a wide swathe of society to defend the Revolution against German militarism. This mood was reflected in the Petrograd Soviet's policy on bringing an end to the war, a policy crafted by the Georgian Menshevik I. Tsereteli, and published as a proclamation 'To the Peoples of the World' on 14 March. Although it called for the army to defend the Revolution, its 'revolutionary defencism' was more radical than that of the

Workers' Group of the War Industries Committees insofar as its accent was very much on internationalism and on the achievement of a peace without territorial annexations or the imposition of indemnities.[14] Hopes were placed in the Stockholm peace conference, which had been proposed by socialists of neutral countries and eventually backed by the British Labour Party and the French and Italian Socialist Parties. However, the conference was soon scuppered by the Allied governments, whose determination to achieve a decisive victory was strengthened by the entry of the USA into the war on 4 April. Initially the moderate socialists hoped that this might actually help the achievement of a peace in which neither side was victorious, since this was a position that Woodrow Wilson had until recently supported, but the German advance in spring 1917 seems to have persuaded him that the Allies should not be dictated to by Russian revolutionaries whose contribution to the war effort was now in serious doubt.[15]

Outside the capital dual power did not really exist.[16] The line-up of political and social forces in the provinces varied a good deal, but in most places committees of public organizations or committees of public safety were set up to fill the power vacuum. These brought together the educated public and workers and soldiers and acted to remove police and tsarist officials, maintain order and food supply, and later to supervise elections to the municipal dumas and rural zemstvos. In March, 79 such committees were set up at provincial level, 651 at county level, and about 1,000 at township level.[17] The committee of public organizations in far-away Irkutsk was typical in defining its aim as being to 'carry the revolution to its conclusion and strengthen the foundations of freedom and popular power'.[18] The committees, however, did not survive for more than a few months, since the Provisional Government was determined to stamp its authority on the localities by appointing commissars, most of whom were chairs of the county zemstvos and thus representatives of landed or business interests. In the provinces energetic and respected individuals were far more important than political parties in shaping local politics. In Saratov province, for example, there were no political parties in three-quarters of township-level committees of public organizations. This began to change as elections to the zemstvos and municipalities got under way between May and October, but in 418 county towns just over half the votes still went to non-party lists, in contrast to the fifty provincial capitals where Mensheviks and SRs were dominant.[19]

In spring of 1917 some 700 soviets sprang up, involving around 200,000 deputies, as representative organs of the working people. By October 1,429 soviets existed in the empire: 706 of them comprising workers' and soldiers' deputies; 235 comprising workers', soldiers', and peasants' deputies; 455 comprising peasants' deputies; and 33 consisting just of soldiers' deputies.[20] It has been estimated that soviets represented about one-third of the empire's population. This network represented working people, but peasants were much slower to form soviets than workers and soldiers. The moderate socialists tended to describe them as organs of 'revolutionary democracy', a bloc that comprised not only workers, soldiers, and peasants, but also the 'toiling intelligentsia', such as teachers and journalists, and professionals such as lawyers and doctors and even (as in Omsk) representatives of ethnic minorities. This 'revolutionary democracy' had historically defined itself against the *tsenzoviki*, a somewhat antiquated term that referred to those under the tsarist regime who possessed sufficient property to participate in the zemstvos and municipal governments, but which was used more loosely to denote the propertied classes. The basic principles of soviet democracy were that deputies were directly elected by those they represented and that they were accountable to and recallable by their constituents. In contrast to the committees of public organizations, soviets were subject to regular democratic election and representatives were drawn almost exclusively from the different socialist parties. At the First All-Russian Congress of Soviets at the beginning of June, out of 822 delegates with voting rights 285 were SRs, 248 were Mensheviks, 32 were Menshevik Internationalists, and 105 were Bolsheviks.[21] The Mensheviks and SRs generally saw the soviets as temporary bodies whose task was to exercise 'control' over the local organs of government in the interests of revolutionary democracy. In contrast to what Lenin would later argue, soviets did not see themselves as representing a 'higher' form of democracy than that of parliamentary democracy.[22] Indeed much of their energy went into campaigning for the Constituent Assembly which, everyone assumed, would establish a parliamentary regime. Yet in actuality soviets quickly became organs of local government, concerned with everything from food and fuel supply, to education, to law and order, usually competing with democratized organs of local government. As early as late April, Left SRs and Bolsheviks in the Tsaritsyn soviet affirmed it to be the town's ruling body. In May the Kronstadt Soviet—which consisted of 96 Bolsheviks, 96 non-party deputies, 73 Left SRs, 13 Mensheviks, and 7 anarchists—caused a furore when it refused to recognize the Provisional Government. But these were odd exceptions before the autumn.[23]

Although in January 1912 the conference in Prague had constituted the Bolsheviks as a separate party, in the provinces many local Social Democratic organizations remained 'unified' with, at best, Mensheviks and Bolsheviks operating as factions within a single party. It is thus not easy to estimate the numbers in the two factions. By May there may have been as many as 100,000 Mensheviks, 40,000 of them in Georgia, where their position was unassailable. Their stance of critical support for the Provisional Government had proved popular, and in the spring they grew much faster than they had in 1905–6. By autumn the party may have had almost 200,000 members.[24] As in the Bolshevik party, intellectuals dominated the leadership of the party, but the membership consisted overwhelmingly of working people. More so than the Bolsheviks, the Mensheviks suffered serious splits during the war between defencist and internationalist wings. Tsereteli's policy of 'revolutionary defencism' went some way to bridging that split, but divisions soon reopened when Mensheviks joined the first coalition government in May. Following the July Days (of which more later), Iulii Martov, leader of the internationalist wing of the Menshevik party, which had opposed the war, agitated for a break with the Kadets and the formation of a government comprising exclusively socialist parties; but the centre-right of the party opted to persist with the coalition with the 'bourgeoisie' until September when the party was plunged into crisis.

The SRs were the largest of all the political parties in 1917. By autumn they had about 700,000 members organized into 312 committees and 124 groups, loosely divided between defencists and internationalists.[25] Their membership embraced peasants, soldiers (who comprised almost half the membership), workers, intellectuals, the urban middle strata, businessmen, and army officers. The SRs were seen as the natural party of the rural population, although as we have seen they had always had significant influence among workers. Like the Mensheviks, the SRs would succumb to damaging splits owing to their determination to uphold a coalition with the 'bourgeoisie'. The right wing of the party called for war to victory and saw the task of the Revolution as being to establish a democratic political system, entrench private property, and oppose the cruder forms of capitalist exploitation. The centre, in which the dominant figure was Viktor Chernov, saw the Revolution as one of popular toilers, destined to move towards socialism; but most of the centre were more committed than he to preserving a broad popular alliance that included the bourgeoisie. Only in September did Chernov manage to pull the party away from its adherence to the coalition government. From May left-wingers in the SRs began to crystallize as an embryonic party, by virtue of their support for the peasants' seizure of landowners' estates, their hostility to the 'imperialist' war, and their backing for a pan-socialist government. Their influence grew fast, and by autumn most party organizations in the provinces had come out in favour of power to the soviets. On the extreme left, the SR Maximalists wanted socialization of both land and industry and a toilers' republic, as the first step to socialism. In reality, long before elections to the Constituent Assembly, the SRs had ceased to be a single party: the right reflected the trajectory of the democratic intelligentsia who were willing to postpone social reform until the Allies had won the war, whereas the left sought to advance the social revolution by calling for power to the soviets.

Lenin and the Bolsheviks

On 3 April Lenin returned to Russia from Switzerland, having passed through Germany in a sealed train.[26] Despite the volley of accusations made at the time and since, there is no evidence that the Bolsheviks were in the pay of the Germans. Lenin had been away from his native land for nearly seventeen years and, apart from a six-month stay in 1905–6, up to this point his career as a revolutionary had been largely one of failure. The left-wing Menshevik Nikolai Sukhanov described his arrival at the Finland Station in Petrograd:

> He wore a round cap, his face looked frozen, and there was a magnificent bouquet in his hands. Running to the middle of the room, he stopped in front of Chkheidze, as though colliding with a completely unexpected obstacle. And Chkheidze, still glum, pronounced the following 'speech of welcome' with not only the spirit and wording but also the tone of a sermon: 'Comrade Lenin, in the name of the Petrograd Soviet and the whole Revolution we welcome you to Russia… But we think that the principal task of the revolutionary democracy is now the defence of the Revolution from any encroachments either from within or abroad. We consider that what this goal requires is not disunion but the closing of the democratic ranks'… Lenin stood there as though nothing taking place had the slightest connection with him, looking about him… and then, turning away from the Executive Committee delegation altogether, he made this 'reply': 'Dear Comrades… The piratical imperialist war is the beginning of civil war throughout Europe… the hour is not far distant when… the peoples will turn their arms against their own capitalist exploiters… The worldwide socialist revolution has already dawned.'[27]

Bolshevism was always broader than the views of its leader, yet Lenin was the towering figure within the party and stamped his views upon it. He was a man of broad intellect and tremendous industry, of iron will and self-discipline, self-confident, and intolerant of opponents. Personally, he was modest, indifferent to the trappings of power, fastidious, and capable of deep emotional attachments.[28] As Aleksandr Potresov, a right-wing Menshevik and former comrade, observed: 'Only Lenin was that rare phenomenon, rare especially in Russia, a man of iron will and indomitable energy who combined a fanatical faith in the movement with no less a faith in himself. If Louis XIV could say "I am the state", then Lenin without wasting words consistently felt that he was the party.'[29] Lenin's politics were rooted in Marxist theory, yet he had a profound grasp of the workings of power and a capacity to take tough and unpopular decisions and to make sharp changes to policy. He applied Marxism creatively to a country that lacked the level of capitalist development that Marx had assumed (not always consistently) was necessary for the building of socialism. Yet theory also distorted his perception of Russian realities. He persistently exaggerated the degree of class differentiation among the peasantry, for example, and called for a policy of turning the imperialist war into a civil war that had no more than a handful of supporters. He expended quantities of ink in denouncing ideological deviations within the RSDLP—from 'economism' to 'empiriomonism'—that were largely of his own imagining. Despite his principled internationalism and familiarity with foreign cultures, he was a product of Russian political culture, particularly in his obsession with ideological purity, his belief in his own ideological rectitude, his unwillingness to compromise, and in his authoritarian habits of thought and action. While he recognized the role of mass action in revolution, the distinctive feature of his thought was his stress on the vanguard party, a highly centralized organization whose task was to lead the proletariat through revolution. Ironically, the party that carried out the seizure of power in October bore only a distant resemblance to this model, although it would come into existence not as an instrument of insurrection but as one of state building.[30]

The war had convinced Lenin that capitalism was bankrupt and that socialism was now on the agenda internationally.[31] In Russia, he argued, the 'bourgeois' stage of the Revolution was already passing and a transition to socialism was possible, although he remained unsure how far in a socialist direction Russia could go if her Revolution remained isolated. One might question his optimism about the prospects for international socialist revolution, but he displayed a perspicacity about developments in 1917 that he had not shown in 1905 (when he was obsessed with armed insurrection and slow to recognize the potential of the soviet). His detestation of liberalism and parliamentarism, his conviction that the Provisional Government could not deliver what the people wanted, his implacable opposition to the imperialist war, and his appreciation of the potential of soviets oriented him well to a political situation in which society was polarizing along loosely class lines. Prior to his return, the Bolsheviks were in some disarray: in Petrograd there were three different party centres, unable to settle upon a clear line of policy. The return from exile in Siberia of Lev Kamenev (1883–1936) and Iosif Stalin (1878–1953) had committed the party to limited support for the Provisional Government, to a revolutionary defencist position on the war, and to negotiations with the Mensheviks to reunify the RSDLP. In his *April Theses*, delivered to a largely uncomprehending party, Lenin denounced each of these policies, insisting that there could be no support for a 'government of capitalists and landlords', that the character of the war had not changed one iota, and that the Bolsheviks should campaign for all power to be transferred to a state-wide system of soviets.[32]

In 1917 the Bolshevik party was a very different animal from the tightly knit conspiratorial party conceived by Lenin in 1903.[33] Alongside cadres who had endured years of hardship, tens of thousands of workers, soldiers, and sailors flooded into the party after February, knowing little of Marx but seeing in the Bolsheviks the most implacable defenders of the interests of the common people. At the time of the February Revolution the number of Bolsheviks may have fallen as low as 10,000, owing to wartime persecution, but by October it had risen to over 350,000.[34] Though considerably more united than the SRs, Mensheviks, or anarchists, the Bolsheviks still embraced a rather wide range of opinion. Even after Lenin's *April Theses* became official party policy, the more moderate, gradualist views of Kamenev—erudite, conciliatory, redolent of Chekhov, with his spectacles and goatee beard—and of Grigorii Zinoviev (1883–1936), a tub-thumping orator dubbed 'Lenin's mad dog' by the Mensheviks, continued to enjoy support within the party.[35] On the left of the party, meanwhile, Nikolai Bukharin, a major influence on Lenin's thinking that imperialism represented the highest stage of capitalism, believed that Russia's backwardness did not in any way disqualify it from moving rapidly towards socialism.

Upon his return from the USA on 4 May, Lev Trotsky joined the Inter-district group.[36] Trotsky had clashed with Lenin on many occasions in the past, but welcomed Lenin's conversion to the view that revolution in Russia could trigger international socialist revolution. In July the Inter-district group amalgamated with the Bolsheviks, bringing some 4,000 members into Bolshevik ranks, including such highly talented individuals as Anatolii Lunacharskii (1875–1933), soon to be become Commissar of Enlightenment, Adol'f Ioffe (1883–1927), who would be tasked with making a peace treaty with Germany in January 1918, and Moisei Uritskii, who would become head of the Petrograd Cheka only to be slain by Left SRs in August 1918.[37] Although Trotsky's views overlapped with those of Lenin to a considerable extent, the overlap was not as complete as Lenin might have wished. Trotsky, for example, does not appear ever to have endorsed the utopian model of the 'commune state' outlined in Lenin's *State and Revolution*, a text begun in 1916, completed while he was in hiding in Finland in August, but not published until 1918. In that text he advocated smashing the old state and creating a much reduced state similar to that which had flickered into life during the Paris Commune of 1871, in which the police, standing army, and bureaucracy were abolished and the tasks of government reduced to ones of simple administration that any 'cook or housekeeper' could administer.

The control exercised by the Central Committee over the lower levels of the party organization was rather weak. Despite Lenin's demand that Bolsheviks separate from unified RSDLP organizations, for instance, many were loath to do so. At the front most RSDLP organizations remained unified until September or October. And even when Bolsheviks did split from unified organizations it was often to form 'internationalist' factions. In Vitebsk, for example, such a faction was formed on 3 July by 58 Bolsheviks, 11 Mensheviks, and 28 members of the Inter-district group. At the Sixth Party Congress, held from 26 July to 3 August in Petrograd, representatives from the provinces complained that the Central Committee had failed to inform them of crucial policies, such as the adoption of the slogan of workers' control of production, and that they had been ill informed about the party's planned demonstration on 10 June and the July Days.[38] The city committees were the most important agency coordinating Bolshevik activity at the grass roots and, to an extent, they were left to their own devices. This meant, for example, that the city organizations in Moscow and Kyiv could oppose the plan to seize power in October. And the Moscow city committee, dominated by moderates, clashed with the Moscow regional bureau, responsible for activity in the central industrial region, which was dominated by left-wingers. Arguably, far more important in winning the party popular support in 1917 was not so much its organizational discipline, or even its ideological unity, but its ability to talk a language that ordinary people understood, and to rearticulate in terms of class struggle and socialism their very urgent and desperate concerns.

The Aspirations of Soldiers and Workers

There were around 9 million men in uniform in 1917 and soldiers proved to be a major force in mass politics.[39] Though they lacked the high level of organization of workers, they were more influential in taking revolutionary politics to the countryside and, ultimately, in securing soviet power. Soldiers and sailors hailed the downfall of the autocracy, seeing it as a signal to overthrow the oppressive structure of command in the armed forces. Hated officers were removed and sometimes lynched (lynchings were worst among the Kronstadt sailors, where about fifty officers were murdered).[40] Celebrating the fact that they were now citizens of free Russia, soldiers demanded the abolition of degrading practices such as the use by officers of derogatory language, the right to meet and petition, and improvements in pay and conditions. Crucially, they began to form committees from the level of the company up to the level of the front in order to represent their interests. This drive to democratize authority relations in the armed forces was given expression in the most radical act undertaken by the Petrograd Soviet, namely, the promulgation of Order No. 1 on 1 March, forced upon it by soldiers' deputies. Order No. 1 ratified the election of committees at all levels, put the issuance of weapons under their control, and advised them to look to the Petrograd Soviet for political direction. On duty soldiers were to observe military discipline, while off duty they had full rights as citizens.[41] General M. V. Alekseev pronounced the Order 'the means by which the army I command will be destroyed'. In fact the committees were dominated by fairly educated men, such as non-commissioned officers, doctors, clerical workers, and junior officers, who had little desire to sabotage the operational effectiveness of the army. Most soldiers wanted a speedy peace, but did not wish to see Russia overrun by German troops. Nor, initially, was there much mistrust of the Provisional Government, the sailors in Kronstadt being something of an exception in this regard. Indeed mistrust was probably more in evidence among workers, whose demands, particularly for an eight-hour day, struck soldiers rotting in trenches as excessive.[42] The many resolutions passed by soldiers called for a Constituent Assembly, a democratic republic, and a whole raft of social and political reforms, including compulsory education and progressive income tax. At the same time, if the democratization of the army did not mean its disintegration as a fighting force—at least in the spring and early summer—it was by no means certain that it could be relied upon to wage the all-out offensive the Allies were demanding. It certainly could not be relied upon to perform its conventional function of suppressing domestic disorder. When workers took to the streets to demand the resignation of Foreign Minister Miliukov, on 20–1 April, General L. G. Kornilov ordered troops to leave their barracks and disperse the demonstrators but his order was ignored (during the July Days, however, Soviet leaders were able to bring in troops from outside the capital).[43]

The Petersburg Committee of the Bolshevik party (it refused to change its name to Petrograd) was quick off the mark in setting up a Military Organization to recruit soldiers in the garrison into the party and to promote the party's politics. It published a newspaper, *Soldatskaia Pravda* (*Soldiers' Truth*), which had a circulation of 50,000 to 75,000. On 10 April it became an official organ of the Central Committee responsible for recruiting, agitating, and organizing soldiers on all military fronts and in the garrisons of the rear. On 16 June an All-Russian Conference of the Bolshevik soldiers' organizations took place in the capital, and was attended by 167 delegates who claimed to represent 26,000 members in 43 front and 17 rear organizations.[44] The Military Organization of the Petrograd garrison, where soldiers awaited dispatch to the front, is said to have been 5,800-strong by autumn, although that figure may be exaggerated.[45]

Throughout 1917 industrial workers were the most politicized and organized of the social groups involved in mass politics and the social group that had the most capacity to shape the course of events.[46] By 1917 there were at least 18.5 million workers of all kinds in the empire, about 10 per cent of the population. In Petrograd and its suburbs there were 417,000 industrial workers, of whom 65 per cent were metalworkers, 11 per cent textile workers, and 10 per cent chemical workers. In Moscow there were about 420,000 workers of whom one-third were textile workers and one-quarter metalworkers. In the central industrial region there were over a million workers, of whom 61 per cent were textile workers. In the Urals 83 per cent of 350,000 industrial workers were employed in mining and metallurgy. In Ukraine there were about 1 million workers, including 280,000 miners and metallurgical workers in the Donbass. This regional concentration of the working class was complemented by concentration in large units of production (in Petrograd more than 70 per cent of workers were in enterprises of more than 1,000 employees). It was young, male, mainly skilled workers, especially in the metalworking industries, on the railways, and in printing, who were most active in building a labour movement and in launching strikes. Something like two-thirds of workers were recent recruits to industry, either peasant migrants or women who had taken up jobs in the war industries (women comprised well over a third of the workforce in 1917), and most of these unskilled, low-paid, minimally literate workers did not have a sophisticated level of political understanding.[47] Nevertheless in the course of 1917 they would be drawn into a mass strike movement, would join trade unions, and their disaffection would be given political articulation by socialist activists on the shop floor.

Following the general strike in February, workers determined to overthrow 'autocracy' on the shop floor. Hated foremen and administrators were driven out and old rule books torn up. Factory committees were elected, mainly by metalworkers and mainly in the state-owned defence sector, to represent workers' interests to management. These committees demanded an eight-hour working day and substantial wage rises to compensate for wartime inflation, both demands reluctantly conceded by the same employers who had hitherto resisted them. A plethora of other labour organizations came into being, notably trade unions, but extending to worker cooperatives, worker militias, and worker clubs and dramatic societies.

Factory committees took on tasks such as guarding the factory, overseeing hiring and firing, ensuring labour discipline, and organizing food supplies. Had economic conditions been more favourable, it is possible that they might have served to establish a form of corporatist industrial relations, since more enlightened employers favoured co-responsibility and compulsory arbitration of disputes. However, conditions in industry worsened by the day and by summer the economy was in free fall. In this context the committees mobilized to ensure that jobs were preserved and that companies did not act in ways that hurt their employees. Significantly, the factory committees were the first of the popular organizations to register the shift in workers' attitudes from support for the moderate socialists to the Bolsheviks. At the end of May, the first conference of Petrograd factory committees overwhelmingly passed a Bolshevik resolution on control of the economy. And by the time of the first national conference of factory committees in October, two-thirds of delegates said they were Bolsheviks. By that stage, over two-thirds of enterprises employing 200 or more workers had set up factory committees (although more than three-quarters of factories of all types did not have them).

Trade unions were somewhat slower to get off the ground after February, and Mensheviks played a more important role in these organizations than they did in the factory committees. By May about 120 unions were affiliated to the Petrograd Central Bureau of Trade Unions, compared with 38 to its Moscow counterpart. By summer in faraway Irkutsk some 8,000 workers had enrolled in 20 unions, and in Baku 27 unions were active, including a seamen's union of 4,800 and an oilworkers' union of 3,000. By the Third All-Russian Conference of Trade Unions in June there were 976 unions throughout the empire with a total membership of 1.4 million. In regions such as the Donbass and the Urals, however, unions never achieved influence comparable with that of factory and mine committees (Figure 3.2).

Figure 3.2 A factory meeting on May Day 1917. The banners read: 'Long live the holiday of the world proletariat' and 'If we repair a single steam engine it means we bring the end of hunger and poverty nearer and thereby bring an end to capitalism'.

And the coexistence of unions and factory committees led to clashes concerning their respective spheres of competence. By autumn, trade unions were in theory responsible for defending wages and working conditions of their members (by that stage they numbered around 2 million) and factory committees were responsible for workers' control. The trade unions underwent the same process of 'Bolshevization' as other mass organizations, but a few—notably the printers', chemical workers' and glass workers'—held out as redoubts of Menshevism.

Whereas workers had backed moderate socialists in factory-based elections to the soviets in spring, the decision of the moderate socialists who joined the government in May to support continuation of the war alienated hundreds of thousands of working people. However, the radicalization of the mass of workers over the summer was driven as much by the speedy deterioration of their economic situation as it was by a desire for peace.

Strikes spread out from Petrograd and the central industrial region to all corners of the empire. In July the number of strikers rose to half a million and reached 1.2 million by October, and as strikes multiplied employers began to take a tough line, locking out recalcitrant workers and laying off employees. An analysis of workers' resolutions in Moscow reveals that from May declining real wages, shortages, and the threat to jobs supplanted the war as the issues that most exercised working people.

The Provisional Government in Crisis

By May the Provisional Government was in crisis.[48] In spite of the talk of 'unity of all the vital forces of the nation' the issue of the war had proved deeply divisive from the first. The Minister of Foreign Affairs, Pavel Miliukov, was strongly of the view that Russia must continue the war until Allied victory. By contrast, the leaders of the Soviet wished to bring the war to an end with no side claiming victory. For a few weeks it looked as though Tsereteli's policy of 'revolutionary defencism' might provide a compromise around which both the Soviet and government could unite, but in a note to the Allies that was made public on 20 April Miliukov made clear his support for the 'secret treaties' that promised Russia the Black Sea straits as the fruit of victory. This provoked the first crisis of the government and revealed how tenuous was its support. Soldiers took to the streets to demand Miliukov's resignation and Bolsheviks bore banners proclaiming 'Down with the Provisional Government'. They clashed with counter-demonstrators who carried banners proclaiming 'Down with anarchy', 'Down with Lenin'. On 29 April the Minister of War, Guchkov, resigned, without bothering to consult his colleagues, and three days later, Miliukov was also forced to resign. Prince L'vov, the Prime Minister, demanded that members of the Soviet Executive Committee join a coalition government to resolve the crisis, and it fell to Tsereteli to persuade his reluctant colleagues to participate in a 'bourgeois' government. He did so by convincing them that this would strengthen the chances for peace. On 6 May the moderate socialists assumed six places in a coalition government, against eight occupied by 'bourgeois' representatives, giving them limited influence but full responsibility for government policy.

Having entered the government to hasten the conclusion of peace, they found themselves at once involved in preparations for a new military offensive that was being championed by Kerensky, the new Minister of War. Kerensky's enthusiasm for a new offensive was motivated by a desire to see Russia honour her treaty obligations to the Allies and by the belief that a truly revolutionary army could assist in the creation of a comity of democratic nations once victory was achieved. General Alekseev, perceived to be too cautious, was replaced as Commander-in-Chief by General Brusilov. For their part, the Allies had few illusions about the fighting capacity of the Russian army but they were keen to keep Germany tied down on the Eastern Front. Meanwhile soldiers were becoming radicalized, thanks to SR and Bolshevik agitators, so it was not at all clear whether morale would hold up long enough for an offensive to be carried out. Kerensky, with a crewcut and wearing military fatigues, tirelessly toured the front, calling on divisions to prove to the world that they were fighting not for 'autocratic adventurers' but for a 'free Russian republic' (see Figure 3.3).

Meanwhile the Bolsheviks planned a demonstration against the new government for 10 June, but were forced to back down when this was condemned by the All-Russian Congress of Soviets then taking place in the capital. Instead the Congress agreed to sponsor a demonstration for 18 June in support of the Soviet. On that day, to the chagrin of the Soviet leaders, some 400,000 workers and soldiers marched through the capital with banners declaring 'Down with the ten capitalist ministers' and 'All power to the soviets'. A detail in a newspaper report of the demonstration tells of a 'tall, thin man with a haggard face' who tore down what he called a 'Jewish banner', expressing confidence in the government, reminding us that antisemitism inflected left-wing as well as right-wing radicalism.[49] On the same day as what became known as the 'June crisis', the offensive finally got under way, targeted once more on L'viv, pivot of the 1914–15 fighting, and the focus of Brusilov's offensive the previous summer. In the event, only forty-eight battalions refused to take part. For two days the attack went well, but the

Figure 3.3 Kerensky tours the front June 1917. He here is greeting the Czech Legion.

crack units in the lead became demoralized when those behind them refused to take their place. Between 18 June and 6 July, casualties climbed to 1,968 officers and 56,361 soldiers—including 3,860 deserters—and it was crack units that were mainly affected.[50] By the end of June it was clear that the offensive had been a fiasco. More shock detachments and death battalions were created but the army had began to unravel. Despairing of seeing an end to the bloodshed, soldiers now itched to lay their hands on gentry estates. The Bolsheviks, SRs, and other anti-war activists now found a receptive audience for their denunciation of the imperialist war.

On 3–5 July a major crisis occurred in Petrograd which affected both the Soviet leadership and the Bolshevik party. Historians differ as to whether what is known as the 'July Days' was a calculated attempt at insurrection by the Bolshevik party—'Lenin's worst blunder', as Richard Pipes opines—or a fairly spontaneous initiative by rank-and-file anarchist and Bolshevik soldiers and workers who presented party leaders with a semi-insurrectionary fait accompli.[51] On 2 July four Kadet ministers resigned from the government, ostensibly over concessions being made to Ukrainian nationalists, thereby bringing the first coalition government to an end. The same day, the First Machine-Gun Regiment, the largest unit in the garrison with 11,340 men and nearly 300 officers and a stronghold of the Bolshevik Military Organization, passed a resolution denouncing Kerensky for the measures that were then under way to move troops from the capital to the front. On the afternoon of 3 July, soldiers of the Regiment appeared armed on the streets along with thousands of workers to demand that power be handed to the soviets. By the evening counter-demonstrators had appeared on the street and there was shooting from the roofs of buildings. That night, the Bolshevik leadership, having earlier called for the demonstration to be wound down, fearing that any attempt to overthrow the Provisional Government was premature, changed its mind and resolved to lead the movement. Tsereteli, now Minister of Posts and Telegraphs, denounced the demonstration as 'counter-revolutionary': 'the decisions of the revolutionary democracy cannot be dictated by bayonets'.[52] Steps were taken to bring in Cossacks and other reliable troops to restore order in the capital. The following day even more workers and soldiers surged onto the streets and that afternoon, with sailors from Kronstadt to the fore, tens of thousands made their way to the Soviet headquarters at the Tauride Palace to denounce the Menshevik and SR leaders for having surrendered to the 'landlords and bourgeoisie'. The Menshevik Sukhanov describes how a hard-pressed Trotsky struggled to pacify the crowd which threatened to seize the SR leader Chernov:

> 'You hurried over here, Red Kronstadters, as soon as you heard the Revolution was in danger... You've come to declare your will and show the Soviet that the working class no longer wants to see the bourgeoisie in power. But why hurt your own cause by petty acts of violence against casual individuals?' Trotsky stretched his hand down to a sailor who was protesting with especial violence, but the latter firmly refused to respond... It seemed to me that the sailor, who must have heard Trotsky in Kronstadt more than once, now had

a feeling that he was a traitor: he remembered his previous speeches and was confused.[53]

By 5 July troops loyal to the government were in full control of the capital, vigorously crushing the insurgency. With Kerensky demanding 'severe retribution', orders were issued for the arrest of more than half a dozen leading Bolsheviks, and the party's newspapers were shut down. On 7 July a 'government of salvation of the revolution' was formed in which Kerensky arrogated unlimited powers to himself.

The semi-insurrection, known as the July Days, appears to have welled up from the grass roots and to have taken the Bolshevik leadership by surprise, but rank-and-file militants felt unable to resist—or may positively have encouraged—the pressure that was building up among the most radical sections of the working class and soldiery for action to bring an end to the war and to force the soviet leaders to take power. Clearly, too, in parts of the Bolshevik leadership there was sentiment in favour of taking decisive action: on the Moscow oblast' bureau, for example, leftist Bolsheviks demanded that an armed but peaceful demonstration planned for 4 July in Moscow seize the post and telegraph offices and the headquarters of the *Russian Word* (*Russkoe Slovo*) newspaper.[54] But the semi-insurrection received little support in the provinces: indeed at the Sixth Party Congress of the Bolshevik party, which took place while Lenin was in hiding in Finland, provincial leaders complained about how ill informed they had been about the events in the capital.

Revolution in the Village

Few peasants mourned the passing of the Romanov dynasty.[55] They drew up thousands of resolutions to greet the arrival of the democratic order, to applaud the fact that they were now citizens of a free Russia, and to demand that the entire social and political order be reconstructed on the basis of self-government at the lowest possible level. Land captains, township elders, village policemen were driven out and replaced by township committees elected by the peasants. The Provisional Government hoped to make its writ run via these committees—by July they existed in most of the country's 15,000 townships—but they were very much under the control of the peasants themselves. Later some rebranded themselves as 'soviets'. The Revolution strengthened the authority of the village gathering, 'democratizing' it by allowing younger sons, landless labourers, village intelligentsia (scribes, teachers, vets, and doctors), and some women to participate in the affairs of the community. The level of political awareness of the peasantry remained limited and socialist parties and labour organizations busied themselves sending agitators and literature into the villages. Among the myriad pamphlets produced was the 'Ten Commandments of the Russian Citizen' ('In unity is strength', 'Respect your fellow man', 'Maintain order', 'Do not forget the war'). The Petrograd Soviet of Peasant Deputies, established on 14 April by soldiers in the garrison, sent 3,000 agitators into the countryside, and workers in the capital raised 65,000 rubles to pay for agitational literature. Soldiers returning from the front were a key conduit through which radical political ideas passed into the countryside.

The key issues for the peasants were war and land. But the first issue that brought villagers into conflict with the government was neither war nor land, but that of food.[56] Worryingly for the army and civilian consumers, only one-sixth of the harvest was now being sold on the market, compared with one-quarter before the war. The new government responded by introducing a state monopoly on grain, but its attempts to force peasants to sell their grain at fixed prices provoked them to conceal stocks or turn it into alcohol. In Iashevka village in Tambov county a food-supply official was 'dressed in a woman's skirt, a bag adorned with 30 ruble banknotes was placed over his head, and a spade thrust in his hands to which was attached an inscription: "For thirty pieces of silver he sold our freedom"'.[57] Nevertheless as the new harvest came in, there was still little sense that by the winter an enormous food crisis would be looming, especially in Petrograd.

Peasants expected that the overthrow of the autocracy would mean that the estates of the gentry, Crown, and Church would finally pass into their hands. From late spring a struggle against the landed nobility quietly got under way. Initially, peasants were cautious, testing the capacity of local authorities to curb any illegal action. They unilaterally reduced or failed to pay rent, grazed cattle illegally on the landowner's estate, stole wood from his forests, and, increasingly, took over uncultivated tracts of gentry land on the pretext that it would otherwise remain unsown. In the non-black-earth zone, where dairy and livestock farming were the mainstays of the agricultural economy, peasants concentrated on getting their hands on meadow land and pasture. Seeing the inability of local commissars to stop these illegal actions, the number of 'disturbances' began to increase, levelling off during harvest time from mid-July to mid-August, but climbing sharply from September. By autumn the movement to seize gentry land was in full swing, especially in Ukraine. Peasants were seizing land, equipment, and livestock and redistributing it among themselves. Generally, the village gathering took the initiative, but returning soldiers were a disruptive and disorderly element who spurred their communities into action. In Borisov county in Minsk, just behind the positions of the Third Army, 'Six healthy young men dressed in army greatcoats came into our village on three carts. They called us together: "Get ready, lads, harness your horses, let's go and sack the estate of landlord L."'[58] The intensity of the agrarian movement varied by region, but the main battlegrounds were the overcrowded central black-earth and middle Volga regions. In a province such as Voronezh, landowners and private peasant proprietors only owned about one-fifth of arable land, yet widespread land hunger meant that peasants cast greedy eyes upon their estates. In Belorussia, where there was less pressure on arable land, peasant protest was intense mainly because grazing land and timber were in short supply. There gentry estates were more numerous than in Voronezh but smaller in size and run on more commercial lines. By contrast, in the northern non-black-soil province of Tver' there was little unrest, since for many decades peasants had been forced by poor soil and climate to migrate in search of wage work.

The government nationalized the lands belonging to the imperial family, but it had no enthusiasm for tackling the land question while the war was ongoing, knowing that it was likely to encourage desertion in the armed forces. As an earnest of its seriousness, however, and to prepare a land reform in detail, the government set up a rather bureaucratic structure of land committees at provincial, county, and township levels, topped by a Main Land Committee. Its proceedings proved laborious and the committees at township level were taken over by restive peasants. The Kadet ministers (and Prince L'vov) resisted any concessions to the peasantry, insisting that landlords (and the banks to which much of their land was mortgaged) be fully compensated for any land compulsorily taken from them. For its part, the Union of Landowners and Farmers accused the government of failing to defend the rights of private property, and of giving in to anarchy. And though the government did send troops into some of the most volatile provinces, it had little effect in quelling the growing insurgency.[59] Viktor Chernov, towering leader of the SRs, was the one socialist minister in the coalition with a critical portfolio, having been appointed Minister of Agriculture in May. He rejected the demand of his Kadet colleagues that landowners be compensated for land that was taken from them, but his hope was to see an orderly transfer of land through the land committees. Over July and August several thousand members of land committees were arrested for illegal land seizures, but this was a drop in the ocean. In the countryside a revolution was under way.

One of the first acts of the Bolshevik government was to issue a Decree on Land. This simply recognized what was taking place, namely, a massive and spontaneous movement to seize landed estates.[60] Although the gentry were the overwhelming targets, during the winter internal conflict within the peasant community appeared, as peasants who had taken advantage of the Stolypin reforms to separate from the commune also found their land being snatched. This was especially evident in the black-earth provinces. In the Baltic, Belorussia, and in parts of Ukraine, where capitalist farming existed, agricultural labourers formed unions, just as Lenin had urged in the *April Theses*. Overall the movement was fairly organized, since the paramount aim was to cultivate the land that was being seized; but by late 1917 the sacking of manors and burning of symbols of aristocratic privilege, such as pianos, became more widespread. In December it was reported from Korsunskii county in Simbirsk: 'On the estate of Arapov in the village of Mar'ianovka there was a riot and spontaneous seizures beginning on 15 November. They divided everything in two, half going to Mar'ianovka and half to the two communities of Fedorovka and Berezniakov. All three communities auctioned off livestock, inventory and buildings... but domestic property was sacked. The money raised was divided equally according to the number of mouths to feed in each household.'[61] The movement was largely spontaneous and largely local, but peasants knew that in order to legalize their hold on the land they would have to participate in the Constituent Assembly election, and so most duly voted for the party they considered to be the party of the peasantry, namely the SRs.

The Nationalist Challenge

The First World War had boosted nationalist sentiment, especially in the western borderlands, the Baltic, and the Caucasus, regions which bore the brunt of foreign occupation and forced evacuation.[62] The idea that the war was intended to promote national self-determination began to circulate well before Woodrow Wilson articulated his Fourteen Points in January 1918, Germany for example promising Poland independence in the event of victory by the Central Powers.[63] Nationalism, however, was still unevenly developed across the empire and the problems of giving it effective political articulation became apparent once the February Revolution offered the promise of democratic government. Initially, most nationalist groups pressed for varying degrees of autonomy within a free Russia. Demands ranged from relatively modest ones relating to schooling or religious services in native languages, to more ambitious ones for extensive decentralization of powers. The typical goal was encapsulated in the slogan of the Ukrainian National Council, known as the Rada, a coalition dominated by liberals and moderate socialists: 'Long live autonomous Ukraine in a federated Russia.' Only in Poland and Finland did movements emerge that demanded complete separation from the empire. Both the liberal politicians of the Provisional

Government and the Soviet Executive Committee fatally underestimated the revolutionary potential of nationalism, content to assume that the abrogation of all discriminatory laws would be enough to assuage nationalist opinion.

With approximately 22 per cent of the empire's population, Ukraine was by far the largest minority area and its resources of grain, coal, and iron, as well as its strategic position, made it of paramount importance to the government in Petrograd.[64] Initially, the Provisional Government resisted the Rada's demands for a degree of administrative devolution and for Ukrainian military units, fearing that Ukrainian nationalism was being exploited by Germany. The consequence was that the Rada, in a bid to stay in touch with the escalating radicalism of soldiers and peasants, stepped up its demands for autonomy, so that by July it had pronounced itself to be the 'sole supreme organ of revolutionary democracy in Ukraine'. The effectiveness of the Rada was, however, limited by the fact that most Ukrainian speakers were peasants, while nearly a quarter of the population were Russian speakers, Jews, or Poles, and concentrated in the cities. The landowning class mainly comprised Russians and Poles, the latter in the provinces west of the Dnieper, and the administration was dominated by Russians. So the socio-economic grievances of the Ukrainian peasantry acquired an ethnic coloration. In addition, in right-bank Ukraine Jews controlled much petty trade and small industry and were the peasantry's main creditors. This situation compelled the middle-class socialists and liberals who dominated the Rada to take a radical stance on the land question, promising the peasants that the rich black earth of the region belonged to them alone. However, in eastern Ukraine, in Kharkiv and other cities, and in the Donbass, there was a militant working class comprised of Russian and Russianized Ukrainians who supported soviet power on a pan-Russian scale.

In neighbouring Belorussia, by contrast, with a population of only 4.5 million, nationalism was weakly developed. The Belorussian Socialist Hramada, formed in 1903, was based on the small intelligentsia and after February it was outflanked by the Jewish parties and by the all-Russian parties, notably the Bolsheviks, whose support was based on the garrisons stationed in this critical zone of military operations. Political developments were determined largely by the shifting battle front that ran through the region, and war-weary Russian soldiers took the lead in forming soviets. Peasants made up a majority of the population, and as in Ukraine, the towns were populated by Jews, Russians, and Poles.[65] Nearly three-quarters of the rural population were illiterate, and spoke up to twenty different dialects. Indeed into the twentieth century the Belorussian language lacked a standardized grammar. As in Ukraine the peasantry was primarily concerned to see a division of the large estates that existed in the region.

Finland had enjoyed unprecedented autonomy after its annexation in 1809, and following the February Revolution, all political parties campaigned for complete independence.[66] The Provisional Government did its best to shelve the question, but there was little doubt that Finland was destined to secede in the same way as Poland had effectively done. In the event Finland would descend into a civil war of notable savagery, especially considering that its territory had been largely spared the ravages of the First World War. At its root was a severe economic crisis: Finland's agriculture, paper and pulp, and metalworking industries had benefited from the war, but Russia's withdrawal from the conflict caused major economic problems. Serious shortages emerged and the Finnish mark fell in real terms to 22 per cent of its 1913 value. As in Russia, the workers' movement reacted fiercely to the supply situation and to escalating unemployment. By autumn, street fighting had broken out between armed detachments of workers, known as Red Guards, and civil militias, loosely backed by Germany, known as White Guards. On 13 November a general strike was declared after conservatives blocked key political reforms, but the Social Democrats, having pushed through the reforms, baulked at actually taking power. Talks with the Social Democrats having come to naught, a bourgeois government took office on 4 December, to the fury of Red Guards.

In the Baltic region the landowning class was largely German and periodic campaigns of Russification in the late nineteenth century had fostered a vigorous nationalist movement. Here, too, ethnicity tended to reinforce class sentiment. In the provinces that would become Latvia and Estonia,

German landowners faced indigenous peasantries, but these were divided between a stratum of prosperous farmers and a landless proletariat. In Latvia, especially, the latter was large and hated the 'grey barons', that is, wealthy Latvian farmers, almost as much as they did the German nobility. Both Latvia and Estonia had substantial urban middle classes and important centres of industry, especially Latvia, where a largely Latvian working class and urban lower middle class faced a commercial and industrial bourgeoisie that was Jewish, Russian, or Polish. The Social Democrats had long been a powerful political force in Latvia, having a base among workers and among landless peasants. Here liberals and moderate socialists, who initially dominated the nationalist movement, lost ground rapidly to the Bolsheviks who enjoyed exceptionally strong support in the working class. The famous Latvian riflemen, a militia formed in 1915 to resist German invasion, would go on to play a distinguished role in the Red Army. Estonia, by contrast, was much less industrialized, and the Social Democrats were correspondingly weaker. During 1917 the elected assembly, known as the Maapäev, clashed with the Provisional Government over the extent of the autonomy it should enjoy. Estonian Social Democrats backed demands for self-determination, but the Maapäev soon found itself outflanked from the left by soviets in Revel', Narva, and Dorpat, where mainly Russian workers and soldiers put their weight behind the Bolsheviks and Left SRs.

Nationalism among the Muslim peoples had made some strides since 1905 but it remained weak in 1917. The February Revolution raised the issue of whether religion or ethnicity should be the basis of political organization, pitting the proponents of pan-Islamism—who advocated extra-territorial, cultural autonomy for all Muslims within a unitary Russian state—against those who wished to see different ethnic groups exercise political autonomy over a clearly defined territory. Overlapping this division was one between the reformist jadids, who advocated the modernization of Islam, especially in education, language, and social reform, and the more conservative mullahs and notables who cleaved to the idea of an unchanging Islamic tradition, and opposed, for example, the resolution in favour of women's equality that was passed by the first All-Russian Muslim Congress in May. After February,

Muslims were primarily concerned about promoting their religious and cultural identity, establishing control over education, and the right to form Muslim military units. Only gradually did demands for political autonomy surface. In the Kazakh steppes, where Islamic scholars (*ulama*) were weaker than in Turkestan proper, a significant nationalist party, the Alash Orda (*Alaş Orda*), did emerge. A moderate semi-socialist party, it was based on the Russian-educated sons of the Kazakh aristocracy. Initially, it confined its demands to limited autonomy and use of the Kazakh language, but by December had moved towards claiming full-scale autonomy. In the course of 1917, the proponents of ethnic nationalism began to gain the upper hand over the advocates—mainly Tatar—of pan-Islamic or pan-Turkic projects. Even so, the radicalization of nationalist movements among Muslim peoples was slow compared with other regions. Russian settlers, whose actions were at the root of the rebellion of 1916, dominated the Tashkent Soviet, the most powerful political body in Central Asia. Controlled by Bolsheviks and SRs, it attempted unsuccessfully to seize power as early as September. It would act both as the principal bearer of soviet power in Central Asia and as the instrument through which Russian settlers sought to keep the native population in subjection.

In the Caucasus nationalism was well developed among the Georgians and Armenians, who had long histories as political entities and possessed their own Christian Churches.[67] However, whereas Georgians (and Azeris) lived on compact territory, the Armenians were dispersed between Russia, Turkey, and Persia. After February, traumatized by the genocide, the moderate socialist Dashnak party gave its backing to the Provisional Government. In Georgia the salient social conflicts were between Georgians and tsarist officials and between Georgian workers and peasants and the Armenian middle class. The nationalist intelligentsia used Marxism to forge a national movement based on the working class and—somewhat unusually—also on the peasantry. After February, Mensheviks dominated political life, seizing control of the duma in Tbilisi from the Armenian middle classes and dominating the soviet. The main challenge they faced was from the Russian-dominated garrison. In Azerbaijan to the east the largely Azeri peasantry were Shi'ite Muslims who lacked a national identity.[68] Educated Azeris were variously drawn to pan-Turkism, pan-Islamism, socialism, and liberalism. The towns were stratified, with Muslim workers at the bottom, Armenian and Russian workers in more skilled positions, and Christian and European capitalists in control of the oil industry. Baku, long a centre of militant socialism and a cosmopolitan city where Social Democrats and Dashnaks dominated revolutionary politics, became the bastion of soviet power in the region.

The reluctance of the Provisional Government to concede meaningful autonomy was partly motivated by fear that nationalist movements were a Trojan horse insinuated by Germany, a not unreasonable supposition if one looks at the record of the latter in the Baltic and Ukraine. At a deeper level such reluctance stemmed from the emotional commitment to a unified Russian state, which was especially strong among the Kadets. When, in September, Kerensky finally endorsed the principle of self-determination 'but only on such principles as the Constituent Assembly shall determine', it was too little and too late. If nationalism grew in importance in 1917, the greater salience of class identity at this time was never in doubt. Nationalist politicians were forced to take up the concerns of the masses, notably the land question and the eight-hour day. In general, however, workers were more responsive to class than to nationalist issues, whereas peasants, though concerned above all with the land and an end to the war, preferred parties that spoke to them in their own language and that defended local interests.

Class, Nation, and Gender

A discourse of citizenship was put into circulation by the February Revolution, but it quickly ceded to a discourse of class, in some places as early as the April crisis. The pamphlets and newspapers of the socialist parties addressed ordinary people in the language of class, and strikes and demonstrations, red flags, banners and images, the singing of revolutionary songs, the election of representatives, meetings in the workplace and on street corners, the passing of a resolution, the raising of funds for a political cause, all served to entrench this discourse, so that ordinary folk began to see themselves and the world around them in class terms. The appeal of class politics cannot be seen simply as a reflection of socio-economic realities, since Russia was not yet a fully developed class society. Certain social estates such as those of the townspeople, craftsmen, and merchants, had been in decline since the late nineteenth century, yet estates were still, arguably, more important in structuring social relations than the classes brought into being by industrial capitalism, if only because the vast majority of the population belonged to the peasant estate and because the nobility maintained its privileged status up to 1917. Moreover, groups of critical importance to mass mobilization in 1917, such as soldiers and the non-Russian nationalities, did not fit easily into a class-based schema. The success of the discourse of class derived less from its accuracy in describing social relations than from the fact that it played upon a deep-seated division in Russian political culture between 'them' and 'us', upon a profound sense of the economic and cultural gulf between the *nizy*, that is, those at the bottom, and the *verkhi*, those at the top. The socialist parties articulated this deep social division in somewhat different class language: the Mensheviks talked in terms of 'revolutionary democracy', that is, a broad bloc of popular forces that stretched to include the intelligentsia; the SRs talked in terms of the 'toiling people'; the Bolsheviks talked mainly in terms of the 'proletariat and poor peasantry', although they too drew easily on ideas of the 'toiling people'.

One index of the pervasiveness of the discourse of class was the huge popularity of socialism. All kinds of groups pinned their colours to the socialist mast. The Orthodox Church Council, which finally convened in 1917, set up a special commission to root out 'Bolshevism in the Church'. Deaf people formed a Socialist Union of the Deaf. The journal of the Inter-district group expressed indignation at the fact that even the 'yellow boulevard press' now called itself 'non-party socialist'.[69] In the duma elections in Saratov in July 82 per cent of votes were cast for socialist parties of different kinds and in the Constituent Assembly elections 85 per cent of the national vote went to socialist parties, including their nationalist variants.[70] Millions still had only the vaguest idea about the ideological differences between the socialist parties but were captivated by an idealized vision of socialist society. A typical pamphlet, entitled *What is Socialism?*, published in Minusinsk in eastern Siberia, explained: 'Need and hunger will disappear and pleasures will be available to all equally. Thefts and robberies will cease. Instead of coercion and violence, the kingdom of freedom and brotherhood will commence.'[71] This idea of socialism as the dawn of universal happiness resonated with the apocalyptic strain in Russian culture.

The historian Mark Steinberg has called the language of class a 'flexible designation of otherness', a way of condemning the rich and powerful, or anyone else perceived to be acting against the interests of the common people.[72] Class enemies were landowners, employers, officers, government officials, the police, and sometimes even priests, village elders, or foremen. It could be used against those who were believed to have profited from the war, for example, but also against those believed to have undermined the war effort. In Smolensk, where the Bolsheviks had only 80 out of 220 places in the soviet by October, moderate socialists explained the collapse of the local economy as being due to bourgeois greed and incompetence.[73] The discourse of class could thus pick up and transmute the most diverse grievances, hopes, fears, and ideals of those Dostoevsky had called the 'injured and insulted'. But it was, above all, the term *burzhui*, a corrupted form of the foreign-sounding word 'bourgeois', that was most readily used by the less politically conscious to blacken those of whom they disapproved. As one pamphleteer observed: 'Soon it will be dangerous to put on a collar, tie, hat or decent suit without being called "bourgeois".' *Burzhui* was as much a moral as a sociological designation of otherness. According to another pamphlet, a '*burzhui* is a person who leads an egotistical, meaningless and aimless life, unilluminated by the vivid and wonderful goals of any valuable or spiritual labour'.[74]

As this suggests, if the discourse of class could be suffused with idealism, it could also communicate hatred and threaten retribution. As a leaflet put out in June by the Free Association of Anarchists and Communists in Kyiv roared: 'Down with the Provisional Government! Smash the Bourgeoisie and the Jews!'[75] The portrayal of enemies as 'vampires' or 'vermin' helped to legitimize the use of violence and terror.[76] Many ordinary people called on the new Bolshevik government to show no mercy towards the old ruling classes. 'There must be freedom only for the oppressed. For the exploiters there can be only the stick. Only with the stick can we introduce justice in our land.' Another correspondent proposed that the 'highest nobility', the 'landowners who own 100 *desiatina* (146 hectares) of land', and the 'officials who served in the Okhrana' be sent to Solovki monastery 'once the monks have been removed'. 'This filth should have been put in a safe place a long time ago so that they can no longer poison worker-peasant Russia with their cursed breath. Thanks to the crowned blockheads and their retinue, they drank a lot of workers' blood... Be firm with these creatures, show them no mercy.'[77]

The political orientation of the urban middle strata in 1917 is particularly interesting since they did not fit easily into the 'them' and 'us' framework.[78] In 1913 it is reckoned that the urban middle strata numbered about 12 million—37 per cent of the urban population and 8 per cent of the general population—but they were highly differentiated in terms of employment, ownership of property, level of education, and in relation to the state.[79] They included what might be called the old petty-bourgeoisie, such as artisans and petty traders, and new strata such as white-collar employees in public institutions, banks, industrial enterprises, and transportation. These new strata, known as *sluzhashchie*, or service personnel, were loosely defined by the fact that they were employees whose work was not physical in character. Their upper layers overlapped with professional groups such as teachers (195,000 in 1916), students in higher education (127,000), and doctors (33,000).[80] After February 1917 the *sluzhashchie* tended to side with the labour movement, as they had done in 1905–7. They formed their own unions—sometimes in the face of hostility from blue-collar workers—as well as forming a few mixed unions with manual workers. In Siberia out of 416 trade unions in July, 156 comprised white-collar employees and 40 comprised blue- and white-collar workers.[81] In general the degree of unionization among white-collar employees was high but in politics they mainly oriented towards the moderate socialists. Nevertheless their identities were increasingly articulated in terms of the discourse of class. The Petrograd union of foremen and technicians declared, 'we have always regarded ourselves as an integral part of the proletariat' (a view that would have been contested by the latter). Similarly, the Petrograd Council of Elders of Industrial Employees passed a resolution in August: 'Comrades, at this dread hour of political shifts and state financial crisis, we must rally around freedom's red flag and stand up for the toilers' freedom and rights.'[82] Door-keepers and yard-sweepers refused any longer to be called 'servants', insisting they were part of the working people. Many of the intelligentsia also sought to align themselves with the working people, albeit more reservedly. There were fifty organizations affiliated to the Moscow Soviet of Toiling Intelligentsia but despite their name, they pledged to 'serve democracy and the public interest' rather than the proletariat. The more traditional sections of the petty bourgeoisie, while responding positively to the Revolution, tended to keep their distance from socialism and class politics. The local associations of townspeople, for example, held an All-Russian Congress of Representatives in June and later demanded representation at the Democratic Conference, but their political orientation was either to right-wing socialist groups or to the Kadets. They valued social stability, political compromise, law and order, and longed for a reformist solution to the crisis facing the country. They were for a Constituent Assembly and sometimes for a homogeneous socialist government but after October they soon became disillusioned with party strife.[83]

The salience of the discourse of class was in part linked to the absence of a nationalist politics that could be used by ordinary people. It was of this that the veteran liberal P. V. Struve was thinking when he stated in 1918 that the Russian Revolution 'was the first case in world history of the triumph of internationalism and the class idea over nationalism and the national idea'. Yet what was striking in 1917 was the failure of the radical right to mobilize a popular constituency on the scale it had in 1905–7. It fell to the Kadets to act as the principal exponents of nationalism, outlining a vision of the nation under siege. At the Conference of Public Figures—from which the public was excluded—Miliukov announced on 8 August that 'in the name of Russia's salvation and the rebirth of freedom, the government must immediately and decisively break with all servants of utopia'.[84] Yet it is facile to counterpose nation and class in a starkly antithetical fashion. For even the most enthusiastic exponents of the discourse of class did not entirely abjure the idea of the Russian nation, insofar as SR and Bolshevik propaganda often played on the double sense of the word *narod* in Russian, which means both 'nation' and 'common people'. These class-inflected conceptions construed the nation as one rooted in the toiling people. So even when the language used by ordinary people seemed to be at its most extravagantly divisive, one can often discern a sense of 'us', the true nation, the nation of the toiling people, versus 'them', the exploiting classes, the betrayers of the nation. The Military Horseshoe Works condemned the State Conference on 13 August in the following terms:

> We consider that horse-trading with the bourgeoisie, which is bogged down in its narrow class interests, will not lead the country out of the cul-de-sac into which it has been driven by war and imperialism. Only the poorest classes of the population, led by the proletariat, can decisively suppress the greedy appetites of the plunderers of world capitalism, and lead this worn-out country back on to a broad path, to give peace, bread, freedom and to liberate mankind from the bonds of capitalist slavery.[85]

Here, beneath the shrill language of class there is a subliminal identification with their 'worn-out country'.

Though the Bolsheviks resisted all concessions to patriotism, they were not able to ignore its force. Upon his return to Russia Lenin had lauded fraternization between Russian and German soldiers (which had actually gone on from the winter of 1914 without the initiative of socialist parties). Yet faced by the charge that they were allowing the enemy to take over Russian land, the party quietly dropped this idea. When it looked as though Riga would fall to the Germans in August, the Bolsheviks hotly disclaimed the charge that they had allowed this to happen by demoralizing the army, claiming implausibly that it was a deliberate act by the generals 'who intend to betray the revolutionary Baltic fleet, the pride and glory of the Russian

Revolution, and are preparing to surrender the vanguard of the revolution, Red Petrograd'.[86] Through 1917 they strenuously denied that they would conclude what a group of 'sick and injured Russian warriors' described as a 'shameful and dishonourable' peace with Germany, although they had little choice but to do so after October.[87]

The identity of 'youth' acquired considerable political purchase following the February Revolution, but it, too, was articulated through the discourse of class. As urbanization and education expanded, the period of adolescence had extended, and a distinctive youth subculture had begun to emerge in the cities. During the war the numbers of young workers in the workforce rose, even as their working conditions deteriorated. After February, young workers, mainly male, hastened to join trade unions and political parties. In Petrograd they pressed for an improvement in wages, a six-hour working day, representation in the factory committees, and the right to an education out of working hours. They also campaigned to have the right to vote (which was restricted to those over the age of 21). Out of these initiatives a militant youth organization known as Labour and Light emerged, which had 50,000 members by summer. Its charter of 12 July 1917 promised 'to develop the feeling of personal dignity and class consciousness that are precious to the working class, as youth creates its social organization and becomes enlightened and educated at the technical and professional level'. It was a non-party body committed to the acquisition of culture and education by working-class youth. Krupskaia, who made contact with it, contrasted it to the 'senior pupils of high schools (who) often came in a crowd to the Kshesinskaia mansion and shouted abuse at the Bolsheviks'. She noted the remarkable fact that the organization required its members to learn to sew. 'One lad—a Bolshevik—remarked: "Why should we all learn to sew? I can understand if it's a girl having to learn it, because otherwise she won't be able to sew a button on her husband's trousers when the time comes, but why should we all learn!" This remark raised a storm of indignation.'[88] As politics became more stridently partisan, a Socialist Union of Working Youth was formed in Petrograd which soon stole a march upon Labour and Light. It defined its aim as the 'preparation of developed, educated fighters for socialism'. At the Sixth Congress of the Bolshevik party in August 1917 one-fifth of the delegates were under 21 and the median age was 29. This adoption of a militant class identity by working-class youth was often accompanied by a repudiation of the recreational side of youth culture. In Moscow some members of the Third Youth International condemned those 'harmful elements' in their midst who were organizing evenings of entertainment and dancing.

Women's involvement in revolutionary politics was also configured through the lens of class. It was the demonstrations on International Women's Day by women workers and housewives, demanding bread and an end to the war, that sparked the events that led to the fall of the dynasty. On 19 March 1917 feminists organized a big demonstration to demand the vote which, to judge from photographs, was supported by lower-class women who wore kerchiefs whereas middle-class women wore hats.[89] This, however, was a rare moment in 1917 when gender rather than class was the axis of organization. After a few weeks dithering, the Provisional Government passed a law granting women the right to vote. It also enacted legislation that allowed female lawyers to represent clients in court, women civil servants equal rights with men, and, following the introduction of coeducation in high schools, women teachers equal rights with their male colleagues. In addition, the government introduced restrictions on night work for women and children.[90] These were significant achievements, the result of decades of campaigning by women's organizations. Yet for all their achievement, the feminist movement, firmly labelled 'bourgeois' in class discourse, went into decline. Indeed some feminists signed up fully to the nationalist agenda of the liberals and right-wing socialists. Mariia Pokrovskaia, founder of the Women's Progressive Party in 1905 and a doctor who worked with the poor, called on women to be 'guided by ideals and aspirations, not by coarse material incentives'. And from this perspective, which played on the deep association in Russian culture of women with higher spiritual things, the woman soldier Mariia Bochkarëva formed the Women's Death Battalion in the summer of 1917 in a rearguard effort to reverse the disintegration of the army. 'Our Mother (Russia) is perishing . . . I want women whose tears are pure crystal, whose souls are pure, whose impulses are lofty. With such women setting an example of self-sacrifice, your men will realise their duty at this grave hour.'[91] Bochkarëva carefully selected 300 women out of a couple of thousand volunteers but the only combat they saw was in defending the Winter Palace against unruly Bolshevik soldiers and Red Guards. Incidentally, the pattern of relatively high female participation in military action would continue in the Red Army, where some 50,000 to 70,000 women enlisted by 1920. Some served as riflewomen, as commanders of armoured trains, and even as machine gunners, although most served in medical units or did clerical work. The challenge to patriarchal gender roles was thus by no means insignificant.[92]

Lower-class women tended to act first as members of the subordinate classes and second as women. The most notable example of women acting as wives and mothers as well as workers came from the *soldatki*, or soldiers' wives. By 1917 there were around 14 million *soldatki* and they had been involved in food riots (called, somewhat confusingly, 'pogroms' in Russian) and demands for increases in family allowances during the war.[93] Not surprisingly, they took a very different attitude to the war from that of the aforementioned feminists. 'Enough of this horrible bloodshed, which is utterly pointless for working people', women in Smolensk declared in May.[94] Despite relatively low levels of formal organization—the Petrograd Soviet did organize a national union of *soldatki* in June—*soldatki* made quite an impact on local politics, demanding that city treasuries raise allowances to compensate for soaring prices. Given the rather vocal and aggressive character of their protests, they tended to be portrayed in the press as a 'dark', unwomanly force motivated by greed rather than by quintessential female qualities.

Female workers, including those in domestic service and in such service sectors as restaurants and laundries, threw themselves into the strike movement in 1917.[95] When the director of the Vyborg spinning mill in Petrograd explained that he was unable to afford a wage increase, women shoved him in a wheelbarrow and carted him to the canal bank where, poised perilously on the edge, he shakily signed a piece of paper agreeing to a rise.[96] This, however, was not militancy that translated into formal, durable organization.

Thanks to a small number of socialist women, mainly Bolsheviks, who worked around the newspaper *Woman Worker*, female factory workers, domestic servants, shop assistants, and waitresses were persuaded to join trade unions. These Bolshevik women opposed separate organization of women workers, warning that this would bring division into the ranks of the proletariat. The textile workers' union successfully recruited substantial numbers of female workers, but women proved reluctant to take up positions of leadership. This was partly a matter of time and domestic priorities, for they had a dual burden as wives and mothers as well as workers; partly a matter of lack of confidence; and partly a disposition to defer to men in the public sphere (women workers' levels of literacy were lower than those of men). Also to blame were the leaders of labour and socialist organizations who were ever ready to criticize 'the backwardness, downtrodden position and darkness of many of our sisters', but loath to do much about it.[97] In fact the evidence suggests that when they felt their interests were at stake, women did show interest in politics. During the elections to the Constituent Assembly, 77 per cent of women in the countryside participated in elections compared with 70 per cent of men, believing that this would secure their title to the land.[98]

So far as leadership of the socialist parties was concerned, the position of women may actually have deteriorated following the February Revolution. Under tsarism women in the RSDLP were almost as likely as men to hold office in city-level organizations, though the same was not true of the SRs. This changed as men rushed to join the socialist parties in spring 1917 and as old leaders returned from exile.[99] The culture of the socialist left was male dominated, despite the extraordinary aura that attached to certain revolutionary women, notably female terrorists in the Populist and SR tradition, such as Vera Figner, Ekaterina Breshko-Breshkovskaia, and Maria Spiridonova. Spiridonova, in particular, commanded enormous admiration for the dignified way in which she had endured brutal treatment during the eleven years she was imprisoned for shooting a police official in 1906. In 1917 the central leaderships of all the socialist parties were overwhelmingly male. Among the members of the Council of People's Commissars, the government established by the Bolsheviks after the October seizure of power, only one woman, Alexandra Kollontai, was given a ministerial position (as Commissar of Welfare).

Political Polarization

By summer the economy was falling apart at the seams. Russia was saddled with a gigantic debt to the Allies that had been incurred to buy war matériel that had not always arrived when it was needed. The Provisional Government continued the policy of paying for the war by printing money to meet its obligations. From March to June, currency emissions amounted to 3 billion rubles; in July and August to 2.3 billion.[100] New currency notes, known as *kerenki*, after the Prime Minister, were so worthless that people began to hoard the hugely devalued tsarist currency. The result was an astronomical rise in inflation. Between July and October prices rose fourfold, so that the ruble possessed about 6 per cent of its real pre-war value. Production of most fuel and raw materials had fallen by at least a third by summer and, faced with shortages, many plants closed temporarily. By October nearly half a million workers had been laid off. The economic crisis was aggravated by mounting chaos in the transport system, which meant that grain and industrial supplies could not get through to the cities. Bread was in particularly short supply.

The value of real wages fell by 50 per cent in the two capitals in the second half of 1917. Workers began to strike on a monumental scale. In the eight months between February and October 2.5 million workers downed tools and the average strike increased in size as the year wore on.[101] Yet strikes also became harder to win, especially on wage issues. As they became less effective, the trade unions made efforts to negotiate collective wage agreements for entire industries. But negotiations proved intractable and no sooner had new contracts been ratified than they were nullified by inflation. The other response to the economic crisis, pursued by the factory committees, was to implement workers' control of production to prevent what workers believed was widespread 'sabotage' being practised by employers. Workers' control of production had ideological origins in the idea of worker autonomy that had arisen in 1905, but it was essentially a practical response to economic crisis, a means of *monitoring* the activities of the employers, with a view to preserving jobs. However, as supplies of fuel and raw materials dried up and as orders declined, factory committees encroached ever more radically on employers' 'right to manage' in order to ensure that workers were not laid off simply so that companies could maintain their profits. In areas such as the Donbass and the Urals, mining and metallurgical companies abandoned unprofitable companies and the mine and factory committees struggled to keep them going. By October there were no fewer than ninety-four unified centres of factory committees (in towns, provinces, or branches of industry), together with an All-Russian Central Council of Factory Committees, committed to establishing workers' control of production across the entire economy. Apart from anarchists and SR Maximalists—whose numbers were few—only the Bolshevik party officially supported the slogan of workers' control, although even they were happier with the idea of state control of the economy (something all the socialist parties could sign up to). The moderate socialists argued that since the writ of a factory committee could only run in one enterprise, workers' control could only aggravate the economic chaos by fragmenting efforts at state regulation of the economy.

One of the symptoms of social disintegration that now became visible, one that would get steadily worse during the civil war, was an upsurge in crime, especially violent crime. Prior to the February Revolution the level of violent crime In Petrograd had been exceptionally low. In 1914 there were fourteen murders, whereas the press reported ninety between March and October 1917. As regards property-related crime, the victims, at least in Petrograd, tended to be either the well-to-do or the poorest sections of the population. The breakdown in law and order had several causes. Some 7,652 prisoners were freed from the city's jails during the February Revolution and by July there were some 50,000 deserters in the capital, all with firearms. The problem of combating crime was hampered by the fact that the civil militias established to replace the tsarist police were underfunded and poorly organized and quickly found themselves in competition with workers' militias and, somewhat later, with Red Guards, both strongly class defined organizations that were elected directly from the factories.[102] A similar pattern was replicated in provincial cities. In Nizhnii Novgorod the provincial soviet made a rather forlorn request to the military commissar to disarm the 25,000 workforce at the Sormovo locomotive plant and ensure that firearms were only held by permit.[103] In Smolensk the number of reported cases of violent crime was lower than in the capital, but the instance of thefts, burglaries, drunkenness, and sales of spirits was significantly higher than in 1916 . Here the numbers jailed or registered as criminals also increased, which suggests that the civil militia was not completely ineffective.[104]

It was against this background of economic and social disintegration, and in the wake of the apparent triumph of the Provisional Government during the July Days, that Kerensky became Prime Minister. He ruled very much in a personalistic fashion, cultivating an ascetic image as a 'man of destiny' summoned to 'save Russia'. He was still popular but his hubris masked increasing political impotence. On 19 July, in a bid to halt the disintegration of the army, Kerensky appointed General Kornilov Supreme Commander-in-Chief of the armed forces. All who knew Kornilov were aware that he was a man profoundly out of sympathy with the Revolution, and he agreed to take up the post only on condition that there be no interference by soldiers' committees in operational orders or in the appointment of officers and that the death penalty for insubordination be extended from soldiers at the front to those in the rear (something Kerensky had already agreed to on 12 July). Kerensky hoped to use the reactionary general to bolster his own position, by strengthening the military force at his disposal and by restoring the frayed political tie with the Kadets. By summer 1917 the Kadets had at least 70,000 members, organized into more than 300 organizations, but now a majority within the party believed that only military dictatorship could save Russia from anarchy.[105] By mid-1917, moreover, at least twenty different organizations had formed that were committed to overthrowing the Provisional Government and establishing some form of dictatorship. They included the Society for the Economic Recovery of Russia, formed by bankers and industrialists in May, the Republican Centre, and the Officers' Union, based at general army headquarters in Mogilëv in Belorussia.

Only with the State Conference, which opened in Moscow on 12 August to rally support for the coalition government, did these groups put their weight behind Kornilov as saviour of the Russian nation.[106] How far Kornilov was bent on the overthrow of the Provisional Government is disputed by historians. He and Kerensky undoubtedly shared a common objective of destroying the Bolsheviks and bringing the Petrograd Soviet to heel, but Kerensky baulked at Kornilov's demands that the railways and defence factories be placed under military discipline—replete with the death penalty. Each man appears to have hoped to use the other to strengthen his personal position, but when on 26 August Kerensky received what appeared to be an ultimatum from Kornilov, demanding that all military and civil authority be placed in the hands of a supreme commander, he turned on him, accusing him of conspiring to overthrow the government. On 27 August Kornilov ignored a telegram relieving him of his duties and ordered troops to move towards Petrograd. If this was a coup, it was a poorly planned one, and the Republican Centre, an underground organization in Petrograd, failed to rise up as planned. In a humiliating bid to save his feeble government, Kerensky was forced to turn to the soviets to stop troops reaching the capital. Railway workers scuppered Kornilov's advance by diverting his troops along the wrong railway line. Kornilov's action can be seen as marking the emergence of the White cause, a military and political movement bent on restoring order by establishing a 'strong power'. By dramatizing the threat of counter-revolution and by revealing the impotence of the government, Kornilov's rebellion seemed to confirm that the stark choice facing Russia was between soviet power and military dictatorship.

The second coalition collapsed and Kerensky formed a five-man 'directory', a personal dictatorship in all but name, in which he had virtually total responsibility for military as well as civil affairs. Notwithstanding efforts to create a new coalition government, many Mensheviks by now would no longer countenance a government that included the Kadets, since they were blatantly implicated in the Kornilov rebellion. The depth of the crisis among the moderate socialists was revealed at the Democratic Conference, called on 14–22 September to rally 'democratic' organizations behind the government. This proved quite unable to resolve the question of whether the government should continue to involve 'bourgeois' forces. On 25 September Kerensky went ahead and formed a third coalition, but this failed to win ratification from the Petrograd Soviet, under Bolshevik control since early that month. This deprived the government of any chance of success, yet the divisions within the 'Preparliament', a council set up to advise the government on 7 October, highlighted the fact that even without the Soviet, its chances of success were close to zero. A majority in the Preparliament could not accept that the army was no longer a fighting force and rejected a proposal to declare a truce, agreeing only to ask the Allies to clarify their war aims. Politics had become a theatre of shadows in which the real battles for power were going on in society.

The paradoxical outcome of Kornilov's attack on the Provisional Government was to strengthen massively the forces of those who attacked it from the left. In most localities the moderate socialists retained their hegemony until the rebellion, but thereafter their collapse was swift. In autumn 1917 there was a break in the public mood—the euphoria of the spring had given way to anxiety, to a sense of impending catastrophe—and the Bolsheviks ably capitalized on this to suggest that they alone could avert it. As living standards plummeted and the threat of mass unemployment mounted, the slogans of 'Bread, peace and land', 'Down with the imperialist war', and 'Workers' control of production' grew in popularity. Many now believed that Kerensky, previously the embodiment of the hopes of 'democracy', had proved himself a traitor to the Revolution. On 31 August the Petrograd Soviet and on 5 September a unified plenum of the workers' and soldiers' soviets in Moscow passed a Bolshevik resolution 'On Power'. And in the first half of September eighty soviets in large and medium towns backed the call for a soviet government. In towns such as Tsaritsyn, Narva, Krasnoiarsk, and Kostroma soviet power was already a reality. The Menshevik Sukhanov, describing the dogged efforts of the Bolsheviks to popularize the idea of soviet power, wrote:

> The Bolsheviks were working stubbornly and without let-up. They were among the masses, at the factory-benches, every day without a pause. Tens of speakers, big and little, were speaking in Petersburg, at the factories and in the barracks, every blessed day. For the masses they had become their own people, because they were always there, taking the lead in details as well as in the most important affairs of the factory or barracks. They had become the sole hope.[107]

Yet if the slogan 'All power to the soviets' gained huge popularity, its meaning was ill defined. The slogan belonged not only to the Bolsheviks, but also to Left SRs, anarchists, and a few Menshevik Internationalists. Generally, it was not understood to mean a demand for the type of state that Lenin advocated in *State and Revolution* but rather a demand that the Provisional Government sever its coalition with the 'bourgeoisie' and form a government of all parties represented in the soviets, pending the convocation of the Constituent Assembly.[108] And even for most Bolsheviks, support for the slogan did not entail an armed seizure of power.

The October Seizure of Power

In the context of growing support for the Bolsheviks, Lenin concluded that internationally as well as nationally the time was ripe for them to seize power.[109] From his hiding place in Finland, where he had gone after Kerensky ordered the arrest of key Bolshevik leaders, he blitzed the Central Committee with demands that it prepare an insurrection, even threatening to resign on 29 September when his demands were ignored: 'History will not forgive us if this opportunity to take action is missed.' The majority of the leadership was unenthusiastic, believing that it would be better to allow power to pass democratically to the soviets by waiting for the Second Congress of Soviets, which was scheduled to open on 20 October. Returning in secret to Petrograd, and still a wanted man, Lenin on 10 October succeeded in persuading the Central Committee to commit itself to the overthrow of the Provisional Government. However, no timetable was set. Zinoviev and Kamenev, two of Lenin's most trusted lieutenants, were bitterly opposed to the decision, believing that the conditions for socialist revolution did not yet exist and that a foolhardy bid for power would see the party crushed. As late as 16 October, the mood in the party was against an insurrection in the immediate future, and in an effort to delay plans for a seizure of power Kamenev published a letter in Maxim Gor'kii's newspaper on 18 October announcing to the world that he and Zinoviev considered it 'inadmissible to launch an armed uprising in the present circumstances'. Lenin was driven to a paroxysm of fury and demanded their expulsion from the Central Committee.

The die had been cast and the issue was now about how a seizure of power should be carried out. On 6 October the sweeping advance of Germany towards Petrograd had led the Kerensky government to announce that about half the garrison would be moved out of the capital to defend the approaches to the city. The Petrograd Soviet, under the chairmanship of Trotsky, interpreted this as a sign that Kerensky wished to relieve the capital of its revolutionary garrison. On 9 October the Soviet formed a Military-Revolutionary Committee to prevent any such move. This was the organization that Trotsky would use to unseat the Provisional Government. Trotsky favoured waiting for the Second Congress of Soviets to convene in order to gain its mandate to unseat the government, whereas Lenin reckoned that the different parties in the soviet were unlikely to support decisive action and argued that it was vital that the party seize power before the Congress convened so that it could be presented with a fait accompli in the form of a soviet government. As late as 16 October the Bolshevik Military Organization, its fingers burned by the experience of the July Days, expressed scepticism that the garrison could be relied upon to carry out such action, so Lenin toyed with the idea of bringing in sailors and soldiers from the northern front. In the event, the insurrection followed Trotsky's plan, becoming associated with defensive action by the Military-Revolutionary Committee to resist Kerensky's plans to move soldiers out of the capital.[110] Lenin's demand that the seizure of power take place before the Second Congress convened was only made realisable by the decision of the moderate socialist majority on the Central Executive Committee of the Soviets to postpone the opening of the Congress from 20 to 25 October. What is striking is just how late the plans for a seizure of power came together.

Fully informed that the Bolsheviks were laying plans to overturn his government, Kerensky took steps to strengthen his defences, moves that the Military-Revolutionary Committee interpreted as a sinister plot to hand over Petrograd to the Germans. It ordered garrison units not to move without its permission and on 23 October to only obey orders signed by the Committee. When on the night of 23–24 October the government shut down the Bolsheviks' printing press as a preliminary to moving against the Military-Revolutionary Committee, Trotsky declared that action was now imperative to prevent Kerensky crushing the Revolution. On 24 October reliable military units and Red Guards took control of bridges, railway stations, and other key points in Petrograd. Unable to muster a credible military force, Kerensky fled. Just after midnight Lenin emerged from hiding and went to the Bolshevik headquarters at the Smol'nyi Institute where he proceeded to enforce a more offensive tactic on the part of the insurgents. By the morning of 25 October all strategic points in the city were under their control and only the Winter Palace, headquarters of the Provisional Government, remained to be taken. That afternoon Lenin, appearing for the first time in public since July, told the Petrograd Soviet that the government had been overthrown and that 'in Russia we must now set about building a proletarian socialist state'. On the night of 25 October the Winter Palace was 'stormed' and the Provisional Government arrested. At 10.40 p.m., against the background thud of artillery bombardment of the Winter Palace, the Second Congress of Soviets finally opened. About 300 out of the 650 to 670 deputies were Bolsheviks, so ratification of the seizure of power had to rely on the support of the 80 to 85 Left SRs, who were active in the military-revolutionary committees that were everywhere being set up. For their part, the Mensheviks and SRs denounced the overthrow of the government as a declaration of civil war and demonstratively walked out. Trotsky bellowed after them: 'You are miserable bankrupts; your role is played out. Go where you ought to be: into the dustbin of history.' In Moscow, where the Bolsheviks had made no preparations for a seizure of power, neither setting up a military-revolutionary committee nor strengthening the factory-based Red Guard, the commander of the military district, a Right SR, put up spirited opposition when soviet power was declared on 25 October. The SRs were strong in the garrison and city duma, and it was only after a week of bitter fighting, with several hundred casualties, that Red Guards were able to proclaim soviet power on 2 November.

The seizure of power is often presented as a conspiratorial coup against a democratic government. It certainly had the elements of a coup, but it was a coup much advertised, and the government it overthrew had not been democratically elected. It is noteworthy how few military officers were willing to come to the aid of the government, since many despised Kerensky for what they saw as his betrayal of Kornilov. The coup would certainly not have taken place had it not been for Lenin; and thanks to the decision of the moderate socialists to postpone the Second Congress, his plan to present the latter with a fait accompli was achieved. But the execution of the insurrection was entirely Trotsky's work, cleverly disguised as a defensive operation to preserve the garrison and the Petrograd Soviet against the 'counter-revolutionary' design of the Provisional Government. In the last analysis, however, the Provisional Government had expired even before the Bolsheviks finished it off.

4

CIVIL WAR AND BOLSHEVIK POWER

It was a matter of utmost urgency for the Bolsheviks to show that they were going to take action on all the issues that had alienated workers, soldiers, and peasants from the Provisional Government. Decrees on the burning issues of peace and land were thus passed by the Second Congress on 26 October.[1] That evening, the Bolsheviks formed a government, the Council of People's Commissars (*Sovnarkom*), all of whose fifteen members were Bolsheviks. This was patently at odds with the idea of 'soviet power' that had been current up to this point, since those who had rallied to the slogan 'All power to the soviets' envisaged this to mean that the Central Executive Committee of the Soviets, known as VTsIK in its Russian acronym, would form a government of all the socialist parties in the soviets. It was in protest at the Bolsheviks forming a one-party government that on 29 October the anti-Bolshevik executive of the railway workers' union threatened to call a strike unless talks to form a pan-socialist government got under way. Leading Bolsheviks, led by Kamenev, insisted that the party negotiate in good faith, but Lenin threatened to 'go to the sailors' to scupper what he considered to be a bid on the part of right-wing socialists to play for time. Given that Right SRs in Petrograd and Moscow were fighting to overthrow the new regime, this was not an unreasonable consideration. Moreover, the Mensheviks and SRs, by refusing to countenance Lenin or Trotsky as members of a soviet coalition government, certainly overplayed their hand. Despite this, when negotiations broke down, five Bolsheviks resigned from the Council of People's Commissars, on the grounds, as moderate Bolshevik V. P. Nogin put it, that 'we consider a purely Bolshevik government has no choice but to maintain itself by political terror'. Hard-liners in all parties, however, bear a measure of responsibility for scuttling the effort to form a democratic socialist government, which might have stopped the drift to civil war.

In the end, the Bolsheviks did form a coalition government. On 17 November, seven Left SRs entered the Council of People's Commissars, despite their unhappiness that this body was not clearly accountable to the Soviet CEC and that the Bolsheviks had closed 'bourgeois' newspapers.[2] The entry of the Left SRs into government allowed the Bolsheviks to claim that theirs was an authentic soviet government, based on the two parties that represented, respectively, the proletariat and the toiling peasantry. The Left SRs would play a decisive role in helping to undermine the All-Russian Soviet of Peasant Deputies, whose Right SR-dominated executive had supported military resistance to the Bolsheviks. Over the next months the CEC and Council of People's Commissars issued a torrent of decrees and orders on matters as diverse as the eight-hour day, workers' control of production, the abolition of the death penalty at the front, the abolition of social estates and ranks, the rights of the non-Russian peoples, the nationalization of the banks, the election of army officers, civil marriage, reform of the alphabet, and the cancellation of foreign debts.[3] This served to buttress the image of the government as one that represented rule by the toiling people and that was committed to reorganize social life on the basis of equality and justice.

Hopes ran high that the Bolshevik seizure of power was but the prelude to worldwide revolution. These hopes were captured in a manifesto issued by the Moscow Military-Revolutionary Committee on 3 November 1917, after it crushed the SR resistance:

> Comrades and Citizens! The whole world is experiencing a colossal crisis. The war, caused by capital, led to a profound shock that shook the working masses in all countries. Everywhere the revolution of the proletariat is growing. And the great honour has fallen to the Russian working class to be the first to overthrow the rule of the bourgeoisie. For the first time in history the labouring classes have taken power into their hands, having won freedom by their blood. This is freedom that they will not let fall from their hands. The armed people is guarding the revolution.[4]

Interestingly, this manifesto made no mention of socialism—although that was not uncommon at the time—and it represented the new political order variously as one representing the 'people', 'the proletariat', 'workers, soldiers, and peasants', and the 'toiling classes'. This suggests that Left SR members of the Military-Revolutionary Committee may have had a hand in its composition.

Despite much enthusiasm for the new government, it was clear from the first that the Bolsheviks would have to fight to secure the new order. Scholars disagree as to when civil war began, but it seems sensible to see it building up gradually from Kornilov's rebellion and intensifying after what many saw as the illegal seizure of power by the Bolsheviks. Kerensky, who had fled to Pskov on 25 October, rallied the Cossack general Petro Krasnov to move troops to retake the capital and these soon took control of Tsarskoe Selo, some twenty kilometres south of Petrograd. On 29 October students of the *junker* (military cadet) schools in the capital rose up in his support, led by the Committee for the Salvation of the Motherland and Revolution, which was dominated by Right SRs. In Moscow the Military-Revolutionary Committee declared soviet power on 2 November after five days of fierce fighting against the SR-dominated Committee of Public Safety, which had seized the Kremlin and shot several dozen Bolsheviks after they had surrendered. About 350 military-revolutionary committees were formed, mainly in the central industrial region, the Urals, and the Volga, most attached to the local soviet and tasked with defeating the 'counter-revolution'. Though some were set up by Bolsheviks alone, most represented a coalition of left-wing parties including Left SRs, anarchists, Menshevik Internationalists, and even the occasional SR.[5] During November in the southern Urals and the Don, respectively, atamans A. I. Dutov and A. M. Kaledin summoned their Cossack followers to overthrow soviet power, while far to the east, Soviet forces managed in mid-November to take Irkutsk after fierce skirmishes with Cossacks and army officers. But civil war proper would commence in the Don region of Ukraine, where a Volunteer Army, comprising officers, cadets, students, and Cossacks, was being formed in Novocherskassk under the leadership of Generals Alekseev and Kornilov.

The first test of the Bolsheviks' popular support came with elections to the Constituent Assembly in November and December. In the preceding months the Bolsheviks had made political capital out of the fact that the Provisional Government had postponed the elections to the Assembly. Following the October seizure of power, however, Lenin argued that some form of parliamentary democracy would merely serve as a fig-leaf for capitalist rule and that a government based on directly elected soviets was a superior form of democracy. Some Bolsheviks saw no reason why soviet power should not be combined with a parliament and they were successful in ensuring that elections to the Constituent Assembly went ahead, optimistic that the coalition with their new Left SR allies might bring them victory. From 25 November the elections commenced, in some areas dragging on for several months because of lack of telegraph contact with outlying regions, or lack of ballot papers and polling stations. In the Kuban Cossack region elections did not take place until 2–4 February by which time civil war was in full swing. According to the full or partial returns for 75 out of 81 electoral districts (including seven at the front), of 48.4 million valid votes cast, the SRs gained 19.1 million (39.5 per cent), the Bolsheviks 10.9 million (22.5 per cent), the Kadets 2.2 million (4.5 per cent), and the Mensheviks 1.5 million (3.2 per cent).[6] Among the non-Russian peoples over 7 million voted for non-Russian socialist parties, including two-thirds of the population in Ukraine who voted for Ukrainian SRs, Ukrainian nationalists, or Ukrainian Social Democrats. The SRs were the clear winners—especially when one takes into account the votes for their sister parties in the non-Russian borderlands—but their vote was concentrated in the rural population. The Bolsheviks argued that had their new allies, the Left SRs, been able to stand as an independent party, they would have won the lion's share of the SR vote; but it must be said that in the six electoral districts where Left SRs did stand on a separate ticket, they did not do particularly well, except in the Baltic fleet. The main supporters of the Bolsheviks were workers, soldiers, and sailors, with 42 per cent of the 5.5 million votes in the armed forces going to the party that had consistently called for an end to the war. In Siberia the Bolsheviks won only 8.6 per cent of votes—compared with

75 per cent for the SRs—but 55 per cent of votes among soldiers stationed in the garrisons.[7] This result probably represented the pinnacle of popular support for the Bolsheviks, which would dwindle significantly over the next months.

On 5 January the Constituent Assembly opened in dispiriting circumstances, delayed in part because sailors, soldiers, and Red Guards fired on a group of demonstrators supporting the Assembly, killing twelve (including eight workers from the Obukhov artillery plant) and wounding at least twenty. A leaflet denounced the demonstrators as 'enemies of the people'.[8] The long-time SR leader and former Minister of Agriculture, Viktor Chernov, was elected chair of the Assembly by 244 votes against 151 cast for Maria Spiridonova, leader of the Left SRs. The delegates then voted by 237 to 146 to discuss the political agenda put forward by the SRs, which prioritized the questions of peace and land but did not endorse the principle of soviet power. By the small hours of the morning, the anarchist leader of the Baltic sailors, A. G. Zhelezniakov, announced that 'the guard is getting tired' and closed the proceedings—for ever, as it turned out. Realistically, it is hard to believe that the Constituent Assembly could have provided stable government, for political conflict was now immeasurably more inflamed than it had been in summer 1917, and the majority of delegates were not prepared to give way on what was for the Bolsheviks the central issue: the abandonment of parliamentary democracy in favour of a dictatorship of the proletariat. The 70 per cent of the peasants who had turned out to vote in the Constituent Assembly, believing that it would legalize their title to the land, watched its closure with equanimity, confident that the land was now theirs.[9]

The most consequential act of the new government was the promulgation of the peace decree on 26 October, which called on all the belligerent powers to begin peace talks on the basis of a repudiation of territorial annexations and indemnities and national self-determination. The Bolsheviks then proceeded to publish the secret treaties concluded by the Allies to expose the 'filthy machinations of imperialist diplomacy'. The rejection by the Allies of the peace proposal led the Bolsheviks on 2 (15) December to sign an armistice with the Central Powers at Brest-Litovsk, and on 9 (22)

December they began negotiations with Germany for a separate peace, something they had hitherto rejected. German terms were harsh, and included the detachment of Ukraine, the annexation of the Baltic, and the creation of a rump Polish state. The Bolsheviks played for time. On 5 (18) January the Central Powers issued an ultimatum, demanding the secession to them of all lands currently occupied by Germany and its allies. Lenin insisted that the German ultimatum be accepted, arguing that the Soviets had no means to resist it, and that if they temporized, worse might follow. This provoked what was arguably the deepest split ever inside the Bolshevik party. Bukharin and the left—now organized as the Left Communist faction—insisted that to capitulate was tantamount to abandoning the struggle to spread the Revolution to Germany. From 17 (30) January Trotsky, who favoured a policy of demobilizing the army but of not signing a peace agreement, sought to drag the negotiations out, but on 28 January (9 February) he withdrew, refusing to sign a treaty. On 27 January (8 February) the Central Powers signed a separate treaty with the Ukrainian Rada. On 18 (5) February (now according to the new calendar) the German High Command lost patience, sending 700,000 troops into Ukraine and Russia where they met virtually no resistance. On 23 February it proffered terms more draconian than those previously on offer. At the crucial meeting of the Central Committee that evening, the left gained four votes against Lenin's seven, while four supporters of Trotsky's formula of 'No war, no peace' abstained. Lenin's insistence that the terms be accepted so outraged the left that they briefly discussed with the Left SRs the possibility of removing him as head of government and resuming a 'revolutionary war'. On 3 March the peace treaty was signed at Brest-Litovsk. It was massively punitive: the Baltic provinces, a large part of Belorussia, and the whole of the Ukraine were excised from the former empire, with the result that Russia lost one-third of its agriculture and railways, virtually all its oil and cotton production, three-quarters of its coal and iron. The Treaty effectively made Germany dominant throughout eastern and central Europe, although Lenin's calculation that the treaty would be short-lived proved to be correct, albeit not for the reason—a socialist revolution in Germany—on which he banked.[10]

Meanwhile the Bolsheviks were also facing external pressure from Finland. On 18 December the Soviet government recognized the independence of Finland, confident that the forces of socialist revolution were on the rise in the former Grand Duchy. Following the declaration of independence, former tsarist general C. G. E. Mannerheim incorporated the White Guards into a Finnish White army, which swung into action against the Red Guards after they seized Helsinki on 27/8 January and declared a Finnish Socialist Workers' Republic. For the next four months Finland was plunged into a vicious civil war. The Kaiser and General Erich Ludendorff settled on a plan to wipe out the Finnish Reds and then march south towards Petrograd, but icy weather delayed General von der Goltz's expeditionary force until April. Having joined up with the White Guards, however, von der Goltz inflicted a crushing defeat on the Reds, clearing Helsinki of Red Guards on 12–13 April and taking the main industrial city of Tampere. The civil war ended on 15 May but the killing did not. White terror claimed the lives of more than 5,600, and about 12,500 more would die of famine and disease in prison camps. All this in a country of just 3.1 million people.[11] The Finnish war has been rightly called the first of the 'savage counter-revolutionary campaigns that would open a new chapter in twentieth-century political violence'.[12]

The Expansion of Soviets

Despite the insecurity of the new regime, soviet power advanced during winter 1917–18 across the length of the former empire. Beginning in late November, the Bolsheviks organized a series of 'echelons', special detachments that travelled along the railways, to make contact with the more than 900 soviets that had come into existence since the February Revolution. Many were in the hands of SRs and Mensheviks who had no inclination to declare 'soviet power', and it fell to local garrisons or ad hoc military-revolutionary committees to neutralize them. By January 1918, the Bolsheviks could claim to have the allegiance of local governments in most major towns, although support was by no means solid. A host of factors, such as the political coloration of the local soviet, the vigour of local Bolsheviks, the presence of a garrison or a sizeable phalanx of workers, the existence of ethnic divisions, all influenced the ease with which soviet power was established. In Siberia soviet power was carried along the Trans-Siberian railway and by the beginning of 1918 the overwhelming majority of chairs of town and county soviets were Bolsheviks, mainly professional revolutionaries who had been exiled there in tsarist times. Given that workers were few, however, and that 90 per cent of the peasantry in Siberia were independent farmers, here as elsewhere Bolshevik power remained tenuous.[13]

In the countryside soviets were created at county and township level, often at the instigation of soldiers returning from the front. Hundreds of resolutions from provincial, county, and township soviets in the Volga region, for example, show that most peasants saw the soviets as putting power in the hands of the toiling people. In the Urals support for soviet power was more uneven. There were eleven counties in Perm' province, and in Kamyshlovksii county 'almost all townships came out for soviet power and recognised the necessity of merging with the soviet of workers' deputies on a proportional basis'. By contrast in Krasnoufimskii county

> wealthy people, even kulaks, have been elected to the township soviets and have tried by all manner of means to slow down the work of the soviets… Many times we have had to take repressive measures to reorganize them. With the arrival of the county Red Guard, the local population was terrified so the soviet was speedily organized.[14]

There were very few soviets at village level, the land redistribution having served to strengthen the traditional village commune. And although the zemstvos had undergone democratic re-election in summer 1917, there was generally little support for these institutions except among the SRs. Moscow, which became the new capital on 12 March 1918—as the German army threatened to take Petrograd—had little control over county and township soviets, so the latter ignored central government decrees with impunity. On 2 May 1918 the Commissar of Internal Affairs, G. I. Petrovskii, complained that county and township soviets 'prefer their local interests to state interests, continuing to confiscate fuel, timber, designated for railways, factories and works'.[15] The establishment of soviet power in the countryside thus intensified the tendency for power to devolve to the lowest level.

The 'triumphal march of Soviet power', once a favoured trope of Soviet historiography, was not a myth, but it proved to be short-lived. By spring 1918 in many provincial soviets there was a backlash against the Bolsheviks, which was sometimes due, as in the cities of Kaluga and Briansk, to the demobilization of the local garrison. More worryingly, the rapid escalation of unemployment and the deterioration of food supply caused many workers, who had imagined that Bolshevik victory would bring an end to their economic woes, to become disillusioned. In Tver', a textile town, the local commissars, especially the Left SR, A. Abramov, alienated the populace, not least because of a number of arbitrary killings. On 26 March the Bolsheviks managed to retrieve the situation by removing Abramov, increasing the food ration, and by fierce campaigning against 'non-party' candidates. On 16–17 April new elections gave Bolsheviks 67 seats, Mensheviks 31, Left SRs 11, non-party candidates 8, and SRs 7.[16] In Iaroslavl', another textile town, the partial re-election of the soviet of workers' deputies in late April gave Mensheviks 47 places, Bolsheviks and Left SRs 38, and the SRs 13. The Bolsheviks promptly dissolved the soviet and arrested Mensheviks, thereby triggering strikes and leading to the imposition of martial law.[17] In many provincial capitals the economic situation led to a revival of the Mensheviks and the SRs, although political disagreements between the two parties meant that they were seldom able to offer effective opposition to the Bolsheviks. New elections to the Moscow Soviet from 28 March to 10 April, although marred by malpractice, gave the Mensheviks and SRs only a quarter of the vote.[18] Elsewhere the challenge came from the left. In March SR Maximalists gained control of the Samara provincial congress of soviets, and the city of Samara fell under the control of detachments of 'communards', backed by the garrison, who dispersed the Red Guards. V. V. Kuibyshev, at this time on the left of the Bolshevik party, brought in military units that replaced the soviet with a revolutionary committee.[19] This attests to a more general process that was taking place whereby the loose bloc of left parties that often cooperated in 1917, comprising Left SRs, Menshevik Internationalists, anarchists, and Bolsheviks, was splitting apart.

The Bolsheviks did not hesitate to reorganize or shut down soviets that fell under the control of forces they dismissed as 'petty bourgeois'. Yet the unambiguous assertion of party control over the soviets was primarily a response to an unnerving international situation and to the worsening food crisis within the country. Early in May alarm swept through the Bolshevik leadership as the Allies intensified their intervention (discussed in the section 'Civil War') and as the Czech Legion, which had been fighting the Central Powers, rose up in rebellion. On 10 May Lenin recommended that they seek the economic cooperation of Germany, as a counter to the Allies, and there was serious consideration of moving the government beyond the Urals. It was in this context of anxiety about the survival of the new regime that the Bolshevik leadership suppressed the soviets as multi-party organs. On 29 May a Central Committee circular declared: 'Our party stands at the head of soviet power. Decrees and measures of soviet power emanate from our party.'[20] On 14 June the Soviet CEC expelled Mensheviks and SRs on the grounds that they were 'using all means from shameless slander to conspiracy and armed insurrection' to destabilize the government.[21] Henceforward the function of the CEC would be reduced to ratifying decisions taken by the Council of People's Commissars, which, following the withdrawal of the Left SRs in protest at Brest-Litovsk, once again comprised only Bolsheviks. Despite occasional concessions made to the socialist opposition during the civil war, discussed below in the section on the suppression of the socialist opposition, the Bolsheviks would henceforth run a one-party state.

Civil War

The years between 1918 and 1922 witnessed a level of chaos, strife, and savagery that was unparalleled since Russia's 'Time of Troubles' at the beginning of the seventeenth century (1605–13).[22] It has been estimated that between May 1918 and the end of 1920 nearly 4.7 million members of the Red and

White forces, partisan detachments, and nationalist armies died as a result of combat or disease, or simply disappeared.[23] The population on Soviet territory (within 1926 borders) fell from its 1917 level by 7.1 million in 1920, by 10.9 million in 1921, and by 12.7 million in early 1922.[24] Up to 2 million of this loss was due to emigration, but the overwhelming majority who died perished not in battle but as a result of the ravages of typhus, typhoid fever, cholera, smallpox, dysentery, hunger, and cold. In December 1919 Lenin warned: 'Either the lice will defeat socialism or socialism will defeat the lice.' In 1920 drought compounded the cumulative effects of food requisitioning in the countryside by triggering a catastrophic famine that peaked in summer and autumn of 1921 but continued through to the end of 1922. As many as 5 million would die of starvation.

The civil war was dominated by the cruel and gruelling conflict between the Red Army and the White armies. Yet its constituent conflicts were far more complex than the battle between those committed to building a socialist society and those seeking to restore some version of the old regime. Up to autumn 1918, probably the biggest threat to Bolshevik power came from the so-called 'democratic counter-revolution', led by the Right SRs, who were determined to restore the mandate they had received in elections to the Constituent Assembly. The Cossacks, for their part, whose eleven 'hosts' stretched across the southern and eastern borders, fought to maintain their distinctive caste (and increasingly ethnic) identity and sided mainly, but not exclusively, with the Whites. Another ingredient was added to the civil war by the nationalist armies which struggled to achieve different degrees of autonomy. In 1918 the epicentre of nationalist conflict was in Finland and Ukraine; in 1919 in Ukraine, Estonia, Latvia, Lithuania, and Finland; in 1920 in Poland, Azerbaijan, Armenia; in 1921 in Georgia; and in 1920–2 in Central Asia. Added to this were conflicts between ethnic groups that flared up as emerging nations struggled to carve out territories for themselves, notably clashes between Armenians and Azeris, Georgians and Armenians, Poles and Lithuanians, and Poles and Ukrainians. In addition, the incipient Bolshevik state found itself in conventional warfare with powerful existing states (Germany and then the Allies) and with newly formed nation-states

(Poland and Finland). The civil war thus had a vast international and geopolitical dimension, initially significant in relation to the outcome of the First World War and soon significant for the prospects of nation-building in Eastern Europe and for socialist revolution across Europe, and to a lesser extent the Far East.

Another element in the civil war was the activities of warlords, usually known as *atamany*, or *otomany* in Ukrainian, in Siberia, the Far East, and Ukraine. These were men possessed of armies, usually based on personal ties, which struggled for control of territory and resources. They displayed varying levels of political consciousness. Someone like Nestor Makhno was a committed anarchist whose revolutionary army put up fierce resistance to all who sought to impose external authority on southern Ukraine. More typical of the erratic political loyalties of most *otomany* was Nykyfor Hryhor'yev (1885–1919) whose irregulars carried out fearsome atrocities in Ukraine. Having been awarded the Cross of St George for bravery in the tsarist army, Hryhor'yev become a lieutenant colonel in the National Army of Ukraine following the Bolshevik seizure of power. When the Germans installed Pavlo Skoropads'kii in Kyiv in April 1918 he transferred his loyalty to him, but in November he joined the uprising against the hetman. When the new ruler, Symon Petliura, leader of the Directory government, forbade him to fight French interventionists, he deserted to the Reds, before revolting against them in July 1919 and joining Nestor Makhno's anarchist army. Red partisans—often well outside the control of the Bolshevik party and sometimes little different from bandits—also played a major role in Siberia, Transbaikal, the Amur region, and the Far East where they were critical in fighting the *atamany* and the Whites.[25] Finally, there were the irregulars who fought to defend the interests of local communities, violently confronting food detachments and anti-desertion squads, but often without allegiance to the contenders for national power.[26] Such 'Green' formations were particularly strong in south-central Ukraine, Tambov, and western Siberia; once Red victory looked likely, some grew to the point where in 1920–1 they became mass peasant armies that rose up against the Bolshevik regime.

All protagonists in the civil war practised extreme violence. Reds as well as Whites buried or burned their enemies alive; prisoners, though usually incorporated into their captors' army, might be slaughtered if there were no resources to support them; rape was a regular weapon of war; populations were 'pacified' by the use of massive artillery fire or mass executions. The White general Pëtr Wrangel recalled that after his forces swept the Reds from the Northern Caucasus in January 1919:

> On the outskirts of one of the Cossack settlements we met five young Cossacks with rifles…'Where are you going, lads?' 'We're going to beat up some Bolsheviks. There are a lot of them hiding in the reeds. Their army has fled. Yesterday I killed seven.' This was said by one of the boys, about twelve years old…as though he had achieved some great feat. During the whole of the intestinal conflict I never felt as sharply as I did at that moment the utter horror of fratricidal war.[27]

The meanings of violence were manifold. Most obviously it was a way of crushing enemies and of inspiring fear in one's opponents. It was often inspired by ideology but, as Wrangel's example attests, it could be a depraved form of pleasure. Violence was central to the way in which combat groups cemented bonds and forged identities. Violence also spilled over into the civilian population. Peasants disembowelled members of the food detachments and local communities wreaked havoc on neighbours they believed to have appropriated their land or resources. Violence could thus be predatory or a desperate reaction by a community facing threat.

On 27 December 1917 in Novocherkassk the formation of a Volunteer Army was announced by General Alekseev, who had been Commander-in-Chief of the Russian armed forces from March to May 1917. Kornilov, who loathed Alekseev, was appointed Commander- in-Chief.[28] Some 4,000 officers, cadets, and students flocked to the Don to join the fledgling White army. The hope was to enlist the Don Cossacks, who prided themselves on their history of defending Russian statehood, in the battle to overthrow the upstart regime. Relations between the Volunteers and Don Cossacks were strained from the first, since the Cossacks' prime interest was in defending their new-won autonomy rather than in seeking to re-establish a unified Russian state. In January, enthusiastic but poorly trained Red Guards and sailors, 35,000 Latvian riflemen, plus a motley collection of foreign prisoners-of-war, organized into an International Legion, surged into the Don region from the north and quickly captured Taganrog (Figure 4.1). Mortified, General Aleksei Kaledin, ataman of the Don Cossacks, committed suicide on 29 January. On 23 February (10 February o.s.), as Red forces entered Rostov-on-Don, Kornilov began a heroic march south across the frozen steppe—the so-called Ice March—deep into the territory of the Kuban Cossacks. His attempt to take Ekaterinodar between 9 and 13 April was a disaster, but he died fighting. Command of a somewhat battered Volunteer Army now passed to General Anton Denikin. In May the Don Cossacks sought an accommodation with the German occupation regime, and this set them further at odds with the Volunteer Army. On 23 June, the Volunteers, now 8,000 to 9,000 strong as a result of the incorporation of 3,000 officers from the former Romanian Front, launched the brilliant second Kuban campaign, followed in autumn by the equally successful North Caucasus campaign. Subsequently the Kuban and Don Cossacks would accept the leadership of Denikin, who, with backing from the Allies, became Commander-in-Chief of the Armed Forces of South Russia on 8 January 1919.

Meanwhile, following the Treaty of Brest-Litovsk, Trotsky, now Commissar of War, began the process of creating a conventional army.[29] Initially, the

Figure 4.1 German prisoners-of-war demonstrate in Moscow in 1918. Their banner reads 'Long live the World Revolution!'

hope was that young workers and peasants would volunteer to join a new Red Army, but by 1 July only 360,000 men had signed up. In the teeth of opposition from Bolsheviks who on ideological grounds rejected a standing army in favour of a citizens' militia, Trotsky determined to build a regular army. On 29 May, he reinstated compulsory military service (although as late as 1920, 17 per cent of soldiers were still volunteers), but it was his decision to recruit former tsarist officers as 'military specialists' that particularly incensed his opponents. These specialists were given considerable leeway in the field but were subject to close oversight from 'political-military commissars'. By spring 1919 more than 200 former generals and about 400 former colonels and lieutenant colonels were fighting for the Reds (Figure 4.2).[30] Some were coerced and others saw their families held hostage for their good behaviour, but a surprising number, including some top generals, chose to join the Red Army. By early 1921 the latter had 217,000 commanders (as officers were now called), one-third of whom had held positions in the tsarist army. In order to weld a mass of poorly equipped and

Figure 4.2 Red Army soldiers going off to fight.

ill-disciplined conscripts together, vigorous steps were taken to instil discipline. Summary executions and the decimation of units—'first the commissar, and then the commander', as one of Trotsky's orders read—were applied in cases of mass flight, although in practice only 0.6 per cent of ordinary deserters were ever shot, usually when they had fled their units two or three times or had stolen arms. On 2 September 1918 a Revolutionary-Military Council of the Republic was formed to preside over field operations, and soon each front had its own council, made up of one military specialist and two political commissars. In October elected party committees were abolished and replaced by 'political departments', consisting of the commissar and his assistants, a form of organization that Trotsky later tried to extend to the trade unions.

The civil war proved to be Trotsky's finest hour. He emerged as a brilliant military leader, remarkable in one whose only previous experience had been as a journalist in the Balkan wars. As a tactician he was flexible and, though certainly not infallible, he was able to learn from his mistakes. Above all, as a magnificent orator, he was an inspirational figure for his men, as he toured from front to front in the train that served as his mobile headquarters. His colleague Anatolii Lunacharskii summed up his role in the civil war in 1923 (a time when it was still possibly to speak frankly):

> It would be wrong to imagine that the second great leader of the Russian revolution is inferior to his colleague (i.e. Lenin) in everything: there are, for instance, aspects in which Trotsky incontestably surpasses him—he is more brilliant, he is clearer, he is more active. Lenin is fitted as no one else to take the chair at the Council of Peoples' Commissars and to guide the world revolution with the touch of genius, but he could never have coped with the titanic mission that Trotsky took upon his own shoulders, with those lightning moves from place to place, those astounding speeches, those fanfares of on-the-spot orders, that role of being the unceasing electrifier of a weakening army, now at one spot, now at another. There is not a man on earth who could have replaced Trotsky in that respect.[31]

Not surprisingly, Trotsky's haughtiness, as well as his controversial policies in forging a Red Army, made him many enemies. Stalin and Kliment

Voroshilov, political commissar of the First Cavalry Army, were deeply distrustful of the military specialists. In May 1918, during the campaign against the Don Cossacks Stalin was dispatched to Tsaritsyn, where he held show trials of former tsarist officers working for the Red Army and executed dozens of prisoners-of-war. He ignored repeated orders from Trotsky who, with Lenin's backing, recalled him from the front in October. In March 1919 opposition to Trotsky's policies came to a head at the Eighth Party Congress. Stalin's proposal to strengthen the status of the party's military organizations was accepted, but Lenin supported Trotsky on the issue of military specialists.

During the first six months of civil war, the counter-revolutionary cause was led by the resolutely anti-socialist Volunteer Army of General Denikin, but during the summer of 1918 the centre of gravity of the anti-Bolshevik cause shifted to the SRs. In May 1918 the Czech Legion, a body of 38,000 men recruited by the tsarist government from Austro-Hungarian prisoners-of-war, was making its way along the Trans-Siberian railway to Vladivostok, whence it was due to be evacuated to join the Allies in Western Europe. After clashes with local soviets, Trotsky issued an unenforceable order on 14 May that the Czechs be disarmed. This immediately sparked a rebellion that quickly spread along the railway from Cheliabinsk. Czech rebels now provided the Right SRs with the armed backing they so sorely needed—a 'People's Army of the Komuch', that is, an army supporting the Constituent Assembly. Within months, the Legion held a vast area east of the Volga. The Right SRs set up anti-Bolshevik governments in the Volga and the Urals regions to enforce the mandate they had received in the elections to the Constituent Assembly. From this time on, one can speak of full-scale civil war, with large armies fighting along defined fronts. There was, however, none of the positional warfare that had been an intermittent feature of fighting during the First World War, much of the fighting taking place along railways or involving cavalry.[32]

The rebellion by Czech troops caused consternation in Bolshevik ranks. In April 1918 the imperial family had been taken from Tobol'sk, where Nicholas II had demonstrated his carpentry skills by building a platform on the roof of the orangery, to Ekaterinburg in the Urals. As the Czech Legion advanced on Ekaterinburg, the local soviet decided that the imperial family must be eliminated. Some historians believe that a secret order to this effect came from Lenin and Iakov Sverdlov, chair of the Soviet CEC, but it has never been found.[33] On the night of 16–17 July 1918, the local Cheka (the political police), led by Iakov Yurovskii, a watchmaker who had been a Bolshevik since 1905, carried out the shooting of Nicholas, Alexandra, their four daughters, their son Alexei, and four servants. Their corpses were taken to an abandoned mine shaft where they were covered with vitriol and set alight. On 25 July the Czech Legion captured Ekaterinburg to discover the royal family had vanished.

Despite the military backing of the Czech Legion, the 'democratic counter-revolution' of the SRs proved an abortive experiment. On 8 June SRs and Kadets created an 'All-Russian' government in Samara, a city on the east bank of the middle reaches of the Volga, which pledged to resume the war against Germany and overthrow the Bolsheviks. It made no attempt to reverse the land redistribution, but its resort to conscription was not popular with the local peasantry. In Omsk on 30 June the western Siberian Commissariat of the SRs broke with the rhetoric of 'people's power' and threw in its lot with the Council of Ministers of the Temporary Siberian Government, which comprised Right SRs, advocates of Siberian autonomy, and White officers. This temporary government proceeded to abolish soviets, arrest Bolsheviks, and return estates to their former owners.[34] In Ekaterinburg a Urals Provisional Government sought to act as a buffer between the Omsk and Samara administrations, but clashed with the Omsk government when the latter refused to recognize its borders and imposed a 50 per cent surcharge on the grain it sent it from Siberia. Under pressure from the Czechs, the Samara and Omsk governments agreed to meet in Ufa in September 1918 with a view to uniting their forces. This led to the formation in Omsk of the Directory government in which the SRs, having made substantial concessions to the Whites on the agrarian question, gained only two of the five places. The fate of these SR-sponsored attempts to create a 'third way' between the dictatorships of right and left was sealed on

18 November when Cossack officers arrested the SR members of the Omsk Directory and installed Admiral Aleksandr Kolchak as 'Supreme Ruler'.

Meanwhile far to the north in Arkhangel'sk province a somewhat more moderate coalition of socialists, liberals, and army officers had been set up in August 1918 with the help of British interventionist forces.[35] This too was pushed in an increasingly right-wing direction as it grappled with deep social conflicts, and ended up in turn the victim of a coup by Kolchak. The fate of the 'democratic counter-revolution' is interesting not least because it reveals the impossibility by this stage of democratic government in Russia. In the face of conflicts over land, industrial management, and law and order, the SRs proved unable to translate the electoral support they had received in the Constituent Assembly into solid government. Crucially, they proved unable to establish viable armies. Having gone to considerable lengths to secure the cooperation of conservative military elements, they ended up in hock to them, abandoning democratic politics and compromising what were for the peasants the most important gains of the Revolution.

Admiral Kolchak, the Supreme Ruler in Omsk, now became the principal leader of the White cause. Appointed commander of the Black Sea Fleet in 1916, he had offered his services to the British army following the Bolshevik seizure of power. General Alfred Knox, head of the British mission in Siberia, was his great champion, seeing in the vain and suggestible admiral the only hope for crushing the Bolsheviks. The head of the French military mission, General Maurice Janin, was less impressed by the capacities of a man who had had no experience of land warfare; but despite French and American reservations, the Allies threw in their lot with the Supreme Ruler in spring 1919. Denikin reluctantly accepted Kolchak's supremacy, although in practice he enjoyed more power than his rival, who was constrained by the 'Council of the Supreme Ruler', the formal Omsk government, as well as by thuggish warlords such as G. M. Semenov, ataman of the Transbaikal Cossack host, and I. M. Kalmykov, whose atrocities brought disgrace on his regime. Nevertheless the consequence of Allied recognition was that Kolchak received a huge volume of weapons and advice. Moreover, to his great good fortune, the capture of Kazan' by the Czech Legion back in August 1918 had placed the tsar's reserve of 700 million gold rubles at his disposal, which meant the Omsk government could issue loans backed by the reserve.

The Whites represented the interests of the old elites, but they were not a class movement in a sociological sense. An analysis of seventy-one generals and officers involved in the Volunteer Army's first Kuban campaign showed that only 21 per cent were from hereditary nobility and only five had owned landed estates, although in later White armies the proportion of officers of noble blood may have been higher.[36] This reflected the democratization of the officer corps that had taken place during the First World War, and reminds us that many who joined the White cause did so not in order to maintain their family's privileges, but out of a patriotic sense of honour or some personal connection. The Whites were, first and foremost, Russian nationalists who aspired to re-establish 'Russia One and Indivisible', which meant suppressing 'anarchy' and restoring a strong state and the values of the Orthodox Church. What united them emotionally was a passionate detestation of Bolshevism, which they saw as a 'German-Jewish' conspiracy inflicted on the Russian people. In White propaganda, the words 'Jew' (*zhid*) and 'Communist' were interchangeable. Naturally, they detested class conflict, and they feared and hated the revolutionary masses (that 'wild beast', as the journalist and Kadet politician Ariadna Tyrkova-Williams called them). Contemptuous of 'idle talkers', they saw themselves as men of action. In their view only a 'strong power' could stop Russia sliding into the abyss. V. V. Shul'gin, a supporter of Denikin, wrote of the Volunteer Army that 'having taken on itself the task of purging Russia of anarchy, [it] raised as an immutable principle of firm government a dictatorial power. Only an unlimited, strong and firm power could save the nation and restore the torn-down temple of state-mindedness'.[37] Some leading members of the White administrations favoured a restoration of the monarchy—Wrangel was one—but others believed that a period of firm government might eventually lead to the reconvening of a Constituent Assembly.

White officers liked to see themselves as being 'above class' and 'above party'—a familiar trope of Kadet discourse. They sought to keep political differences at bay by avoiding thrashing out detailed political programmes, justifying this in terms of what they rather pretentiously called a principle of 'non-predetermination', that is, the postponement of policy-making until after they had won the civil war. However, faced by opponents who had a detailed social and political agenda, 'non-predetermination' proved to be a non-starter. In the course of 1919, the White administrations were forced to grapple with the thorny issues of land reform, national autonomy, labour policy, and local government. Generally, the policies they concocted proved too little and too late, and laid bare internal divisions. Kolchak's government, more stable and ramified than Denikin's peripatetic Special Conference of the Armed Forces of South Russia, tended to take the lead in policy-making.[38] In March 1919 it issued a proposal to allow peasants to rent land from the state; but a month later, not to be outdone, Denikin put forward a plan to bolster peasant smallholding through compulsory expropriation of gentry land, albeit with compensation. However, he was overruled by his Special Conference, which called for the return of all land seized at the time of the Revolution, and insisted that any expropriation could only be considered three years after the end of hostilities. It is true that as the Whites faced the prospect of defeat, their policies became less uncompromising. Wrangel's land reform law of 1920 was fairly progressive, envisaging a land fund created from the compulsory alienation of lands above a certain norm, to which recipients of land would be obliged to give part of their harvest, thus enabling those whose land had been taken gradually to be compensated.[39]

The Achilles heel of White policy was their failure to devise a policy on national self-determination for non-Russian ethnicities. Located on the peripheries of the empire, the Whites inevitably had to deal with national minorities, yet their commitment to Russia 'One and Indivisible' inhibited them from making serious concessions towards aspirations for political autonomy. For Denikin, the 'sweet poisonous dreams of complete independence' were hateful, and he refused to recognize a 'separatist' Ukrainian state, although he was prepared to concede cultural autonomy. His administration in the North Caucasus in 1919 had no alternative but to recognize autonomous districts of Ossetians, Ingush, and others, but whereas the Terek Cossacks mostly supported the Whites, these mountain peoples resisted efforts to conscript them. In western Siberia Kolchak was less troubled by the 'national question', yet when the Finnish general Mannerheim offered him support by taking Petrograd in July 1919, in return for recognition of an independent Finland, Kolchak spurned the offer. ('History will never forgive me if I surrender what Peter the Great won.') None of the White leaders would recognize the independence of Finland and the Baltic states—though General Nikolai Iudenich could have been persuaded—and nor would they negotiate with Józef Piłsudski, the 'First Marshal of Poland'.

The Allies had intervened in Russia in spring 1918 with a view to maintaining the war effort on the Eastern Front. Indeed when the British Royal Marines landed at Murmansk in March 1918 it was with the blessing of Trotsky, who feared that the Finns and their German allies were about to capture the Arctic port. By August 1918, 50,000 foreign troops occupied the region south of Arkhangel'sk and along the North Dvina River. The landing of British and Japanese troops in Vladivostok in April was harder to justify in terms of support for the war effort and it provoked strenuous protests from the Bolsheviks. The Japanese military opportunistically sought to exploit the power vacuum in the Far East in order to facilitate their ultimate goal of controlling Manchuria and of reversing their declining influence in domestic politics. Their intervention was a factor—along with general concern to ensure the defeat of the Central Powers—that persuaded Woodrow Wilson in July to agree to US participation in expeditions to north Russia and Siberia in order to assist Russian 'patriots'.

Logically, the signing of the armistice with Germany in November should have led to the Allies scaling back their intervention but the opposite happened. The lifting of the German blockade in the Baltic and Black Seas led to an increase in the number of soldiers and weapons being brought into Soviet Russia, while the Allied blockade of Russia, imposed after Brest-Litovsk, was maintained. By 1919 there were 150,000 foreign troops in Siberia and the Far East, including the Czech Legion, although this was not many in relation to the size of Eurasia. In the Transcaucasus there were over 20,000 British troops by 1919—their initial aim being to secure the railway from Baku to Batum. In the Black Sea Prime Minister Clemenceau sent six French divisions to occupy Odessa and Sebastopol, so by February 1919 there were nearly 60,000 foreign troops across southern Russia (including southern Ukraine and the North Caucasus). French troops showed little keenness to fight, however, and following the mutiny by the French Black Sea fleet, they evacuated in April 1919. From around this time, the Allies grew increasingly lukewarm about military involvement, yet they stepped up their supplies to the Whites and to certain nationalist forces. Britain sent matériel worth more than £100 million, mainly to Denikin and Kolchak, and the USA allowed the Russian embassy in Washington to utilize credits to the tune of more than $50 million dollars. These funds and supplies were vital to equipping the anti-Bolshevik forces, but were not decisive in shifting the balance of military advantage towards the anti-Bolshevik cause. Supplies often failed to arrive when they were needed and pressure from the Allies caused Kolchak to launch his spring offensive of 1919 prematurely.

The most critical phase of the civil war came in spring 1919. Of fateful significance was the fact that Kolchak's spring offensive was not coordinated with Denikin's 'Moscow offensive' in July. In March Kolchak's forces moved with impressive swiftness west from Omsk across the Urals towards the Volga, with the aim of moving north to connect with General Evgenii Miller's White forces in Arkhangel'sk. By the time they reached Samara and Simbirsk, the crossing points on the Volga, their supply lines had become overstretched. The Reds counter-attacked and, under the gifted commander Mikhail Frunze, pushed the Whites back east, taking Ekaterinburg on 15 July. In May a north-western front opened up around Pskov after 6,000 Whites crossed from Estonia into Soviet territory. This Northwestern Army was under the command of General Iudenich, who in September drove the Reds back to within sight of Petrograd. 'Red Petrograd' came perilously close to falling to the counter-revolution. Lenin was minded to see the city abandoned, but Trotsky helped organize a heroic defence of the former capital, repelling the invaders. The most dramatic of the White offensives, however, was led by Denikin from the south. Between January and March the Red Army had managed to capture the Don region from the Cossacks, but in May General V. Z. Mai-Maevskii, commander of the Volunteer Army within the Armed Forces of South Russia, scattered the Red forces controlling this vital grain region. In July Denikin's forces drove north along the railway and by October reached Tula, less than 200 km from the capital. The Reds improvised cleverly, exposing the precariousness of Denikin's supply lines and the exhaustion and unreliability of his 100,000-strong army. Harried by partisan attacks in his rear, especially from the Ukrainian anarchist forces of Makhno, the Armed Forces of South Russia were forced into headlong retreat. After an appalling winter, in which many were captured, some 34,000 Volunteers and Cossacks managed to get to Novorossiisk, whence they were evacuated by sea in March 1920. Meanwhile in Siberia the Reds pushed Kolchak's forces eastward until in November they captured Omsk, the headquarters of his government. On 5 January 1920 the 'Political Centre', set up in November 1919 by the All-Siberian Conference of Zemstvos and Towns, seized Irkutsk, showing that there was still some life left in the moderate socialists. The Centre arrested Kolchak upon his arrival in Irkutsk, and he was executed by local Bolsheviks on 7 February.

At the start of 1920 it looked as though Red victory was at hand. However, in order to thwart Soviet expansion, Marshal Piłsudski had hatched a plan to create a federation of Ukraine, Belorussia, and Lithuania under Polish leadership. In return for Eastern Galicia, he offered to support the Ukrainian nationalist leader Simon Petliura in his bid to establish an independent Ukraine. On 7 May the Polish-Ukrainian army captured Kyiv. However the brilliant Red commander Mikhail Tukhachevskii pushed Polish forces back across the Bug River by 1 August. Tukhachevskii proclaimed that 'across the corpse of White Poland lies the path to world conflagration. We shall bring happiness and peace to the toilers of humanity on our bayonets.' For a few weeks the normally level-headed Lenin (Figure 4.3) imagined that the Red Army would march through Poland and bring revolution to Germany, where the right-wing Kapp putsch had recently been crushed. The Bolshevik decision to take the war into Poland proved disastrous, the Polish people rising

Figure 4.3 Lenin speaks to troops being sent to the Polish Front in Moscow, 5 May 1920. Trotsky and Kamenev are standing on the step of the platform.

up against their historic enemies. On 13 August, as the Reds neared Warsaw, the Polish army counter-attacked with astonishing success (the 'miracle on the Vistula'). Overstretched and outnumbered, the Reds were battered into retreat. In October the Bolsheviks signed an armistice with Poland, the prelude to the Treaty of Riga in March 1921. This partitioned Ukraine between the Soviet state and a hugely expanded Poland and recognized the boundary with the Baltic states that had been drawn up by Germany in 1918. The treaty reflected the weakness of both Soviet Russia and Poland and, as it turned out, marked the end of Bolshevik hopes for a rapid extension of socialist revolution into Europe.

The coda to the civil war came in March 1920 when 35,000 Whites who had been evacuated from the Don arrived in Crimea. Baron P. N. Wrangel, who had been ousted by Denikin, was recalled from exile in Constantinople to head the Armed Forces of South Russia. He removed incompetent generals and formed a cabinet to draw up political reforms designed to mollify the Allies. Despite his fierce criticism of Denikin's government, he proved no better at tackling rampant inflation, speculation, and embezzlement. Between April and October prices of food rose sixteen to twenty-fold, fuel fifty-fold, and industrial goods twelve-fold. Wrangel's military reforms, based upon elite units, were more successful, allowing him to break out of his confinement in Crimea and capture the grain-growing region of north Tauride in June. Once the Polish front had stabilized, however, the Red Army launched a crushing offensive on 28 October 1920, which forced Wrangel to effect a huge seaborne evacuation of 146,000 men and families from Crimea. Meanwhile in eastern Siberia the Bolsheviks resolved that with Kolchak out of the way, it was better to do a deal with the SRs and Mensheviks. In April 1920, they set up a Far Eastern Republic as an independent buffer between Soviet Russia and Japan, comprising Bolsheviks and moderate socialists, although Moscow quietly exerted influence behind the scenes. The most ghastly of the Siberian warlords, R. F. von Ungern Sternberg, seized Mongolia from its Chinese occupants in 1920–1 and restored Bogdo Gegen, the Eighth Reincarnation of the Living Buddha, with a view to establishing a base from which to overthrow Soviet power. Apprehended by Reds, he was executed in September 1921. The Japanese army remained in occupation of the southern Maritime Province and northern Sakhalin until 1922, providing a refuge for the remnants of the White army, but in summer of that year it began to withdraw. Following the fall of White-controlled Vladivostok in October 1922, the Far Eastern Republic was wound up.

The reasons for Red victory are manifold. One should begin by noting that a White victory was never beyond the realm of possibility. If Kolchak and Denikin had advanced on Moscow simultaneously in 1919, rather than five months apart, or if Kolchak had struck a deal with Mannerheim, then the Red Army could easily have gone under. Its operations over the course of the war were uneven in quality, sometimes brilliant, sometimes poorly planned and executed. Nevertheless the Reds had certain military advantages over the Whites. Firstly, they had a larger army: in the course of 1919, the Red Army grew from 800,000 to nearly 3 million and by autumn 1920 to over 5 million, but at no point did the number of front-line troops exceed half a million. The combined total of the White forces was larger than used to be supposed, and may have approached 2 million by spring 1920. By that stage, of course, it no longer comprised mainly officers, Cossacks, cadets, and students, but peasants, townspeople, intellectuals, and even some workers. Both sides found it difficult to recruit and retain troops and both suffered from massive levels of desertion. Deserters mostly left because of material shortages in their units or because they needed to sow their fields. The Bolsheviks got on top of this problem by giving deserters a second chance, but threatening to cut the tax exemptions and special rations enjoyed by their families if they deserted a second time.[40] Secondly, so far as the quality of the Red and White armies was concerned, the two sides were initially fairly evenly matched, but over the course of the war the Reds gained an edge. Many experienced officers joined the Volunteer Army in early 1918, but this ceased to be an advantage once Trotsky employed military specialists. Moreover, the Reds proved better at nurturing young talent: gifted commanders who rose from the ranks included S. M. Budënnyi, commander of the First Cavalry Army, V. K. Bliukher, four times recipient of the Order of the Red Banner, who became the senior military adviser to the Guomindang in China in 1924–7, and Frunze, who not only led the counter-offensive against Kolchak in 1919 but also dealt the coup de grâce to Wrangel in 1920. Consequently, over the war, the proportion of military specialists in the officer corps fell from three-quarters in 1918 to just over a third by the end of 1921.[41] As regards the quality of the White cavalry forces, the Cossack cavalry certainly offered a significant military advantage, given that the front line moved so fast. Yet they were never at ease fighting beyond their homelands and their dream of autonomy was ultimately incompatible with the White commitment to a reunified empire. A third factor influencing the balance of military advantage relates to the relative unity of leadership on the two sides. The White armies were riven by personal animosity, between Alekseev and Kornilov, Denikin and Kolchak, and Denikin and Wrangel.[42] In the leadership of the Red Army, too, there were no few grudges, notably between Stalin and Trotsky and Stalin and Tukhachevskii, but they proved less damaging, since the Bolsheviks shared a binding ideology and a recognized leader in Lenin. Fourth, the Bolsheviks were undoubtedly superior in the sphere of organization. The Red Army had a unified centre of command—the Revolutionary Military Council of the Republic—that was accountable to a tightly knit political oligarchy. The Council of Workers' and Peasants' Defence, which fused the civilian and defence sectors, was another expeditious innovation, as were institutions such as the political commissars, the Cheka, and the underground party network in White-occupied areas. By contrast, the White armies, beset by communications difficulties, were organizationally fragmented and unable to coordinate strategy.

Perhaps the key strategic advantage enjoyed by the Reds lay in their possession of a compact, integrated territory. This meant that they could send forces from one front to another without great difficulty. By contrast, the Whites were disadvantaged by their location along the periphery of European Russia. The Don base of the Volunteer Army was nearly 1,000 km from Moscow; Omsk, the seat of Kolchak's government, was almost 3,000 km from Petrograd. Any advance into the heartlands of Soviet power, therefore, created a problem of long supply lines and coordination of armies strung out along the periphery. Railways radiated outwards from Moscow, and lateral lines, which would have been beneficial to the Whites, were underdeveloped. Moreover, the possession by the Reds of a core territory, where the majority of the population and resources were concentrated, gave them control not only of the stocks of the tsarist army but also of the key defence industries. The Whites, by contrast, were better supplied with coal but had control only of secondary centres of the defence industry in the Donbass and Urals. As against that, they had an abundance of food, especially in Siberia and the Kuban region, which remained under White control throughout 1919. Soldiers in the White armies were generally better fed than their Red counterparts whose ration norm of one *funt* (0.4 kg) of bread a day was lower than in the tsarist army and even then was not always fulfilled.

The significance of Allied support for the Whites as a factor determining the outcome of the civil war is contentious. The scale of military support should not be underestimated. By mid-1919 Britain had supplied the Whites in the Baltic with 40,000 rifles, 500 Vickers and Lewis machine guns, and numerous tanks and aircraft. By the end of 1919 the Armed Forces of South Russia had received 198,000 rifles, 6,177 machine guns, and 1,200 artillery pieces plus 100,000 rifles from the USA.[43] Nevertheless the divisions within Allied governments concerning the wisdom of supporting the anti-Bolshevik cause, combined with mistrust between the interventionist governments, meant that material aid was never offered on the scale the Whites expected. They thus had cause to feel aggrieved: for if London, Paris, and Washington had been determined to overthrow Bolshevik power, they could have committed men and resources on a vastly greater scale than they did. But Allied governments faced war-weary publics, and growing left-wing opposition to intervention, so this option was never on the political table. Even the French, who wished to redeem their huge pre-war investments in Russia, were more concerned about the restraint of Germany than about Russia. Nevertheless, while Allied support made the 1919 campaigns of Kolchak and Denikin possible, their ultimate failure can hardly be blamed on the inadequacy of that support.

If military and strategic factors were paramount in explaining the defeat of the Whites, socio-political factors were also significant. If the White generals were politically inexperienced, this was hardly true of their right-wing Kadet and monarchist advisers. First, their failure to come up with credible schemes of land reform made them suspect in peasant eyes, and there were enough cases of officers returning former landowners to their estates—for instance Major General Uvarov in Stavropol' in 1918 and the Ufa Directory in 1919—to fix in peasant minds the notion that a White victory would mean the return of the landlords. The Reds certainly did not win because they had mass peasant support: their policies of requisitioning and conscription created intense animosity on the part of the rural population. Nevertheless, they were certainly seen as the lesser of two evils. Indeed it was the willingness of the rural population to swing behind the Bolsheviks whenever a White takeover threatened which meant that so long as the civil war lasted, endemic rural unrest did not pose a serious threat to

Bolshevik power. Secondly, the arbitrariness, looting, and brigandage of White armies, especially the Cossacks, were a factor that alienated the population. In Siberia, for example, the brutalities of the atamans caused many wealthy peasants to join the partisans who fought deep behind Kolchak's lines. Thirdly, the failure of the Whites to deal with the 'national question' had more damaging consequences than did the frequent alienation of nationalist movements by the Bolsheviks. However much national self-determination was subordinated to Moscow's military priorities, it was known that the Bolsheviks were willing to negotiate on the matter of self-government. Fourthly, despite trumpeting their devotion to the Russian people, the Whites failed to forge a conception of the nation with which the peasants could identify. They could probably have done more to play on the Orthodox faith that was still shared by a majority of the population—they had, after all, the Church on their side—yet they proved too inflexible, too hidebound by a militaristic ethos to adapt traditional values to the new world of mass politics. Moreover, and with savage irony, the Bolsheviks—tribunes of proletarian internationalism—could play for propaganda purposes on the White reliance on foreign assistance to present them as false patriots, as the playthings of foreign capital. Karl Radek would go so far as to describe the civil war as a 'national struggle of liberation against foreign intervention'.[44] One consequence was that following the war with Poland, some leading conservatives began to see in the Bolsheviks the one hope for preserving some form of Russian statehood.

Finally, the Bolsheviks had a huge advantage over the Whites when it came to propaganda. They understood the lesson of the First World War about the need to maintain military and civilian morale, and from the start they recognized the importance of what they called 'political enlightenment'. In April 1918 compulsory classes were introduced for all ranks in the nascent Red Army, and 'cultural and enlightenment commissions' were attached to every unit, each having sections for political literacy, literature, theatre and music, and physical culture. Given the fact that a majority of the population was illiterate and that paper was in critically short supply, 'political enlightenment' depended to a large extent on the spoken word.

In 1920, 1,415 Red Army and Navy theatre groups staged 'agit-plays' that dramatized what the soldiers and sailors were fighting for. Ideas were expressed simply and often in ethical more than political terms. Red Army soldiers were advised: do not wish for more than you have; be independent; do not wish for a slave when you yourself have no desire to be a slave; respect science, art, culture, and handicrafts. About 3,100 political posters were produced which, in stylistic terms, drew on popular, biblical, classical, and French revolutionary traditions, and the Russian Telegraph Agency, under the inspired direction of the poet Vladimir Mayakovskii, developed a distinctive, agitational style of bold, colourful cartoon frames, duplicated by means of cardboard stencils.[45] All these forms of propaganda popularized a manichean view of the war: Red versus White, proletariat versus bourgeoisie, poor peasant versus kulak. The *burzhui* were represented as corpulent males, often in a top hat and with a watch chain, the worker often as a muscular blacksmith. New symbols, such as the hammer and sickle and the red star—the logo of the Red Army—were created, red being a sacred colour in popular culture and thus capable of investing the working class and the Bolshevik party with a quasi-religious aura. Five agit-trains spent 659 days in the field and welcomed 2.8 million members of the public at 775 different locations (by autumn 1919 Denikin also had three). They carried projectors that showed short didactic films that inter alia allowed the populace to see what their new leaders looked like. It was claimed that 2 million people saw such films, many exposed to this miraculous medium for the first time. The White generals did not leave the field of propaganda wide open to the Bolsheviks: the Armed Forces of South Russia also had an 'information and agitation agency', which put out posters and leaflets recounting lurid 'tales from the commune' but it had little experience of working with peasants and workers and its efforts were fitful.

As a result of the civil war, the Red Army quickly became the largest institution of state, numbering 5.5 million by 1920, including half a million former workers. In the absence of a numerous or politically reliable proletariat, it became by default the principal social base of the regime. Fighting to defend the socialist motherland, living together in collective units, exposed to political education, the army proved to be a training ground for the core of activists that would staff the party and state apparatuses in the 1920s.

National Self-Determination and the Reconstitution of Empire

Between October 1917 and the end of 1918 some thirteen new states came into existence in what had been the Russian empire. Finland, Transcaucasia, the Baltic provinces, and the western borderlands, including Ukraine, seceded and Russia quickly retreated to the frontiers she had enjoyed before the time of Peter the Great.[46] Power passed in the non-Russian borderlands to sections of the nationalist intelligentsia, but did so partially by default. This was not an empire brought to its knees by powerful national liberation struggles. Most nationalist movements did not have a strong popular base and most were weakened by internal political conflicts, especially regarding land redistribution, which threatened landowning interests. Some nationalist movements were torn between the Reds and Whites, and many turned to the Central Powers or the Allies for support. Ultimately, the Bolsheviks would take advantage of the weakness and division to reintegrate the bulk of the territories of the former empire into a Soviet Union. This raises an obvious question about the sincerity of the Bolshevik commitment to national self-determination.

The Declaration of the Rights of the Peoples of Russia, issued on 2 November 1917, abolished all restrictions on nationalities and religions and asserted the right of the peoples of Russia to self-determination, including the right to secede from the Russian polity. Prior to 1914 Lenin's intransigent rejection of 'Great Russian chauvinism' and support for national self-determination had probably made him the leader in the pre-1914 socialist movement most sympathetic to the aspirations of 'oppressed nations'. For him, international working-class solidarity could only be built on the free, voluntary union of different peoples. The Declaration of the Rights of the Toiling and Exploited People on 3 January 1918 defined the new state as a 'federation of soviet national republics'. Yet it soon became clear that there was little agreement in the Bolshevik party about the relationship of national self-determination to class struggle. At the Third Congress of Soviets on 15 January 1918, Stalin, who had been made Commissar of Nationalities in December, pointed to the ongoing conflict with the Ukrainian Rada and baldly stated that 'the principle of self-determination must be a means of struggle for socialism and must be subordinated to the principles of socialism'. A huge range of opinion on the question was reflected at the Congress. Evgenii Preobrazhenskii, representing the left wing of the Bolshevik party, took a harder line than Stalin, arguing that nationalism could only be supported when it was directed against imperialism, and that in Soviet Russia it must be struggled against mercilessly since it was being used by bourgeois forces to undermine socialism. The Right SR L'vovich-Davidovich castigated Stalin for a 'speech that was saturated with the politics of centralism', arguing that the Austrian Social Democrats had tried and failed to subordinate national self-determination to class struggle. For his part, the anarcho-communist Ge demanded class self-determination not national self-determination, while for the Menshevik-Internationalists, Martov insisted that one could not dictate in advance that national minorities choose a soviet form of government.[47] All these views—including those of non-Bolsheviks—would influence party policy during the civil war.

The Bolsheviks recognized the independence of Finland, but were less willing to recognize that of the three Baltic states, not least because there were movements across the Baltic region—of varying strength—in support of soviet power. In Latvia, in particular, the Bolsheviks enjoyed considerable support in the working class. By February 1918 the Germans had occupied the whole of the territory and helped set up a nationalist government. At the end of 1918, the Red Army retook the country and installed Pēteris Stučka, a prominent jurist and educator, as head of a Latvian Soviet Republic. Despite having been a member of the Latvian New Current movement in the late nineteenth century, he showed little sympathy towards nationalist aspiration and his ultra-left policy of collectivizing land angered the rural population. In May 1919, Germans forces—allowed by the Allies to remain in the Baltic to help clear it of Reds—spearheaded the storming of Riga. This subsequently led to the restoration of a nationalist government under Karlis Ulmanis. In Estonia, where soviets ran many towns in 1918, Bolshevik indifference to nationalist sentiment, combined with their failure to expropriate the Baltic barons and their hostility to other parties, strengthened support for the nationalist assembly, the Maapäev. When the Red Army tried to invade in early 1919, the forces of the Maapäev, with assistance from Whites, British naval units, and Finnish volunteers, repelled them. In June 1919 a conflict flared up between German and Estonian forces which was quelled by British troops, keen to see German forces swept from the Baltic now that the Treaty of Versailles was signed. In February 1920 Soviet Russia recognized Estonia's independence, and in August 1920 the independence of Latvia, including its acquisition of the Latgale area.

In Belorussia and Lithuania the armistice with Germany left a power vacuum, in which Poles and Reds vied for control of a borderland where the population was neither predominantly Belorussian nor Lithuanian and had a strong admixture of Poles and Jews. In February 1918, the nationalist Taryba proclaimed a state of Lithuania with its capital at Vilnius in 'eternal and strong' association with Germany. The new state envisaged incorporation of most of the former Russian provinces of Vilna, Kaunas, Grodno, and Suwałki, an area in which Poles formed a strong minority. Its existence was imperilled first by the invasion of the Red Army in January 1919 and then by that of the West Russian Volunteer Army (a White Russian force backed by German Freikorps who had no intention of leaving the Baltic) in September 1919. In Belorussia the occupation by German troops during the Brest-Litovsk negotiations allowed the creation of a national government, but the peasantry, in contrast to its Ukrainian counterpart, lacked national consciousness, and once the Germans withdrew the government fell. On 1 January 1919 the Red Army set up a Belorussian Soviet Socialist Republic, but the western provinces of Mogilëv, Smolensk, and Vitebsk refused to be part of it. In March 1919 it was merged with Lithuania to form the Litbel soviet republic. In April, with the Polish–Soviet war under way, Poland occupied Vilnius, reinstated landowners, and made Polish the official language. Lithuanian nationalists, installed in Kaunas, though lacking a mass base, managed to take advantage of the war to declare an independent Lithuanian state, albeit within much reduced borders. In Belorussia the Red Army retook Minsk from the Poles in July 1920, but Belorussia continued to be a zone of conflict between the Poles and the Soviets until October, when a Belorussian Soviet Republic was formed.[48]

If the Bolsheviks could live with the loss of many parts of the former empire, the secession of Ukraine was something they could not easily contemplate, since it was hard to envisage a viable soviet regime that was deprived of access to the immense cereal resources and mining and metallurgical industries of what many Bolsheviks considered 'South Russia'. In Ukraine today historians argue that Great Russian chauvinism coloured the whole of Bolshevik policy towards Ukraine in this period, but it should be noted that some of the most implacable opponents of Ukrainian autonomy were themselves Ukrainian. After October, faced by Red forces bent on setting up a soviet government in Khar'kiv in the east, the Rada turned to Germany for help. The Reichswehr pushed out the Reds, but then proceeded to dissolve the moderate socialist Rada and impose a 'hetmanate' under Skoropads'kii. Following the withdrawal of Germany, a largely peasant army swept Petliura into power allowing him to set up a Directory in Kyiv. Its record was unimpressive. Squeezed between Reds to the north and the Volunteer Army to the south, weakened by personal and political rivalries, the Directory was driven out of Kyiv on 4 February 1919 by the Red Army. Petliura fled to Vinnitsa where he formed a more right-wing regime purged of Social Democrats and Socialist Revolutionaries. The second soviet government from February to August 1919 revealed just how hostile many leftist Bolsheviks were towards Ukrainian national aspirations, and a disastrous campaign of Russification deepened splits within the feeble Ukrainian Communist Party. By May 1919 Ukraine was in turmoil. Villages turned in upon themselves out of self-protection, while armed peasant bands roamed the countryside, led by warlords, who fought for control of territory in the name of the peasant revolution. Unable to get a grip on the chaotic situation, the soviet government was toppled by Denikin, which allowed Petliura once again to resume power. However, divisions within nationalist ranks were widening. Those in eastern Galicia, historically part of the Austro-Hungarian empire, had joined a 'united Ukraine' in 1919, but then opted to support the Whites rather than the Poles with whom Petliura had made a deal. By June 1920, as a consequence of the Russo-Polish war, a third soviet government gained full control of Ukraine. Thanks to Lenin's intervention in December 1919, Russian chauvinists had been removed from the leadership of the Ukrainian party, and the absorption of the Borot'bisty, a left-wing splinter from the Ukrainian SRs, finally gave the party cadres who could speak Ukrainian and who had some understanding of the needs of the peasantry.

No fewer than nine different governments came and went in the space of three years in Ukraine, testifying to the inability of any one political force to take decisive control. Caught between Reds and Whites, the various nationalist administrations were forced to seek protection from Germany, the Entente, or Poland. Themselves torn by division, and increasingly at odds with an insurgent peasantry, nationalists by 1920 could be under no illusions about their fundamental weakness. Yet the experience of independent statehood, however brief and conditional, strengthened identification with the Ukrainian nation, especially on the part of the peasantry. The Bolsheviks gained Ukraine by military not political means—as a result of three major campaigns—and their claims to offer self-determination proved distinctly hollow until 1920, when the Ukrainian Communist Party finally learned some unpalatable lessons. Yet more radical nationalists, recognizing that in a less than ideal world they must defer to one superior force or another, opted in the end for the Ukrainian Soviet Socialist Republic, since that alone offered a genuine degree of political autonomy, however much it was ultimately on Moscow's terms. This set a pattern that was replicated elsewhere.

Ukraine was the region of the former empire with the heaviest concentration of Jews, some 9 per cent of the population. They chiefly comprised artisans, traders, tavern keepers, and estate managers. Relations between Jews and the Ukrainian peasantry were laden with tension. Although the

Rada offered Jews personal-national autonomy, Jews were unenthusiastic about independence, fearing that Ukrainian 'separatism' would split the Jewish community of the former empire, interrupt trade with Russia, and foment prejudice. Jews would suffer massively as civil war whipped up antisemitism. In 1903 Lenin had declared that 'the idea of a Jewish nationality runs counter to the interests of the Jewish proletariat', and assimilated Jews in the Bolshevik leadership, such as Trotsky, Zinoviev, Kamenev, and Sverdlov, shared his animus against Zionism and separate organization of Jewish workers. Nevertheless amid an intensifying climate of antisemitism, the party agreed in January 1918 to the creation of a Jewish Commissariat and later to Jewish sections within the party. Formerly barred from public office and on average more literate than the Russian population, Jews were over-represented in the soviet, party, and Cheka, and it was their new public visibility that helped to inflame anti-Jewish hostility. The civil war inspired a massacre of Jews on a ghastly, historically unprecedented scale, with the loss of between 50,000 and 200,000 lives. Another 200,000 Jews were injured and thousands of women were raped. Some in the local soviets were even boiled alive ('communist soup'). Most of the perpetrators were soldiers of Petliura's armies, Whites, or camp followers of the various warlords.[49] Red Army soldiers—notably Budënnyi's cavalrymen—were certainly responsible for some pogroms, but the generally better record of the Red Army was a key reason why many in the Bund and the other Jewish socialist parties came over to the Bolsheviks.

Cossacks, as the backbone of the White forces, failed to make the transition from being a social estate to becoming an ethnically defined group. Following the Bolshevik seizure of power, the Volunteer Army looked to create a social base among the Cossacks, principally among those of the Don and Kuban—the two largest of the eleven Cossack 'hosts'. The ruthlessness of the Red forces which invaded the Don in spring 1918, and the increasingly bitter war over land between Cossacks and peasant incomers, strengthened Cossack allegiance to the anti-Bolshevik camp. However, Cossack society had become differentiated socially, and one-fifth of all Cossacks under arms actually fought with the Reds. Nevertheless by summer

1918, 50,000 Cossacks had answered the call to arms from ataman Krasnov, who was now committed to complete independence. The Bolsheviks were absolutely unwilling to make any concession to Cossack autonomy. In their eyes, the Cossacks were not a nation in the making, but a superannuated estate, economically privileged by virtue of their military service to the old regime. The conflict in the Don region was ferocious. Nevertheless, it is noteworthy that much of the violence perpetrated by Krasnov while he was in control of the Don from May 1918 to February 1919 was targeted at fellow Cossacks (estimates of the number killed range from 25,000 to 45,000).[50] Indeed it was rebellion within his own ranks that enabled the Reds to re-enter the territory in January 1919. Any shift in sentiment towards the Reds, however, was soon snuffed out by the chilling order of 24 January 'to carry out mass terror against wealthy Cossacks, eliminating them to a man, and to conduct merciless mass terror in relation to all Cossacks who have participated directly or indirectly in the struggle against Soviet power'. Several thousand were slaughtered, and the terror provoked an uprising by some 15,000 in March. The Bolsheviks quickly withdrew the order, but too late to prevent the Red Army from being swept out of the Don region in June.[51] Following their military defeat, the Cossacks were deprived of the right to political autonomy and tens of thousands were forcibly deported to Kazakhstan, the Urals, and Ukraine.

The collapse of the Caucasian Front at the end of 1917 undermined tenuous Bolshevik support in that region. In November a Transcaucasian Sejm (parliament) was set up in Tbilisi, headed by the former chair of the Petrograd Soviet, Chkheidze, based mainly on the Georgian Mensheviks and the Musavat, the moderate Azerbaijani Muslim party. The declaration of independence by the Sejm on 10 February 1918 gained only lukewarm support from the SRs and the Armenian Revolutionary Federation, the Dashnaktsutyun, who were alarmed at the rapid advance of Ottoman forces into the Caucasus and felt that their best protection lay in preserving the alliance with Russia. In Baku, the sole outpost of Soviet power, Bolsheviks and Dashnaks joined forces in March 1918 to defend the soviet against the Musavat, slaughtering several thousand Muslims. When the Turks finally seized Baku in September, Azerbaijanis took revenge, massacring 10,000 Armenians. British forces fled the city. The Georgians turned to Germany for protection, offering substantial economic and political concessions in return for recognition. At the last meeting of the Sejm on 26 May 1918, Tsereteli declared Transcaucasian unity a fiction and its three constituent peoples formed independent republics.

Independent Azerbaijan proved politically unstable from the first: nationalist politicians had little support from the peasantry, whose supra-local identity was with the universal community of Islam, and in Baku nationalist sentiment took second place to class sentiment. Isolation from Russian and foreign markets caused a fall in oil revenues, which led to high unemployment and rocketing inflation. Following the defeat of Turkey in the First World War, the Azerbaijani government looked to the British for protection, and once the latter withdrew from Transcaucasia in August 1919, it was left vulnerable. For its part, independent Armenia began its existence in a catastrophic condition. Confined to a small landlocked territory around Erevan, which was contested by all its neighbours, it faced an inundation of refugees and a population racked by starvation and disease. The Dashnak government dropped its pretensions to socialism and formed a government of national emergency. Georgia proved to be the most viable of the three Caucasian states. In parliamentary elections in February 1919 the Mensheviks won 80 per cent of the vote. Despite facing fearsome economic problems, the government oversaw the formation of trades unions, cooperatives, and industrial arbitration courts and carried out a moderately successful land reform. The chief blot on its record lay in the brutality with which the Georgian National Guard treated ethnic minorities within its borders. Again, it relied on the protection of the British, who were keen to maintain control of the oil pipelines, and British withdrawal left independent Georgia vulnerable to a Soviet takeover.

The Bolsheviks were determined to regain Transcaucasia, not least because of its petroleum and mineral resources, and to counter British intervention. In late 1919 an Azerbaijani Communist Party was formed and the Caucasus regional committee, led by S. M. Kirov, funnelled millions of rubles into the region. In April 1920 an overwhelmingly Russian army invaded Azerbaijan. In Armenia Turkey retook territory ceded to Armenia by the Treaty of Sèvres, which ended the war between the Allies and the Ottoman empire. After failing to gain support from the Allies, the Dashnak leaders turned to the Bolsheviks, but within days of the Red Army's arrival, they were expelled from government. In May 1920 the Bolsheviks recognized the independence of Georgia, but Sergo Orjonikidze, backed by Stalin, pressed for the overthrow of the Menshevik government. Defying orders from Moscow 'not to self-determine Georgia', the Red Army marched into the country in January 1921. Throughout Transcaucasia civil war, economic collapse, and inter-ethnic conflict undermined moderate socialism and nullified moves to multi-national cooperation. All three states came into existence at a time when their sovereignty was rocked by internecine disputes over territory, and all looked to the protection of stronger powers, whether the Turks, the Germans, the British, or Soviet Russia. Unable to withstand external pressure, many nationalists in Azerbaijan and Armenia came in 1920 to see the formation of their own soviet autonomies as the least bad option for national self-determination.

On 24 November 1917, the Bolsheviks invited Muslims to order their national life 'freely and without hindrance'. A year later, they set up a Central Bureau of Muslim Communist Organizations to carry revolution to the Muslim peoples of the former empire. In the course of 1917 jadidist intellectuals had faced mounting opposition to their programme of reform from the conservative mullahs and, following the October Revolution, many looked to achieve national salvation through popular mobilization. The publication by the Bolsheviks of the secret treaties between Russia and the Allies served to shift their politics from liberal constitutionalism to anti-imperialism.[52] Nationalist sentiment was fluid with respect to the desired form of political autonomy. Most jadids envisaged a single Turkic-Muslim nation based on a large swathe of territory in Turkestan and Bukhara. Such pan-Turkism was most developed among Volga Tatar intellectuals, merchants, and mullahs, the most wealthy, educated, and urbanized of the empire's Muslim communities. A pan-Turkic state under Tatar dominance, however, was not to the liking of the Bashkirs in the Urals. And in Central Asia pan-Turkism did not appeal to Persian-speaking peoples and nomadic groups such as the Turkmen, Kazakh, Kyrghyz, or Karakalpak. But it was Tatar jadids, such as Mirsaid Sultangaliev and Mullanur Vakhitov (shot by the Czechs in August 1918), who were the most sophisticated nationalists among the Muslim populations. Faced with a barely existent proletariat and a semi-nomadic populace, they formed a Muslim Red Army with a view to creating a Tatar-Bashkir state stretching from the mid-Volga to the Urals. In July 1918 its 50,000 members were incorporated into the Red Army. These Muslim units, in which soldiers were taught to read in Tatar, were seen as proof of Bolshevik commitment to self-determination.

Everywhere in the Muslim areas Russian settlers were at the forefront of establishing soviet power and they evinced a classically colonialist attitude towards the indigenous population. In February 1918, for example, the Kazan' Soviet crushed efforts by moderate nationalists to form a Tatar-Bashkir state. In Turkestan, in particular, racism ran rampant. In the Fergana valley, following the Bolshevik seizure of power, the jadidist Shura-i-Islam and the conservative clerical Uläma Jamiyäti formed a Turkestan Autonomous Government in Kokand, but the Russian-dominated Turkestan Council of People's Commissars in Tashkent refused to recognize it. On 5 February 1918 the Council sent Red forces to Kokand, where the moderate government was resisting 'soviet power', and put the city to the torch, slaughtering almost 60 per cent of the population. Elsewhere in the Fergana valley armed Russian settlers terrorized the natives. In late April an alarmed Moscow sent P. A. Kobozev to form a Turkestan Autonomous Socialist Republic which, though Russian-dominated, included ten liberal or radical Muslims. Yet the policies pursued by the Autonomous Republic of seizing land belonging to religious endowments (*waqf*) and closing religious schools and sharia courts did little to win the support of the native population.[53]

Among the Bashkirs in the Urals a small nationalist movement had emerged in 1917, led by a young scholar and moderate socialist, Ahmed Zeki Validov. This aspired to differentiate Bashkirs ethnically from their close Tatar neighbours by stressing their nomadic past and their former status as a Cossack host. These Bashkir nationalists resented the move by the Soviets in March 1918 to set up a Tatar-Bashkir Soviet Republic—a pre-emptive move designed to thwart an attempt by anti-Bolshevik forces to set up a Volga-Ural state. In reaction, they allied with the Orenburg Cossacks, and later with the 'democratic counter-revolution'. Following Kolchak's abolition of Bashkir territorial autonomy, however, Validov and his men came to an agreement with the Bolsheviks, and in March 1919 were granted a Bashkir Autonomous Soviet Socialist Republic (ASSR), the first such award by the Bolsheviks of autonomy on the basis of a clearly defined territory. By June 1920, however, in disgust at the continuing interference by Russian settlers and Red Army soldiers in Bashkir self-government, Validov went off and joined the guerrillas (*basmachi*).[54]

In the Kazakh steppes the jadids who led the nationalist Alash Orda, which was close in its politics to the Kadets, proclaimed Kazakh autonomy in December 1917 in Orenburg, which was also the centre of Bashkir nationalism. The Red Army's advance along the Orenburg–Tashkent railway caused the Alash to split between a western group in Orenburg, who allied with anti-Bolshevik Bashkirs, and an eastern group who eventually joined up with Kolchak's forces in Omsk. By spring 1919, however, Kolchak's hostility to nationalist aspirations swung Alash Orda towards a compromise with the Bolsheviks. In March 1920 the Kyrghyz (i.e. Kazakh) Revolutionary Committee dismantled the Alash Orda government and in August a Kazakh ASSR—confusingly named Kyrghyz—was formed, in which Alash Orda leaders were influential. This gave Kazakhs their own political community for the first time and clan and village structures were reconfigured in the guise of soviets. In 1925 it was renamed the Kazakh ASSR.

As this suggests, as the Red Army began to gain the upper hand in the civil war, the Bolsheviks could afford to be more accommodating towards nationalist movements. This, together with the dispiriting experience of White policies, pushed many Muslim nationalists back towards the Reds. In Crimea the left wing of Milli Firka, the Muslim nationalist grouping, joined the Communist Party, and after Wrangel's exodus and the Cheka's extermination of political opponents, a Crimean Tatar ASSR was proclaimed in

October 1921. Meanwhile among the Tatars of the middle Volga an ASSR was formed in May 1920, though some three-quarters of Tatars in the region were outside its borders. The supporters of Sultangaliev, who formed the core of the Tatarstan Communist Party, emerged as the most adept exponents of 'national communism'. This combined jadidist opposition to conservative clerical forces, a desire for modernity, and Leninist anti-imperialism. Galiev argued that Muslim society, not yet being class-divided, occupied a position analogous to that of the proletariat, thus subtly eliding the concepts of an oppressed class and an oppressed nation (his concept of the nation playing on the familiar Islamic concept of *'umma*, or commonwealth of believers). Commenting on his speech to the Second Congress of Peoples of the East in December 1919, the journal of the Commissariat of Nationalities noted disapprovingly: 'The impression was created that comrades might be proposing the East was virgin land more receptive to the ideas of communism than the decadent West.'[55] Despite the whiff of heresy that clung to them, 'national communists' succeeded for a while in abrogating the legislation confiscating *waqf* lands, closing religious schools, and abolishing sharia courts. By 1923, however, Stalin felt strong enough to bring them to heel and Sultangaliev was thrown into jail. Trotsky would later repent of the fact that he played an inglorious part in securing this outcome.[56]

In Turkestan, as the civil war drew to a close, the situation remained fraught. By 1919 in the Fergana valley more than 20,000 natives had joined a surging guerrilla movement, known as *basmachi*, in response to the abuses of Russian settlers. The unpopular policies of the Moscow-backed Turkestan Autonomous Socialist Republic were tempered when Turar Ryskulov, scion of a Kazakh aristocratic family, was installed as its head in July 1920. However, the sovereignty of the Republic was compromised when Moscow placed the task of quelling the *basmachi* in the hands of a Turkestan Commission, which was accountable directly to the Council of People's Commissars in Moscow. The situation in Turkestan was further complicated by the continuing existence of the emirates of Khiva, Bukhara, and Kokand. In September 1920 Red Army forces under Frunze expelled the amir of Bukhara, which gave a further boost to the guerrilla movement. The latter soon acquired an Islamist coloration, partly under Sufi influence. Meanwhile the Khwarezm (Khiva) and Bukhara people's republics were established, which were not called 'Socialist', in view of their pre-industrial economies. By 1921, the Red Army appeared to be gaining the upper hand over the guerrillas, but the movement was revitalized in November 1921 when former Ottoman War Minister Enver Paşa, architect of the Armenian genocide, after a brief dalliance with the Bolsheviks, joined it. By late 1923 the guerrillas in Fergana had been pacified, but it was two more years before the *basmachi* strongholds in Bukhara were smashed. A further complicating factor was the struggle between those, like Ryskulov, who favoured a pan-Turkic solution to the national question and those who wished to see the vast territory of Turkestan divided into ethnically based territorial states. The latter won out and in 1924 the Turkestan ASSR was divided into the autonomous soviet socialist republics of Uzbekistan and Turkmenistan and the autonomous republics of Tadzhikistan and Kazakhstan.

In October 1917 it looked as though the Russian empire was destined to go the way of its Austro-Hungarian and Ottoman counterparts. Yet by 1922 the Bolsheviks had reconquered most of the former tsarist empire, the Soviet state being shorn of 818,000 sq. km (3.7 per cent) of pre-war territory and 31–32 million people. The logic of Soviet expansion, however, had been determined not by the dynamic of international revolution but by the contingencies of war and by the wider geopolitical and security considerations that had governed the growth of the tsarist state. Following the largely peaceful takeover of Azerbaijan by the Red Army on 28 April 1920, Lenin wrote: 'The Baku proletariat has taken power in its hands and overthrown the Azerbaijani government.' In fact, everywhere it was the army, not the proletariat, which served as the agent carrying the Revolution forward, something Lenin tacitly recognized when he supported intervention in Persia or plans to capture Constantinople in 1921. This, however, did not make the Bolsheviks old-style imperialists. Despite the racism of Russian settlers in the borderlands, who were the mainstay of soviets in the large urban centres, internationalism was at the heart of Soviet policy in this period and it is impossible to explain the energy with which the government established alliances with national movements if one assumes that its objective was simply to re-establish a Russian empire. It is true that self-determination for non-Russian minorities was a policy objective that took second place to the practical exigencies of suppressing anti-Bolshevik movements, ensuring the operational effectiveness of the Red Army, or securing food. Moreover, hostility to self-determination in some sections of the party, along with the ability of local actors to thwart the best-laid plans of the centre, meant that policy on national self-determination was subject to improvisation and to sharp changes of tack. Haphazardly, however, Moscow succeeded in restructuring the former empire as a federation of soviet republics constituted along ethno-national lines, each with its own territory, starting with the Bashkir ASSR in February 1919. For the Bolshevik leadership such a system came to seem the optimal means of reconciling the centrifugal impulses of nationalism with the centralizing impulse of the dictatorship of the proletariat.

Overall, the civil war had intensified nationalist sentiment; yet it had also deepened divisions within nationalist ranks. There were huge differences in the degree of socio-economic development of the different non-Russian areas and thus in the degree to which they were amenable to class or nationalist politics. Nationalist movements generally lacked solid popular support (although there were exceptions, such as Georgia) and were forced to compete with political movements that appealed to class. Even in Ukraine, where a majority of the population by 1920 regarded themselves as Ukrainian, national identity proved incapable of transcending class divisions. Recognizing their weakness, nationalist movements turned at different times to the Reds or Whites, to the Allies or to Germany, to Turkey or to Poland. This surrender to superior force further exacerbated political divisions within nationalist ranks. Despite egregious instances of Russian chauvinism practised by Bolsheviks on the ground, and despite the fact that 'class self-determination' always counted for more than national self-determination, it is fair to say that by the end of the civil war, the Bolsheviks offered nationalists far more than was on offer from their adversaries, even if this was less than many would have liked (although it is worth remembering that in 1917 few nationalists had aspired to complete national independence).

Violence and Terror

On 7 December 1917 the Council of People's Commissars set up an emergency commission to 'liquidate all attempts and acts of counter-revolution and sabotage'.[57] This commission, known as the Cheka, quickly became a key organ of government—far more powerful than the underfunded and poorly organized police force known as the civil militia. Though its overwhelming priority was to crush counter-revolution, the Cheka was involved in everything from combating speculative trade to caring for orphans. By 1921, 60,000 personnel worked for the organization. The threat of counter-revolutionary conspiracy was real. The Right Centre, formed in spring 1918, brought together monarchists and right Kadets, who plotted to restore the monarchy. Its pro-German orientation, however, caused a majority to leave to form the National Centre, which looked to a military dictatorship to save Russia. Left Kadets, unhappy at their party's reactionary orientation, turned to the SRs and formed the Union for the Regeneration of Russia. In March 1918, the former SR terrorist Boris Savinkov created the Union of Defence of the Motherland and Freedom, based on guards officers, which launched uprisings in Iaroslavl', Rybinsk, and Murom. From 1920 its successor, based in Warsaw, received funding from the Polish and French governments. Many of these counter-revolutionary groups had only a tenuous existence, and many of their conspiracies were risible affairs, abysmally led, and poorly funded. Nevertheless the fact that they existed was a source of acute anxiety to a regime that was very far from being secure.

The Cheka's mission to hunt down counter-revolution placed it outside the crumbling framework of law, although it was never completely unaccountable for its actions. According to its own statistics, in 1918–19 the Cheka arrested 128,010 people in the Russian Soviet Federative Socialist Republic

(RSFSR), of whom 42.4 per cent were released, 28.5 per cent imprisoned, 10.9 per cent sent to concentration camps, 7.5 per cent shot, 7.5 per cent taken hostage, and 3.2 per cent sent to do hard labour. Of the 9,641 shot—a considerable underestimate of the true figure—7,068 were found guilty of counter-revolution, 632 of abusing their positions of authority, 217 of speculation, and 1,204 of criminal activity.[58] Throughout the civil war, leading Bolsheviks regularly expressed concern that the Cheka was out of control. Executive committees of provincial and city soviets were loud in their denunciations of an overweening body that showed them contempt (from Pskov: 'they bring nothing but harm to the revolution. They have the character of institutions behind walls that violate all human norms, and even have a despotic-monarchist character').[59] In 1919 it was deprived of the power to carry out death sentences in areas not under military jurisdiction, but within four months that power had been reinstated. Every bid to curb the Cheka failed, not least because of Lenin's refusal to accept that institutional checks and balances were a necessary means to inhibit lawlessness and corruption within the emerging state.

Nauseated by the hypocrisy of bourgeois governments that talked about morality yet sent millions to their deaths, and inspired by the example of the French Revolution, the Bolsheviks insisted that terror was a legitimate means to defend the dictatorship of the proletariat. Initially, the hope was that terror would be used only as a last resort. Yet as early as January 1918 Lenin warned ominously that 'until we use terror against speculators—shooting them on the spot—nothing will happen', prompting the Left SR I. N. Steinberg to ask, if that were the case, why he was needed as Commissar of Justice. As civil war escalated, inhibitions about the unrestrained use of violence lessened on all sides. During the first Kuban' campaign Kornilov told the Volunteer Army, 'Take no prisoners. The greater the terror, the greater will be our victory.' But it was only with the near-fatal attack on Lenin on 30 August 1918 that the Bolsheviks elevated terror to official policy. In Petrograd the leading Bolshevik newspaper shrieked: 'For the blood of Lenin...let there be floods of blood of the bourgeoisie—more blood, as much as possible.' Five hundred hostages were shot at once—in alphabetical order—on the orders of Zinoviev. One scholar estimates that between October 1917 and February 1922, 280,000 were killed either by the Cheka or the Internal Security Troops, about half of them in the course of operations to suppress peasant uprisings.[60] This would suggest that perhaps 140,000 were executed directly by the Cheka—a bloodcurdling number, to be sure, but it should be compared with the 50,000 to 200,000 Jews killed at this time in pogroms in Ukraine and Belorussia and the 200,000 who were forced to flee to Poland.

Even allowing for the savagery that is intrinsic to all civil wars, the brutality of the Cheka vitiated the Bolshevik claim to stand for a higher ethical principle than their opponents. Those accused of counter-revolutionary crimes were supposed to be subject to a trial, but some local organs did not scruple to execute opponents on the spot. The assumption that any means was justified in the fight to the death with the Whites quickly became entrenched.[61] G. A. Atarbekov, an Armenian Old Bolshevik who had had legal training at Moscow University, provides an extreme example of how fear of counter-revolution fostered moral degeneration. At the beginning of 1919, as the Eleventh Red Army and the Caspian-Caucasian Front disintegrated, he was promoted by Sergei Kirov to head the Cheka in Astrakhan', a fishing port of vital strategic importance in preventing any link-up between the forces of Kolchak and Denikin. The supply situation was utterly desperate, made worse by the arrival of demoralized Red Army soldiers; and on 6 March the Military-Revolutionary Committee set up to rule the town cut the bread ration to 400 grams. This provoked a strike which caused Atarbekov to place the port under siege on 10 March. All strikers who refused to return to work had their ration books cancelled. According to the official version of events, a striker fired on a cordon of sailors, causing them to open fire on demonstrators, killing as many as 200. This triggered an armed rebellion by workers, led by a Cossack officer. In the face of this 'White' threat, Red Army soldiers launched an artillery bombardment of three working-class districts, killing perhaps as many as 1,000; 184 strikers' leaders were subsequently shot.[62] Over the next couple of months, Atarbekov seems to have succumbed to paranoia about a 'White Guard plot', and presided over the shooting or drowning of up to 4,000 people, including fishermen who were accused of plotting the destruction of the Volga-Caspian flotilla at Aleksandrovsk. K. Ia. Grasis, a political commissar in the Cheka, recorded 'the discontent with the current power that exists among the local population, especially Kalmyks and Kyrghyz, as a result of the unheard-of violence and contempt of the commissars'. On 4 September, Atarbekov was summoned to Moscow, but after a long investigation, his supporters, who included Kirov, Kamo (Simon Ter-Petrosian), and Stalin, ensured not only that he went unpunished but that he was promoted.[63]

Because it was never official policy, White terror has received less attention than its Red counterpart; yet violence unconstrained by law was practised by all sides, including the SR-dominated governments of summer 1918. Whereas in theory Red terror was 'bureaucratic', carried out by professionals usually after the formalities of a trial, much White terror was the consequence of officers allowing their men to go on the rampage. Among the most wanton perpetrators were the 'atamans' of the Far East: the 'bloody baron', von Ungern Sternberg, who unleashed a reign of terror across the Amur and Ussuri regions, and Grigorii Semënov, who boasted of personally supervising the torture of 6,500 people. The logic of terror ratcheted ever upwards, both symptom and cause of a general brutalization that affected all sides. On 29 April 1920 General Wrangel ordered 'the merciless shooting of all commissars and communists taken prisoner', prompting Trotsky to issue his own order for the 'extermination one by one of all members of Wrangel's command staff, caught bearing arms'. When Wrangel's forces were swept out of the Crimea in the autumn, the Military-Revolutionary Council of the Fourth Army initially promised an amnesty to those who had served in the White army and who registered with the authorities. This relatively humane policy was cancelled when Rozaliia Zemliachka, Bela Kun, and others arrived from Moscow in mid-November, bent on purifying the peninsula of all 'class aliens'. Sultangaliev, one of a commission sent from Moscow to investigate the bloodbath that ensued, reported that 20,000 to 25,000 White officers were shot, but added that locals—soon full of hate for their new rulers—put the true figure at nearer 70,000, three-quarters of these being working people.[64] Wrangel's officers had never been squeamish in carrying out reprisals against Reds—General Ia. A. Slashchёv, for instance, was a notorious butcher—but such slaughter was unparalleled in its magnitude and, moreover, took place after the fighting was over.

Not all 'Red' terror emanated from the Bolsheviks. Colonel M. A. Murav'ёv, formerly an officer on the south-western front, came over to the Left SRs following the Kornilov rebellion. He led the defence of Petrograd against the forces of Kerensky and Krasnov in October. Although he may not be considered typical of officers fighting for the Reds—he was soon implicated in the Left SR rebellion in July 1918 (see below: 'The Suppression of the Socialist Opposition')—Murav'ёv wreaked terror when taking Kyiv for the Red forces in January 1918. The Red Cross estimated that up to 5,000 were killed, including 3,000 officers. Some 15,000 shells destroyed key buildings and a 'contribution' of 5 million rubles was exacted from the 'bourgeoisie' of the Ukrainian capital. A detester of Ukrainian nationalism, Murav'ёv oversaw the liquidation not only of 'counter-revolutionaries' but of 'Austrian spies' and 'Mazepan traitors' (Ivan Mazępa, ataman of Ukraine, had risen up against Peter the Great, in alliance with Charles XII of Sweden, in 1708). Following his arrest in April 1918 he wrote:

> We establish Soviet power with fire and sword. I took the city (Kyiv) and wreaked havoc on the palaces and churches…showing mercy to no one. On 28 January the Duma asked for a truce. In response I ordered them to be choked with gas. Hundreds, perhaps thousands of generals were killed without mercy…Thus did we take our revenge. We could have stopped the fury of revenge, but we didn't, because our slogan was 'Be Merciless!'[65]

Murav'ёv's hyperbole unwittingly echoed the words of former tsarist Chief of Staff Ianushkevich who, when asked by the Minister of Agriculture about the devastation wrought in Galicia in 1915, replied: 'War proceeds by fire and sword, and whoever happens to get in the way must suffer.'

Like Murav'ёv, a large proportion of combatants in the civil war had been conscripts in the tsarist army. It is thus tempting to argue that the First World War produced 'brutalization', which in turn produced unparalleled levels of political violence once the tsarist regime broke down. A note of caution, however, is called for. Certainly, the violence of the First World War had inured men to sickening levels of brutality but what was crucial was the ability of the state to preserve its domestic monopoly of violence. Most First World War combatants, once removed from combat, settled back into civilian life without too much strain, and in some countries such as Britain (with the notable exception of Ireland) the level of violence decreased after 1918. Civil war violence grew out of the violence of the First World War, but it had features that are better explained in terms of a situation of revolution and counter-revolution and of the collapse of social order.[66] In addition, some of the violence was of a type that had antecedents that went back long before 1914. The pogroms in 1919, for example, were the third such wave of anti-Jewish violence since 1881–4 and 1905–6, although on an altogether unprecedented scale and now galvanized by revolutionary and counter-revolutionary fear and revenge. More generally, much popular violence had little connection either with the First World War or with the Revolution, but derived from the disintegration of 'settled patterns of quotidian authority', from a situation that allowed pre-existing social tensions, community rivalries, and the desperate struggle for scarce resources to find violent expression.[67]

Some historians stress the 'modernity' of violence in the civil war. They see the First World War as a watershed that led to a massive expansion and militarization of practices designed to shape the 'social body', practices such as categorization, information gathering, policing, incarceration, and deportation, which had their origins in the nineteenth century.[68] In such episodes as 'de-Cossackization' in March 1919, civil war violence appears to arise not so much from the drive to crush political enemies as from an aspiration to create a society purged of contaminating elements.[69] The tell-tale word used in connection with de-Cossackization was *istreblenie*, 'annihilation' or 'extermination', which seems horribly to anticipate events of two decades later. The word crops up in other contexts too. When Komuch forces seized Kazan' on 7 August 1918 and executed scores of Soviet sympathizers, Lenin wrote to Trotsky: 'In my opinion it is wrong to spare the city and delay things further, because merciless annihilation (*istreblenie*) is essential once Kazan' is in an iron ring.'[70] Mercifully, this did not actually happen. How far such words were literal in intent is unclear, but even if figurative they adumbrate the grisly practices of later totalitarian regimes. Nevertheless violence designed to eliminate entire groups perceived to be socially harmful—through mass deportation, for example—was not a common phenomenon, though 'bourgeois elements' or 'aristocrats' were subject to discrimination, internment, and, occasionally, execution.

So far as forms of warfare were concerned, the civil was far less 'modern' than the First World War. To be sure armoured trains, bearing two to four 3- to 6-inch artillery pieces plus four to sixteen machine guns, were deployed. The Reds initially had an advantage in this area, although by mid-1919 the Whites had bridged the gap, thanks to the Allies. The Allies also supplied the Armed Forces of Southern Russia with tanks, a weapon that the Reds lacked, but tank warfare remained limited. Both sides did engage in aerial bombardment —for example during the battle for Kazan' in August and September 1918 —but generally aerial warfare was limited and neither side used poison gas.[71] Use of such weaponry indicates some continuity of military practice with the First World War, but most of the fighting was different in character: a war of manoeuvre, entailing much advance and retreat along railways and reliance on the mobility provided by cavalry. And despite the high-tech nature of some of the weaponry used, the civil war more commonly relied on close combat, using the rifle or sabre.

The Suppression of the Socialist Opposition

During the civil war the socialist and anarchist parties proved unable to mount a concerted challenge to the Bolsheviks.[72] This is often ascribed solely to Bolshevik repression, but though this was the prime factor, it too easily exonerates the opposition for its failures. The SRs were by far the biggest threat to the Bolsheviks, and after the dissolution of the Constituent Assembly the 'centre' of the party was increasingly outstripped by its right wing, which advocated armed resistance to the new regime. Following the revolt of the Czech Legion, the SRs as a whole swung behind that policy. Kolchak's overthrow of the Omsk Directory, however, caused the majority to distance itself from armed rebellion.[73] Indeed, in the wake of the revolution in Germany, the SR Central Committee came to the view that a transition to socialism based on cooperatives and collective forms of ownership was on the cards. In late November 1918, hard on the Red defeat at Perm', the Bolsheviks began to make overtures to the SRs. In late February 1919, after the party proclaimed itself a 'third force' and renounced armed struggle against the Bolshevik dictatorship, the party was legalized. Because the party's newspaper continued to denounce the regime, however, relations remained extremely strained. Each rapprochement proved short-lived. In May 1919 the SR Central Committee agreed to prioritize the battle against the Whites and to postpone armed struggle against the Bolsheviks. However, its hold over its provincial organizations was weak: in Kyiv the local party actively supported Denikin and was expelled, whilst in Siberia SRs collaborated with Bolsheviks and were censured by the centre. By this stage, most SRs accepted that the priority was the contest against the Whites, but they were unable to agree as to whether this required the suspension of struggle against the Bolsheviks. The attempt to act as a 'third force' ended in failure, and by 1920 the majority of the SR Central Committee were in jail.

For several months after October the Mensheviks were convinced that the Bolsheviks could not retain power. Their disastrous showing in the Constituent Assembly election and their rapidly falling membership (from around 150,000 in December to less than 40,000 by late 1918) to some degree lessened divisions within the party.[74] The 'centre' led by Dan, and the left led by Martov, rejected armed struggle and sought to create a strong working-class movement that could press for civil liberties and democratic government. In summer 1918, however, a handful of Mensheviks entered the anti-Bolshevik governments in Samara, Omsk, Ekaterinburg, and Baku, including Ivan Maisky who would later be Soviet ambassador to the United Kingdom. Following Kolchak's coup, the Mensheviks rallied in support of the Red Army which they now saw as 'the defender of the revolution' and railed against the

Allies for their failure to leave Russia. For the first three months of 1919, the party operated largely legally, but Menshevik determination to support strikers and to revitalize the soviets and the trade unions brought them into regular collision with the Cheka. By autumn 1921, the national membership of the Mensheviks was about 4,000, but in a few places, such as Tula, they remained dominant in the city soviet despite every Bolshevik ploy.[75] And Menshevik groups continued to be uncovered through the 1920s.

Incensed by the Treaty of Brest-Litovsk, the Left SRs withdrew from the Council of People's Commissars, which thus reverted to being a one-party body. But local cooperation with Bolsheviks, for example, in the Council of Commissars of the Northern Oblast', continued for a couple more months. The announcement of a 'food dictatorship' in May alienated the party still further. On 4 July the Left SR Central Committee authorized the assassination of the German ambassador in the hope that this would reignite the war with Germany. Two days later, Iakov Bliumkin, a high-ranking Cheka operative, slew Wilhelm von Mirbach, and this was followed on 30 July by the assassination of Field Marshal von Eichhorn in Kyiv. When the Bolsheviks arrested the Left SR fraction at the concurrent Fifth Congress of Soviets, its members retaliated by occupying the Cheka headquarters in Moscow and arresting Dzerzhinskii. This quixotic 'uprising' was designed more to force the Bolsheviks to break with 'opportunism' than to overthrow the regime, but it proved to be a self-destructive move. In June 1918 the Left SRs had nearly 100,000 members and, given their support in the countryside, had the potential to force a change of government policy, yet they managed to squander this advantage. Over the three months following the 'uprising' membership collapsed by two-thirds. By October, when the party's fourth congress took place, a bewildering number of splits had appeared in its ranks. The congress condemned the Bolsheviks for 'supplanting the dictatorship of toilers with a dictatorship of the Bolshevik party' and for creating 'corporate socialism'. Curiously, however, it did not seek to capitalize on the widespread peasant hostility to the food dictatorship, and a majority of the congress even approved the Bolshevik decision to set up committees of poor peasants in order to promote class struggle in the village, a policy that was already proving counter-productive. The congress rejected a policy of carrying out terrorist actions on Soviet soil, but in Ukraine Bliumkin was tasked with organizing partisan activity behind Petliura's lines, which was obviously of assistance to the Red Army. The redoubtable Spiridonova was unhappy at what she saw as the prioritization of the struggle against the Whites, but by April–May 1920 the majority of the Left SR Central Committee had come to reject armed struggle against the Bolsheviks. This did not prevent the latter from arresting the so-called 'activists' in Ukraine, once they retook control of the territory, and from banning a Left SR congress. This triggered a final, suicidal burst of activity on the part of a minority of partisans (who, inter alia, tried three times to assassinate Bliumkin who was now collaborating with the Bolsheviks). Yet the former Commissar of Justice, Steinberg, led the majority of the party towards a rapprochement with the regime and in October 1920 the party was briefly legalized.

The Bolsheviks viewed the socialist opposition parties with contempt, as opportunists at best and counter-revolutionary accomplices at worst. From the first Lenin was prepared to establish a one-party dictatorship if that was the only way to preserve 'soviet power'; but others in the leadership, such as Kamenev, recognized that soviets were quintessentially multi-party bodies, and took the commitment to soviet power much more seriously. However, as working-class opposition increased in spring 1918 and, above all, following the outbreak of full-scale civil war in May, even verbal criticism of the regime came to be seen as intolerable by many Bolsheviks. Seeing themselves as caught up in a life-and-death struggle to preserve the workers' state, any opposition appeared treacherous. At critical junctures, it is true, Bolshevik leaders did make tactical compromises, but never of a substantial or lasting kind. It is not hard to see why they should have distrusted those who claimed to prioritize the struggle against the Whites yet reserved the right to take up arms against the regime, or those who professed to support the regime yet subjected it to withering attack. As civil war intensified, what began mainly as pragmatic restriction on the opposition parties hardened into a principled rejection of the right of 'petty-bourgeois' parties to exist at all. One was either for or against the Bolshevik order. The result of the Bolshevik repression of the opposition can be seen in the dramatic fall in representation of the opposition parties in the soviets: from 14.2 per cent in 1918 to 0.2 per cent in 1920, to their total disappearance by 1922.[76] The Soviet experience has been confirmed by civil wars elsewhere, suggesting that the chances for 'third parties'—whether the anarchists or POUM in the Spanish Civil War or the Democratic League in China in the late 1940s—are slender to non-existent.

A partial exception to this were the anarchists, who fought bravely on the Red side during the civil war, while being swingeing in their criticism of the 'commissarocracy'. The influence of anarchists grew after October, but perhaps not surprisingly, they failed to develop sustained and effective organizations. Many criminal gangs filched the 'anarchist' label in the winter of 1917–18 and many anarchists were happy to operate in a semi-criminal milieu, as they appropriated private property at will. In April 1918 the Cheka forcibly disbanded 'black guards' in Petrograd, Moscow, Ekaterinoslav, and Vologda who had taken over valuable residences, and in Moscow the clash was bloody and led to the death of forty anarchists and about a dozen Chekists. More serious were the established anarchist groups, divided into two main ideological tendencies. A. A. Karelin convened the first congress of anarcho-communists in autumn 1918, and out of this emerged a federation of anarchist youth that sprouted branches in twenty-three towns. Generally better organized were the anarcho-syndicalists, who had enjoyed some influence in the labour movement in 1917. During the civil war, the Voice of Labour group, headed by G. P. Maksimov, fought to defend factory committees and free trade unions and held a series of conferences. However, the 'Free Voice of Labour' in Moscow was shut down because of its acerbic criticism of the Bolsheviks. Only in October 1920 was the All-Russian Federation of Anarcho-Syndicalists formally established. The heartland of anarchist activity was Ukraine, where Makhno's Revolutionary Insurgent Army of Ukraine, with its base in the fertile province of Ekaterinoslav, played a key role in fighting the Whites and Petliura. His army fought for free soviets, elected by all the toiling population and committed to carrying out a far-reaching social revolution. At different times his army fought for the Bolsheviks (thanks mainly to Red Commander V. A. Antonov-Ovseenko who, unlike Trotsky, considered them 'genuine fighters of the revolution'), at other times against. In Ukraine other influential anarchist groups included the Tocsin (Nabat) group in Kursk, led by V. M. Volin and P. A. Arshinov, which linked up with Makhno in a bid to create a united confederation of Ukrainian anarchist organizations. In Siberia and the Far East anarchists also formed the backbone of many Red partisan units.

The key responsibility for the creation of a one-party dictatorship lay with the Bolsheviks, yet the opposition parties bear a measure of responsibility for their own fate. After October they confronted a scenario for which their ideologies left them ill prepared, and they had difficulty orienting themselves to a situation where the ruling power claimed to be socialist. With the partial exception of the Mensheviks, the opposition proved unable to handle internal dissent or forge a unified policy, and the Cheka learned to exploit such divisions to its advantage. The left parties were also hampered by lack of finance. At the same time, in contrast to the Bolsheviks, they revealed how encumbered they were by the 'intelligentsia' psychology characteristic of the pre-revolutionary movement, with its predilection for talk over action. The result was that although popular disaffection was rife, only the Left SRs and Mensheviks managed to secure a foothold in leading strikes and peasant insurrections (and the latter only in winter 1920–1).

One-Party Dictatorship in Action

The outbreak of civil war made it imperative to reverse the extreme decentralization of power that had taken place in the first six months of 1918. According to the 1918 Constitution, the Soviet Central Executive Committee was the 'supreme legislative, administrative and controlling organ of the RSFSR', yet during its first year it ratified only 68 of the 480 decrees passed by the Council of People's Commissars. After the Mensheviks and SRs were expelled in June 1918, the CEC lost its role as a forum in which the opposition could make its voice heard and during 1919 it barely met. Soon a new Council of Workers' and Peasants' Defence came to overshadow the CEC, its founding decree of 30 November 1918 stating that its task was to coordinate the work of the economic agencies with the needs of defence. Lenin was its chairman, and it was this body that allowed him to put his ample organizational talents at the service of the war effort. Within the core area that remained under Bolshevik control, soviets, whose leading personnel were now appointed rather than elected, continued to be the bodies responsible for implementing the policies of the central ministries and higher party bodies. In the huge swathe of territory recaptured from the Whites or in areas close to the front, however, revolutionary committees, rather than soviets, became the supreme authority in military and civilian matters. These were emergency organs established on an ad hoc basis at provincial, county, or local level, usually by the political departments of the Red Army. Tasked with guaranteeing order and ensuring that the Red Army was properly supplied, the aim of the revolutionary committees was ultimately to re-establish politically reliable soviets. By 1920 there were some 500 revolutionary committees in the Don and Terek Cossack regions alone, and about 700 in the Kuban–Black Sea region.[77] Once victory hove into view, the committees should have been wound up, but they substituted for soviets after the Caucasus was recaptured, and they continued to exist into the mid-1920s in parts of Siberia, the Far East, and Central Asia.

Although the trend was towards centralization of power in the hands of the party oligarchy, the command-administrative system functioned more like a loose set of rival and overlapping jurisdictions than a centralized bureaucratic hierarchy. At provincial level party organizations struggled to impose control over soviet authorities, and both in turn fought off intrusion by the provincial Cheka or provincial organs of the economic and food commissariats. In localities closer to the front, revolutionary committees might clash with local party organs and both might clash with food detachments or with special emissaries sent by the centre to finesse particular problems. In the absence of a clear division of authority, the system relied for cohesion on powerful individuals. Party officials thus developed networks of clients to consolidate their control and fend off outside interference. While the centre disapproved of influential power blocs—as its decision to disband the Central Committee of the Ukrainian Communist Party in April 1920 showed—in practice it knew that letting local bosses amass power was the only way to get things done. With remarkable speed a new word—*komchvanstvo*, or 'communist arrogance'—appeared, which described the airs adopted by these new bosses. Poorly educated and inexperienced, they made up for their inadequacies by throwing their weight around, by being rude to subordinates, and by parading their 'proletarian' credentials. Their style of leadership was heavily influenced by army life: their hallmark being a peremptory command, underscored by the brandishing of a Mauser.

The quality of those who represented the public face of the soviets in the localities, particularly in the countryside, was often dismal. In 1919 and 1920 the Commissariat of State Control received tens of thousands of complaints about abuses and corruption by soviet officials. Cheka reports were frank about the scale of bribery, speculation, embezzlement, drunkenness, and sabotage. A report from the Penza provincial Cheka in summer 1920 was typical: 'In the countryside we must quench the appetites of those "commissars" who on going into the village consider it their sacred duty to get blind drunk, and then take other pleasures, such as raping women, shooting and so forth. Crimes such as bribery and illegal requisitions of anything they fancy flourish everywhere in the counties and when repression is applied it does little to help.'[78]

Meanwhile the number of those employed in Soviet institutions spiralled. In 1917 about 1 million people were working in state institutions, but by 1921 this had risen to 2.5 million. In 1913 officials comprised 6.4 per cent of the working population of the Russian empire; in 1920 13.5 per cent. Already in 1922 the number of white-collar employees working for the Supreme Council of National Economy was 1.2 million, compared with 6,000 in autumn 1918.[79] As early as June 1918 the Cheka in Perm' district in the Urals reported:

> Robbery quickly established a nest for itself in the organizations that is difficult to root out, as the gentlemen of fortune who, on seeing the shortage of personnel in the first days of the revolution, declared themselves fervent supporter of soviet power and took up positions in the offices and departments… Theft, embezzlement, waste and sabotage have become an almost daily phenomenon and the struggle against them absorbs much strength and energy of the young Cheka.[80]

Few among the army of typists, filing clerks, cashiers, accountants, storekeepers, and drivers felt much sympathy towards the new rulers: they worked in order to get a food ration. Most had a low level of education, were inefficient, reluctant to take initiative, and imbued with an ethos of red tape and routinism.

The Bolshevik party, which renamed itself the All-Russian Communist Party (Bolshevik) (RKP(b)) in 1918, was rapidly transformed from a subversive organization into a governing party concerned to build a functioning state.[81] The Central Committee of the party was no longer just responsible for party affairs, but also had a remit to determine the broad direction of policy of the Council of People's Commissars, the individual commissariats, and other organs of government. By 1921 the Central Committee had doubled in size to cope with an ever-growing volume of business. Since its meetings were relatively infrequent, a Politburo of five was established in 1919 to deal with urgent matters. This met at least once a week and quickly became the party's most powerful decision-making body. The sudden death from influenza in March 1919 of Sverdlov, a man of indefatigable energy who had served as secretary to the Central Committee, but who relied mainly on a phenomenal memory, accelerated the effort to improve record-keeping. The Secretariat grew from six to over 600 officials by 1921, but still could not meet the needs of registering and assigning new recruits and of sending activists to the different fronts so long as the war lasted. It was partly its inefficiency that caused Lenin to put Stalin in charge in April 1922.[82]

The Central Committee was dominated by an oligarchy consisting of Lenin, Trotsky, Kamenev, Zinoviev, Stalin, and Bukharin, but there was never any doubt that Lenin was first among equals. He enjoyed towering moral authority and it was his extraordinary talent as a political leader, in particular his ability to balance intransigence with compromise, that held the oligarchy together. The Central Committee generally, but not invariably, followed Lenin's direction: in August 1921, for example, he was unable to engineer the expulsion from it of Aleksandr Shliapnikov, the leader of the Workers' Opposition. There were no deep factional divisions in the Central Committee, but there was a loose group that resented Trotsky's talent and influence. The sovereign policy-making body continued to be the party congress, of which four took place during the period 1917 to 1921, and the degree of political conflict evident at the congresses was intense. Factions such as the Democratic Centralists inveighed against the 'dictatorship of party officialdom', hoping to reconcile centralization of authority with rank-and-file participation in the party and soviets. For their part, the Workers' Opposition campaigned for the trade unions to run industry. None of this prevented the range of permitted dissent from gradually narrowing. By the end of the civil war, it was inconceivable that a Bolshevik should argue—as had been perfectly permissible in October 1917—that other socialist parties should be represented in the soviets or that freedom of the press should extend to 'bourgeois' publications. In March 1921, against the background of the Kronstadt rebellion, discussed in Chapter 5, the Tenth Party Congress banned factions as a temporary measure: but it was never revoked.

Between the Eighth Congress (March 1919) and the Tenth, the party grew from 313,000 to 730,000. This was still tiny in relation to the population and in 1920 the majority of the 10,000 townships in European Russia had no party organization. Worker members comprised 41 per cent of the membership, as opposed to 60 per cent in 1917, but most of these were workers by social origin who no longer worked on the factory floor, having been promoted to positions in the state administration, economic organs, or the Red Army. The rest of the membership was more or less equally divided between peasants (mostly soldiers) and white-collar employees (most of whom worked in the state apparatuses). On the eve of the Tenth Party Congress, L. B. Krasin declared: 'The source of the woes and unpleasantness that we are currently experiencing is the fact that the Communist Party consists of 10% convinced idealists who are ready to die for the idea, and 90% hangers-on without consciences, who have joined the party in order to get a position.'[83] Krasin articulated a growing sense that the party had been hijacked by careerists; and if the purge of 1921 is any guide, he was right; for no fewer than 24 per cent of the 732,000 party members were excluded for 'idleness', 'lack of firmness', 'unreliability', 'discrediting soviet power', 'self-seeking', careerism, drunkenness, a 'bourgeois lifestyle', and a 'dissolute way of life'.[84]

Not surprisingly, many rank-and-file party members began vociferously to attack the privileges enjoyed by 'those at the top'. In June 1920 Preobrazhenskii reported to the Central Committee that the 'majority of rank-and-file members' supported slogans such as 'Down with the privileged caste of the communist elite!'[85] What these privileges might entail can be seen from the diary entry for 24 November 1919 of the writer Kornei Chukovskii: 'Yesterday I was at Gorky's on Kronverskii. Zinoviev was there. At the entrance I was amazed to see a magnificent car on the seat of which was carelessly thrown a bear skin. Zinoviev—short and fat—spoke in a hoarse and satiated voice.'[86] In reality, most of the party oligarchy were men of spartan habits, but the fact that Kremlin staff were eligible for 'armoured' rations caused disgust at a time when tens of thousands were starving. At the Ninth Party Conference in September 1920 Zinoviev admitted that the gap between the *nizy*, 'those at the bottom', and the *verkhi*, 'those at the top', was the 'most acute issue' within the party and a commission was set up to investigate 'Kremlin privileges'. Its recommendations were never implemented.[87]

By 1920–1 there was a severe crisis of morale inside the Communist Party. A discourse about 'bureaucracy' had become influential in the party which fused exasperation at red tape and careerism with disaffection at the arbitrary transfer of cadres and the substitution of political departments, such as Trotsky had created in the Red Army, for party committees. At a deeper level, it expressed dissatisfaction with authoritarianism and the suppression of democracy. Everyone could agree that 'bureaucracy' was a bad thing and party members tended to concur that it sprang from the entry of 'class aliens' into the soviet and party administration, a diagnosis that conveniently relieved party leaders of responsibility for the pathology. Both leadership and left oppositionists, moreover, agreed that one solution to 'bureaucracy' lay in 'workerization', that is, the promotion of workers to positions of responsibility. Yet it was clear that proletarians promoted into positions of authority often behaved little differently from those officials who had moved seamlessly from positions in tsarist ministries or zemstvos into commissariats or soviets. It was, however, the calls from the opposition factions for a restoration of internal party democracy that most rattled the leadership.

When the former house painter Timofei Sapronov, leader of the Democratic Centralists, called for greater accountability of the Central Committee at the Ninth Party Congress, Lenin retorted: 'soviet socialist democracy is not incompatible with one-person management or dictatorship…a dictator can sometimes express the will of a class, since he will sometimes achieve more alone and thus be more necessary'. Lenin never revoked that position, even when he became tormented by the problem of bureaucracy towards the end of his life. In his view—probably realistic in the conditions that prevailed—centralized dictatorship was vital if the Revolution was to be safeguarded: the most that could be allowed was for the masses to monitor those who governed on their behalf. Measures to combat the many different issues that were condensed into the word 'bureaucracy', therefore, proved feeble. The most significant were the creation of a Workers' and Peasants' Inspectorate (Rabkrin), to check on the activities of government organs, and of a Central Control Commission, to monitor the activities of the party. These two bodies may have added to the problem they were intended to solve, since each organ quickly acquired its own staff and generated vast quantities of paperwork. What no one could admit was that the principal causes of 'bureaucracy' lay in the massive expansion of the state itself and in the absence of a culture of rational and impersonal authority and legal regulation.

Neither could the discourse of 'bureaucracy' allow any discussion of the moral degeneration that the civil war had engendered within the party, particularly the ingrained assumption that any measure, however repulsive, could be justified if it could be said to preserve the workers' state. To her surprise, Angelica Balabanoff, the Russian-Jewish-Italian revolutionary, was appointed secretary of the Third International (see Chapter 6) in 1919. Yet she proved too free a spirit and began to criticize the 'partisan, factional, dogmatic, authoritarian, manipulative, organizational' approach of Lenin and Zinoviev.[88] In tsarist times, she noted:

> the actions of those who, to attain the desired end, resorted to objectionable means were regarded as purified by the sacrifices they endured…But when,

> with the accession of the Bolsheviks, the same principle was applied by people who acted not in the interests of an idealistic end, but in their own interest...the debacle began, dragging with it the destruction of principles, scruples, inhibitions, idealism and ideals...If the head of the government declares, as Lenin did many times in his speeches and writings, that to penetrate reactionary trade unions 'the communists must, if necessary, distort the truth and resort to subterfuge, cunning and mental reservations', and if Lenin, speaking as Bolshevik leader, said one time that in order to 'finish' a group of dissidents, slander was acceptable, one should not wonder that people within and outside the party later used the same methods to reach their own ends.[89]

But it was Karl Kautsky, the leader of the German Social Democrats and the arch-renegade in Bolshevik eyes, who most cogently set out the case that the means used to achieve an end can easily distort and undermine it. In his book *Terrorism and Communism*, written in June 1919, he argued: 'The Bolsheviks are prepared in order to maintain their position, to make all sorts of possible concessions to bureaucracy, to militarism, and to capitalism, whereas any concession to democracy seems to them to be sheer suicide.'[90] This provoked a furious response from Trotsky in May 1920 in a pamphlet that bore the same title as Kautsky's:

> Who aims at the end cannot reject the means. The struggle must be carried on with such intensity as actually to guarantee the supremacy of the proletariat. If the Socialist revolution requires a dictatorship...it follows that the dictatorship must be guaranteed at all cost...It is only possible to safeguard the supremacy of the working class by forcing the bourgeoisie...to realize that it is too dangerous an undertaking for it to revolt against the dictatorship of the proletariat, to undermine it by conspiracies, sabotage, insurrections, or the calling in of foreign troops...The man who repudiates terrorism in principle—i.e., repudiates measures of suppression and intimidation towards determined and armed counter-revolution, must reject all idea of the political supremacy of the working class and its revolutionary dictatorship.[91]

Trotsky was, of course, correct scornfully to point out that it was easier to write 'tearful pamphlets' than to win a civil war, but the fury of his response suggests that Kautsky's critique had touched a raw nerve.

In October 1917 when the former turner Aleksandr Shotman ventured to doubt whether 'even a cook or housekeeper' could administer the state,

Lenin retorted: 'Rubbish! Any worker will master any ministry within a few days.' In 1921, however, an exasperated Lenin expostulated: 'Does every worker really know how to run the state? Practical people know that this is a fairy story.... Who of the workers can rule? Only several thousand—no more—throughout the whole of Russia.'[92] The Bolsheviks had eliminated private property in the means of production with astounding ease, but a by-product of that was the collapse of a working class. Absent the force that was supposed to make socialism, Lenin came to believe that the state had become the guarantor of progress towards it, and that any strengthening of the state broadly equated to the strengthening of the 'proletariat'. He had no inkling that the state itself could become an instrument of exploitation and showed little understanding of how the Bolsheviks could themselves be 'captured' by the apparatus which they notionally controlled.

5

WAR COMMUNISM

The civil war brought about a demographic collapse and a calamitous breakdown in social relations.[1] The economic crisis that had been building up since 1914 and that erupted in 1917 led to an implosion of the industrial economy after October. By 1920–1 gross national income had fallen by more than 60 per cent, owing mainly to the collapse of industrial production. Industrial output fell to one-fifth of its 1913 level; coal production and consumer goods production to one-quarter of their pre-war levels. Plummeting output was compounded by chaos in the transport system: by 1921–2, two-thirds of railway engines were unusable and 1,885 km of railway had been destroyed. Inflation soared to unimaginable levels: in 1922 a one-ruble banknote (*sovznak*) was worth 10,000 1918 rubles. An Allied blockade added to the catastrophe.[2] Labour productivity may have fallen as low as 18 per cent of its pre-war level, brought on by the exhaustion of machinery, depletion of stocks, the breakdown of transportation, bottlenecks in supplies, a big deterioration in labour discipline, and, above all, by a decline in labour intensity brought on by hunger, malnutrition, and cold. Some recent historiography has emphasized the extent to which the Bolsheviks brought this upon themselves, but while it would be foolish to deny that their ideas and policies played a part in bringing these things into being, the socio-economic collapse was rooted in structural problems that had their origins in the First World War.

The collapse of industry together with grave food shortages led to the near breakdown of urban life, which was particularly acute in Petrograd and, to a lesser extent, in Moscow. Between 1917 and 1920, the percentage of the population living in towns fell from 18 per cent to 15 per cent, but in Petrograd the city's population fell from 2.4 million to 722,000 and in Moscow it fell by almost half.[3] Life was reduced to a constant search for food, fuel, shelter, and warm clothes, and to trying to avoid disease and crime. As a result of military conscription and the closure of factories, women came to outnumber men in the urban population. In spring and summer 1918 and again in summer 1919 many cities came close to starvation. In the provinces that were net consumers of food the urban population survived on about 396 grams of grain a day.[4] In 1919 over 600,000 people in Petrograd (out of a population of 800,000) and over 800,000 in Moscow (out of a population of just over 1 million) survived thanks to the disagreeable fare on offer in free public cafeterias, schools, and workplaces. People stoked their furnaces with wooden fences, furniture, any available tree, until the fuel ran out. The literary critic Viktor Shklovskii wrote: 'People who lived in housing with central heating died in droves. They froze to death—whole apartments of them.'[5] This was an urban community whose every ounce of energy was drained by the exigencies of survival. In Moscow the death rate, which had fallen to 231 per 10,000 in 1910–14, shot up to a staggering 504 in the first half of 1919, falling to 390 in the second half of that year, only to rise again to 462 in the first half of 1920. In Petrograd it rose from 215 in 1914, to 437 by 1918, soaring to 506 in 1920. Nationally, almost one baby in three died before the age of one.[6] By 1920 life expectancy had fallen to 19.5 for men and 21.5 for women.[7]

Against a background of perishing cold, poor diet, unsanitary conditions, and health facilities at breaking point, epidemic disease erupted on a devastating scale. Epidemics were a far greater killer than rifles and sabres. Between 1917 and 1922 around 3 million died of disease, and to this may be added the 5 million who died of starvation in 1921–2. Typhus alone claimed 1.5 million lives in 1918–19.[8] But the struggle to survive also exacted a psychological cost. The eminent psychologist V. M. Bekhterev observed, 'along with a weakening of the organism there is a reduction of nervous-psychological energy as a result of which there develops general abjection of the personality, passivity, a more or less significant weakening of mental capacity, psychological lethargy and an insufficiency of willpower'.[9]

Mobilizing Industry

Such was the context in which the Bolsheviks fought to hold on to power. To mobilize the battered forces of industry and agriculture in order to meet the needs of war, they gradually put in place a set of policies that they retrospectively labelled 'War Communism'.[10] These comprised an extremely centralized system of economic administration; the complete nationalization of industry; a state monopoly on grain and other agricultural products; a partial ban on private trade; rationing of key consumer items; and the militarization of labour. Historians differ in their assessment of how far these policies were dictated by the collapse of the economy and the exigencies of fighting a civil war or how far derived from Bolshevik antipathy to the market and determination to place the whole of production and distribution in the hands of the state. As we shall see, the terms of the debate are overly polarized: to offer a broadly structural explanation of War Communism is not to deny the strong influence of ideology.

There was no unanimity in the Bolshevik leadership concerning how far and how rapidly Russia could travel along the road to socialism. After his return to Russia in April, Lenin had talked of taking 'steps towards socialism', but by this he meant such measures as confiscation of land, nationalization of the banks, and state regulation of the economy, all measures that were compatible in principle with the continued existence of capitalism. There was agreement in the leadership on the need to impose state regulation of the economy, but opinions differed as to how far this would commence a transition to socialism. For Lenin the model to be emulated was the German war economy, which he characterized as 'military-state monopoly capitalism', and which he believed provided a material foundation for a gradual transition to socialism. In *The Impending Catastrophe and How to Combat It*, written 10–14 September 1917 while he was in hiding in Finland, he elaborated on this perspective, calling for the nationalization of banks; the creation of 'syndicates', that is, cartels that would set sales quotas and wholesale prices in major industries; and for the compulsory organization of the population into consumer communes.[11]

In the weeks after October 1917 many Bolsheviks were in a state of elation and believed that it would only be a short time before revolution broke out in more developed capitalist countries, thus accelerating the advance to socialism on an international scale. The factory committees were particularly optimistic, despite the fact that they were fighting a rearguard action to save their jobs. The Central Council of Factory Committees pressed for an All-Russian Council of Workers' Control to regulate the entire economy. The Decree on Workers' Control, issued on 14 November, vested the committees with the right to monitor all aspects of production and to make their decisions binding on employers. By and large, the trade unions were sceptical about the potential of workers' control to stem the fall in industrial production. They favoured state regulation of the economy but were lukewarm about plans to nationalize industry, since they doubted that the government had the wherewithal actually to manage factories. On 2 December 1917, the Supreme Council of National Economy (VSNKh) was created, a central organ of economic regulation that was vested with the right 'to confiscate, requisition, sequester and forcibly syndicate the different branches of industry and trade and to take other measures in the sphere of production, distribution and state finances'.[12] This was broadly what the Central Council of Factory Committee had been pressing for, although the Supreme Council was somewhat broader in composition than it would have liked. Under its chair, the Left Communist N. Osinskii, the Supreme Council, like the factory committees, believed it was laying the foundations of a socialist mode of production.

Over the winter of 1917–18, factory committees and local soviets clashed sharply with employers over their attempts to close unprofitable enterprises. This led between November and March 1918 to 836 enterprises being spontaneously 'nationalized', that is, taken over by workers' organizations, which then turned to the government for financial support to keep them running. The Supreme Council of National Economy took bold steps to intensify state regulation of the economy. On 14 December private commercial banks were nationalized, their capital being transferred to the State Bank on 23 January. On 21 January the loans incurred by the tsarist government were repudiated (an action that infuriated the French and was a key reason for their intervention in the civil war). On 26 January the marine and river fleets of private and joint-stock companies were nationalized, although the railway system was not nationalized in its entirety until 28 June. On 22 April a state monopoly on foreign trade was declared, although like much of the legislation at this time it remained a dead letter, since contraband trade across Soviet borders continued into the 1920s.

For a brief moment Lenin seems to have shared the optimism that the advance to socialism could be rapid, to judge from his support for a radical interpretation of workers' control of production and for the 'red guard attack on capital'. The difficult negotiations over the peace treaty, however, and the ever mounting chaos in the economy disabused him of any notion that Russia could progress to socialism in current conditions. In the 'Immediate Tasks of the Soviet Government', which he published in March 1918, he declared that 'state capitalism will be our salvation'. By this he envisaged that most industrial enterprises would remain in private ownership but be amalgamated into syndicates under the supervision of the government. Lenin insisted that 'iron discipline' was vital to the 'main objective', which he defined as 'the introduction of the strictest and universal accounting and control of the production and distribution of goods, raising the productivity of labour and socializing production in practice'. This perspective of 'state capitalism' enraged the Left Communists, who had formed a faction within the party in January 1918 to oppose the peace treaty. They wanted to see the socialization of all large-scale industry under the direction of the *sovnarkhozy* or local councils of national economy.[13] Lenin further riled his left-wing critics by stating: 'It would be extremely stupid and absurdly utopian to assume that the transition from capitalism to socialism is possible without coercion and without dictatorship.' In the event, state capitalism proved to be a non-starter, since capitalists who had not already opted to take themselves and their assets abroad had little incentive to cooperate with a revolutionary socialist state.

For a time the government tried to resist the momentum for nationalization that was coming from the grass roots, but its desire to avoid paying compensation for shares owned by German nationals in private Russian companies, as stipulated by the Treaty of Brest-Litovsk, led it to issue a far-reaching decree on 28 June 1918 that nationalized without compensation up to 2,000 joint-stock companies in major branches of industry, railway transportation, and urban amenities. The Supreme Council of National Economy and the Commissariats of Transport and Food were charged with running these sectors. Under the pressure of civil war, the need to establish monopoly control over scarce supplies of materials, fuel, and manufactures led to the nationalization of more and more enterprises. There is no doubt that this was driven by ideology, in particular, by hostility to the market and by the Bolshevik preference for centralism. For example, in spring 1918 there was a serious proposal to give state orders and credits to rural artisans by organizing them into cooperative associations, a policy that might have eased the shortage of manufactures. But the Supreme Council of National Economy took over responsibility for this and did little to implement it. Similarly, in January 1920 the All-Russian Congress of Councils of National Economy recommended that the promotion of artisanal manufacture be done through the cooperative network—which the Bolsheviks disliked for political reasons—but the Supreme Council opted instead for nationalization. On 29 November 1920 the government declared that all mechanized enterprises hiring more than five workers and all unmechanized enterprises hiring ten or more workers were now under state ownership.[14] The decree would have been completely unworkable, but it remained a dead letter because within weeks there was a dramatic about-turn in policy, known as the New Economic Policy, or NEP.

The powers of the Supreme Council of National Economy grew exponentially in response to the urgent demands of civil war, coming to embrace all sectors of industrial production, finance, procurement and distribution of supplies, transportation, and labour. The Council was organized by industrial-branch boards (*glavki*) and 'centres', each underpinned by a hierarchy of subordinate organs. These functioned independently from a geographically organized hierarchy of councils of national economy (*sovnarkhozy*) at provincial and county level that was also subject to the Supreme Council. While the *glavki* were supposed to integrate activity within particular industries on a national basis, the regional councils of national economy were supposed to integrate economic activities of all kinds within a particular geographical area. The Bolshevik preference for centralism, which they equated with efficiency, tended to favour the top-down approach advocated by the industrial-branch boards, but reality was one in which dozens of vertically structured organizations overlapped and competed for resources, operating with little knowledge of the needs of a particular locality. Within the localities a multiplicity of inexperienced soviets, local councils of national economy, trade unions, and factory committees vied with one another to commandeer resources and resolve local supply problems.[15] Trotsky described how in the Urals one province ate oats, while another fed wheat to horses: all because nothing could be done without the approval of the Food Commissariat in Moscow. To try to obviate these problems, on 30 November 1918 a Council of Workers' and Peasants' Defence was set up with extraordinary powers to mobilize material and human resources for the needs of the Red Army and to coordinate activities between the front and rear. From the outset, it was considered virtually the equal of the Council of People's Commissars, its powers being extensive and its decisions unchallengeable. The most that can be said is that this hyper-centralized system of economic administration kept the army supplied. In other respects, however, it led to serious imbalances in supplies, strain on the transport system, lack of incentives for grass-roots producers, and to terrible waste. The centralization of productive activity in the hands of the state also led to a vast increase in the numbers of people employed in running the economic organs. In industry the ratio of white-collar employees to workers rose from one in ten in 1918 to one in seven by 1920.

The Food Dictatorship

The grain shortage, which first emerged during the First World War, was exacerbated by the Revolution.[16] The break-up of the landowners' estates and the consolidated farms of wealthier peasants strengthened subsistence farming at the expense of cash crops. Crucially, the separation of Ukraine for much of the civil war deprived Moscow of access to a region that had produced 35 per cent of marketed grain before the war, and grain supply was further weakened by the fact that the grain-growing Volga region and Siberia became arenas of military conflict. It has been reckoned that twenty-one provinces relied on imports of grain ('consumer' provinces) and that twenty-four exported grain ('producer' provinces), and whereas all the consumer provinces were under permanent Bolshevik control during the civil war, only five of the producer provinces were. The supply situation in general was aggravated by the crisis in transportation. Chaos on the railways steadily mounted, owing to fuel shortages, the deterioration of track and rolling stock, the loss of engines to the Whites, and the control exercised by local railway unions. The problems of transportation meant much of the food that actually made it to a railway station either went to waste or was pillaged. Of 1,065 million kilograms of potatoes procured in the Urals in 1920, only 81.9 million reached the urban population; the rest were left to rot or be stolen.

The winter of 1917–18 proved to be exceptionally severe and the food authorities were simply unable to fulfil rations: by early 1918 the bread ration in Petrograd fell at times to as little as 50 grams a day, driving many back to the countryside. Workers' organizations and local soviets clamoured to buy bread where they could and, despite the continuance of the grain monopoly, petty trade (and profiteering) flourished. In the deficit province of Ivanovo-Voznesensk so-called 'baggers' (*meshochniki*) imported about 49 million kilograms of grain between 1 August 1917 and 1 January 1918, two-and-a-half times the amount procured by the official food agencies. Having bought grain for 10–12 rubles a *pud* (16.38 kilograms) in surplus provinces (the fixed price was still only 3–4 rubles), they sold it for 50–70 rubles. The black market created inequality but it functioned as a supply network.

The hope of the new government was that peasants could be induced to exchange more grain for manufactured goods such as fabrics, salt, sugar, or kerosene. But the fall in production of such goods, together with rocketing inflation, meant that peasants held on to their diminishing stocks of grain. They either ate them because they were hungry, fed them to their livestock, or turned them into alcohol. In Siberia it was estimated that in the first half of 1918, 196.6 million kilograms of grain were requisitioned, whereas 409.5 million were converted into illegal moonshine (the ban on alcohol continued during these years). Faced with an extreme food shortage in the major cities and lacking the means to induce peasants to part with their grain voluntarily, the Bolsheviks turned to coercion. On 14 May they announced the establishment of a 'food dictatorship' whereby all surpluses above a fixed consumption norm would henceforward be subject to confiscation. The decree warned darkly that any undisclosed surpluses would be seized and the guilty parties—'enemies of the people'—jailed for not less than ten years. In theory, peasants were to be recompensed—25 per cent of the value of requisitions would be in the form of goods, the rest in money or credits—but by this stage industrial production was geared largely to meeting the needs of the Red Army, so very little in the way of consumer goods was produced. According to the most generous estimate, only about half of the grain requisitioned in 1919 received some form of compensation, and in 1920 only around 20 per cent. The campaign to confiscate grain was targeted on the black-earth provinces of Saratov, Samara, Penza, and Tambov, the other main grain-growing regions already being in the hands of anti-Bolshevik forces. Food detachments, consisting of some 76,000 workers, of whom around one-third were Bolsheviks or sympathizers, barged into the villages. Needless to say, peasants responded by hiding their grain or by violent resistance: over the course of 1918, 7,309 members of food detachments were killed. Leaving to one side the conflict it provoked, the food dictatorship was hardly successful even judged as a desperate measure to feed the towns: by December about 982.8 million kilograms had been taken, but because of the chaos on the railways and waterways, some of the grain seized was left to rot at dispatch points while livestock starved because of lack of fodder.

The food dictatorship was not just a measure of desperation forced on a government by the prospect of starvation in the cities. It was what Aleksandr Tsiurupa, the Commissar for Food, on 9 May called a 'war on the rural bourgeoisie'. Tsiurupa had after 1905 been the manager of the estates of Prince Viacheslav Kugushev. The Bolsheviks were convinced that 'kulaks' were deliberately holding back grain and the hope was that by establishing committees of the rural poor (*kombedy*) poor peasants would rise up against their richer neighbours, providing the regime with the social base in the countryside that it so sorely needed. In reality many of the members of the *kombedy* were activists in the food detachments, military personnel, and party workers. A study of more than 800 village-level *kombedy* in Tambov showed that one-third of members had never engaged in farming. The *kombedy* assisted the food detachments in seizing grain and other forms of property, imposing fines, and generally carrying out arbitrary acts and illegal arrests. Unsurprisingly, rural communities did not welcome the intruders. In August 1918 the congress of peasants in Kargopol' county in Arkhangel'sk province declared: 'We consider the organization of *kombedy* unnecessary, since thanks to the equal division of land across the county the former division of the population into classes has passed away.'[17] This is not to say that there was no resentment of rich peasants on the part of poorer peasants. In Kolovskaia in the forested province of Olonets peasants petitioned the Pudozhskii county soviet on 18 June 1918: 'Send us help, even if it is only a small Red Army detachment, so that we shall be saved from an early death from hunger. Let it persuade or force our neighbours to act like decent people if only for a time and share with us their grain surpluses at this terrible moment. We will point out to you the well-fed grain kings who shelter by their treasure chests.'[18] This plea was motivated less by class consciousness, however, than by a desire to restore the mechanisms of mutual aid of the commune. In autumn 1918 the tempo of creating *kombedy* accelerated, even as the central leadership was beginning to have doubts about the wisdom of the policy, since they facilitated the formation of rural party cells. In thirty-three provinces over 70 per cent of the 139,000 township and village *kombedy* that existed in late November had come into existence since

September. Yet as early as August Lenin had begun to have misgivings, calling for more compromise with the middle peasantry; and in November the VI Congress of Soviets came out in favour of their abolition, owing to 'bitter clashes between *kombedy* and peasant organs of power...during autumn of 1918'.

The turn to the middle peasantry was accompanied on 11 January 1919 by the introduction of the *raszverstka*, or quota assessment, under which the Food Commissariat sought to calculate the amount of grain required by the country as a whole and then divide it up between provinces, on the basis of its estimates of 'surpluses'. This *razverstka* in theory introduced a degree of predictability into food requisitioning, since each county and village knew the quota it had been assigned, but in reality the food detachments continued to squeeze as much as they could from a reluctant peasantry. The quota assessment system did lead to an increase in the amount of agricultural produce squeezed from the countryside. Between August 1918 and August 1919, it is reckoned that 1,767 million kilograms were raised in European Russia—only 41.5 per cent fulfilment of the quota set. The second procurement of 1919–20 raised 3,481 million kilograms (about 85 per cent of which came from European Russia, the rest mainly from Siberia). The third procurement of 1920–1 raised 3,882 million kilograms from the provinces of European Russia alone. This was no more than the grain procurement of 1916/17, yet it represented a huge burden of suffering for the peasantry, since output had almost halved in the intervening period, owing to the reduction of sowing and the decrease in yield.[19] During these years the word *vykachka*, literally the 'pumping out' of the peasantry, passed into common parlance. By December 1920, there were 62,043 activists in detachments directly responsible to the Food Commissariat plus 30,560 in detachments responsible to the Military Food Bureau. On 7 March 1920, the chair of Novgorod provincial soviet wrote to the Food Commissariat: 'The food detachments are completely unable to carry out their task. They stir up the villages where they go against soviet power. Rudeness, illegal demands for food for themselves, confiscation of cattle and their demonstrative slaughter in case of refusal...Cases of straightforward theft (accordions, rings, kerchiefs etc.). The province is starving. A huge quantity of peasants is eating moss and other rubbish.' Perhaps the gravest indictment of requisitioning was that it encouraged peasants to farm less land, so that in the major grain-growing regions the area put to seed was 15 per cent to 24 per cent less than in 1913. This was also a consequence of lack of manpower, livestock, and ruined equipment.

The hostility of the Bolsheviks to markets did not improve the supply situation. Draconian penalties for 'speculation' were prescribed—of ten years' hard labour plus confiscation of property—yet this did not deter hundreds of thousands of 'baggers' from scouring the countryside for food to sell to townsfolk. If baggers were found to be carrying more than the permitted amounts of goods, they risked arrest by the Cheka or the roadblock detachments that were set up to search rail passengers and those entering towns on foot. The behaviour of these detachments was described by the Soviet CEC in January 1919 as a 'shocking disgrace'. Many arrested for 'speculation' were just ordinary folk forced to truck and barter. In November 1918 a girl from Gzhatsk wrote to the Council of People's Commissars: 'My father is a peasant and I work now on the railway. My mother sells things at the station and forces me to do the same. I have always been against speculation, but as they say, hunger can make us do anything. Even Communists have to eat.' This does not mean that organized speculation was a figment of the Bolshevik imagination: Cheka reports suggest that there was a market in everything from machinery to land, buildings, enterprises, and even stocks and shares. And the activities of organized networks undoubtedly pushed up prices. In July 1919 the British historian Sir Bernard Pares, at this time seconded to the British embassy in Petrograd, was shocked when merchants in Ekaterinburg, where the supply situation was dire, attempted to sell off hoarded food at knock-down prices before the city fell into Bolshevik hands.

Yet the fight against the illegal and semi-legal market was never consistent, for the Bolsheviks were forced to recognize that without it townspeople would starve. Astonishingly, it is reckoned that at least half the food requirements of the urban population were met through the market. Even as the nationalization of trade was being proclaimed, the authorities were forced to allow peasants to sell 24.6 kilograms (1.5 *pud*) of food per family member. This is not to suggest that complete reliance on the market could have fed the Red Army, the towns, and the consumer provinces. Even if the Bolsheviks had not taken a single *pud* of grain from the peasants, the latter would still have had little incentive to produce more than was necessary for subsistence, since there were no manufactures to buy and money had become almost worthless. Even in Siberia, where Kolchak's regime had far greater surpluses at its disposal and where there was no forced requisitioning, lack of manufactures, inflation, and chaos in the monetary system led peasants to withhold grain and to cut back their sown areas. The Bolsheviks thus had 'to take from the hungry to give to the hungrier', as one official put it. That said, this does not mean that there was no alternative to the policy that was pursued. Much more use, for example, could have been made of the cooperative network, not only with respect to improving food supply but also in relation to stimulating artisanal manufacture in the countryside. If congresses of peasant soviets are any guide—most of which were dominated by Left SRs—peasants were willing to exchange grain for manufactured goods on an organized basis, preferably through the cooperatives, and so long as this was at a price that did not discriminate in favour of manufactured goods. Yet the Bolsheviks were deeply suspicious of the cooperative movement—not without reason, since it had initially opposed soviet power—and were reluctant to recognize that it had a far more effective network of distribution in place than did the Commissariat of Food. So the regime expended more energy trying to oust the moderate socialists from leadership of the cooperative movement than it did in seeking to tap its potential to mitigate the food-supply crisis. It is ironic that within a couple of years Lenin should be hailing the cooperative movement as a framework for slow advance towards socialism.

War Communism in Crisis

As we have seen, the Bolsheviks counterposed the anarchy and inequality generated by the market to a system of state-wide distribution via the compulsory organization of the population into consumer communes. Attempts to introduce rationing had begun before the February Revolution, and in spring 1917 the Provisional Government introduced rationing of bread and sugar, followed later by some other grain and fat products. In July 1918 the so-called class ration was introduced in Petrograd, and soon extended to Moscow and other towns. This classified the population into a hierarchy of four different ration categories: the highest was for skilled workers; the lowest was designed, in Zinoviev's words, to give the 'bourgeoisie' just enough bread so that they would not forget the smell of it. From the end of 1918 the shrunken ranks of industrial workers were almost completely reliant on rations. Yet food shortages meant that it was frequently impossible to fulfil ration norms even for specialized workers in the first ration category. A joke did the rounds: 'A religious instruction teacher asked his secondary school, "Our Lord fed 5,000 people with five loaves and two fishes. What is this called?" To which one wag replied: "the ration system".' Inability to meet ration norms fuelled pressure on groups to get themselves into a higher ration category. By April 1920 in Petrograd 63 per cent of the population was in category one and only 0.1 per cent remained in the lowest category.[20] The complexity of the ration system, plus the fact that it came to be used not only to punish the 'bourgeoisie' but also to reward key groups, such as academics and artists, or to defuse industrial unrest, meant that the system became a major source of corruption. In 1920 the urban population of the RSFSR (minus Turkestan) numbered 12.3 million yet there were 22 million urban ration cards in circulation.[21]

A stupendous crisis was building up, yet the scent of victory encouraged the Bolsheviks to believe that the draconian methods used to win the civil war could now be turned to building socialism. 'Universal labour conscription' had been instituted as early as January 1918, as a means to 'eliminate the parasitic layers of society and organize the economy'.[22] And throughout the civil war members of the 'bourgeoisie' were drafted into clearing snow, unloading food, repairing roads and railways, and even teaching the illiterate to read. In 1918 workers in the defence industries and on the railways were also put on a semi-military footing, ordered to fulfil fixed norms of output and losing the right to change jobs. In 1919 the Defence Council extended militarization to employees in marine and river transport, certain mines, and other fuel sectors. Only at the start of 1920, however, was the proposal made to implement labour conscription on a mass scale. In January the Defence Council transformed the Third Red Army, which had been fighting in the Urals, into a labour army tasked with agricultural reconstruction. During the first half of the year as many as 6 million people were drafted to work in cutting timber and peat. In March—with absenteeism on the railways now running at between 20 per cent and 40 per cent—Trotsky took over the Commissariat of Transport and set about imposing military-style discipline on the workforce. Trotsky emerged as the major exponent of the idea that labour conscription could be used to build socialism. In *Terrorism and Communism*, he declared: 'Obligation and compulsion are essential conditions in order to bind down bourgeois anarchy, to secure socialization of the means of production and labour, and to reconstruct economic life on the basis of a single plan.' Not all Bolsheviks were convinced, and some were repelled by the idea that the labour army offered a microcosm of socialist society. For the best part of a year, however, the leadership committed itself to a vision of army and economy fused into a single, all-embracing military-economic body run on hierarchical and commandist lines. Yet the capacity of stubborn individuals to overwhelm the grandest of plans quickly became apparent. In the first nine months of 1920, for example, no fewer than 90 per cent of the 38,514 workers mobilized for work in thirty-five armaments plants left their jobs. This prompted a volley of measures to punish 'labour deserters', including dispatch to concentration camps, but these were a sign of impotence not of strength.

As the civil war drew to a close, utopian thinking in the All-Russian Communist Party (RKP(b)) reached its apogee. By the beginning of 1920, the amount of money in circulation was 150 times the level of 1917; prices had risen to 6,290 times the 1914 level.[23] As the year wore on, efforts to stabilize the currency and maintain monetary taxes gave way in some quarters to the comforting delusion that money might be eliminated altogether. Lenin cautioned that 'it is impossible to abolish money at once', yet gave his blessing to plans to replace currency with 'labour units', known as *tredy*, defined by the Menshevik economist S. G. Strumilin as the expenditure of 100,000 'kilogram-meters' during the workday of a single worker.[24] A flurry of decrees abolished rents on housing, payments for heating and lighting, fares on trams and railways, charges for the postal service, health services, and even for the theatre and cinema. In the first half of 1920, 11 million people ate in public canteens, including 7.6 million children, though the food was meagre and badly cooked and conditions often filthy. These measures seemed to augur a moneyless society, and there were those who were willing to justify them in ideological terms. Yet they were fundamentally dictated by practical exigencies, notably the fact that it now cost more to collect money payments than it did to make these services free.

In February 1920 Trotsky proposed that requisitioning be replaced with a tax in kind as an incentive to peasants to sow more grain, but he was rebuffed. In keeping with the commandist spirit of the times, the government in December opted to back a plan by Osinskii to set up sowing committees. As a Left Communist, Osinskii had resigned from the chairmanship of the Supreme Council of National Economy when the Treaty of Brest-Litovsk was signed. Sowing committees were a typical 'War Communist' measure that envisaged the committees distributing seed, organizing sowing, and instructing peasants on how much area was to be sown. The idea was to combine coercion, 'shock work', and incentives (peasants were to be allowed to keep a higher proportion of grain as a reward for fulfilling state planting obligations). But the days of War Communism were numbered. The devastating consequences of food requisitioning could no longer be ignored. In autumn 1920, the first signs that people were beginning to starve in the Volga region appeared. The following year a severe drought ruined the harvest, bringing mass starvation to millions, mainly in the Volga provinces and the southern Urals. The famine raged from autumn 1921 into the summer of 1922, only diminishing gradually thereafter. In all up to 5 million people died, not only from hunger, but also from diseases, such as typhoid fever, cholera, bubonic plague, and smallpox.[25] The Commissariat of Enlightenment received grotesque reports that mothers were tying their children to separate corners of their huts for fear they would eat one another. The government struggled none too impressively with the situation, but was strapped for resources. In Orenburg province, where as many as 100,000 people perished, 4.3 million kilograms of rye, tens of thousands of kilograms of rice, and 105 wagons of seed corn were shipped in by September 1921, and all children and 30,000 adults were evacuated to Turkestan.[26] Without the sterling efforts of the American Relief Administration and the International Red Cross, however, millions more would have died. Foreign aid workers found party officials in the famine areas 'fearful men, jumpy, flying off into violence on very slight provocation; so insecure had been their hold on power that they were suspicious of the most innocent acts'.[27]

War Communism was abandoned at the Tenth Party Congress in March 1921 and in October Lenin admitted that it had reached a dead end a year previously. In answer to the question posed at the start of this section—whether the package of policies was dictated by circumstances or by ideology—Lenin confessed that it had been dictated by 'desperate necessity' but also by 'an attempt to introduce the socialist principles of production and distribution by "direct assault", i.e. in the shortest, quickest and most direct way'. The collapse of industrial output, the need to feed the population, chaos in the transport system, destruction of assets as a result of warfare, had all placed severe constraints on the Bolsheviks' scope for action. That the exigencies of war did much to dictate policy can be seen from the fact that even White administrations, favourably disposed to the free market and to reprivatizing industry and the banks, resorted to measures of economic compulsion in the 'interests of state'. Moreover, one of the policies that became associated with War Communism, the imposition of fixed prices on agricultural products, was a continuation of the policy introduced by the tsarist regime. Yet this one policy did much to stoke inflation and undermine the value of the ruble. Thus structural constraints, contingencies, and unintended consequences all served to shape the policies that constituted War Communism, but Lenin was correct to suggest that Bolshevik ideology also played a crucial role in determining policy. Policy choices were not unilaterally 'imposed' by objective circumstances: they were defined by the dominant conceptions and inherited dispositions of the RKP(b), sometimes as matters of explicit choice, sometimes as unconscious reflexes. Antipathy towards the market, a penchant for centralism, and the equation of state ownership and state regulation with advance to socialism all served powerfully to shape the policies that came to typify War Communism. And though it was abandoned in 1921, the command-administrative system and the militarized ideology that had inspired it would prove to be lasting elements in the Soviet system.

Social Order Overturned

The crime wave that began in 1917 soared during the civil war. During the October seizure of power there had been orgies of drunkenness as soldiers ransacked wine stores and looted shops, and in 1918 the incidence of robbery and murder in Moscow was estimated to be ten to fifteen times the pre-war level.[28] Those involved were professional gangs and bandits, who used the class war against *burzhui* to enrich themselves, along with a large number of deserters and refugees. However, many ordinary people also turned to crime in the struggle to survive. There were daily reports in the press of hideous mob lynchings (*samosudy*) by desperate civilians, directed against thieves and, especially, those suspected of hoarding. As one newspaper put it: 'Mob justice occurs when there is no justice, when the people has lost confidence in government and the law.' These acts of violence were often spectacularly barbaric, with a strong antisemitic tinge. In a huge riot in Kazanskaia *stanitsa* in Kuban' in early 1918 forty presumed speculators were killed, four of whose bodies were quartered.[29] Crime was facilitated by the weakness of the militia and the widespread availability of weapons. From the first the Bolsheviks made no bones of the fact that they were determined to stamp out crime. On 27 October 1917, the Military-Revolutionary Committee in Moscow, having taken steps to seize stocks of weapons, warned that 'any attempt at a pogrom, any attempt at robbery or riot, will be crushed with the most merciless measures'.[30] Within weeks the new regime restored capital punishment and Lenin began to make minatory noises about the need for an 'iron hand' to suppress lawlessness.

At the same time, and in a rather different spirit, the incoming government abolished the old court system—seen as a linchpin of the tsarist order—and pledged to construct a system of 'proletarian justice'. The courts, the procuracy, and the bar association were abolished and in their place people's courts were set up, comprising an elected judge and two lay assessors, all drawn as far as possible from the working classes. Marked leniency was shown towards criminals from the 'toiling classes'. Juvenile courts and prison sentences for the under-17s were abolished, juvenile crime being handled by special welfare commissions. The system of courts gradually bedded down, but since a new Criminal Code was not drawn up until 1922, the people's courts continued to rely mainly on the pre-revolutionary law code except where specific laws were repealed. Over the course of the civil war local commissariats of justice were gradually brought under the control of the Commissariat of Justice, and the influence of local soviets was reduced. According to the Commissariat of Justice, in 1920 popular courts dealt with only 22.3 per cent of criminal cases.[31] Of 582,571 people found guilty, only one-third were given prison sentences, and of these about 40 per cent were suspended.[32]

The majority of criminal cases were dealt with by new 'revolutionary' organs, notably the revolutionary tribunals (which dealt with 35.3 per cent of criminal cases in 1920), by the Cheka (which dealt with 30.4 per cent), and by military tribunals (which dealt with 12 per cent of cases). The military tribunals, as well as operating in the armed forces, also operated on the railways and waterways, where theft was rife. The revolutionary tribunals were initially set up (as part of the law on courts of 22 November 1917) 'to struggle against counter-revolutionary forces by way of taking measures to protect the revolution and its gains, and equally to decide cases of marauding and looting, sabotage and other abuses of traders, industrialists, officials and others'.[33] Their scope soon expanded and in May 1918 they were put in charge of prosecuting espionage, riots ('pogroms' in the extended Russian meaning of the term), bribery, forgery, and hooliganism. Though their rhetoric was often bloodcurdling, the punishments meted out by the tribunals were generally fairly mild. By April 1918, the tribunal in Stavropol had sentenced 177 people, but the harshest punishment it had imposed was three months in jail. In the Urals all punishments entailed service in the community. In 1919 in Viatka province 5 per cent of sentences resulted in the death penalty—although not all were carried out—mainly for corruption in public office.[34] As this suggests, revolutionary tribunals tried many criminal cases that should have come before the popular courts. In 1920 more than 80 per cent of the cases they heard were non-political.[35] Indeed in Tambov a large part of their activities involved petty enforcement of taxes in kind on hay, meat, eggs, bread, butter, and wool.[36] In part, this was because the Cheka took charge of cases it deemed most serious.

One facet of the breakdown of the old social order was the incredibly rapid way in which the privileged elites disappeared. The major assets of the nobility were, obviously, taken when peasants seized landed estates; and capitalists lost their assets with the nationalization of industry, commerce, and banks. By autumn 1918, 90 per cent of landowners in Orël province and about two-thirds in Iaroslavl' had been thrown off their estates. But middle-class people with property also found themselves 'taxed' by local soviets, Cheka organs, and Red Guards who divested them of cash and valuables. Local soviets, in particular, strapped for finance, exacted 'contributions' and 'confiscations' and carried out evictions on all those they deemed to be 'bourgeois'. On 8 January 1918 the soviet in Tver' demanded sums ranging from 20,000 to 100,000 rubles from local traders and industrialists and threatened to send those who did not comply to Kronstadt, to be dealt with by the sailors. In Tambov even bicycles were requisitioned and rumours that sewing machines and gramophones were next in line for confiscation caused some 'bourgeois' families to entrust 'soviet' families with their valuables for safekeeping. In theory, all such requisitions were to be properly inventoried—a typical protocol of the Moscow Cheka for 27 October 1919 carefully described a Guarneri and a Stradivarius violin taken from Citizen Zubov—but local authorities flouted central directives with impunity. A judicial ruling that the property of a Red Army soldier could not be confiscated was overturned by the Moscow provincial soviet on the grounds that he was the son of a landowner: 'Smirnov is one of those parasites for whom there is no place in the ranks of the fighting proletariat and who should be thrown overboard from the revolution.' And local authorities proved powerless to prevent the huge proportion of expropriations carried out by criminals, sometimes posing under a political banner. In Rostov-on-Don the Brotherhood of Revolutionary Cossacks and Sailors warned of a 'Bartholomew's Night' against the bourgeoisie, under the slogan 'Kill all the *burzhui* and the Jews'. As the leading Chekist Latsis put it: 'Our Russian reckons: "Don't I really deserve those trousers and boots that the bourgeoisie have been wearing until now? That's a reward for my work, right? So, I'll take what's mine."'

Hit by 'requisitions' and 'indemnities' and forced to do humiliating work assignments, landowners, capitalists, and government officials sold what they could, packed their bags, and headed for the White areas or for emigration. In its editorial to mark the New Year in 1919 *Pravda* mused: 'Where are the wealthy, the fashionable ladies, the expensive restaurants and private mansions, the beautiful entrances, the lying newspapers, all the corrupted "golden life"? All swept away.' The age-old gulf between the world of the propertied and educated and that of the common people had been wiped out in a matter of months. Between 1.8 million and 2 million fled abroad between 1917 and 1921, overwhelmingly from the educated and propertied groups. Yet a significant number of former landowners and industrialists, tsarist generals and officers, opted to remain in Russia. A. A. Golovin, scion of an ancient boyar family, found a job in the garage of the Malyi Theatre in 1921. Yet his son managed to get a place at the Moscow Arts Theatre school and became famous for his film portrayals of Stalin. Sergei Golitsyn, son of Prince M. V. Golitsyn, managed to get into a higher literature course and became a famous children's writer. His mother and other aristocratic ladies formed an embroidery cooperative whose products were sold abroad.[37] At the end of 1927, there were still 10,756 former landowners in the RSFSR who lived on their estates, having been granted a portion of land during the land redistribution; but their days were numbered.[38] Typical was Maria Livinskaia, widow of a railway-company director, who lived in Kozel'skii county in Kaluga province with her wastrel son Sergei and her servant Avdot'iia, who had three children, the youngest fathered by Sergei. At land redistribution she had been allowed to keep the house and orchard and her son and Avdotiia had each been given the standard allotment of 4.4 hectares. In a scene that might have been taken from Chekhov, we are told: 'The rose garden, which once boasted thirty-five different types of rose, is now thick with nettles and burdock and the local peasants tramp through the orchard on the way to the fields.'[39] These 'former people'—a term once applied to criminals but now used to describe these remnants of the *ancien régime*—did their best to conceal their origins and fought shy of politics. Yet despite being reduced to the humblest of circumstances, they were viewed with deep mistrust by the regime, seen as a potential fifth column for any White Guard restoration.

For the multifarious middle classes the Revolution brought a sharp diminution in privilege, although opportunities to adapt to the new order were fairly plentiful (Figure 5.1). While Lenin despised the intelligentsia, he was quick to see that the Revolution could not survive without 'knowledgeable, experienced, business-like people' and he insisted that they should be paid for their skills and that their authority should be respected. Doctors, dentists, architects, and other professionals continued to practise privately. In industry technical specialists—*spetsy*—remained relatively privileged: their authority as engineers and administrators was upheld and they were paid relatively high salaries. It was not unusual for industrialists, especially those who had been members of the regulatory organs for industries such as textiles, leather, and tobacco, to end up as members of the *glavki*, the industrial-branch boards of the Supreme Council of National Economy. A White professor who reached Omsk in autumn 1919 was surprised to see so many former owners of leather factories sitting on the board of the leather industry.[40] Former merchants might end up working in the soviet supply organs. D. A. D'iakov, owner of a large trading company in Nikol'skaia township in Kursk province, became its chairman when it was turned into a cooperative in 1918. He later served in the provincial food commissariat of Kursk, living all the while in one of his former houses.

Figure 5.1 The bourgeoisie doing compulsory labour service.

For the lower-middle strata with education there were plenty of jobs in local soviets and commissariats as clerks, secretaries, and minor functionaries, and this entitled them to a second-grade food ration ('responsible' soviet officials qualified for the first grade). Such petty functionaries were generally exempt from conscription. The Vladimir journalist S. Pospelov wrote in February 1919: 'There only needs to be a conscription summons sent to some typist, clerk, accountant or secretary to provoke howls of protest and hundreds and thousands of certificates and petitions insisting that the person is irreplaceable.'[41] As we have seen, petty trade and handicraft production also provided a meagre livelihood for the many without paid employment. In Voronezh in summer 1918 there were more than 500 applications to trade in fruit and vegetables.[42]

The intelligentsia was the only elite group to survive the Revolution intact, though its self-image was badly shaken.[43] Most were moderate socialist in sympathy, but the war and revolution had killed any naive belief they might once have entertained about the innate goodness of the people. Their sense of themselves as the conscience of society, called upon to oppose tyranny and to preserve Russia's heritage, led most to oppose the Bolsheviks.

They deplored the strident demagogy of the new rulers, the violence of the mob, the closure of the 'bourgeois' press, and the lawlessness on the streets. Particularly significant, in comparison with other social revolutions, is that students were generally hostile to the Revolution, with the overwhelming majority of student organizations remaining resolutely 'non-party', and secretly sympathetic to the Kadets and SRs. The intelligentsia in general, however, had had enough of politics and tried to maintain a neutral stance during the civil war. Many writers, artists, actors, and musicians moved to the southern cities that were under White control, mainly to the Crimea, but also to Rostov-on-Don, Kyiv, Kharkiv, or Tbilisi—all of these being places that managed to sustain a lively cultural life amid the privation. Notwithstanding this, the regime took a pragmatic approach. Anatolii Lunacharskii, head of the Commissariat of Enlightenment, was the Bolshevik leader most sympathetic to the intelligentsia, convinced that they would eventually come over to the Revolution. During the civil war crippling cold, the threat of starvation, appalling shortages—not least of paper—were facts of life for everyone, artists included. The composer Aleksandr Grechaninov recalled: 'my health was undermined to such an extent that I could hardly drag my feet. My hands suffered from frost bite and I could not touch the piano'.[44] Most *intelligenty* were not well paid and had few reserves to fall back on. The collapse of the economy meant that income from performances, writing, teaching, and private patronage all dried up. Simon Dubnov, founder of the liberal Jewish National Party and author of a ten-volume *World History of the Jewish People*, wrote in his diary on 13 December 1919: 'I got up early, dressed, got into my overcoat, galoshes and hat (it was minus 7 degrees in the room) and sat at my writing desk. With numbed fingers I wrote about the Dominicans and the Inquisition in France in the 13th century. At 10am I had something to eat, looked at the newspaper and then went to the firewood department of the district soviet to receive a warrant for firewood. For two hours I stood amid the dense mass of unhappy, anxious people and, like hundreds of others, came away with nothing.'[45] Morale, however, was not necessarily as low as this might suggest. In 1920 Nikolai Berdiaev was elected to a professorship in philosophy at Moscow University: 'I gave lectures in which I openly and without hindrance criticised Marxism.' He did not mind having to do obligatory labour: 'I did not feel at all depressed and unhappy despite the unaccustomed strain of the pick and shovel on my sedentary muscles ... I could not help realising the justice of my predicament.'[46]

In many ways, the appeal of the Red cause was as much to generation as it was to social class, in particular, to urban working-class men in their late teens. Youth was a powerful trope in Bolshevik propaganda, which represented young people as the generation that was destined to build communism. The first congress of the Komsomol (Communist Union of Youth) met in November 1918 and proclaimed:

> Youth represents the vanguard of the social revolution. Youth is more perceptive, and has not been poisoned by the prejudices and ideas of bourgeois society. The adult generation of the working class lived through the horrors of the imperialist war; the war exhausted its strength and sometimes it yields to feelings of fatigue.[47]

As Lenin told the Third Congress of the Komsomol in October 1920, 'the generation of those who are now fifteen will see a communist society, and will itself build this society'. 'You are faced with the task of construction, and you can accomplish that task only by assimilating all modern knowledge, only if you are able to transform communism from cut-and-dried memorized formulas, counsels, recipes, prescriptions and programmes into that living reality which gives unity to your immediate work.'[48]

There were many who responded to this rousing call. Following the seizure of power, young men and a few women launched themselves into the struggle for soviet power, erecting barricades, digging trenches, and setting off to join the Red Army. During the civil war the Komsomol recruited between 50,000 and 60,000 into the Red Army and the food detachments. The main focus of its activities, however, lay in political education in clubs and factory schools, and it arranged a broad programme of recreational activities, including dramatic, choral, literary, sports, and sewing societies. By 1920 the Komsomol claimed 400,000 members, a not insignificant number. Yet it still represented only 2 per cent of eligible youth.[49] The Komsomol had almost no base in the countryside and among students in the cities its influence was extremely limited. In 1919 it was reported that the 'basic element' of school pupils 'have no interests or thoughts about matters other than food'.[50] Soon there was muttering from lower-class youth that young people from middle-class backgrounds were taking advantage of free access to university in order to gain exemption from conscription and compulsory labour service. This reminds us that the privileged classes of the old order might have lost much of their property but they had not lost their cultural capital and social connections.

Fighting the Church

The Bolsheviks came to power bent on disestablishing and dispossessing the Orthodox Church which had been a pillar of the old order.[51] The Decree on the Separation of Church and State of 23 January 1918 declared freedom of conscience and the right to practise religion or not (though people did not have the right to refuse civic obligations on religious grounds). Schools were taken out of the hands of the Church, and religious education in schools was banned. Icons and other images were to be removed from all public buildings and processions were to be allowed only with the permission of the local soviet. The practice of religious rituals in state and public institutions was forbidden. Churches were deprived of their status as judicial personages and thus forbidden to possess property. Legislation in August explained that property that had belonged to the Church was to pass into the hands of parish councils. The registration of births, marriages, and deaths was also taken out of the hands of the Church and transferred to the soviets.[52] The response of the new patriarch Tikhon was swift: in January 1918 he pronounced an anathema on the Bolsheviks, warning that they would 'burn in hell in the life hereafter and be cursed for generations'. The ending of financial subventions hit the central and diocesan administrations hard, but made little difference to parish clergy, who depended on parishioners for financial support. During the land redistribution even the pious took an active part in seizing church lands, but villagers provided local priests with an allotment of land and some financial support. The Bolshevik leadership was largely content to leave ecclesiastical institutions and the network of parish churches intact. The major exceptions were the monasteries. By late 1920, 673 monasteries in the RSFSR had been dissolved and their 1.2 million hectares of land confiscated. In that year the Commissariat of Justice announced the 'painless but full liquidation of the monasteries as chief centres of parasitism, as powerful screws in the exploiting machine of the old ruling classes'.[53]

The Bolsheviks portrayed the clergy as inveterate reactionaries: posters depicted priests as drunkards and gluttons, monks and nuns as sinister 'black crows', the faithful as innocent dupes of ruling-class lackeys. For their part, a majority of the church hierarchy, appalled at the breakdown of social order, portrayed the Bolsheviks as Christ-haters, German hirelings, 'Jewish-Masonic slave-masters', men who led the simple people astray by false promises of worldly bliss. Patriarch Tikhon urged the faithful to resist the Bolsheviks only by spiritual means, but in many areas clergy openly sided with the Whites. The scale of opposition on the part of the Church to the Bolshevik regime remains unclear. In the Urals, a major zone of civil war conflict, there were 78 cases of resistance to the decree separating Church and state; 4 cases of refusal to hand over church registers; 18 cases of clerics 'giving their blessing' to armed actions against the Bolshevik regime; and 4 cases of clergy active in underground activity.[54] Estimates of the number of clergy killed across the former empire are contentious. They vary from 827 priests and monks shot in 1918 and 19 in 1919 (along with 69 imprisoned) to 3,000 clergy shot and 1,500 punished in 1918, and 1,000 shot and 800 punished in 1919.[55] Most of these killings were at the hands of the Cheka or sailors and soldiers. Archbishop Andronnik of Perm', who had supported Kornilov's coup, met a particularly gruesome death, drowned by the Cheka on 20 June 1918, after he called on his clergy to refuse to carry out church services.

Although the party programme of 1918 called for 'systematic anti-religious propaganda to free the masses from their prejudices but without irritating the feelings of others', little effort was made to carry out such propaganda during the civil war. The one exception was the campaign to expose the fraudulence of sacred relics. There were over sixty such cases, following the opening of the massive silver coffin of St Alexandr Svirskii which was found to contain not a miraculously preserved body but a wax effigy. In February 1919 G. I. Petrovskii, the Commissar for Internal Affairs, issued a circular setting out the rationale for such exposures:

> In certain places, workers and peasants have ceased to believe what was drummed into their heads by their former masters, and with their own eyes and hands have examined 'relics' and, to their understandable surprise, have not found what they expected. In the decorated boxes are large dummies made of wadding, sawdust and other junk dressed in appropriate costume. The exposure of this ancient deception does not in any way contradict freedom of conscience and does not contravene any law of the Soviet republic. On the contrary, malicious and deliberate deceivers of the toilers must be brought to strict judicial account.[56]

The exposures stirred up much hostility in the laity and the campaign never had strong backing from the party leadership. The prevailing view inside the RKP(b) at this time was that religious belief would wither away once the economic and political foundations of socialism were in place. By the end of the civil war the campaign to expose relics had run out of steam (although it revived briefly in the late 1920s).

Worker Unrest

It was only a matter of months before the new incumbents in power realized that they had greatly overestimated the level of their working-class support. Crucially, what had been a phalanx of supporters in the industrial working class soon either left the factories or became politically much less reliable. Over a million workers fled the towns for the villages, several hundred thousand left to join the Red Army, and tens of thousands took up administrative positions in the soviet, trade-union, and party organs. The result was that between 1917 and 1920 the number of factory and mine workers fell from 3.6 million to 1.5 million. The fall was dramatic in Petrograd, where by July 1918 the industrial workforce was only about 100,000, 30 per cent of its size on 1 January 1917.[57] The Bolsheviks defined this process as one of 'declassing' and explained the phenomenon of worker unrest, which was endemic during the civil war, as being due to a strengthening of 'petty-bourgeois elements' in the working class. It is true that many of the Bolsheviks' most ardent supporters left industry, but less proletarianized workers with ties to the land were also more likely to leave the factories and head for the countryside, as jobs and food disappeared from the cities, than those who had been resident in the cities for a generation or more. Moreover, a much depleted working class continued to exist: even in Petrograd, where shrinkage was greater than elsewhere, the city's industry produced half the country's artillery and shells, half its explosives, as well as overcoats, boots, and so on to meet the demands of the Red Army.[58]

During the civil war, workers experienced a massive drop in their living standards. By 1920 the real value of the average 'wage' was reckoned to be 38 per cent of the 1913 level, but this was made up largely of rations, free housing, transport, clothing, and other goods. Money wages had lost most of their importance. By 1920 in Petrograd the average real wage was 9.6 per cent of its 1913 level.[59] The search for food, the necessity of doing work on the side, such as making cigarette lighters, together with a huge increase in susceptibility to disease, led to staggering levels of absenteeism and a decline in the already dismally low level of productivity. In September 1920 at the huge Motovilikha works in Perm', absenteeism stood at 50 per cent and theft and deliberate damage to steam engines were rife.

The vision that the factory committees had upheld in 1917 of sustaining production by entrenching workers' power at the level of the shop floor faded within months. The First All-Russian Trade-Union Congress in January 1918 resolved that factory committees should be absorbed into the trade unions, becoming their workplace cells and trade unions, as organizations embracing whole branches of industry, were tasked with overseeing the implementation of the government's economic policy. There was no intention as yet, however, to do away with worker participation in industrial management. The First Congress of Councils of National Economy in late May 1918 agreed that the management boards of nationalized enterprises should comprise one-third worker representatives, alongside representatives from technical staff, trade unions, and state economic organs. This was not to Lenin's liking, for he had come to the view that the only way of improving labour productivity was to put a single individual in charge of each enterprise. Up until the end of 1919, the defenders of collegial management in the trade unions put up stiff resistance to this idea: in 1919 only 11 per cent of enterprises were run by individual managers, although by autumn 1920 this had risen to 82 per cent. Convinced that the Russian worker needed to 'learn how to work', Lenin also demanded that technical specialists and managers be offered high salaries and superior conditions of employment in return for their expertise. This was a policy that was deeply unpopular with many workers. A worker told the Ninth Party Conference in September 1920: 'I'll go to my grave hating *spetsy*.... We have to hold them in a grip of iron, the way they used to hold us.'[60] The Workers' Opposition, the faction that emerged in 1919 to promote the role of the trade unions in the management of the economy, counterposed mass enthusiasm to hierarchy, compulsion, and privileges. But Lenin insisted that technical competence was more important than 'zeal', 'human qualities', or 'saintliness'. By the end of the civil war, therefore, not much was left of workers' control as practised in 1917. The official justification was that it had become outmoded since the economy had now passed into the ownership of a workers' state, allowing worker control to be institutionalized at a higher level, in trade-union inspectorates and organs of state inspection, such as the Workers' and Peasants' Inspectorate (Rabkrin), which was responsible for scrutinizing the state administration.

The civil war saw the autonomy of the trade unions severely curtailed. The First Trade-Union Congress rejected the Menshevik view that trade unions in a workers' state could remain 'neutral' or 'independent', and took the view that since the state itself had taken on the task of defending workers' interests, their chief function must now be to 'organize production and restore the battered productive forces of the country'. To some, this seemed to deprive unions of any capacity to defend the day-to-day interests of workers, and certain unions, such as those of printers and chemical workers, remained bastions of Menshevism. The Bolsheviks tried rather desperately to undercut their influence by manipulating trade-union elections, by arresting die-hard defenders of trade-union autonomy, or by the simple expedient of closing a union and setting up a 'red' one instead (as was done with the printers' union in Petrograd in November 1918). Other unions also proved resistant to Bolshevik takeover, such as those of railway workers, commercial and industrial employees, and bakers.[61] At the same time, Bolshevik trade-union leaders retained a certain independence from government, and were able to resist one-person management and the militarization of labour. In August 1920 this led to such tension that Trotsky peremptorily replaced the elected boards of the railway and water-transport unions with a Central Committee for Transport, which combined the functions of economic commissariat, party organ, and trade union. The All-Russian Central Council of Trade Unions condemned this action, for importing 'bureaucratic methods and orders from above' into trade-union affairs. In the three months preceding the Ninth Party Congress in March 1920, a fierce debate took place concerning the role of trade unions. Trotsky, Bukharin, and others called for the 'planned transformation of the unions into apparatuses of the workers' state', while the Bolshevik trade-union leader Mikhail Tomskii, a metalworker from the age of 13, demanded that the unions retain some autonomy while insisting that their principal task was to oversee the implementation of economic policy. For its part, the Workers' Opposition argued that trade unions should become organs actually running the economy—a position that the Eighth Party Congress had appeared to support in March 1919, but which was condemned as an 'anarcho-syndicalist deviation' by the time of the Tenth Party Congress in March 1921. That Congress overwhelmingly supported a resolution of Lenin which rejected Trotsky's proposal to make the trade unions state organs, instead defining them as 'schools of communism' in which their members would learn how to administer the economy.[62]

As early as spring 1918 worker support for the government started to erode, as unemployment, food shortages, and declining wages began to bite.[63] Mounting bitterness was manifest in a revival of support for Mensheviks and SRs in the soviets. Not untypical was the giant steel and locomotive plant at Sormovo near Nizhnii Novgorod where discontent over food shortages and abuses by local commissars led to new elections to the soviet on 10 April, in which the Bolsheviks won 5,306 votes, the SRs 4,887, Mensheviks 2,887, Left SRs 433, SR Maximalists 346, and non-party white-collar employees 238 votes.[64] The Bolshevik response was simply to bypass the soviet by forming a new Sormovo bureau of the Nizhnii Novgorod soviet. From early March the Mensheviks in many cities launched a campaign to create assemblies of factory plenipotentiaries as alternatives to the soviets, which they said were 'rigged by the Communist majority'. In Petrograd, where the movement was strongest, the assembly grew to 200 delegates, drawn from 72 factories, who claimed to represent over two-thirds of the city's workforce, mainly in the metal and paper industries. The assemblies campaigned for civil rights, independent trade unions, and free soviet elections, with the ultimate aim of reconvening the Constituent Assembly. Yet delegates conceded that worker grievances were predominantly about unemployment, bread rations, and freedom to leave and enter the city. Plans to call a general strike in Petrograd on 2 July were stymied by the Cheka, but it is clear that rank-and-file attitudes were inconsistent and divided. As the delegates ruefully noted, 'the masses have still not turned away from the Bolsheviks and are not completely disenchanted'.[65] In the Volga and Urals a section of the working class welcomed the revolt of the Czech Legion. Podvoiskii, chair of the Supreme Military Inspectorate, reported: 'With rare exceptions workers are hostile to soviet power. The unemployed from the demobilized factories are the most hostile towards us and a certain number of workers at the Pipe and Cartridge factories in Samara have gone over to the Cossacks.'[66] In Siberia railway workers, the most active contingent of organized labour, also assisted the Czech Legion. At Izhevsk in Viatka province, an overwhelmingly working-class town, SR Maximalists in the Red Guard so alienated the local populace through harsh requisitions, searches, and arrests that Mensheviks and SRs won 70 per cent of the 135 seats in new elections to the soviet in May. Desperate to maintain control of one of the country's most important munitions plants at a time when the 'democratic counter-revolution' was in the ascendant, the Bolsheviks promptly disbanded the soviet. On 5 August, as the Czech Legion drew near, the Bolsheviks announced a compulsory draft, which led to the SR-dominated veterans' union, with backing from workers at the plant, seizing control of the town. Thousands of workers, including those at the neighbouring Votkinsk works, joined the People's Army of the SRs, while those who did not remained neutral, until they were subdued by the Second Red Army in mid-November.

In general, workers had no illusions about the nature of the Kolchak regime, however. Between January and November 1919 there were 1,130 mainly economic conflicts, involving 82,000 strikers in the regions it controlled and in cities such as Krasnoiarsk, Irkutsk, and Vladivostok workers remained strong supporters of the Bolshevik cause. On 21 December 1919 the SR Political Centre, which favoured cooperation with the Bolsheviks, instigated an uprising at the Cheremkhovo coal mines, which had been nationalized by the Kolchak regime for pragmatic reasons. Quickly, workers' militias and partisans seized the initiative for the Bolsheviks, marking a turning point in the revival of Red fortunes in Siberia.[67] Similarly in the Donbass, where General S. V. Denisov had hundreds of miners in Iuzivka hanged—a throwback to the days of Stolypin—the experience of White rule firmed up support for the Bolsheviks. All the White administrations suppressed trade unions and restored the authority of the factory owners, so they were extremely unpopular with workers.

This is not to say that worker support for the Red cause was by any means solid. Throughout the civil war there were regular stoppages—most of them limited in scope and duration—caused mainly by dissatisfaction over food supply. By spring 1920, more than 1 million workers were on special rations, but on average these were fulfilled by only one-quarter to one-fifth. In Petrograd in spring 1919, an average worker's daily calorie intake was 1,598, less than half of what it would be four years later.[68] In 1920 there were 146 strikes involving 135,000 workers in eighteen provinces, including Petrograd and Moscow.[69] These strikes were mainly over failure to fulfil rations, but since the regime was now responsible for supplies, they inevitably took on a political coloration. Moreover, the fanatical way in which the Bolsheviks often reacted to worker protest served to politicize discontent still further. From 1919 this mainly took the form of attacks on the privileges enjoyed by officials: 'the communists receive high salaries and food rations, eat three dishes in their canteens, while we are given slops as though we were pigs'.[70] It was often possible to defuse such discontent by bringing in emergency supplies, but the regime had few qualms about using repressive methods if it believed they were necessary. These included confiscation of strikers' ration cards, lockouts, mass dismissals followed by selective rehiring, and, in extremis, the deployment of armed force. In autumn 1920, after the civil war had ended, the chairman of the provincial party committee in Ekaterinoslav reported:

> In September the workers here rose up against the formation and despatch to the countryside of food detachments. We decided to pursue an iron policy.... We closed down the tram park, fired all workers and employees and sent some of them to the concentration camp, some (of the appropriate age) we sent to the front, and others we handed over directly to the Cheka. This had a beneficial effect and the flow of workers into the food detachments intensified.[71]

The Bolsheviks saw the hand of the opposition parties at work in every outburst of worker unrest. While it is doubtful whether Mensheviks and SRs were in a position to instigate worker protest on any significant scale, not least because Cheka repression had left them without unified leadership or effective organization, they were able at times to channel grievances into demands for free soviets, free trade unions, freedom of speech and assembly, and an end to coercion and dictatorship. Most notably this occurred on 10 March 1919 when Putilov workers, angry at the absence of bread, passed a Left SR resolution by 10,000 votes to 22 with four abstentions, excoriating the 'servile yoking of workers to the factories', and calling for the destruction of the 'commissarocracy' and for the transfer of factory management into the hands of free trade unions. It was endorsed by workers at the Skorokhod shoe factory, the Aleksandrovskie railway workshops, and possibly several other workplaces. When Lunacharskii spoke to the workers of the Rozhdestvenskii tram park he was assailed with cries of 'White Guard!', 'Toff!', 'Take off that fur coat!' The suddenness with which worker protest escalated into an attack on the regime prompted the authorities to bring in sailors from Kronstadt to restore order. At an emergency session of the Petrograd Soviet Zinoviev said that only 'backward' workers were left at Putilov and, in a neat reversal of the standard stereotype, women at the Nevskaia cotton mill were induced to pass a resolution condemning the Putilov workers, which was published under the headline 'The voice of the conscious workers'.[72] Yet support for such political opposition was an expression of anger and frustration rather than of principled commitment.

The next major crisis came in Petrograd in February 1921, discussed further below in the section on the Kronstadt rebellion, following endless disruption of supplies and failure to meet ration norms. The Mensheviks were able to revive the assembly of factory plenipotentiaries as a counterweight to the soviet, which had lost the confidence of workers, but the assembly was not as successful as in spring 1918. On 25 February martial law was declared, which proved to be one cause of the Kronstadt rebellion. Tukhachevskii informed Lenin that the 'workers of Petrograd are definitely unreliable' but in fact the fears of the authorities that the city's workers might rise up came to nothing. Once the rebellion in Kronstadt had been suppressed, worker activists were rounded up and fired from their jobs. The key to defusing worker militancy, however, lay essentially in the use of the 'carrot': workers were given a ration of meat, and some basic goods, and roadblock detachments were removed to allow them to trade with the peasantry. In April the Bolsheviks also organized a non-party worker conference at which workers were allowed—for the first time in several years—to vent their grievances.[73]

So long as civil war dragged on, it is probably fair to say that in spite of deep bitterness at the conditions they were forced to endure, the majority of workers had no desire to jeopardize the fortunes of the Red Army. When Iudenich threatened Petrograd in autumn 1919, many worked a sixteen-hour shift to produce the weapons to defeat him. At the beginning of 1920 the Menshevik leader Martov conceded: 'So long as we criticised Bolshevism, we were applauded; as soon as we went on to say that a changed regime was needed to fight Denikin successfully...our audience turned cold or even hostile.'[74] The majority of workers were disgruntled at aspects of the regime but not solidly behind the socialist opposition. During the general strike in Petrograd in February 1921 (mentioned above and further discussed below) Gazenberg, who was responsible for safeguarding the Skorokhod shoe factory, asked strikers on the streets what their demands were: 'We want a bit more bread, we want to purge the high-ups, there are too many *burzhui* among them, and we want new elections to the Soviet.'[75] There were some who raised demands for a Constituent Assembly (some railway workers and some metalworkers in Petrograd and Sormovo) but generally workers wanted a soviet system that lived up to its ideals. If the level of political sophistication was not high, it is clear that many ideals of the Revolution had bitten deep. Workers evinced fierce hostility to *burzhui*, counterposing 'us', the toiling people, to 'them', the parasites. They believed passionately in equality and detested privilege—especially when enjoyed by Communists. When judged against these ideals, they found the Bolsheviks gravely wanting, yet they were not confident that the overthrow of the regime would do anything to further their ideals.[76] There was no credible alternative.

Peasant Wars

Having assisted the Bolsheviks' rise to power through a tumultuous agrarian revolution, the peasants within six months came to be seen as a grave threat to the regime, by dint of their capacity to starve the population.[77] Sporadic uprisings against detachments procuring food occurred in the Urals and the Moscow industrial region as early as spring 1918, at a time when soviet power was generally welcomed by the peasantry. But it was the launch of the food dictatorship in May that triggered a wave of peasant protests in autumn 1918. In 1919 there were hundreds of uprisings, mostly small in scale, prompted by the seizure of grain, conscription, labour or cartage obligations, or abuses by soviet officials. Of the eighty-nine uprisings in the Volga region in 1919 by far the biggest was that of the kaftans (*chapanny*), named after the smock worn by the rebels. Armed mainly with pikes and pitchforks, they rose up in Samara and Simbirsk after the imposition of an emergency tax in March. The rebellion spread fast and at its peak involved over 100,000 people. It worked to the benefit of Kolchak, whose army at that time was advancing east towards the Volga. Red Army units, backed by special Cheka units, abandoned the eastern front in order to suppress the rebellion, which they did with the utmost ruthlessness. The Volga region saw another large rural insurgency in 1920. The pitchfork (*vilochnoe*) uprising was concentrated in Ufa and parts of Samara and Kazan', and the 35,000 insurgents were mainly Tatars. It was provoked by the severe food requisitioning that was being carried out now that the Reds had captured the area. 'Better to die at once than expire from hunger and disease' was a widely reported reaction. The 'black eagle' uprising, which formed a part of this larger uprising, centred on Samara, revealed a rising level of politicization: 'We are the peasant millions. Our enemies are the communists. They drink our blood and oppress us like slaves.'[78]

Peasants frequently behaved in bestial fashion towards soviet and party officials. In Penza in March 1920 Shuvaev, the local commissar, had his nose cut off, then his ears, then his head. The report concluded: 'Now everything is peaceful and quiet. The peasants were calmed with the help of the lash.'[79] As this suggests, Bolsheviks retaliated ruthlessly, taking hostages and shooting leaders. Their military superiority was always decisive. In one battle 15 from the Soviet forces were killed and 47 wounded, whereas 1,078 peasants were killed, 2,400 wounded, and 2,029 captured.[80] In the Volga region in 1918 rebels killed 387 officials and their families, in retaliation for which 1,972 rebels were shot. The kaftan rebels killed about 200, but the punitive detachments killed 1,000 in combat and executed a further 600. In Bolshevik eyes these uprisings were the work of 'kulaks', 'counter-revolutionaries', and 'Black Hundreds'. In the kaftan uprising kulaks were a not insignificant force—many centres of insurgency in Simbirsk and Samara were former trading settlements where up to 40 per cent of households were wealthy—but almost everywhere rebellions were supported by the entire peasant community. In January 1919 in Vedlozerskaia township in Olonets county one official admitted that 'those taking part were mainly from the poorest population'[81] Incidentally, it is noteworthy that in comparison with the peasant movement in 1917, women played a far less significant role.

It is doubtful that the many forms of peasant resistance can usefully be lumped together as a single 'Green movement'. The Soviet authorities used the term 'Greens' to denote the roving bands of deserters from the Red Army who lived in the fields and forests beyond the villages. These deserters survived by banditry, periodically attacking requisition squads and soviet officials. Their bands were more structured and politicized than those of the peasants who rose up spontaneously. Generally, they could rely on the sympathy of villagers, but whenever they tried to organize peasants into a more permanent structure or to draw them into compulsory labour duties, it would provoke discontent.

The truly massive peasant movements that indubitably threatened the regime came after the White threat had been eliminated and lasted for about a year from autumn 1920. These movements saw peasant protest escalate to a new level as 'Green' bands formed peasant armies, commanded by men with combat experience. The movement was most intense in the areas where the *razverstka* was applied most ferociously in summer 1920, namely Tambov and western Siberia. In Tambov villagers in Kamenka rose up against requisition agents on 12 August, killing seven. A. S. Antonov, a former Left SR who had served the soviet cause with distinction until summer 1918, quickly put together an army that eventually had territorial divisions and hierarchies of command, supply lines based on the villages, and 'unions of toiling peasantry' as its political base. This partisan army overthrew the structure of soviet authority, killing more than 2,000 soviet and party officials. The Union of Toiling Peasantry, set up at the end of 1920, set as its tasks:

> To overthrow the Communist-Bolshevik power, which has brought the country to misery, ruin and shame. In order to destroy this violent government and its regime, the Union is organizing voluntary partisan units to conduct armed struggle to bring about: 1) political equality of all citizens without division into classes, excluding the Romanov household; 2) all-round furtherance of a lasting peace with all foreign powers; 3) the summoning of a Constituent Assembly on the basis of universal, direct and equal suffrage,

> without predetermining its will in choosing and establishing a political system, and preserving the right of voters to recall representatives who do not express the will of the people.[82]

The Antonov movement promised freedom of expression, conscience, the press, association, and assembly; complete socialization of the land; the satisfaction of the urban and rural population with means of subsistence, in the first place food, through the cooperatives; regulation of prices of labour and factory produce via the state; partial nationalization of factories, with heavy industry (mining and metallurgy) in the hands of the state; workers' control and state inspection of production. Significantly there was no mention of soviets.[83] By February 1921 practically the entire territory of the Volga had fallen under the control of 40,000 partisans. Thereafter, the Red Army poured forces in, using light aircraft and possibly poison gas, with Tukhachevskii displaying a mercilessness that was shocking even by the dismal standards of the civil war.

The biggest of the peasant wars in terms of participants and scale was that in western Siberia. Here the peasants had supported the partisan movement against the Whites, but the commencement of brutal food requisitioning in summer 1920 created widespread disaffection. Handwritten notices began to circulate: 'Long live the Jewish leaders'; 'If you are hungry, comrades, then sing the Communist Internationale'. The rebellion broke out at the end of January 1921 in a number of centres, notably Ishimskii county in Tiumen' province, then spread to the entire province, and then into various counties of Omsk and Ekaterinburg provinces. The initial resistance was led by women, but it soon took on military form, involving mainly peasants but also Cossacks, local intellectuals, and white-collar workers. By mid-February rebels had overthrown Bolshevik power across 1 million square kilometres of western Siberia—rising to 1.5 million at the peak of the rebellion—and had severed railway contact with European Russia. On 21 February they seized the city of Tobol'sk, where a soviet was formed that proclaimed civil liberties, free trade, equal rations, denationalization of industrial enterprises, and the restoration of the old courts. There may have been as many as 100,000 men fighting (almost the size of the force that Kolchak had had at his disposal). Yet the different divisions, groups, and armies were never subject to a unified command. Cavalry detachments and couriers succeeded in coordinating action across thousands of kilometres, yet peasant detachments were effective mainly when fighting on home territory. The battle for the town of Petropavlovsk was particularly bitter, the town changing hands several times before being seized by the Red Army. Not until autumn 1921 did the Red Army regain full control. Particularly worrying for the authorities was the way the peasant Communists of the Altai region, far to the south-east, deserted to the peasant unions. It is claimed that at least 10,000 party members, soviet officials, members of their families, and Red Army soldiers perished in the fighting, but the casualties on the side of the insurgents probably ran into tens of thousands.[84]

In 1921 there were over fifty large-scale peasant uprisings in regions as far-flung as Ukraine and Belorussia, the North Caucasus, and Karelia. What worried the Bolshevik government was that in a loose way the different regions saw themselves as united in a common cause to overthrow the dictatorship. The Antonov partisans, for example, fought in the expectation that Makhno would come to their aid, even though unbeknownst to them he had fled to Romania. More especially, the Bolsheviks were anxious lest Red Army soldiers go over to the insurgents (there were mutinies in Gomel', Krasnaia Gorka, Vernyi, Nizhnii Novgorod, and elsewhere). The political influence of the SRs was evident in most of the peasant insurgency, but generally the rebels were more supportive of soviets than the SR party centre. It is true that there were a number of demands for the return of the Constituent Assembly—in Zlatoust' district in Ufa a band of 1,000 horsemen roamed under the slogan 'Down with Trotsky, long live Lenin and the Constituent Assembly!'—but the most popular slogan called for 'soviets without communists'.[85] Organizationally, the leaderships of the different uprisings acted independently of the SR party. Rebels were angry at the cruel policies of War Communism and the widespread corruption in the soviet and party apparatus, and desperate to see the Communist regime overthrown, yet a majority remained attached to the ideal of soviet power, which they associated with the victory over the landlords and with land redistribution.

The Kronstadt Rebellion

Those who pushed hardest to restore the ideals of the 1917 Revolution were the sailors and soldiers of Kronstadt, a naval base on Kotlin Island in the Gulf of Finland, some 30 km from Petrograd (see Figure 5.2).[86] They had been the 'flower' of the Revolution in 1917, in the eyes of contemporaries. On 27 and 28 February 1921, disturbed by the way in which the authorities were dealing with the general strike in Petrograd, meetings were held on board the battleship *Petropavlovsk*. On 1 March 16,000 met on Anchor Square and passed a resolution, drafted by the senior naval clerk, Stepan Petrichenko, and the artillery electrician, P. Perepelkin, which called for the dismantling of War Communism and, crucially, for the devolution of power to freely elected soviets, in which all left parties would compete freely, and for freedoms of speech, the press, and association. In addition, it called for political departments, special military units, the Cheka, and 'all privileges of Communists' to be abolished. Unlike the peasant rebels, these sailors did

Figure 5.2 The Red Army crosses the ice to crush the Kronstadt rebellion, 1921.

not expressly call for the overthrow of the Bolshevik regime but did wish to see the dismantling of one-party dictatorship. Theirs was not the programme of any single party, although it was probably closest to that of the SR Maximalists, and it was considerably to the left of the political demands then being raised by strikers in Petrograd and Moscow. When the town fell under the control of the rebels, about 200 local Communists escaped across the ice. But about 900 tore up their party cards and threw in their lot with the rebels; 300 who refused to do so were placed under arrest. Perhaps 12,000 out of 18,000 military and 8,000 to 9,000 adult male civilians (out of a total civilian population of 30,000) backed the rebellion.

On 7 March the Bolsheviks began military operations to crush the insurgency, confident that a speedy victory would coincide with the opening of the Tenth Party Congress the following day. However, effective leadership from professional officers on the island led to Red forces being repulsed with very heavy losses. Scores of Red Army soldiers were shot for refusing to 'pacify' the rebels. On 16 March riflemen of the 27th Omsk Division, who had excelled against the Whites, mutinied with an appeal to 'go to Petrograd and beat the Jews'. Nevertheless news that food requisitioning was to be abolished seems to have stiffened Red Army morale. On 17 March the final assault by some 45,000 troops got under way, and by the following morning the island had been retaken by the Reds. By that stage, some 700 Soviet troops had been killed and 2,500 injured. Over the next couple of months, 2,103 prisoners were sentenced to death—though the number actually shot was in the hundreds—and 6,459 sentenced to terms of imprisonment (1,464 of whom were released).

Lenin depicted the Kronstadt rebellion as a 'White Guard plot'. However in a post-mortem report of 5 April, the Chekist S. S. Agranov, who rose to become head of the NKVD (the successor to the Cheka) at the time of the show trial of Zinoviev and Kamenev in 1936, characterized it accurately as 'a disorganized uprising of the sailor and worker mass' and denied that it had any connection with the Whites.[87] The rebels' dream of local autonomy and their loathing of privilege were anathema to the Whites, and they turned down a request by former SR leader Viktor Chernov, then in Estonia, to visit the island under the banner of the Constituent Assembly. The Bolsheviks claimed that the true leader of the rebellion was Major-General Aleksandr Kozlovskii, a former tsarist officer who had joined the Red Army and been appointed director of artillery on the island. The evidence for this is thin, although White agents certainly intervened once the rebellion got under way. Petrichenko persuaded a reluctant Revolutionary Committee to accept aid from the monarchist Baron P. V. Vil'ken, leader of the naval officers' organization, who visited the rebels as a representative of the Red Cross. How far, on the basis of Cheka reports, the Bolsheviks believed the rebellion was a White Guard plot is difficult to say. A couple of months later, the Cheka claimed to uncover a 'Petrograd Fighting Organization', led by geography professor V. N. Tagantsev, which planned to 'set fire to factories, eliminate Jews, and blow up the monument to the communards'. They arrested 833 people, overwhelmingly intellectuals, 96 of whom were shot or died in detention, including the Silver Age poet Nikolai Gumilëv. In 1992 an investigation concluded that the 'Tagantsev Affair' was fabricated by the Cheka. However, there is documentation to suggest that at least some of those arrested were working to overthrow the regime.[88]

Whether or not the Bolsheviks did believe that the Kronstadt rebellion was a 'White guard plot', they had every reason to fear counter-revolution. That said, they could certainly have dealt with the rebels in a less bloody fashion. It is very doubtful that the sailors and soldiers sought armed confrontation with the regime: the rising was poorly timed and ill prepared and the Bolsheviks had a huge military superiority. Moreover, there was definite scope for negotiation, given that the Bolsheviks had decided to end War Communism at exactly the point when they took the decision to use overwhelming military force. Yet they were in no mood to compromise. This intransigence sprang not from confidence, but from fear. They felt themselves embattled, besieged by an insurgent populace, and the fear—unrealistic on any objective appraisal—was that the rebels would link up with the myriad peasant rebellions, strikes, and mutinies and thus provide a bridgehead for the Whites and their foreign backers. Knowing how they were hated, they were convinced that any show of weakness would give sustenance to rebels elsewhere, especially in the armed forces. Yet in their hearts the Bolsheviks must have known that the aspirations of the rebels—for soviet power, equality, justice—were broadly the same as those that had inspired millions to support them in 1917. And in suppressing the rebellion, they bade farewell to the most cherished—and most utopian—ideals of the 1917 Revolution. Utopian because, having gone through unimaginable horrors in the intervening three and a half years, it is hard to believe that soviet democracy could have provided Russia with stable government. The civil war had transformed the meaning of the Revolution. Henceforward nothing more would be heard of power to the soviets, worker participation in management, or a democratic army. As Lenin said, Kronstadt was the 'flash that lit up reality better than anything else'.

When the Bolsheviks had seized power they had imagined that the working class would be at the heart of the political system. By March 1919, Lenin could declare that soviet rule was rule for the proletariat rather than by it. Paradoxically, the end of the civil war increased rather than decreased the determination of the party to substitute itself for the working class. In his report to the XI Party Congress in March 1922 Lenin declared: 'Very often those who go into the factories are not proletarians; they are casual elements of every description.' To which Shliapnikov, leader of the now defeated Workers' Opposition, responded: 'Permit me to congratulate you on being the vanguard of a non-existent class.... We will not have another and "better" working class, we have to be satisfied with what we've got.'[89]

Against all the odds the Bolsheviks had built the rudiments of a state, using an army, party organization, ideology, and terror. This was a state based on a party dictatorship, which monopolized the means of production and the distribution of basic resources, which operated through peremptory decrees, emergency powers, and extra-legal coercion. In form it was a less than efficient bureaucracy, characterized by arbitrariness, commandism, and waste, and it depended for its functioning on powerful bosses and their cliques. Historians debate how far this came into being as a direct result of Bolshevik ideology and how far as a result of the circumstances of civil war. Some argue that the Marxist notion of the dictatorship of the proletariat as the violent suppression of the former ruling classes justified extreme coercion and fostered antipathy to any form of compromise. They point to Lenin's notion of the party as a 'vanguard', which claimed privileged insight into the workings of history. Others put more weight on circumstances, seeing the massive reliance on coercion as a response to the remorseless demands of raising an army and feeding the population, to entrenched localism, passive resistance, and inertia. Once civil war raged, they suggest, the atmosphere of pervasive violence and destruction, starvation and disease, the constant emergencies, the absence of popular support, bred dictatorial habits of rule and a brutalized psychology on the part of the leadership. In 1920 L. B Kamenev explained it thus: 'Yes, we ruled with the help of dictatorship and in view of the colossal events which we have gone through if we had summoned plenums and tried to solve problems by parliamentary methods, then we would have destroyed the revolution because for us winning time was extremely important.'[90]

The political culture of the RKP(b) was significantly shaped by the experience of civil war. The Bolshevik ethos had always been characterized by ruthlessness, determination, authoritarianism, and class hatred; but the civil war turned these qualities into cruelty, fanaticism, absolute intolerance of any views other than those within the range of permitted Bolshevik opinion. These qualities became central to the anti-democratic culture of the new state. The crude belief that the end justifies the means was espoused without any sense that means may corrupt ends. In August 1919 the newspaper *Krasnyi Mech* (Red Sword) declared: 'Everything is permitted to us, because we are the first in the world to raise the sword not in the name of enserfment and oppression but of general happiness and liberation from slavery.'[91] That the Bolsheviks achieved victory—even if at a punishing cost—further strengthened illusions of infallibility and omnipotence and pitilessness towards opponents. The invasion of foreign powers, the failure of revolution to spread across Europe, bred a mentality of encirclement, of Russia as an armed fortress. During the civil war an obsession with enemies developed that became a distinctive element of the psychology of the Communist leadership: 'the enemy keeps watch over us and is ready at any minute to exploit our every blunder, mistake or gesture of vacillation'. And this was not only a fear of the external enemy, but of the enemy within. On 3 October 1919 party members in the western sector of the troops for the internal defence of the republic (the Cheka's armed force) were told: 'Vigilantly pursue and listen to every conversation on the streets, in order to catch the mood of the philistine public. By this means we can gradually root out all harmful elements from the population.'[92] Such paranoia would grow during the 1920s.

6

THE NEW ECONOMIC POLICY: POLITICS AND THE ECONOMY

In March 1921 Lenin told the Tenth Party Congress that Russia was like a man beaten 'to within an inch of his life'.[1] Against the background of the Kronstadt rebellion and nationwide peasant insurgency, the congress initiated what soon became known as the New Economic Policy (NEP), a massive reorientation of economic and social policy away from War Communism towards the market and private enterprise. As early as January 1920, Iurii Larin had proposed on behalf of the Supreme Council of National Economy a partial shift from grain requisitioning towards commodity exchange with the peasantry, but Lenin demanded he be 'cut down to size'. In March 1920 Trotsky proposed that in selected regions confiscation of agricultural produce be replaced with a tax in kind, but the Central Committee rejected his proposal by 11 votes to 4. From November, however, the prostration of the entire country was too grave to be ignored, and Moscow was bombarded with appeals from the provinces to end War Communism. On 8 February 1921, the Politburo appointed a commission to work out plans for a tax in kind, although this envisaged only a partial legalization of local markets. In the event, a couple of weeks later the Tenth Party Congress gave almost unanimous backing to the universal institution of a tax calculated at 20 per cent of the harvest. More significantly, the Soviet Central Executive Committee (CEC) spelled out that any surplus grain might be sold to cooperatives or on the open market (the word 'trade' was still taboo). In the event, this relatively modest step—recall that a black market had continued throughout the civil war—signalled the beginning of the New Economic Policy (NEP).

The regime moved quickly to restore the market, although within months it would be grappling to tackle the famine. The system of rationing and state distribution of subsistence items was dismantled and in May 1921 much of industry was denationalized, with cooperatives and private entrepreneurs permitted to lease small consumer-goods enterprises. Radical though these measures were, they did not lead to a drastic mitigation of the economic crisis. In parts of the Volga region, the Don, and Ukraine famine lingered into 1923.[2] Nevertheless agriculture recovered quickly and the harvests of 1922 and 1923 were good. However, the trusts that oversaw the different branches of nationalized industry continued to maintain the price of manufactured goods at an artificially high level, and this resulted in 1923 in the scissors crisis. This was the first crisis of NEP. In the scissors crisis the 'blades' of industrial and agricultural prices opened ever wider to the point where by October 1923 industrial prices were 290 per cent above their 1913 level, while agricultural prices were only 89 per cent.[3] The bias against agricultural prices worsened in 1924 as peasants, eager to pay taxes in money rather than in kind, released a considerable volume of grain onto the market, further pushing down prices. The government responded by introducing stringent fiscal, credit, and price measures to lower industrial prices. Through massively cutting public expenditure, slashing subsidies to the state sector, and requiring state-owned enterprises to make a profit, the scissors crisis was overcome. In addition, by 1924 a stable currency had been restored, in which the ruble was backed by gold, a remarkable achievement given the inflationary anarchy that had prevailed. By this stage, the NEP had emerged in full: it was a hybrid, mutating system that combined a peasant economy, state industry subject to 'economic accounting', private trade and industry, a state and cooperative network of procurement and distribution, a credit system, and a rudimentary capital market. However, even after the scissors crisis had been overcome, the system continued to experience problems, not least because of the reluctance of government economic organs to allow market forces too much sway.

While all Bolsheviks agreed that NEP was a 'transitional' phase, the nature and duration of that transition proved to be a matter of bitter dispute. Lenin was ambivalent, speaking of NEP both as a 'retreat' and as a policy intended to last 'seriously and for a long time'. In his last writings, such as *On Cooperation*, penned in January 1923 when he was already seriously ill, he went so far as to concede that 'there has been a radical modification in our whole outlook on socialism' and that the 'system of civilized cooperators is the system of socialism'. He sketched a perspective of a gradual transition to socialism based upon a 'cultural revolution' (discussed in Chapter 7) and the expansion of cooperatives among the peasantry.[4] Some historians argue that these valedictory meditations demonstrate that Lenin had come to embrace a market-based alternative to statist socialism, in which the Soviet Union would evolve gradually from state capitalism to socialism.[5] Yet neither he nor his party seriously deviated from the conception of socialism as entailing the elimination of the market and state ownership of the entire means of production. Equally, however, it is clear that Lenin did come to see NEP as more than a 'retreat', namely, as a system in which market mechanisms of private trade, profit and loss, and monetary relations would gradually be used to strengthen the state sector at the expense of the private sector, over a period of at least 'one or two decades'.

Bolsheviks and markets were never happy bedfellows, and from the first the government felt impelled to interfere in the operation of the market, not least because the working class tended to suffer from the new system more than the peasantry.[6] In a bid to strengthen state-owned industry, as early as 1923, the Supreme Council of National Economy sought to restrict sources of private credit to private entrepreneurs, and to increase the role of syndicates in distributing commodities.[7] Following Lenin's death in 1924, economic policy increasingly became a bone of contention within the party leadership, at the heart of the struggle to establish who should replace him. The Stalin group, in the ascendancy from the mid-1920s, defended NEP against the Left Opposition, but from 1926 gradually turned against it. Nevertheless from 1924 to 1926 NEP enjoyed a heyday in which market forces were allowed considerable scope, especially in agriculture. This was the period when the official slogan was 'Face to the countryside' and even 'kulaks' were offered significant leeway. Thereafter the Politburo increasingly intervened to direct policy, undermining the authority of the Council of People's Commissars and the Council of Labour and Defence, both organs that were broadly supportive of NEP. The war scare of summer 1927, which was precipitated by Britain's severing diplomatic relations after Soviet espionage was uncovered, was critical in hardening the determination of the Stalin group to step up the rate of investment in heavy industry. A crisis emerged in summer 1928 when difficulties in procuring grain from the harvest year 1927–8 led to the reintroduction of rationing in the cities. This coincided with the onset of the First Five-Year Plan, which had been ratified at the Fifteenth Party Congress in December 1927. The Stalin leadership now became convinced that instead of the state sector gradually gaining dominance over the private sector, the reverse was happening: kulaks were holding the towns to ransom and in the cities 'nepmen' (the business people who seized the opportunities for private enterprise opened up by NEP) and the 'bourgeoisie' were becoming ever more influential. It resolved to be done with NEP.

New Economic Policy and Agriculture

The ideological aim of NEP was, in the jargon of the leadership, to cement the alliance (*smychka*) between the proletariat and the peasantry. Yet NEP never overcame the conflict between the needs of the town and countryside that had first appeared during the First World War. The government recognized the need to invest in modernizing agriculture by introducing new equipment, continuing the rationalization of land use, and by encouraging the resettlement of population, but it was unable and unwilling to commit the large-scale resources that these things required, given that its overwhelming priority was to accelerate industrialization. Moreover, the desire to mollify the peasantry and modernize agriculture strained against the need to squeeze the countryside for grain, raw materials, and timber: not only to feed the towns, but also to extract a surplus of agricultural produce that could be sold for export in return for the import of industrial equipment.

As early as 1923, grain exports resumed even as some areas continued to go hungry.[8] Nevertheless peasant society recovered from its desperate plight with astonishing speed.

By the middle of the 1920s the agrarian economy was back to pre-war levels of output. Farming continued to be prey to the vicissitudes of the weather. The harvest of 1924–5 was disappointing owing to severe drought in many regions, but thereafter harvests were good. By 1926 grain output had recovered to its pre-war level, although per capita output remained somewhat below the 1909–13 average. This was partly due to the destruction of the most commercially developed landed estates in the course of the Revolution, so that in the key southern and central agricultural regions grain surpluses never reached more than 70 per cent and 35 per cent, respectively, of their pre-war levels.[9] The output of non-grain products was far more buoyant, exceeding pre-war levels. By 1925 cattle numbers had almost recovered to 1916 levels and milk production exceeded the 1913 level. The number of horses, however, was still slightly below the 1913 level by 1928.[10] By the mid-1920s peasants, though still very poor by modern standards, were enjoying the best times they would see between 1914 and the 1950s. Having 'over-supplied' the market during the scissors crisis, peasants were increasingly consuming more of their produce, selling just enough to cover their taxes and other expenses. In comparison with the pre-revolutionary period, the burden of direct taxation on land, cattle, and horses had increased, but since land rents had been abolished, the combined burden of indirect and direct taxes on farm incomes fell from 19 per cent in 1913 to just under 10 per cent in 1926–7.[11] Moreover, the tax was broadly progressive, so that in 1924–5 one-fifth of households were exempt on the grounds that they were poor peasants (a proportion that rose to one-third by 1929). Taxes were lowered in spring 1925, so that the economic year 1925–6 may be said to mark the apogee of NEP, the time when official policy, as articulated by Bukharin and at this point backed by Stalin, was at its most favourable to the peasantry. This was also the point when official policy towards the wealthier peasants was at its most lenient, since restrictions on hiring labour and leasing land were relaxed.

The relative decline in the tax burden was thus a factor discouraging peasants from marketing as much grain as they had done before the Revolution.

Another reason for the fall in the amount marketed, in addition to the tax issue just mentioned, was that in spite of the scissors crisis, the terms of trade between agriculture and industry continued to favour the latter. More particularly, they disfavoured grain compared with other types of farm produce and livestock. In 1926 grain accounted for only 35 per cent of net agricultural output, and the proportion of that which was sold on the market was lower than before the war.[12] Between 1926–7 and 1928–9 the terms of trade for agriculture improved, owing to a lowering of industrial prices, but although the total volume of agricultural produce sold continued to rise, sales of grain did not increase. Indeed a lowering of the procurement prices for grain led to a serious shortage by the autumn of 1927, when only 16.9 per cent of the grain harvest was marketed compared with 24 per cent in 1913.[13] Peasants clearly preferred to hold on to their grain, using it to feed a rapidly growing population, to eat better, to rebuild livestock herds, and to turn it into alcohol. On 6 January 1928 the Central Committee issued a circular, signed by Stalin, which criticized local party and state organizations for slowness in handing over 'surpluses', and ordered them to speed up the payment of peasant 'arrears'. 'In recovering arrears of all kinds apply immediately the harshest punishment, in the first instance towards the kulaks.'[14] Shortly thereafter, Stalin took the unprecedented step of leading an expedition to Siberia to oversee the implementation of the decree, announcing while he was there that the 'shock task' of all party and soviet organizations was to keep up maximum pressure on the 'procurement front'—a return to the language of civil war.[15] Nevertheless, Stalin still faced opposition from rivals within the party leadership, notably Bukharin and Aleksei Rykov, and the April 1928 plenum of the Central Committee temporarily reversed course to a more pro-market policy. In summer 1928, however, as rationing was introduced in the cities, Stalin's line of using force to procure grain prevailed.[16]

The 1920s was a period when the underlying resilience and traditionalism of peasant society reasserted itself. The agrarian revolution had strengthened the influence of the commune and left little of the Stolypin reforms in place. The Land Code of 1922 strengthened communal principles of land use by making labour the criterion of eligibility for land and by prohibiting the purchase and sale of land. At the same time, the drafters of the law sought to encourage households to enclose their holdings, in the spirit of the Stolypin reforms, and to discourage the trend for sons to demand their share of land and to set up their own farms. In 1922 almost 99 per cent of peasant land in the RSFSR was under communal control and the percentage would only decrease to about 95 per cent by end of the decade. A few individual farmsteads did survive in the west and north-west, where they comprised 19 per cent and 11 per cent of peasant land, but for most peasants the costs of separating from the commune and consolidating their allotments—through building, digging wells, and drainage—remained beyond their means.[17]

Change was taking place, but not at a pace that could satisfy the regime. The Commissariat of Agriculture, the largest government ministry by the end of the 1920s, pursued many of the policies of its tsarist predecessor. Between 1922 and 1927, 98.3 million hectares were redistributed between and within communities, mainly to the benefit of the neediest households.[18] Land reorganization involved promoting multi-field rotation, merger of strips, reducing the distance between strips, and technical improvements such as the replacement of the scratch-plough by the wooden plough. The Commissariat was one of the ministries—others were the commissariats for trade and finance—which were most committed to NEP, downplaying class differentiation in the countryside and seeking to work with, rather than against, the commune in its effort to encourage innovation. This, plus the fact that many of its staff were former SRs, only served to arouse suspicion in sections of the party leadership and led to the Commissariat's being overhauled at the end of the 1920s.[19] On the eve of the forced collectivization, however, agriculture still remained primitive, with modern equipment such as horse-drawn sowing machines, harvesters, mowers, and threshing machines still a rare phenomenon. NEP proved that it could sustain slow extensive growth of agricultural output, but it could not generate the big increase in productivity that was required if rapid industrialization were to be achieved.

The Communist Party saw the abolition of small peasant farming and the creation of agricultural collectives as the solution to this problem, but so long as Lenin lived this was seen as a medium- to long-term project. In particular, collectivization of agriculture was understood to be a process that the peasantry would undertake voluntarily. In his last writings Lenin argued that the expansion of cooperatives would serve as a brake on private trade and as a bridge to large-scale collective farming. Deliberately squeezed during the civil war, the cooperative movement in 1922 stirred into life, in spite of high taxes on its activities, tight credit, and the general instability of the ruble. Only in December 1923 did the government make a decisive concession to the cooperatives by making membership voluntary. Between January 1923 and April 1924, the number enrolled in cooperatives grew from 4.9 million to 6.9 million, mostly in supply and purchasing cooperatives or credit cooperatives. By 1928 there were 28,600 such cooperatives, embracing nearly half of peasant households, testimony perhaps to the potential that Lenin saw in them.[20] However, producer cooperatives remained few in number and the bulk of peasants preferred to trade on the open market. Moreover, through its insistence on strictly regulating their activities, the party clogged the administration of the cooperatives with staff and cramped their economic freedom. More generally, the robustness of the commune was a factor that inhibited government efforts to promote voluntary collective farms: even by 1928, two-thirds of collective farms were rudimentary associations for common cultivation, attracting relatively small numbers of mainly poor peasants.

In the countryside the forces of tradition still prevailed over those of change, but the burning question of land no longer absorbed the younger generation in the way that it had its parents. A sample of letters sent to the *Peasant Newspaper* between 1924 and 1926—from a total of 1.3 million received—presents a complex picture. Nearly 60 per cent of letters reflect what might be called a 'traditional' orientation to agriculture, insofar as they were not antagonistic to the market, yet urged the state to ensure fairness by modifying its operation through taxation and agricultural subsidies.[21] Such letters were also traditional in that they favoured collective over individual forms of enterprise, seeing the gradual development of cooperatives as most in tune with the 'Russian' way of doing things. The rest of the letters divide more or less equally into three: those that saw individual entrepreneurship as the only way to improve peasant living standards and were distrustful of the state; those—overwhelmingly from poor peasants—that bemoaned continuing inequalities and looked to the state to rectify these; and those—which included letters from Communists and members of agricultural communes—that were genuinely enthusiastic for collective forms of agriculture.

New Economic Policy and Industry

Nearly all large industry, along with the banks and wholesale trade, remained in state hands, and most investment outside agriculture was financed by the state. The industrial-branch boards (*glavki*) under the Supreme Council of National Economy were dismantled and replaced by trusts, which were associations of enterprises in the same branch of industry. By the end of 1922 there were 421 of these. State enterprises under the trusts were subject to 'commercial accounting' (*khozraschët*), whereby they could retain any revenues they made but must also bear any losses. The slashing of state subsidies in 1924, in a drive to bring prices under control, nearly led to the closure of the iconic Putilov works. Eighty per cent of trusts were organized into syndicates, which already existed under tsarism in certain capital goods sectors, which facilitated marketing, supplies, and finance for foreign trade deals and generally controlled sales and wholesale prices. By 1928 twenty-three such syndicates controlled the bulk of wholesale trade. One of the most radical initiatives was to allow foreign firms the right to use state enterprises. In 1926–7 there were 117 such concessions, many of them German, which were mainly involved in extractive industries, such as lead, silver, gold, and manganese. However, these concessions failed to generate substantial foreign investment. More significantly, NEP allowed small factories and artisanal enterprises to return to private enterprise or into cooperative ownership. However, in Moscow by 1924 only a fifth of the city's workforce was employed in the cooperative or private sectors, compared with around four-fifths employed in 422 state enterprises. Moreover, the attempt to subject the state sector to market disciplines was half-hearted. Even in the first half of the 1920s, enterprises under 'commercial accounting' were deprived of complete independence, insofar as state organs increasingly fixed wholesale industrial prices and a growing number of retail prices, allocated credit, attempted to regulate wages, imposed controls on imports, and sought to oversee the country's economic development through an annual state plan (so-called 'control figures').[22]

Nevertheless NEP led to a rapid recovery of industry, especially in war-torn areas such as the Donbass, the Baku oilfields, the Urals, and Siberia. The index of industrial production tripled between 1921 and 1926, and by the economic year 1926–7, production in large-scale industry surpassed the pre-war level. The output of small-scale industry, now largely in private hands, constituted 30 per cent of gross industrial production.[23] Net industrial investment increased—it was perhaps 20 per cent higher by 1927–8 than in 1913—but it is reckoned that two-thirds of investment came from the state budget, so it came at the expense of investment in housing and transport. However, the costs of industrial production were two to 2.5 times higher in 1926 than they had been in 1913, owing to ageing capital stock, and the quality of output was poorer.[24] There was some reduction in industrial costs by 1927–8 but only relative to the extremely high costs of the preceding years. By 1928 gross national income had reached the pre-war level (though it is less certain that this is so if measured on a per capita basis).[25] Overall, therefore, the record of NEP in industry was mixed. It undoubtedly engendered a rapid recovery of industry—in some ways remarkable, given the dire straits into which industry had sunk by 1920. Crucially, however, it failed to narrow the gap in production per head between the Soviet Union and the advanced industrial countries, and the technology gap between them widened during the 1920s. By 1928, it was clear that neither the state nor private capital could raise the funds necessary for the big expansion of factories, mines, or oil extraction that was felt to be urgently required within the framework of NEP.

In contrast to capitalism, socialist industrialization was supposed to be carried out in a rational fashion, through central planning, specialization, and universal norms. Since 1917 there had been talk of a 'single economic plan', and despite the turn to the market, planning began in earnest in the 1920s. Lenin was especially enthusiastic about the plan for the electrification of the country, proposed by Gleb Krzhizhanovskii, who had managed to combine an active career as a Bolshevik with overseeing the installation of the electricity network in Moscow in 1912–14. Lenin hailed electrification as a step that 'will link town and countryside, will make it possible to raise the level of culture in the countryside and overcome, even in the remote corners of the land, backwardness, ignorance, poverty, disease and barbarism'. The image of the peasant seeing his first light bulb was immortalized in posters, stamps, and on lacquer boxes. Thus despite the radicalism of the privatization measures introduced by NEP, major organs of government—the Council of Labour and Defence, the Supreme Council of National Economy, and the new State Planning Commission (Gosplan), chaired by Krzhizhanovskii—worked to lay the ground for state-directed industrialization.

One of the currents within Bolshevik ideology, sometimes called 'productivist', came to the fore during NEP.[26] This saw the advance to socialism as predicated on central planning and on the application of science and technology to the development of the productive forces. 'Productivism' regarded the social organization of labour inherited from capitalism, with its particular technologies and techniques to raise productivity, as politically neutral. One of its more curious expressions was the vogue for NOT, or the 'scientific organization of labour', a Soviet appropriation of F. W. Taylor's theory of scientific management. Advocates of NOT argued that in Soviet

Russia what Lenin had once called the 'refined brutality' of Taylorism could be applied to tackle the most fundamental source of the country's backwardness, namely, the desperately low level of labour productivity. One of its chief proponents was A. K. Gastev, a former syndicalist and 'worker-poet', who in 1920 became the director of the Central Institute of Labour. He dreamed of a socialist society in which man and machine would merge: 'In the social sphere we must enter the epoch of precise measurement, formulae, blueprints, controlled calibration, and social norms.' In 1923 a Time League was formed to agitate for the more economical use of time: 'Instead of "perhaps"—a precise calculation | Instead of "anyhow"—a thought-out plan | Instead of "somehow"—a scientific method | Instead of "sometime"—on 25 October at 20.35' (the latter reference being, of course, to the storming of the Winter Palace).[27] The productivist vision did not go unchallenged. When Gastev proclaimed in 1928 that 'the time has gone beyond recall when one could speak of the freedom of the worker in regard to the machine and still more in regard to the enterprise as a whole', critics at the Eighth Komsomol Congress condemned this conception of the worker as indistinguishable from that of Henry Ford. And with the onset of the First Five-Year Plan in 1928, the impulse to make science the arbiter of industrial relations came increasingly to conflict with the heroic, voluntarist strain within Bolshevism that lauded revolutionary will and collective initiative. Although 'socialist competition' and 'storming' did not become the order of the day until the onset of the First Five-Year Plan (1928–32), as early as 1926 'shock brigades' in the Ukrainian metallurgical industry and the Triangle rubber factory in Leningrad set out to bust scientifically calculated production norms.

With NEP the tight controls over labour associated with militarization in the civil war were lifted, but at the same time managerial hierarchies were restored within state-owned enterprises. The board of each trust now appointed a single director to run each enterprise under the trust, although in 1922 nearly two-thirds of these 'Red Directors', as they were known, were former workers.[28] The director was expected to run the enterprise in collaboration with its party cell and the trade-union committee, and the latter were expected to support him in his efforts to revive and expand production. Along with this came an assertion of the importance of technical and managerial expertise, such as Lenin had argued for since 1918. Workers continued to view the *spetsy* with suspicion: 'The red specialists behave worse than the old owners: they never greet us as they pass by, whereas the boss used to chat and shake our hand.'[29] NEP also saw the power of the foreman substantially restored on the shop floor, although not to the extent that had appertained under tsarism. Cases of foremen behaving rudely to workers, and demanding bribes and sexual favours, quickly resurfaced. In 1927 miners in Shakhty in the Donbass rebelled against an order they received to work twelve-hour shifts to fulfil new production targets. Their rallying-cry was: 'Beat the Communists and the *spetsy*.' During the First Five-Year Plan the regime would cleverly exploit worker resentment against *spetsy* to stiffen support for 'socialist construction'.[30]

Lenin had proclaimed in 1918 that 'the Russian worker must learn how to work' and the 1920s saw a determined drive to overcome low labour productivity by reorganization of the labour process. The low level of productivity was due to a number of factors, including primitive technology, wear and tear on machinery, low levels of skill, and, not least, poor labour discipline. Sometimes the latter was due to the restoration of traditional patterns of industrial relations, as in the textile industry of the central industrial region, where the symbiotic relationships between field and factory revived and work groups based on family or village reasserted themselves.[31] The campaign to raise labour productivity entailed increasing output by reducing piece rates and increasing output norms and, more slowly, by introducing greater mechanization, standardization, and specialization in production. Time-study bureaux were brought into the factories and psychophysiologists, psychotechnicians, and labour hygienists sought to measure and improve the output per worker in a fixed span of time. Achievement fell well short of aspiration, yet by 1927 the rationalization drive had pushed up average hourly labour productivity to 10 per cent above its 1913 level.[32] One baleful consequence was that the industrial accident rate also shot up from an average of 26 per 1,000 for the principal industries in 1925 to 443 by 1927, although fatalities fell in the same period.[33]

New Economic Policy and Labour

By 1926 the numbers employed in large-scale industry (3.1 million), construction (0.2 million), and railways (0.9 million) had recovered to approximately the level of 1913. Of the total number of waged workers (including white-collar employees) in 1926, 7.8 million were employed in the state sector, and just 1.8 million in the private sector.[34] The number of waged workers rose steadily, from 6.7 million in 1924–5 to 10.4 million in 1929.[35] Significantly, in the RSFSR white-collar employees grew as fast as blue-collar workers, each constituting about 26 per cent of the urban population in 1926.[36] By 1929, there were 3.82 million industrial workers, of whom 31.1 per cent were in textiles and 26.6 per cent in metalworking and machine-building. It was reckoned that only 18.5 per cent of the industrial workforce was skilled, the rest being semi- or unskilled. The proportion of women (28.7 per cent) was somewhat lower than in 1913.[37]

The regime set in place a corporatist system of industrial relations, comprising representatives of management and the trade unions, in which wages and working conditions were to be regulated through collective agreements, and disputes resolved through rates-and-conflict commissions. With the restoration of a labour market the right of the trade unions to bargain over wages and conditions—including the right to strike—was gradually restored. The NEP made trade-union membership voluntary, and initially the number of trade unionists fell from 8.4 million in 1921 to 4.5 million in October 1922, many of the drop-outs being artisans who were excluded for being 'owners of means of production'. Thereafter, membership rose steadily to reach 11 million by 1928, and it embraced employees well beyond the industrial workforce.[38] This indicates that workers recognized the benefit of being a trade-union member, not least because the unions now administered welfare benefits, holidays, promotion, and educational opportunities. The number of female trade unionists doubled to reach 2.57 million by 1927, but despite rules and quotas designed to protect the interests of women and youth, the needs of these groups were subordinated in practice to those of adult male workers from the mid-1920s.[39] The unions lost their voice in policy-making, but they could still contest management decisions through the rates-and-conflict commissions and through the courts. In 1924 the Sixth Congress of Trade Unions condemned the so-called 'regime of economy' for worsening working conditions; and as late as 1928, the unions successfully resisted the upward revision of output norms. The unions were expected to prevent conflicts from breaking out, but it was not unknown for them to back workers in disputes. In general, they, along with other mass organizations, were expected to educate workers in the official ideology and to act as 'transmission belts' between the party and the masses, a mechanistic image that suggested that the party-state drove the machinery of society.

A paradoxical development of the 1920s was that unemployment rose even as the numbers in employment also rose. It was a major problem that particularly affected women, which was mitigated only slightly by the introduction in 1922 of rudimentary unemployment insurance. By 1924 the number out of work had reached 1.4 million, mainly due to the demobilization of the Red Army and to the pressure on enterprises to achieve 'economic accounting'. The number out of work dropped slightly in the mid-1920s, but returned to the 1924 level by January 1927, accounting for over 10 per cent of the workforce. In 1928 the figure rose still higher.[40] By this stage, the cause was the resumption of migration from the countryside to the towns. In 1928 over a million people settled permanently in the cities, and there were an additional 3.9 million seasonal migrants.[41] This resumption of the pre-war pattern of migration worsened an already acute housing situation and put strain on the rudimentary network of welfare services.

The number of women in employment rose during the 1920s but their share of the workforce—just under 30 per cent—remained smaller than it had been during the First World War. The Soviet Union became the first country in the world to introduce equal pay, so women's wages rose relative to the pre-war period; yet in 1928 women's average daily earnings were still only two-thirds those of men. In part this was a reflection of women's low skills, but it was, notwithstanding trade-union policy, a reflection, too, of job discrimination. In the early 1920s, the unions insisted that women should not be the first to be laid off in the event of redundancies. The printers' union, for example, declared: 'We should never place [a woman] in dependence on the work of her husband, since this enserfs her materially and therefore morally, turning her into a slave.'[42] From around 1925, however, as unemployment persisted, decisions on who should be laid off first were increasingly made on the basis of family need and, inevitably, it tended to be wives rather than husbands who lost their jobs. Women seem to have accepted this, not least because they generally earned less than their menfolk, but it is noteworthy that the regime adapted to this family-based perspective. It should also be noted that women's unemployment was in part a consequence of the decline in domestic service. In 1912 twice as many women worked in domestic service as in factories, but the number fell during the war.[43] From the end of the civil war, the number of 'domestic workers', as they were now known, grew steadily, and by 1929, 527,000 women lived in with their employers or, less commonly, came to work on a daily basis. This was only half the pre-war figure, but it represented 16 per cent of employed women. Domestic workers were employed by professionals, nepmen, party officials, and even by workers, since their labour was cheap. Now, though, domestic workers were protected by legislation and defended by trade unions, even if their living conditions and treatment by employers often fell short of official standards.[44]

In important respects workers' lives improved during the 1920s. Trade-union members enjoyed free medical care, maternity allowances, disability pensions, and other benefits. Real wages struggled to reach their pre-war level, but subsidized rents and transport meant that most workers were probably better off. Perhaps the greatest improvement was the achievement of an eight-hour working day, a demand first raised by the labour movement in 1905. Working conditions in privately owned factories—though often criticized in the press—do not seem to have been any worse than in state enterprises, mainly because they were now subject to a system of labour inspection, social insurance, and tax inspection.[45] By 1927 most workers were eating better than they had ten years earlier: official figures suggest that per capita consumption of bread had fallen, but that consumption of meat, dairy products, and sugar had risen. Even so, eggs and dairy produce remained luxuries for many.[46] This bird's eye view may mask a bleaker reality, since one factory survey showed that on average men and women weighed 5 kilograms less than the norm, and that calorific intake was no better than it had been in the 1890s. And in 1928–9, shortages of food would once again become a problem and the institution of the queue for subsistence items would become a standard feature of Soviet life.

Labour intensification, cuts in piece rates, highly differentiated wage scales, and shortages of consumer goods were hardly likely to enthuse the average worker, however necessary they may have been as means to industrialize a backward, internationally isolated society. Not surprisingly, there was no shortage of collective protest, albeit on a sectional basis. Up to 1924 the key cause of strikes was delay in the payment of wages; thereafter it was reductions in wage rates, increases in output norms, and changes in the organization of production.[47] According to official figures, strikes peaked in the USSR in 1922, when there were 431 stoppages involving 197,215 strikers. Thereafter the number fell to 196 in 1925, involving 37,600; then rose to 396 in 1927, involving 25,400 workers, before falling sharply in 1928 to 90 strikes and 9,700 strikers.[48] Even if the number of strikes in the second half of the 1920s was higher than these figures indicate, it is clear that stoppages became fewer, shorter, and smaller in scope. The regime thus seems to have been successful in avoiding outright stoppages by channelling worker dissatisfaction through the rates-and-conflict commissions. The threat of unemployment was doubtless a factor that deterred workers from taking strike action. Other factors may have been the co-option of potential leaders through their promotion into semi-official positions, as well as the diffuse ideological influence exercised in state enterprises by the party cells and trade unions. In the private sector, which mainly comprised small workshops, a further factor depressing levels of industrial conflict was that relations between workers and employers were still paternalistic. In Tula the party provincial committee reported that 'between 30% and 40% of workers follow their bosses and consider him their benefactor'.[49] Finally, the likelihood of arrest was also doubtless a deterrent factor, although after 1924 there was less recourse to suppression of strikes than there had been during the civil war. Crucial to understanding the decline in collective protest, however, was the change in political context.

In tsarist times labour militancy had reflected the fact that economic struggles were easily politicized, the factory being construed as a microcosm of the wider autocratic order. This was, obviously, no longer the case. A regime was now in power that hailed the working class as the leading class in society, vested with the task of building socialism. Yet in a different way, this ideological positioning of the working class also facilitated the fusion of economic and political grievances, for workers expected better working and living conditions from a regime that purported to rule in their name. It is not easy to generalize about workers' political attitudes during NEP. It is likely that enthusiastic supporters of the regime comprised a sizeable minority, mainly those active in the workplace party cell, trade union, or the Komsomol: a guess would be that they constituted no more than one-fifth of the workforce, including the one in ten workers who by 1928 had joined the Communist Party. These were idealists, though they also had reason to see their own advancement as proof that socialism was being built. In addition, a small percentage of politically engaged workers saw NEP as a betrayal of the ideals of socialism, these orienting to Trotsky's Left Opposition.[50] At the other extreme was a large minority who were apathetic, apolitical, and alienated from the regime. If they had a political orientation it was likely to be towards nationalism. These were the workers that the official ideology categorized as 'backward'. The male representatives of this group resented official campaigns such as those against alcohol, against what we would now call male chauvinism, or against antisemitism. Among this group, for example, complaints were rife to the effect that the regime gave Jews preferential treatment in respect of promotion, education, and jobs in the state administration. 'There are only Jews on the board of the textile trust and they defend their brothers and oppress Russians.'[51] In between were the majority of workers who believed that the government should rule on their behalf but who were dispirited by the gap between official rhetoric and reality. These workers were not hardened opponents of the regime: turn-out in elections to urban soviets, for example, rose from a low of 36.5 per cent in 1922 to 59.5 per cent in 1926–7.[52] This majority welcomed the improvements to their living and working conditions that were being made, but felt that they were too few and too slow. In particular, they were bitter in their criticism of the privileges enjoyed by party, government, and economic officials. In Gomel' workers were reported as saying, 'soviet power doesn't defend us; the communists are like the nobility, a special privileged class, who hold power and enjoy all the good things of life'. More politically sophisticated were criticisms that held the leadership to account for its failure to abide by the ideals of the Revolution: 'Who can rate the chances for socialism when a worker earns 40 rubles and expends much physical energy, whereas those in power earn 300 rubles.'[53] Such criticism, centring on the absence of equality and collectivism, reflected the gap between workers' aspirations and the realities of NEP, and probably a majority of workers sympathized with this sentiment. At the same time, this majority continued to espouse the ideal of 'soviet power'.

The contradictoriness of worker attitudes provides a clue to why collective protest was less frequent than one might have expected. Leaving aside the fear of reprisals, many workers in some inchoate way still believed that the regime was 'theirs'. This attitude was underpinned by the fact that in spite of poor living and working conditions, they were relatively privileged compared with other social groups. Moreover, official propaganda constantly hammered home the idea that the proletariat was now the ruling class. And therein lay the rub. For class had become a problematic language for the articulation of worker grievances in a way that had not been true up to 1917. Workers could still use it—especially to condemn official privilege—but the most powerful exponent of the language of class, with power to determine its strategic uses through the mass media, organs of censorship, schools, and the like, was the state itself. And through the use of categories such as 'conscious' and 'backward', through the condemnation of many entirely reasonable grievances as an expression of 'petty-bourgeois' consciousness or even—*horribile dictu*—of counter-revolutionary Menshevism, the regime was able to erode the political potency of the language that in 1917 had served to knit together the disparate elements of the workforce into a self-conscious class.

The Inner-Party Struggle

Logically, NEP implied political as well as economic reform, but this was never something the leadership could countenance. Indeed it concluded that liberalization on the economic front required an intensification of the party's monopoly of power and party leaders were increasingly willing publicly to voice the party's absolute right to rule. In April 1923 Zinoviev told the Twelfth Party Congress:

> It is impossible to agree with the paradoxical view that the presidium of the Soviet CEC carries out the same role for the soviets as the Central Committee does for the party. It's totally incorrect. The Central Committee is the Central Committee, whether it be for the soviets, the trade unions, the co-operatives, the provincial executives, or the whole working class. In that resides its leading role, in that is expressed the dictatorship of the party.[54]

Zinoviev would come to rue his words, as the space for dissent within the party dramatically narrowed. The Tenth Party Congress in 1921 imposed a ban on factions that was supposed to be temporary, authorizing the Central Committee 'to apply all measures of party punishment up to and including expulsion from the party in cases of violation of discipline or of a revival or toleration of factionalism'.[55] When in May 1921 Gavril Miasnikov, a worker who had been a party member for fifteen years, wrote an article calling for freedom of expression for workers and peasants, 'from anarchist to monarchist opinion', Lenin demanded that the Perm' provincial committee discipline him. The committee ordered the party branch at the Motovilikha works, where Miasnikov worked, not to elect him to a forthcoming conference on account of his 'unwholesome thoughts'. But his former comrades protested: 'If one discounts lies, slander and abuse, the provincial committee knows of no other way of dealing with those who think differently than repression.'[56] Needless to say, Miasnikov was soon out on his ear.

In the second half of 1921, Lenin's health declined, significantly affecting his ability to work. The Eleventh Party Congress in April 1922 was the last he would lead. In May he suffered a brain haemorrhage and two further strokes towards the end of the year. Skirmishing commenced within the party oligarchy to determine who should succeed him, with the so-called 'troika', or triumvirate, of Zinoviev, Stalin, and Kamenev emerging as the controlling group within the Politburo. In 1920, Lenin had backed these three as a counterweight to Trotsky. In addition, he had backed Stalin's becoming general secretary of the party in April 1922, impressed by his organizational skills. Despite his illness, towards the end of that year he became increasingly concerned about Stalin's personality and modus operandi. In December, seeking to influence the makeup of the party leadership after his death, he wrote a testament in which he compared, in somewhat begrudging fashion, the qualities of six of his lieutenants. Trotsky was praised for his outstanding

Figure 6.1 Soviet leaders in 1919. From left, Joseph Stalin, Vladimir Lenin, Mikhail Kalinin.

abilities, but chided for excessive self-assurance and a preoccupation with administrative matters. Stalin received his harshest criticism, judged as being rude, intolerant, and capricious, and Lenin urged that he be removed from the post of general secretary (Figure 6.1). The intention was to keep the testament secret, but Lenin's secretary told Stalin of its contents, prompting him to keep Lenin incommunicado, under the surveillance of doctors who reported to him alone. Despite his frailty, Lenin struggled to thwart Stalin's pretensions, objecting vigorously to the way he rode roughshod over those Georgian Communists who dared to oppose his plan to absorb Georgia into the RSFSR. When on 4 March 1923 he learnt of an incident in which Stalin had subjected Krupskaia to a 'storm of coarse abuse', he fired off a furious missive, threatening to break off relations with the general secretary. But Lenin's struggle against the 'marvellous Georgian', whom he had done much to promote, though prescient, came too late. On 10 March, he suffered a massive stroke that left him speechless and paralysed. He died on 21 January 1924.[57]

Trotsky was by far the most gifted and charismatic of Lenin's successors and did not lack popularity, particularly in the Komsomol. Yet he was heartily disliked by the triumvirate and this was one reason why he prevaricated in putting himself forward as Lenin's successor. Fearful of appearing to be factionalist, Trotsky let slip several opportunities to consolidate his position, declining to give the political report to the Twelfth Party Congress in April 1923—and thus allowing the triumvirate to consolidate its authority—and refusing to become deputy chair of the Council of People's Commissars. Only in September 1923, against the background of the scissors crisis, did he come out and lambast the regime within the party. The 'Declaration of the 46' marked the inception of the Left Opposition, which condemned the bureaucratization of the party and called for accelerated industrialization in order to strengthen the social weight of the proletariat. During 1924 Stalin and Zinoviev waged a vituperative campaign against the Left Opposition, impugning Trotsky's claim to be a Bolshevik by drawing attention to his many conflicts with Lenin prior to 1917. Since Trotsky had been no friend to earlier opposition groups within the party, his belated conversion to the cause of inner-party democracy was seen by many as little more than a cover for his 'bonapartist' ambitions. At the Thirteenth Party Congress in May 1924 he and Evgenii Preobrazhenskii attempted a compromise with the leadership, but were heaped with obloquy for their pains. So determined were the seven other members of the Politburo to block what they considered to be Trotsky's self-aggrandizing ambition that from August 1924 they met as a caucus before each Politburo meeting. In late 1924, to counter the left's claim that international revolution was the only means to ensure Russia's survival as a socialist state, Stalin enunciated the new doctrine of 'socialism in one country', thereby initiating a process that ended in the 1930s with the rehabilitation of Russia's imperial history and traditions.

In January 1925 Trotsky was removed from the presidency of the Revolutionary Military Council. Zinoviev and Kamenev, who had no illusions about Stalin's ambitions, were increasingly alarmed at his attempts to undermine their position, but they concentrated their fire on Bukharin, the most eloquent defender of NEP, since they believed that under his influence excessive concessions were being made to the peasantry. They were, of course, fully aware that behind Bukharin stood Stalin. At the Fourteenth Party Congress in December 1925, they attacked the general secretary's vast concentration of power—to howls of outrage from the floor—but although Trotsky and Zinoviev remained on the Politburo, they were unable to stop Molotov, Kalinin, and Voroshilov, staunch allies of Stalin, being brought in. In summer 1926, an astounding turn of events took place when Zinoviev and Kamenev joined forces with their erstwhile foe, Trotsky, to form the United Opposition. Determined to annihilate this new challenge, Stalin aligned with the right wing of the party, led by Bukharin, Rykov, now head of Council of People's Commissars, and Tomskii, the trade-union leader. In October 1926, Trotsky and Zinoviev were removed from the Central Committee, accused of representing a 'social democratic' deviation—one of the worst insults in the Bolshevik lexicon—and by November 1927 they were expelled from the party. At the Fifteenth Party Congress in December 1927 Rykov, reflecting on the split in the party, declared: 'I think we cannot guarantee that the prison population will not have to increase somewhat in the near future.' In January 1928 Trotsky was exiled to Alma Ata, a preliminary to his deportation and ultimate assassination at the hands of one of Stalin's henchmen in August 1940. As the grain procurement crisis deepened in 1927–8, Stalin distanced himself from the moderate gradualism of the right. Bukharin, though a brilliant theoretician, was no match for him politically, and the 'right opposition' hardly functioned as an organized faction. The denouement came in 1928, when Stalin called for a 'decisive struggle' against 'right opportunism'. By April 1929 Bukharin had been hounded from the Politburo and the right opposition smashed.[58]

At the heart of the inner-party struggle was a conflict about the optimal strategy for industrializing Soviet Russia in conditions of economic backwardness and international isolation. The centrality of class within Bolshevik ideology, however, meant that the debates focused not on technical economic questions but on whether particular policies were 'proletarian' or 'bourgeois' in their implications. Trotsky accepted the framework of NEP—the market, material incentives, and the alliance with the peasantry—but emphasized the primacy of building state industry and supporting the proletariat. His ally, Preobrazhenskii, insisted that investment in industrial growth could be acquired only by squeezing the peasantry through fiscal and financial mechanisms and called for the state to limit the operations of the market through comprehensive planning.[59] On the right wing of the party, Bukharin argued that the preservation of the alliance with the peasantry was the overriding requirement. Peasants should be allowed to prosper: his slogan 'Enrich yourselves' outraged the left. In his view, rising demand for consumer goods would be met by the more efficient state sector, which would gradually squeeze out the private sector. In addition, peasants would be encouraged to join consumer cooperatives and this would give them a competitive advantage over the kulaks. Taxes and profits from state factories would then provide the funds to invest in industry and collective farms. Bukharin squarely recognized that progress would be slow, likening his programme to 'riding into socialism on a peasant nag'; and this left him open to the charge from the United Opposition that his pro-peasant orientation in reality strengthened 'kulak' forces.[60]

So long as NEP seemed to be working, Stalin pursued a middle course, successfully exploiting divisions among his opponents, though his supporters were concerned that too much freedom was being left to market forces. As late as April 1927, Stalin inclined to the right rather than to the left: in 1926 he opposed the Dnieper dam project on the grounds that it was like a peasant buying a gramophone when he should be repairing his plough. However, as the evidence mounted that NEP was running into the sand, he switched course decisively, calling in 1928 for a pace of industrialization far more hectic than anything envisaged by the left. Facing a country that was not only economically feeble, but falling further behind the advanced capitalist powers, the Stalin group came to believe that speed was of the essence: a decisive breakthrough to socialism could come only by breaking with NEP. An often overlooked factor, too, was that military leaders, whose budget had been slashed to stabilize the ruble, were now lobbying for rapid expansion of military as well as civilian production in the wake of the war scare of 1927.[61]

As this suggests, one cannot interpret the inner-party conflict as simply a naked power struggle, although the issue of power was at the heart of the conflict. Lenin had ruled by virtue of his charisma, rather than his formal position, and he bequeathed a structure of weak but bloated institutions that relied for direction on a strong leader. Stanisław Kosior, Polish-born secretary of the Siberian bureau, reported to the Central Committee on 5 April 1923 on the effect of Lenin's illness: 'Among party members there is great anxiety. For many the Central Committee and party leadership are synonymous with Lenin and now it is difficult to imagine how the party can exist without him.'[62] Yet no one in the oligarchy enjoyed anything approaching Lenin's authority. So the question of who should succeed him also raised the fundamental question of how power was to be institutionalized. The Left Opposition, though hardly champions of democracy, stood for collective leadership rather than personal dictatorship, for tolerance of a range of opinion within the party, and against the extreme concentration of power in the central organs of the party. Yet psychologically they were ill fitted for opposition since they believed in the paramount importance of discipline and unity and were terrified of being seen as splitters. This disarmed them ideologically and psychologically—no more pathetic evidence for which exists than Trotsky's admission to the Thirteenth Party Congress in May 1924 that 'the party in the last analysis is always right... I know that one must not be right against the party'. Stalin ably traded on the widespread fear of disunity, building up a reputation as a champion of orthodoxy against assorted malcontents. By harping on Trotsky's differences with Lenin in the past, he was able to attach himself to the growing cult of Lenin, not least through the publication in 1924 of his *Foundations of Leninism*, a book plagiarized from the work of Filipp Ksenofontov (1903–38), which presented Lenin as the unchallengeable touchstone of ideological rectitude. This became the textbook that shaped the political education of tens of thousands of new recruits, who were easily convinced that the 'anti-Leninism' of the opposition deprived them of any right to a fair hearing.

How far Stalin's rise was due to his control of the party machine and his ability to build up a network of loyal clients has been disputed following the opening of the Secretariat archives. From April 1922, he was the only Bolshevik who was simultaneously a full member of the Politburo, the Secretariat, and the weaker Organizational Bureau. We know that one of his first acts as general secretary was to order provincial party secretaries to report to him personally by the fifth of each month. And between April 1922 and March 1923, the Organizational Bureau made over 1,000 appointments, including 42 provincial party secretaries.[63] Yet the Secretariat was barely able to cope with the growing demand for cadres that welled up from below, and Stalin in fact cut the number of positions for which it was responsible from about 22,500 in 1921–2 to 6,000 in 1922–3.[64] Local party and state organs were encouraged to promote their own cadres, and this enabled them to form their own networks of clients. Many local party secretaries did vote for Stalin but more because they approved of his clamping down on factionalism and his calls for party unity. For his part, Stalin maintained good relations with party secretaries, who made up almost half the members of the Central Committee, since they had formal responsibility for electing and removing members of the Politburo. Doubtless Stalin was able to exercise powers of patronage through the *nomenklatura* system, but the control of the Secretariat and Organizational Bureau may not have been as vital to his ascent to power as is often supposed. He had a number of other levers at his disposal, apart from patronage, including influence over the agenda of the Politburo, control of the press, manipulation of delegates to conferences, and use of the party control commission to weed out 'anti-party elements'. Using a combination of these, he was able to break up the power bases of Zinoviev in Leningrad and the supposed 'rightist' stronghold in the capital of Nikolai Uglanov, first secretary of the Moscow Communist Party. In 1928 hundreds of oppositionists were arrested by the political police.

Stalin always believed himself to be the faithful continuer of the work of Lenin, however vehemently his opponents might impugn his Leninist credentials.[65] The issue that his opponents most seized on to prove he was departing from Leninist principles was the issue of 'socialism in one country'. Lenin had never denied that Russia could make some headway towards socialism, in spite of its backwardness and international isolation, and Trotsky, too, did not deny this. Trotsky's clash with Stalin came over the issue of whether the socialist revolution could be completed within the boundaries of a single state. In the years up to the First World War, Trotsky's theory of 'permanent revolution' had maintained that leadership of the bourgeois revolution in Russia—that is, the revolution against the autocracy—must fall to the proletariat, and a consequence of this was that the bourgeois stage of revolution would spill over into the socialist stage. In a similar way, following the conquest of power by the proletariat in Russia, Trotsky—and the party as a whole—believed the Russian Revolution was destined to spill over into more advanced capitalist countries since capitalism was a global system. The political lesson he drew from this was that the overwhelming priority was to hasten international revolution if the Soviet Union were not to be forced into autarchy and a permanently defensive foreign policy. Stalin castigated this perspective as thoroughly Menshevik and 'defeatist': 'permanent gloom' and 'permanent hopelessness'. He and his supporters cast themselves as optimists, as loyal, disciplined 'doers'. He hinted that Trotsky, a Jewish intellectual, was not a true Russian: 'Lack of faith in the strength and capacities of our revolution, lack of faith in the strength and capacities of the Russian proletariat—that is what lies at the root of the theory of "permanent revolution".'[66] By hitching his colours to the mast of 'socialism in one country' in late 1924, Stalin opened up a positive perspective of backward Russia raising herself up by her bootstraps. This played to the latent nationalism of the burgeoning ranks of young party members, mostly working-class men who, while parroting the recently acquired language of class and internationalism, resented the idea that Russia's prospects for achieving a socialist society should depend on revolution in more advanced countries. Stalin recognized the importance of this rank-and-file support and, almost two decades later, informed his inner circle that in 1927, 720,000 members of the party had voted in favour of the 'Central Committee line', that is, his own; compared with between 4,000 and 6,000 who had voted for Trotsky; and a further 20,000 who had abstained. Trotsky's mistake, Stalin reminisced, had been to concentrate attention on winning over the Central Committee rather than the rank-and-file.[67]

It is this ideological and psychological context, as much as a brilliant grasp of machine politics, which explains why Stalin came out on top in the inner-party conflict. But it hardly explains how he ended up as one of the twentieth century's most savage tyrants. To appreciate this, we need to look at his personality. Many historians see his personality as shaped by the fact that he was born into poverty and that his father was a violent drunkard, significant mainly by his absence. But too much can be made of this, since his parents were broadly supportive, certainly of his education. More relevant may be the fact that he became habituated to the use of violence in the Caucasus, with its rebellions and fierce ethnic, religious, and class conflicts.[68] By the time he reached adulthood, Stalin, who had read Machiavelli, appears to have endorsed his cynical view that 'men are ungrateful, fickle, liars and deceivers'.[69] Within the Bolshevik party, outshone intellectually by the likes of Trotsky and Kamenev, he made his mark by his immense capacity for hard work. He had an excellent memory, and was a first-rate tactician, cool and calculating, and averse to the kind of histrionic gestures to which Zinoviev and Trotsky were prone. In the words of M. I. Riutin, leader of the last opposition group to resist Stalin's ascendancy in 1932, he was 'narrow-minded, sly, power-loving, vengeful, treacherous, envious, hypocritical, insolent, boastful, stubborn'.[70] What this misses is Stalin's sociability, his sense of humour, and his apparent lack of side. He appreciated the importance of winning allies, whereas not least of the factors that alienated party members from Trotsky was what Lunacharskii called 'his tremendous imperiousness and inability or unwillingness to be at all amiable and attentive to people'.

The Party-State

NEP saw a drastic reduction in the numbers working for the government. During the 1920s the party steadily increased its control over all organs of government, with the Council of People's Commissars and the CEC of the Soviets becoming firmly subordinated to the Politburo. Yet the party-state was still far from being a monolithic leviathan. The party struggled to impose stability on a state administration that comprised a number of relatively autonomous institutions—the economic commissariats, the GPU (the name of the successor to the Cheka from 1922 to 1923), the soviets, and the trade unions. Among the economic commissariats, for example, the respective spheres of competence of the Commissariat of Finance, the State Planning Commission, and the Supreme Council of National Economy remained uncertain, each seeking to expand its authority at the expense of the others, with the Supreme Council of National Economy eventually coming out on top. In 1925 Stalin complained to Viacheslav Molotov, who was to become one of his most loyal protégés, that on economic questions it was not the Politburo but the State Planning Commission that was in charge.[71] All government ministries, moreover, relied heavily on non-party specialists: even by 1929 only 14 per cent of personnel in the Commissariat of Agriculture were party members, rising to 24 per cent in the Commissariat of Trade. So despite efforts to promote workers and peasants, white-collar employees constituted the largest proportion of staff in the thirteen commissariats of government. In the Commissariat of Agriculture, which employed 40,000 people, 97 per cent of staff in the central offices were white-collar employees by social origin and around a half of specialists had worked for the tsarist government.[72] Naturally, the party looked on these 'alien' social elements with much distrust, yet it could not survive without their expertise.

NEP witnessed the emergence of a new political and social elite. In April 1923 the Twelfth Party Congress ratified the *nomenklatura* system, whereby the Central Committee (or the relevant provincial or district committee in the case of more junior officials) was assigned the right to make appointments to all key positions in the party-state administration. The Congress agreed that responsible party officials down to the level of local party secretaries should be guaranteed rations, housing, uniforms, health care, and rest cures in the Crimea. It was through this mechanism that a new ruling elite began to emerge, comprising party officials at oblast' level and above, senior state officials, and leading industrial managers. In 1927 those appointed via the *nomenklatura* system included some 3,000 to 4,000 higher party officials and about 100,000 officials at middle and lower levels of the party apparatus.[73] When high-ranking officials in the state apparatus, including senior executives in industry and education, are added, the *nomenklatura* elite grew to about half a million people out of a total working population of over 86 million. One could also add to this new socialist elite acclaimed members of the artistic and literary worlds. The elite enjoyed important privileges and access to scarce resources, but it was not a class in the capitalist sense, since it was not defined by its ownership of property and wealth, but by office within the party-state, office in which it had no security of tenure. Formally speaking, moreover, it was not able to bequeath its privileges to its offspring.

In 1925 there were 1,025,000 Bolsheviks in a population of 147 million. A series of 'purges' of party members—a term that had not yet acquired a sinister ring—ensured that the size of membership remained roughly similar at the end of the 1920s. These purges, which began in June 1921, removed several hundred thousand 'alien and hostile elements' from the party but, despite the language of infiltration and conspiracy, most were expelled for passivity, careerism, or drunkenness. The purges helped the RKP(b) to 'proletarianize' itself: by 1927 nearly half of party members were workers by social origin, although over 300,000 'workers' had in fact been promoted to administrative positions. By 1929, 8.5 per cent of all industrial workers were party members, although among workers aged 23 to 29 the proportion was 18.3 per cent.[74] Most had only primary education and their level of political sophistication was not high. In the mid-1920s 72 per cent of party members in Voronezh were said to be 'politically illiterate'. One party secretary finished his report on the celebrations he had organized to mark the anniversary of Bloody Sunday in 1905 with the flourish: 'Let us fulfil to the end the cause begun by Gapon and Zubatov' (Zubatov was the police chief who had set up pro-government unions between 1901 and 1903 and—unfairly—Gapon was officially portrayed as a stooge).[75] The regular purges that took place testified to the ongoing dissatisfaction of the leadership with the quality of cadres and party members. In April 1929 at the Sixteenth Party Conference, the Workers' and Peasants' Inspectorate was ordered to organize a general purge of the apparatus and launch criticism and self-criticism 'from top to bottom and from bottom to top'. The influx of poorly educated workers and peasants was paralleled by the eclipse of the 'Old Bolsheviks'. In 1925, when party membership stood at well over 1 million, fewer than 2,000 had joined the party before 1905.[76] These Old Bolsheviks had suffered imprisonment or exile for their beliefs, and many had lived for periods abroad. They were contemptuous of material comfort, respectful of culture and education, dedicated to a cause whose success was absolutely uncertain. Their values contrasted with those of plebeian incomers, who were doubtless sincere and zealous yet who no longer risked exile or the noose, who had little understanding of Marxist theory, and who saw party membership as, at best, a matter of conscientiously carrying out centrally determined policy or, at worst, a route to self-advancement. Reports by OGPU (the name the GPU acquired in 1923, following the formation of the Soviet Union) regularly comment on the desire of recruits 'to get a higher-paying job and a good apartment'. Those lower-class party members who were promoted into positions of responsibility in government, industrial administration, trade unions, or education—in Votskaia autonomous region, for instance, they accounted for half of party members—saw their own promotion as proof that the proletariat had become the ruling class. At the same time, the extent of upward social mobility by members of the lower classes should not be exaggerated: probably no more than 5 per cent of the industrial workforce ever benefited from such promotion.[77]

Meanwhile the 'bureaucratization' of the party continued, though the trend was universally deplored. In his last years, perhaps under the strain of illness, Lenin's writings took on a dark, pessimistic tone: 'We are being sucked into a foul, bureaucratic swamp.' Yet Lenin continued to believe that the solution to the rampant lack of accountability lay in promoting workers to positions within the bureaucracy and getting the Workers' and Peasants' Inspectorate and the Central Control Committee, the agencies responsible for 'control', or monitoring, of state and party organs, to combat administrative inefficiency and inertia. These agencies themselves, however, rapidly succumbed to the bureaucratic disease they were intended to cure, bombarding lower levels of the administrative hierarchy with demands for plans and reports. The promotion of workers into official positions did nothing to mitigate the problems of bureaucracy. Indeed they often brought new levels of incompetence into administration, and became inured to the hierarchy, subordination, corruption, and careerism that had long been hallmarks of Russian government. The 1920s saw endless exhortations to activists to expose corruption, incompetence, and capriciousness. Yet official discourse failed to register that much of what was termed 'bureaucracy' was actually functional to the entire operation of power. Middle- and lower-level party officials had little security of tenure and little institutional protection against vengeful superiors, so they responded to this uncertain environment by developing networks of clients to bolster their influence and protect themselves against the centre. Moreover, periodic campaigns for 'democracy' compounded their sense of insecurity by exposing them to criticism from the rank-and-file. Thus, in reality, the operation of power was not 'bureaucratic' in the proper sense of that term at all—despite a proliferating division of labour, hierarchies of authority, and an ever-lengthening trail of paperwork—for in the last analysis getting things done depended on personalized authority rather than formal rules. Behind the façade of bureaucratic hierarchy, decision making and the implementation of decisions made was in fact in the hands of local bosses, such as Grigol Ordzhonikidze in Tbilisi, Sergei Kirov in Baku, and Filipp Goloshchëkin in Kazakhstan. These men presided over personal fiefdoms and relied on 'family circles', that is, networks of mutual protection, to get things done. In other words, bureaucracy galvanized by clientelism was what kept the party-state functioning.

One less remarked upon development was the reincorporation of a patriarchal dimension into political relationships. The February Revolution had delivered a sharp blow to the patriarchal principle in political, ecclesiastical, and familial authority and set in its place the fraternal principle of comradeship. As the party-state spawned a more hierarchical division of labour, however, fitness for leadership became ever more associated with models of personalized authority—the military commander, the industrial manager, the scientist—that were thoroughly masculine. The bitter struggle for power among the 'sons' that followed Lenin's death signalled the decline of the idiom of revolutionary fraternity and the reinstatement of a model of patriarchal authority.[78] From the outset notions of revolutionary brotherhood had served to exclude women from positions of power. In 1928 women comprised 13 per cent of party members but only 3 per cent of secretaries of party cells, the lowest position in the party hierarchy. Sidelined to work in the Women's Bureau—referred to derisively as 'Tsentro-baba' (*baba* being a pejorative term for women)—or in agitprop departments, women were reluctant to challenge men for leadership, and in the rare cases they did, incurred resentment.[79] The politburo of the Anzhero-Sudzhenskii township committee reported in November 1921 to the Tomsk provincial committee: 'The responsible secretary and heads of the political departments are women with an intelligentsia psychology.... Frequently we hear party members say "What's the point of going to meetings if we have to listen to womanish claptrap?"'[80] Increasingly, therefore, patriarchal conceptions of authority, still very much alive at the popular level, began to assert themselves. In 1926 a 15-year-old girl in Verkhneudinsk in Siberia wrote to Stalin after she was barred from the Pioneers because her father had been briefly a trader: 'I don't look to you as someone high, great, unapproachable, but as my teacher and elder brother, even as my father.'[81] By the 1930s Stalin would be widely acclaimed as the 'wise father' of the 'great family' of the Soviet people.

Instituting Law

With the end of the civil war, the intention was that the political police, responsible for rooting out counter-revolution, should be rolled back. On 6 February 1922 the Cheka was replaced by the GPU, which changed its name again the following year to OGPU. The numbers employed in the political police were cut drastically. At the end of 1921 there were 90,000 employees on the official payroll of the Cheka, but by end of 1923 only 32,152 worked in OGPU. In the same period the number of those working clandestinely for the political police fell from 60,000 to 12,900, and by late 1923 the total number in the internal troops, border guards, and escort troops had fallen from 117,000 to 78,400.[82] The OGPU was no longer permitted to practise terror but it could try and sentence those arrested for breaches of state security, which included imposing capital sentences (although these could be appealed). After a peak number of capital sentences in 1921 of 9,701, the average over the next eight years fell to 1,654.[83] None of this should be interpreted to mean that the role of the OGPU had diminished. Within the party, the OGPU now operated as the secret police of the emergent Stalinist leadership, and within society at large, surveillance of the population was stepped up. The OGPU produced regular 'information summaries' on the 'popular mood' which were circulated among a select group of high-ranking party officials. These were based on OGPU's own interrogations and inspections, on intercepted correspondence, and on reports from informers in workplaces, markets, railway stations, and the army.[84]

NEP saw a broadening in the scope of law and the emergence of a more uniform judicial system. How far Soviet society should be regulated by law, however, remained a vexed question. In Marxist theory it was assumed that law was an instrument whose function was to uphold property and class relations, and the expectation was that it would eventually wither away as socialist society was achieved. Lenin, though trained as a lawyer, had little time for his profession and certainly did not believe that law had a role to play in curbing the powers of the state or in protecting the individual against the state. Yet the civil war had seen a staggering rise in the crime rate with which the judicial organs had struggled to deal, so if only for pragmatic reasons it was felt to be imperative to re-establish a framework of law and legal institutions. In 1922 a Criminal Code was enacted, followed by a statute on court organization, and the following year by a code of criminal procedure.[85] A tiered court system was put in place that was subject to formal procedures and reliant on trained professionals. The Code drew to a significant extent on elements of tsarist jurisprudence, although the ethos of the judicial system remained one of leniency towards criminals from the 'toiling classes' and one geared towards rehabilitation. This was a period of considerable experimentation in judicial practice. In particular, many imaginative schemes were devised to rehabilitate young criminals, although such schemes were hampered by lack of cash. Lawyers remained thin on the ground, so the system continued to rely on lay judges and assessors who were poorly paid and dependent on the good will of local officials. The office of procurator was restored and soon became the most powerful judicial agency: by 1928 all procurators were party members.[86] Nevertheless the judiciary failed to develop real independence from the state, and its powers to defend the individual against the state were feeble. In seeing law primarily as a means to defend the state, the Bolsheviks unwittingly reproduced an ethos that was deeply rooted in tsarist political culture.

Contrary to expectation, the crime rate did not fall with the end of the civil war, although crimes of violence did. In 1922 the regime resolved that a professional police force was necessary, but it placed the cost on local soviets, which meant that numbers fell by 60 per cent, and salaries remained low. Consequently, through the 1920s, the police survived by graft, and in the countryside especially they relied on the 'law of the fist'.[87] The countryside remained under-governed. Following a slashing of the size of the militia in 1924, the number of police in the RSFSR rose between 1926 and 1929 to around 80,000, but half of these were attached to state institutions.[88] This meant that the ratio of police to population was actually lower than in the tsarist period. In keeping with the return to normalcy, economic crimes such as embezzlement, sabotage, pilfering state property, counterfeiting, production of liquor, and trade in contraband all rose. Around 1925 something of moral panic erupted about the rising tide of 'hooliganism'. This category could legally encompass anything from rape to rowdiness, drunkenness to staying away from work after pay-day. The majority of those convicted were working-class males under the age of 25 (in contrast to the late-imperial period when the average offender was rather older and less likely to be a worker).[89] In the countryside the peasants continued to show confidence in the court system, as they had done in the late tsarist era, often travelling long distances to achieve judicial resolution, especially of cases of assault, slander, divorce, alimony, theft, and damage to property.[90] An effective appeals system now existed, and peasants appealing judicial decisions sometimes modelled their appeals on the traditional ritual lament (as did petitioners to state organs more generally), and threw themselves on the mercy of the judge. Their appeals would decry their fate, but—in a new twist—often place blame for their misdeeds on the harmful social influences to which they had been subject in the old society.[91]

Governing the Countryside

The Revolution had caused the village to turn in on itself, and the commune was in some respects stronger than it had been in the last years of tsarism. It had lost its tax-gathering function, yet was still central in determining issues of land allocation and utilization. Younger men challenged the dominance of older men in the village gathering, and women over 18 now had the right to participate in it, although it was usually only Red Army wives and widows who did so. Generally, peasants preferred to transact business through the village gathering and the executives of township soviets often preferred to deal directly with the gathering rather than go via the rural soviet. That said, after a shaky start, the rural soviets did begin to revive after the devastation of the civil war.

In the early 1920s, the alienation of the peasants from the regime was palpable, evinced in the fact that only 22 per cent of rural voters (and only 14 per cent of women) actually took part in soviet elections in 1922. Indeed rural elections had to be called off in 1924 and the 'Face to the countryside' campaign launched to revitalize the rural soviets and ensure that they were 'polite, attentive, listening to the voice of the peasantry'.[92] As a result, the percentage taking part in soviet elections rose to 47 per cent in 1926–7.[93] The 'youth who doesn't shave', with a record of service in the Red Army and a limited primary education, was the archetypal representative of the rural soviets. In 1922 only 1 per cent of rural soviet members were female, although this rose to nearly 12 per cent by 1927. Young and poor—and seen by many as ignorant of farming—the lower soviet personnel did not command much respect. They compensated for their poor salaries by corruption and embezzlement. In the Tersk region of the Northern Caucasus the party control commission reported that 'drunkenness has infected all responsible officials and its forms exceed all limits—debauches, scandals, consorting with prostitutes'.[94] Complaints about local soviet officials were legion, yet it would be a mistake to assume that peasants universally hated these upstarts. Certainly, they disliked bribery and excessive rigour on the part of officials, but sometimes they commented favourably on the absence of 'nobs' (*bary*) in local government and on the fact that the soviets were led by 'our people whom we can scold and have a cigarette with'.[95] By contrast, there was mainly indifference on the part of villagers to the county soviets, which embraced urban as well as rural soviets: 'We have no objection to government; we need authority, but we don't care how it's organized.' Barely a quarter of members of the executives at this level were peasants, compared with 44 per cent who were 'employees' (mostly professionals who had once worked for the zemstvos).[96]

In the unprecedentedly free election of 1925, Communists were voted out of soviets in some areas and widespread calls were made for the establishment of peasant unions. In 1921 Osinskii proposed that a Peasant Union be permitted under the 'ideological and organizational hegemony of the RKP(b)', but Lenin dismissed the suggestion peremptorily.[97] This was possibly because the idea of peasant unions was one much touted by the SRs in emigration and because peasant congresses that took place in southern Ukraine between 1921 and 1923 had an anti-Bolshevik complexion.[98] In spring 1927 Genrikh Iagoda, deputy chair of OGPU, reported that the initiative group to create an All-Russian Peasant Union had been arrested. Although we cannot rule out the involvement of émigré organizations, the demand for peasant unions—and a few seem actually to have materialized—arose spontaneously, reflecting the sense on the part of the peasants that they were entitled to the same rights to organize as workers.[99] For the political police, however, such demands were a sign that 'kulaks' were in the ascendancy. Meanwhile, the proportion of peasants deprived of the vote fell from 1.4 per cent in 1924–5 to 1 per cent in 1925–6, but then rose to 3.3 per cent in November 1926.[100] As a counterweight to the kulaks, poor peasants were encouraged to form separate organizations within the village to influence the make-up of the soviets. In February 1927, OGPU reported that in Ukraine, North Caucasus, and Siberia leadership in the soviets had passed to organized poor peasants, but it now complained that middle peasants were being ignored.[101]

One of the many reasons why the Communists felt insecure was that party penetration of rural areas was extremely limited. Party control of rural local government was secure only down to the county level, where already by 1922 Communists accounted for 82 per cent of members of the executives. During the 1920s the party made rapid headway in increasing its influence in township executive committees, Communists accounting for 48 per cent of members as early as 1924. However, in that year only 7 per cent of ordinary members of rural soviets were Communists. Even by 1928 there was only one party cell for every twenty-six rural centres of population.[102] Fairly typical of peasant attitudes was Gadyshi in Novgorod, where older villagers disliked the Communists: 'they oppose God, many are Jews and they serve in the communes' (i.e. dominate the soviet administration). Younger members of the village, however, might well view them as 'advanced people, supporters of enlightenment, enemies of darkness and ignorance'.[103]

Peasants were far from being a cowed mass and, to some extent, the regime encouraged them to speak out. Many did so in the relatively traditional form of petitions, appeals, complaints, or denunciations to higher authority. Tens of thousands of petitions were sent to Lenin and to Mikhail Kalinin, president of the Soviet CEC and one of the few party leaders to hail from a peasant background; others were sent directly to institutions such as the CEC and the Commissariat of State Control. Petitioners were not afraid to express their views boldly and there is little of the self-abasement characteristic of petitioners in tsarist times. Petitioners, moreover, were usually able to deploy the language of the new order, however opportunistically: 'Comrade Lenin bequeathed the following important teaching: Do not oppress the toiling people because the tsar-autocrats flayed them enough ... but now local officials oppress us as much as the tsars.'[104]

It is foolhardy to generalize about the political attitudes of 100 million peasants, yet to judge from their intercepted letters it seems that there was a minority of enthusiastic supporters and a minority of foes and that the attitudes of the great majority were shifting and contradictory.[105] Throughout the period, the majority expressed disgruntlement at the slowness with which their conditions were improving, and grumbles about such matters as taxes and the price of industrial manufactures were legion. Tension between the peasants and the regime eased greatly from 1923, but it began to increase again from 1926. A sample of 407 letters from peasants to Red Army soldiers, intercepted by military censors between 1924 and 1925, shows that almost two-thirds were positively disposed to the central government, but that virtually all complained about the local soviets. Analysis of letters sent to the *Peasant Newspaper* between 1924 and 1928, most of which were never published, suggests that the principal concerns of peasants were taxation, the price and poor quality of manufactures, fleecing by middlemen, kulak exploitation, the eight-hour day enjoyed by workers, and the better cultural facilities in the towns. Underlying these complaints was the peasants' sense that they were second-class citizens in the new Soviet order. In 1926 letters offering a negative assessment of the central government (28 per cent of the total) for the first time outnumbered those offering a positive one (23 per cent of the total). The leitmotif of these was that peasants continued to live in great hardship ('unshod and unclothed', 'puffed up with hunger'), mainly due to taxes and unfair pricing of agricultural and industrial goods. One letter from 100 poor peasants inveighed against the party leadership: 'Communists and commissars, you have all forgotten 1917. You parasites sit in your warm berths drinking our blood... We may rot for the cause of justice, but we will wipe you out, you deceivers of the people.'[106] However, the majority of peasants, though disgruntled, appear not to have been deeply hostile to the government and a sizeable minority positively approved the Communist ideal in principle, seeing in it an extension of the values of the collectivism, equality, and mutual aid that were inherent in the commune. The fact that so many took advantage of the opportunity to express their opinions to the government suggests that they expected it to live by the ideals it proclaimed.

The widespread hatred of the Bolsheviks that had erupted in the countryside in 1920–1 had abated. This was, in large part, because the state was no longer violently intervening to seize grain and because, despite persisting economic difficulties, peasant living standards had much improved. The regime, however, felt that its authority was far from secure in the countryside. This anxiety was, in many respects, incongruous. Certainly, the influence of the party was extremely limited, and the reliability of the rural soviets could not be guaranteed. Nevertheless, despite the general weakness of the party-state in rural areas, the state actually penetrated more deeply into peasant society than its tsarist predecessor had done. Moreover, the boundary between state and society was now more porous than it had been when the peasants constituted a separate estate and official administration barely went beneath the county town. Soviets existed at the township level and there were opportunities for the politically committed, mainly young men, to be elected to these bodies.

Foreign Policy and Promoting Revolution

From 1921 Soviet Russia was left isolated as the only socialist state in an international system dominated by the capitalist powers. The Washington Conference in 1921–2 marked the emergence of a new global order dominated by the USA. The Conference accorded equal status to the USA and Britain as the only powers with a naval presence throughout the high seas. Japan was granted secondary status because of its power in the Pacific. The Soviet Union had interests in the Pacific, but it was denied representation.[107] The Treaty of Rapallo in 1922 saw the two pariahs of the Versailles settlement, Germany and Russia, grant each other most-favoured-nation status. Georgii Chicherin, Commissar of Foreign Affairs from 1918 to 1930, bent his energies to minimizing Soviet isolation by securing bilateral treaties with individual governments, in order to prevent the formation of a coalition hostile to the Soviet Union, and to securing commercial agreements that would give Russia the modern technology she so desperately needed. In 1924 it looked as though isolation might be lessening, as Italy, Britain, and France granted diplomatic recognition to the Soviet Union, and by 1925 thirteen governments had recognized the new state. The only new state to join the Soviet fold, however, was Mongolia, where the death in 1924 of Bogd Khagan, head of the Buddhist hierarchy, allowed the Mongolian People's Party to seize power. Developments in Europe between 1924 and 1926 turned in a more worrying direction so far as the Soviet Union was concerned, as Britain and France mended fences over implementation of the Treaty of Versailles and France and Germany achieved a rapprochement with the Locarno Treaty of 1925. By 1926 the major capitalist powers had recovered from the economic devastation of the First World War and from post-war inflation, and pre-war levels of output had been surpassed. As its economy boomed, the USA underwrote this stabilization of the capitalist order with extensive loans. Pulling against—indeed threatening to sabotage—the efforts of Chicherin to repair relations with the capitalist powers were the efforts of the Comintern to promote revolution throughout Europe.

In March 1919, confident that international revolution was just over the horizon, the Bolsheviks called the First Congress of a new (Third) Communist International, known as the Comintern, to promote Bolshevik-style revolution on a global scale. The real activity of the Comintern, however, did not begin until the Second Congress, which took place from 19 July to 17

August 1920. According to the constitution approved by the Congress, the Comintern was to become the 'world party of the proletariat', albeit one based on national sections. The congress ratified 'Twenty-One Conditions for Acceptance into the Communist International', which forbade the entry of 'opportunists and wavering elements' into national communist parties. The aim was to split the international labour movement by making a decisive break with social democratic parties. National communist parties were to create a cadre of professional revolutionaries who would adopt methods of strict conspiracy and underground work, such as had been pioneered by the Bolsheviks in their struggle against tsarism, even as they operated openly in the labour movement. The directing organ of the Comintern was its Executive Committee (ECCI), which was chaired by Zinoviev. Members of the RKP(b) dominated the ECCI and its organizational apparatus from the first, although some delegates from foreign communist parties were summoned to Moscow to work for the new organization. In November 1926 Zinoviev was removed, having failed in his campaign to have Stalin replaced as general secretary, and a permanent delegation of the RKP(b) was installed within the ECCI. Constitutionally, this had no status, yet it became the centre where the key decisions concerning cadres, finance, and politics were made, decisions that were binding on foreign communist parties.

By the time the Third Congress convened from 22 June to 12 July 1921, communist parties had come into existence in forty-eight countries. The previous year Lenin had spoken out against 'the infantile disease of left-wing communism' since many who joined the new movement were unwilling to work with reformists. In December 1921 the ECCI approved the tactic of the 'united front', which advocated cooperation with different currents in the labour movement, above all with social democrats in countries where they had a mass base. The idea was that through practical struggle, through organizing strikes and demonstrations, the 'opportunists' would be revealed in their true colours. Until 1923 hopes ran high that a Bolshevik-style revolution would break out in Germany, but the 'March Action' of 1921, an attempted uprising by the Communist Party in Germany, was a flop. Indeed the chances of revolution in Germany had been highest in the winter of 1918–19, following Germany's withdrawal from the war, but German workers, soldiers, and sailors had opted for a parliamentary rather than a soviet system.

The Fifth Congress of the Comintern, which met from 17 June to 8 July 1924, recognized that 'international capitalist stabilization' had occurred, but judged it 'temporary and partial'. Communist parties were forced to face up to more mundane tasks of strengthening trade-union and parliamentary work, carrying out anti-war work, and organizing solidarity campaigns with colonial peoples. Nevertheless at the first sign of any political crisis—such as the British general strike in 1926—the ECCI would revert to insurrectionary mode, convinced that militant leadership would lead the European working class to the barricades. Bukharin, who replaced Zinoviev as chairman of the ECCI, penned the programme passed by the Sixth Congress, which met from 17 July to 1 September 1928. This depicted the Soviet Union as 'the fatherland of toilers throughout the world' and insisted that the phase of capitalist stabilization was over and that capitalism was now entering its 'third period' of development since the First World War. All cooperation with reformist socialists must end—a tactic known as 'class against class'—and the trade-union movement must be split by the formation a 'red trade-union opposition'. The new policy had devastating consequences in Germany where the refusal of the German Communists to cooperate with the Social Democrats facilitated the rise of Adolf Hitler.[108] Whether oriented to the united front or to 'class against class', the Comintern consistently failed to understand that workers in the developed capitalist countries were unlikely to risk the short-term benefits of reform, however slender, for the terrible costs of revolution Bolshevik style. This was connected to its failure to understand the very specific conditions that engendered revolution in Russia, which inter alia included the feebleness of Russian capitalism and the fact that Russia remained the only country in Europe at the start of the twentieth century where the peasantry was still a revolutionary force.

The Comintern's antennae were better attuned to the prospects of revolution in the colonial and semi-colonial world. The Second Congress of the

Comintern in July 1920 turned its attention to this subject. Indeed it was one of Lenin's great insights to realize that nationalist movements of a 'bourgeois-democratic' character could play a vital part in the global struggle against capitalism. On 1 September 1920 the ECCI called a Congress of the Peoples of the East in Baku, which was attended by some 2,000 delegates, mainly from the Caucasus, Central Asia, and Iran and Turkey. Zinoviev opened the proceedings with a demagogic speech that called on the delegates to take up the 'task of igniting a general holy war against the English and French capitalists', a call that was greeted with stormy applause and furious waving of swords.[109] Karl Radek explained: 'We are united with you by fate . . . Either we unite with the peoples of the East and speed up the victory of the Western European proletariat, or we will perish, and you will be enslaved.'[110] H. G. Wells, who was in Russia at the time, wrote condescendingly: 'They held a congress at Baku at which they gathered together a quite wonderful accumulation of white, black, brown, and yellow people, Asiatic costumes and astonishing weapons. They had a great assembly in which they swore undying hatred of Capitalism and British imperialism.'[111] According to a British intelligence report, a scaffold was erected not far from the congress venue with 'most lifelike' effigies of Lloyd George, French Prime Minister Millerand, and Woodrow Wilson suspended from it, each attired in court dress with a full array of decorations.[112] Although there were only fifty-five women present at the congress, Naciye Hanim from the Turkish Communist Party introduced a resolution that called for equality of the sexes, women's right to education, equality of marriage rights, an end to polygamy, the employment of women in government institutions, and local committees to protect the rights of women.[113] Enver Paşa, architect of the Armenian genocide, was not allowed to attend the congress in person, since his presence would have enraged the Armenian delegates and Turkish supporters of Mustafa Kemal Atatürk, but a statement from this fleeting Bolshevik ally was read out.[114]

Overcoming considerable controversy, the Second Congress agreed that Communist parties in the colonies should ally with bourgeois nationalist movements, whilst retaining their political independence. This was a contradictory policy that came bloodily unstuck in China in 1927, as the national revolution, led by Chiang Kai-shek and the Nationalist Party, unfolded between 1926 and 1928. Under orders from Moscow the Chinese Communist Party had reluctantly joined the Nationalist Party in 1923. In 1926 with Stalin's supporters in control of the Comintern, the Chinese Communists were urged to take power by stealth within the Nationalist Party and the National Revolutionary Army and promote social revolution, while ensuring that unity with the right wing of the Nationalist Party was maintained, a strategy that placed the Communists in a suicidal quandary. In April 1927 Chiang Kai-shek crushed his Communist allies, an act that could have spelled the end of the Chinese Communist Party. Rather belatedly, the failed Comintern policy towards China became one of the burning issues at stake in the inner-party conflict within the RKP(b).[115]

The tension between the Comintern's mission of promoting revolution and the needs of the Soviet state to engage in conventional diplomacy with ill-disposed foreign governments dogged foreign relations through the 1920s. Chicherin pressed for a strict separation of diplomacy from Comintern activity, and inveighed against the Comintern willingness to endanger diplomatic relations. In early 1927, after a series of statements by Bukharin, he wrote: 'Would you please stop equating Chiang Kai-shek with Kemalism? It is absolutely ridiculous and spoils our relationship with Turkey. Isn't spoiling our relationship with Germany enough for you?'[116] In May 1927 the British broke off diplomatic relations with the Soviet Union after evidence of espionage, and relations would not be restored until 1929. By this stage Chicherin's health was failing and his influence had ebbed. He had always favoured an orientation towards Germany in foreign policy, as a counter to Britain and France, but his deputy, Maxim Litvinov, who succeeded him, preferred a more balanced approach. All these developments created a climate of anxiety in the Soviet leadership. The theme of capitalist encirclement now became a leitmotif of any discussion of the 'international question'. The number in the political elite who had experience of foreign countries or who could speak foreign languages had declined drastically by the late 1920s, and the number of people authorized to read foreign literature was tiny. Lack of knowledge of foreign countries fuelled a highly ideologized view of the capitalist world which, in turn, fed on xenophobic elements within Russian culture. This helps explain both the recurrent fears of invasion—notably the 'war scare' of 1927—and the periodic lurches towards an absurd overestimation of the prospects for revolution in Europe.[117]

Nation-Building

The idea of a Soviet Union, in which the RSFSR would be one republic among several, was not formalized until 1922. By that date, a series of bilateral treaties between the RSFSR and Ukraine, Belorussia, Georgia, Armenia, Azerbaijan, Bukhara, Khwarezm (Khiva), and the Far Eastern Republic had brought these states into a federation (although the Far Eastern Republic was merged into the RSFSR in November 1922). Christian Rakovskii, the Bulgarian head of the Ukrainian soviet government, and the Georgian Bolsheviks P. G. Mdivani and F. I. Makharadze favoured a loose arrangement in which the republics would remain sovereign entities, whereas Stalin favoured 'autonomization' which meant absorbing the republics into a Russian-dominated RSFSR within which they would be given a degree of autonomy.[118] Lenin rejected the latter solution as redolent of the chauvinism of the old regime, and insisted on a federation in which non-Russian republics would have equal status with the RSFSR. In a letter to Lenin in September 1922, Stalin frankly opined that during the civil war the 'demonstration of liberalism' in relation to the non-Russian peoples had been no more than 'a game of independence'. For Lenin it was anything but a game. Stalin, however, was fearful that any serious devolution of power to the non-Russian autonomies would weaken the party's dictatorship. The constitution of the USSR, finally ratified on 31 January 1924, left no doubt that the ultimate power lay with Moscow, and where non-Russians resisted incorporation, they were duly crushed. In summer 1925 Iosif Unshlikht, deputy head of the Revolutionary Military Council, led over 7,000 troops, including eight planes and 22 heavy artillery pieces, to 'disarm the bandit nests' of Chechnia.

Within a loosely imperial framework, however, the 1920s saw a unique process of nation-building, as the state entrenched nationality as a major principle of socio-political organization. The 1926 census showed that no fewer than 69 million of the 147 million inhabitants of the Soviet Union were non-Russians, so ethnographers were tasked with classifying and counting ethnic groups, many of which had little understanding of themselves as nations. They eventually distinguished 194 different nationalities. In the 1926 census, those taking the census were instructed to ascribe an ethno-national identity to every person and not accept answers to the question of nationality such as 'I am a Muslim'.[119] This was something of a paradox, since the Soviet Union at one level claimed to represent the transcendence of the nation state and, at various times, deployed a rhetoric of ultimate 'fusion' of the constituent nations of the USSR into a single Soviet people. In practice, however, nationality, once seen as an impediment to socialism, was now viewed positively—as the modality through which the economic, political, and cultural development of the non-Russian peoples would take place.

A series of what historian Terry Martin has dubbed 'affirmative action programmes' were devised to promote native political elites and intelligentsias and to further the use of national languages.[120] Having eliminated traditional elites, Moscow aimed to promote members of the indigenous population—mainly young, politically active males from humble backgrounds—to positions of leadership within their respective polities in order to create a social base of support in the non-Russian republics. This process, known as nativization (*korenizatsiia*), was designed, in Stalin's words, to produce republics and autonomous regions that were 'national in form, but socialist in content'. By institutionalizing the republics as political units and by creating national elites, Soviet rule helped to create quasi-nations, albeit at a sub-state level. Broadly, this policy of indigenizing the party-state was a success. Ukrainian membership of the Ukrainian Communist Party, for example, increased from 24 per cent to 52 per cent between 1922 and 1927, while Kazakh membership of that republic's party grew from 8 per cent to 53 per cent between 1924 and 1933. Yet there were limits to Moscow's support for nation-building. The Kurds, for example, were never recognized as a nation, and the degree of autonomy a nation might enjoy depended on Moscow (Abkhazia, for example, had its full republican status rescinded in 1931). Moreover, at the centre, Russians (and, more broadly, Slavs) continued to enjoy a preponderance of key positions in the political, military, and security apparatuses.

Nevertheless the state-sponsored policy of nation-building through conflating language, 'culture', territory, and a quota-based set of state and party structures was a great success.[121] This was particularly evident in the sphere of popular education and the promotion of literacy and print culture in native languages. Alphabets were devised for people who had no written language. Schools which taught in local languages were opened. By 1927, 82 per cent of schools in Ukraine used Ukrainian. Native intelligentsias were created by giving them preferential access to higher education and professional positions. Hundreds of soviets were created for minority nationalities that lived within autonomies where a different non-Russian nationality was dominant. In the Far East Chinese and Koreans had their own autonomies, schools, and publications. This emphasis on national self-expression did not rule out conflict. The Tatars, for example, favoured updating Arabic as the written medium of their language, whereas Muslims in Azerbaijan and the North Caucasus pressed for a Latin script. Moscow supported the latter, seeing Latinization as a means to undermine the power of Muslim clerics; but neo-Arabists in Kazan' waged a counter-challenge in 1926 and 1927.[122] Moscow genuinely encouraged national diversity, but this did not mean that it considered all cultures to be equal. Firmly committed to an evolutionist view of social development, it had little compunction in attacking elements of Islam it considered 'backward'. In the last analysis, the policy of nation-building was on Moscow's terms. And following Stalin's 'revolution from above', the tensions between the institutionalization of nationality within a federal structure and the centralization of economic and political power in a unitary party-state would become much more evident.

The Limits of NEP

In recent years NEP has been the subject of considerable debate. During the perestroika era of Mikhail Gorbachev in the 1980s many argued that NEP could have delivered balanced economic growth at a rate which matched that which was actually achieved by the crash industrialization of the First Five-Year Plan. Following the fall of the Soviet Union, the argument swung the other way, with historians arguing that NEP was doomed to collapse under the weight of its contradictions. While one does not have to subscribe to the idea that there is an absolute contradiction between plan and market, it is clear that NEP was a deeply contradictory system. From the first, it proved vulnerable to crises, and as it evolved, the temptation to use command-administrative methods to intervene in the workings of the market became irresistible. Yet in 1928 NEP was not in terminal crisis. Grain procurement was certainly a serious problem, yet a change in the price of grain relative to other agricultural goods would have influenced the propensity of peasants to grow and market grain. The problem was that even increased grain sales could not generate the surplus required to sustain the rate of industrialization to which the Stalin leadership had become committed, especially following the war scare of 1927. Ludicrously ambitious though the targets of the First Five-Year Plan became, threatening external and domestic pressures dictated that growth be rapid. Externally, the situation created by the Versailles peace settlement had left the Soviet Union vulnerable to hostile powers, and fear of invasion powered the conviction of the leadership that the Soviet Union must build her economic and military strength as quickly as possible. Internally, the revival of the peasantry and the market set in train social and economic dynamics that, to a considerable extent, eluded the control of the party-state and strengthened the ideological perception that 'class enemies' were in the ascendant. Together these external and internal pressures dictated that the overriding political tasks must be rapid industrialization, the modernization of agriculture, and the rapid expansion of defence capability.

If, objectively, NEP could not deliver the rapid growth wanted by the Stalin leadership, the decision to abandon it was nevertheless more an ideological than a pragmatic one. Both the Left Opposition and the Stalinist leadership were convinced that 'kulaks' were holding the towns to ransom and that if NEP continued, the Soviet state was in danger of becoming engulfed by 'petty-bourgeois' forces. The deep structure of Bolshevik ideology—the sense that all policies served either to strengthen 'bourgeois' or 'proletarian' forces—made a break with NEP likely sooner rather than later. However, this emphatically did not mean that ideology dictated the violent dekulakization, wildly escalating planning targets, the terror and forced labour that Stalin would actually unleash.

7

THE NEW ECONOMIC POLICY: SOCIETY AND CULTURE

The 1920s was a period characterized by a paradoxical combination of anxiety and hope.[1] The power of the party-state expanded, yet the new rulers became uncomfortably aware of the limits of their power, and anxious about the resurgence of 'bourgeois' forces they had assumed had been vanquished by the Revolution. At the same time, NEP was the period when the utopian dimension of revolution flourished, even as efforts to achieve the most limited practical reforms were crippled by lack of finance and personnel. It witnessed radical experimentation in the arts and culture and, to some extent, in daily life. Communists looked impatiently to the future, yet were acutely aware of how trammelled they were by the structural and cultural legacy of the past. For society at large the period brought immense relief after the appalling suffering of the civil war and hopes were high that the Soviet population could look forward to a period of prosperity and stability. Limited social and economic improvement was achieved, but life remained tough for the majority and the limits placed on liberty by the still weak but growing state were palpable. Relative to the civil war and the 'revolution from above', which was to come in 1928–9, this was a period of relative order and civic advance, one that in some ways harked back to the period 1905–14. A civil society re-emerged, yet state intervention to limit and control its development steadily increased.

Social Order Restored

If Russia in the last decades of tsarism was moving away from an estate society towards a class society, the Revolution halted that process by destroying the old elites. In the emerging socialist society class remained a fragile structure, its material underpinnings of ownership of means of production, the employment of wage labour, or exercise of managerial authority weakly articulated. Social relations were fluid, with plenty of opportunities for upward mobility which ranged from leaving one's village, to getting an education, to getting a factory job, to joining the Komsomol (the Communist organization for young people between the age of 14 and 23), or to using one's skills and political commitment to acquire a position in the burgeoning institutions of the party-state. With the onset of NEP, social inequality began to increase. As early as March 1922, Evgenii Preobrazhenskii warned: 'The levelling of class contradictions in our country has come to a halt.' Compared with capitalist societies, of course, NEP society's nascent class relations were still remarkably equal. Yet social differentiations were complex, certainly more so than official categories allowed. Leaving to one side the beginnings of a *nomenklatura* elite, discussed in the previous chapter, there were processes of class formation at work over which the state had relatively little control, caused not only by the resurgence of the market but also by the seemingly unstoppable expansion of bureaucracy. It was in an effort to control such forces that Bolsheviks sought to impose their own design upon the new social order by ascribing rights and duties to social groups on the basis of their place in the new political and juridical order. In imposing its own classification on society, it acted rather as Peter the Great had done in 1722 when he imposed on the hereditary nobility a Table of Ranks, or as the tsarist state had done a century later by ratifying the system of social estates (the system that had been abolished on 11 November 1917).[2]

In 1926 a detailed census was carried out across the newly created Soviet Union, which produced a vast amount of information about the social and ethnic structure of the population. It emerged that the population stood at 147 million, 5.5 per cent higher than in 1914, although later statisticians would estimate that the population might have been a million lower than this because of movement of people during the week it took to carry out the census. The rise in population—despite the demographic catastrophe of the civil war—was remarkable and was almost entirely due to the rapid recovery of the rural population, which was estimated to comprise 82 per cent of inhabitants of the Soviet Union.[3] If one defines 'urban' less generously than the census takers, the rural percentage was even higher than this. However, it is noteworthy that about 5.7 per cent of the population classed as rural was engaged in occupations other than farming, such as artisanal production, transportation, construction, or employment in soviet, cooperative, educational, or other public institutions. The census provided information on such matters as the number of peasant families that employed labour and the number that relied exclusively on the labour of family members, but it could not provide the Stalin leadership—at least directly—with the information it really wanted, which was about the extent to which class differentiation was taking place in the countryside. The leadership was convinced that 'bourgeois' forces were in the ascendant and it yearned to measure and to limit that process.

The agrarian revolution had increased the amount of land at the disposal of peasants and brought about its more equitable distribution. The number of peasant households rose sharply from 18.7 million in 1914 to about 24 million in 1927, as sons split from the parental household, generally at the insistence of their wives. However, there was no reduction in the size of the average household plot. Indeed in European Russia (minus the autonomous republics) it increased in area from 10.08 hectares before the Revolution to 13.23 in 1927.[4] The reality was that the average household sat squarely in the 'middle peasant' category: as a family working mainly for its own subsistence and relying on its own labour.The so-called 'neo-populist' school of A. V. Chaianov, which was well represented in the Commissariat of Agriculture, doubted that social differentiation was taking place, arguing that peasant households were subject to cyclical mobility rather than to long-term stratification. Wealthy households, they argued, were those in which the ratio of workers to consumers was high. When sons split from the parental household, their wealth declined.[5] Marxists, on the contrary, produced studies that purported to show that NEP was allowing kulaks to prosper at the expense of the poor. A large-scale survey of 1927 classified households according to the value of their means of production, and purported to show that 26 per cent of households were poor; that 57 per cent belonged to the 'middle' peasantry; 14 per cent to the 'upper middle'; and 3.2 per cent to the kulaks.[6] Yet all these categories were hard to define, none more so than that of 'kulak'. There was neither popular nor academic unanimity on how kulak households should be defined. Traditionally, kulaks were associated with money-lending or with those whose wealth derived primarily from trade, such as the sale of liquor; but kulaks could also be wealthy farmers, especially if they hired labour, hired out heavy machinery or draft animals, or produced mainly for the market. In addition, the statistics produced could be interpreted in different ways. If one measured the data on a per capita basis, for example, the degree of social differentiation within the peasantry was less than if one measured it by household. Moreover, whereas sown area per capita was distributed fairly equally, per capita holding of livestock, rented land, and hired labour was less equally distributed, and ownership of machinery was concentrated very unequally. Finally, such data did not take full account of off-farm earnings from trade, handicrafts, or wage work.[7] At the other extreme of village society, farm labourers were rather easier to count, since they were defined as those who worked continuously for more than four months each year for wages. In 1927 there were 2.3 million labourers, although it is noteworthy that 1.5 million of these worked for individual peasant households (something that was legal if able-bodied members of a household were working but unable to cope with all the tasks of farming).[8] Because of the problems of definition and statistical interpretation, historians continue to argue about whether social differentiation was actually taking place in the countryside. It is probably fair to say that the Bolsheviks were almost certainly wrong to believe that NEP was increasing the trend for rich and poor to grow at the expense of the middle peasants, if only because it was in operation for too short a time. However, historians influenced by the 'neo-populist' school also probably underestimate the extent of divisions within village society (though they are right to dispute the idea that a trend towards greater division was under way).

If class in the sense of enduring, structured relations of inequality of wealth and power was still a tenuous entity in NEP society, class as a discourse became ever more influential. Distinctions between rich, middle, and poor peasants had always been recognized in village society, but now such distinctions took on a heightened significance, since they were used by the regime as a basis for granting tax exemptions, withdrawing voting rights, or encouraging poor peasants to form separate organizations (from 1926). Indeed, one is struck by the extent to which peasants themselves used the language of class, though whether as a means of self-protection, of legitimizing complaints, or as a convenient way to explain away problems (by blaming them on priests or kulaks, for example) is uncertain. Typical was the schoolchild who wrote of her village: 'We still have some *burzhui*, who squeeze the inhabitants, giving them goods on credit so that they cost two to three times what they cost in the cooperative. We have a lot of them, seven in all. They've been deprived of the vote at the village gathering because they elect one another and support one another.'[9] At the same time, peasant perceptions of village society continued to be at odds with those of officialdom: poor peasants, the cynosure of party leaders, were often regarded as 'idlers' and 'spongers' by their fellow villagers; while kulaks might be praised for their industriousness, on the one hand, or castigated as 'commune eaters' and 'parasites on the *mir* (village gathering)'.

If the regime was alarmed by the increase in influence of 'kulaks', it was just as exercised by the revival of 'bourgeois' elements in the towns.[10] Much public concern centred on the nepmen, that is, the traders, manufacturers, and suppliers who seized the new opportunities offered by NEP to engage in private enterprise. Probably the biggest group of the 3 million traders and middlemen were those involved in manufacture and sale of handicrafts in the countryside, but it was those who traded or ran small businesses in the towns who came in for fiercest criticism. This was because many made substantial fortunes and, if literary representations are to be believed, flaunted their new-found wealth, by dining on caviar and champagne, hiring servants, buying houses, dressing in suits, silk dresses, or expensive fur coats. These were the nouveaux riches, and there was little overlap between them and the pre-revolutionary merchant estate, except among an elite of big wholesalers. For ordinary folk who struggled to feed and clothe their families, nepmen provided a target for traditional hatred of 'speculators'. Popular antipathy was captured in and reinforced by the merciless caricatures of nepmen in magazines, cartoons, films, posters, and schools as flashy, ignorant upstarts, swindlers, and philistines. So far as party leaders were concerned, they existed on sufferance, necessary to revive the devastated economy yet seen as an alien force liable to pollute the social body.

In an effort to master the situation of uncertainty, one discursive strategy of the Bolsheviks was to identify and separate 'exploiters' from 'toilers'. 'Toilers' was more of a Populist than a Marxist category, since it blurred the distinction between the industrial proletariat and the petty-bourgeois mass of peasants, but it was politically useful. 'Toilers' were workers, most peasants and (though they were seldom referred to) the rising number of white-collar employees. 'Exploiters' were kulaks, businessmen, and rentiers, with *spetsy*, technical intelligentsia, and the free professions tending towards the latter.[11] Those deemed 'exploiters' were deprived of the vote and barred from joining the Komsomol or the party; they were also penalized in terms of taxation, and access to higher education and to housing. Discrimination intensified from 1926: in that year there were 1.04 million people deprived of the vote and by 1929 it had risen to 3.7 million. In 1926 43.3 per cent of the disenfranchised were traders and middlemen, 15.2 per cent were clergy and monks, 13.8 per cent were rentiers, and 9 per cent were those who had served as officers or police under the old regime. Among rural dwellers the proportion of the disenfranchised rose from 1.4 per cent in 1924 to 3.5 per cent in 1929.[12] After 1928 the disenfranchised could no longer claim rations and from the same year, when military service was made compulsory for all male 'toilers' aged 19 to 40, 'exploiters' were no longer trusted to defend the motherland, and were required instead to enrol in the home guard and pay a large exemption tax. Compulsory military service thus defined citizenship in the socialist state not only in gendered but also in class terms. In practice discriminatory class labels were applied arbitrarily. Local soviets disenfranchised middle and even poor peasants for hiring nurses or workers during harvest time, on the grounds that this rendered them 'exploiters'. Similarly membership of a religious sect or of an Orthodox parish council might lead to being labelled a kulak (or, in later Stalinist parlance, a 'kulak hanger-on' (*podkulachnik*)). Significantly, by the end of the 1920s, the bulk of those deprived of voting rights were not 'former people' from aristocratic or bourgeois backgrounds, or former White officers, or even priests, but those who had been forced by unemployment and economic necessity to dabble in trade.

Those who appealed against the loss of rights invariably made the point that they were workers and that any lapse into 'non-toiling activity'—that is, trade—had been due to pressure of circumstances: 'I took up trade not for profit but to support my family.'[13] This spontaneous use of the term 'non-toiling activity' suggests the official language of class battened on to deeper peasant conceptions of what was productive labour and what made one a useful member of society. Moreover, the appeals against disenfranchisement attest to the regime's having a certain legitimacy, since even those who complained of being unjustly treated appear to have believed that this was in principle a legitimate means of weeding out those who had become rich at the people's expense. Bolshevik ideology was thus more than an imposed illusion, despite the many contradictions between it and the reality experienced by ordinary Soviet citizens. To some extent, it proved able to engage with the needs and aspirations of ordinary people, to re-inflect them in its own idiom and feed them back in ways that rendered the ideology plausible, even attractive for some. It provided a basis on which members of a very fluid society could fashion a public identity and find motivations for social action.

Designing a Welfare State

In addition to categorizing its population, the Soviet state sought to refashion it through education, health care, housing, urban planning, and social work. In its commitment to improve the welfare of the people, it may be seen as an authoritarian variant of the welfare states that were emerging throughout Europe in this period, where governments massively expanded their remit, mobilizing new forms of knowledge and surveillance, new technologies of control, new means of communication to foster a rational improvement of the social body.[14]

Healthcare was an area where the Bolshevik record in the 1920s was impressive, given the overwhelming poverty of society and the crippling restraints on resources.[15] The war and civil war had brought about a catastrophic deterioration in popular health, evinced in the fact that the average height of male conscripts to the army fell from 169.5 cm in 1908 to 166.5 cm in 1924, while the average weight fell from 66.5 kg to 60.5 kg. From a dismal nadir, however, the health of the population improved during the 1920s to a point where it was superior to the average for 1911–13. In those years, for example, there were 28.6 deaths per 1,000 of the population; a figure that fell to 21 by 1927.[16] That said, the financing of healthcare remained under intense strain and there was a good deal of variation in the level and quality of health provision, above all between town and countryside. Only workers qualified for free health care, and the introduction of charges for services discouraged peasants from using the limited facilities available, since zemstvo medicine had been free. Yet even in the countryside per capita health expenditure on uninsured persons rose from a paltry 69 kopecks in 1924–5 to 1.05 roubles in 1926–7, which still compared unfavourably with 4.41 to 6.26 roubles for townspeople. The ratio of doctors to population rose from 1: 6,900 in 1913 to 1: 2,590 in 1926—a big improvement—but at the latter date there was still only one doctor for every 18,900 people in the countryside.[17] The principal reason was the unwillingness of doctors to practise in the countryside because of low pay and poor working conditions. Furthermore, by the late 1920s a large proportion of medical students were women, many of whom were bound to the city by family ties. The result was that paramedics, many of them trained in the army, remained crucial to rural medical services, even though the policy of the Health Commissariat was to phase them out.

Initially, doctors were hostile to the Bolshevik regime, objecting to its elimination of their institutional autonomy in the zemstvos and professional societies, but they quickly adapted to the creation of a Health Commissariat in July 1918, and a promise of free, accessible healthcare for all. The Commissariat upheld the technical expertise of doctors, and resisted calls from the medical-sanitary workers' union to equalize the status of physicians' assistants and nurses with that of doctors and allow the trade unions to administer health facilities. Central to the policy of the Health Commissariat was a programme of preventive medicine and of sanitary and other measures to alleviate disease and improve living conditions. Through a programme of 'dispensarization', aimed at screening targeted sections of the population for diseases such as tuberculosis, syphilis, or trachoma, local clinics and workplace units implemented preventive measures, such as obligatory vaccination against smallpox, and carried out health education. Sanitary-enlightenment propaganda was systematically developed to raise awareness about disease and public health, with campaigns in the Red Army to 'Help the country with a toothbrush' and 'Help the country by washing in cold water'. Sanitary-enlightenment units were established, which conducted lectures in factories and schools, displayed posters in villages, and staged plays, lantern-shows, and exhibitions—all to convey the message that making every aspect of one's life healthy was a sign of 'consciousness' (see Figure 7.1).

Despite the prohibition of alcohol in 1914, illegal distilling of alcohol was rife, leading not only to the social problems associated with drunkenness, but also to a reduction in grain supply to the cities.[18] In 1922–3, a campaign was launched against illegal distilling which led to a sharp rise in convictions. At the same time, the fiscal pressure on the government caused it gradually to weaken the policy of prohibition, starting with the sale of wine, albeit not without provoking intense argument in the party leadership. By August 1925, prohibition had been lifted and the state's monopoly on the sale of vodka at pre-war strength fully restored. At the Fourteenth Party Congress in December Stalin, noting *en passant* that one cannot 'build socialism in white gloves', argued that the reinstatement of the state monopoly

Figure 7.1 Young Pioneers demonstrate against the dangers of alcohol, 1929.

was the only way to prevent 'slavery to Western European capitalists'. The addition of a tax on vodka, however, further encouraged illegal brewing and this was almost certainly a factor behind the grain crisis of 1928. In October of that year a nationwide campaign against drunkenness was launched in which schoolchildren, in particular, were mobilized ('Instead of vodka, buy us school books').

Another dimension of the drive to enhance the productive and reproductive power of the new socialist society lay in the official promotion of sport, something that had no parallel under the *ancien régime*.[19] By 1929 759,000 were registered as sports club members (still only 0.5 per cent of the population). Trade unions and the Komsomol were given responsibility for promoting team sports such as soccer and basketball, as well as athletics, speed skating, boxing, wrestling, and fencing. There was also working-class interest in spectator sports, although this was not especially encouraged by government.[20] Some activists opposed competitive sports in favour of recreation and all-round fitness for the masses. 'It is necessary to be vigilant that competition does not spoil comradely relations, does not develop in the victors bourgeois feelings of pride, superiority, self-regard, or envy in the defeated.'[21] Social hygienists, an influential group who approached disease primarily as a social rather than a biological phenomenon, objected to games that were potentially injurious to health such as weightlifting, boxing, and gymnastics, preferring sports that were 'rational' and collective in nature. The supporters of Proletkul't, discussed in the section 'Cultural Revolution' below, rejected 'bourgeois' sports in their entirety, favouring 'labour gymnastics', mass displays, and pageants, such as that which was held in 1924 on Sparrow Hills in Moscow, when 6,000 staged a pageant in which British imperialists were thrown out of India. Following party intervention in 1925, the emphasis was increasingly on sport as a means of promoting health and fitness, clean living, collectivism, social progress, and military training.

The Bolshevik record in education has come under more critical scrutiny than that in health, partly because some historians believe the radical experimentalism that characterized it was impractical and merely made a desperate situation worse. The new regime was committed to primary and secondary education for all and free of cost, but in 1921 school fees were introduced. In 1927 they were abolished for primary education since they were discouraging peasants from sending their children to school.[22] The school system was coeducational and integrated—the Church was deprived of any role in education—and entrance examinations, grading, homework, and corporal punishment were all abolished. Education was to embody popular initiative through educational councils, elected at township, county, and provincial level. Building on the progressive educational theories influential in late-imperial Russia, Anatolii Lunacharskii, the Commissar of Enlightenment, together with Krupskaia, promoted polytechnicism—the idea of an all-round education without vocational specialization—and the 'unified labour school', where pupils took part in vocational training as a way of familiarizing them with production. The 'complex' method dispensed with traditional subjects in favour of the pupil's independent, activity-centred learning on themes to do with nature, labour, and society.[23] Children were to be taught proletarian, collectivist, and materialist values and to learn the skills and dispositions needed to transform a backward economy. In reality, lack of resources meant that many initiatives, such as the unified labour school, barely got off the ground.[24] Experimentalism in education was by no means popular. Given that the level of educational achievement was still so low, the Komsomol and the trade unions began to demand more vocational training and greater specialization within the school system. The Commissariat of Education resisted these demands, but from 1926 it took steps towards reinstating a more traditional curriculum, while preserving the principle of polytechnicism. This failed to silence the critics, however, and in 1929, at the height of the 'Cultural Revolution' (see below), Lunacharskii was removed and the Central Committee demanded that the Commissariat be purged of 'alien elements who distort the proletarian class line'.

Relations between the government and teachers got off to a shaky start, after the latter went on strike. The Congress of the Teachers' Union, dominated by Mensheviks and SRs, refused in June 1918 to cooperate with authorities 'in whose activities there are neither creative ideas and principles nor a democratic basis for school education'. During the civil war teachers struggled on, with pitiful salaries, in derelict buildings, and with few textbooks and materials, while the government battled to provide schoolchildren with one square meal a day. Many veteran teachers were conscripted, leaving the profession overwhelmingly female and with a low average level of training and experience. Teachers were generally hostile to principles of child-centred education, and many continued to teach by means of dictation, memorization, homework, grades, and even corporal punishment.[25] As late as 1926, teachers earned less than half what they had earned in 1913. At the same time, the number of teachers grew by 77 per cent between 1922 and 1929, although standards of teaching remained low.

As with education in the tsarist era historians differ in their assessment of the Bolshevik record. Statistics suggest progress; and a fair assessment needs to take into account both the campaign to eliminate illiteracy, which is discussed in the section 'Cultural Revolution' below, and the campaign to develop education in the non-Russian republics. The number of pupils in primary and secondary schools rose from 8.13 million in 1914–15 to 12.24 million in 1928. By 1926–7 eight out of ten children aged 8 to 11 were in school, compared with 49 per cent in 1915; but the average time spent there was only 2.3 years for girls—who comprised only 36 per cent of the enrolment in rural primary schools—and 2.5 years for boys. The numbers at junior secondary level (grades five to seven) increased two-and-a-half times, but again townspeople were the major beneficiaries.[26] It was, however, the actual amount spent by government that is the crucial indicator, as it had been in the tsarist era, and in 1924–5 only 4.4 per cent of the central budget was spent on education, slightly less than the tsarist government had spent by 1914. In some of the non-Russian republics the percentage was higher, but in the RSFSR more seems to have been spent on 'political enlightenment' than on primary and secondary education.[27]

In 1918 a 'revolutionary housing repartition' had been proclaimed under the slogan 'Peace to the hovels, war to the palaces', whereby workers were moved from squalid 'cots' and 'corners', where many had lived before the Revolution, into the apartments of the well-to-do.[28] The quality of the housing stock deteriorated sharply, partly because there was no rental income to pay for upkeep and partly because furniture and fittings were plundered to provide heating. Apartments of the so-called 'nobs' (*barskie*), with their interconnecting rooms, high ceilings, huge stoves, kitchens, and lavatories, often proved quite unsuitable for what were later known as *kommunalki*, communal apartments, where each family had a separate room but shared kitchen, lavatory, and corridor. Kitchens with fuel-hungry stoves, and inhabitants working different shifts, made for much friction. As Woland says in Mikhail Bulgakov's novel *Master and Margarita,* 'People are people. It's just the housing question that spoils them.' With NEP 'housing repartition' was abandoned and much property was returned to its former owners. Private housing construction was permitted and housing associations of various types were formed, often by tenants, to administer the accommodation. In 1922 rents were reinstated and began to rise once the currency was stabilized, although even by 1928–9 only 8.6 per cent of the expenditure of working-class families went on rent.[29] Housing was a low priority in the state budget, but strenuous efforts were made to improve the living conditions of the working class. In Moscow between 1918 and 1924 over half a million workers and their families were rehoused. Nationally, the percentage of worker families with more than one room rose from 28 per cent in 1908 to 64 per cent in 1922, while the percentage living in one room rose to 33 per cent.[30] Yet the resumption of migration to the cities put intense pressure on housing, and this was probably the sphere of urban life where least improvement occurred. In Moscow the amount of living space per person declined from 9.3 square metres in 1920 to 5.5 in 1927, and the average number of inhabitants per apartment grew from five to nine.[31] Housing was also an area in which the government policy increasingly favoured officials and experts. From January 1922, scientific workers were allowed an extra room, a privilege later extended to state and party officials, military and naval administrators, and to doctors and dentists in private practice. In 1926 the official allocation of living space per adult was 4.9 square metres for workers, 6.9 for employees, and 6.1 for others.[32] Anyone having in excess of these norms was likely to be asked to 'self-compress' (*samouplotnit'sia*), that is, to make room for others. Only with the onset of the First Five-Year Plan did the regime return to a policy of allocating housing on class principles.

With NEP, the regime abandoned its grandiose scheme to distribute goods and services through a comprehensive system of rationing. The rapidity with which inequalities in consumption took hold surprised everyone. The hero of Andrei Platonov's novel *Chevengur* returns home in 1921: 'At first he thought that the Whites were in town. At the station they were selling grey bread rolls at the buffet without ration cards and without any queue... A concise and crudely written sign declared: "Everything for sale to all citizens. Pre-war bread, pre-war fish, fresh meat, our own pickles."'[33] If the easing of supplies was widely welcomed, the fact that goods were only available to those with money rankled, especially with idealists. The Belgian anarchist-turned-Bolshevik Victor Serge exclaimed: 'The sordid taint of money is visible on everything. The grocers have sumptuous displays, packed with Crimean fruits and Georgian wines, but a postman earns only about fifty roubles a month...Hordes of beggars and abandoned children, hordes of prostitutes.'[34] From 1926 restrictions on 'speculation' were stepped up, but cooperatives and state trusts were quite unable to substitute for private trade. By 1928 long lines stood for hours outside bakeries in Moscow and Leningrad. While for the mass of citizens, goods were increasingly in short supply—*defitsitnyi* ('in deficit') was one of many new words that entered the Soviet lexicon—members of the *nomenklatura* elite had access to special supplies. At the same time, citizens became versed in the arts of getting access to scarce commodities and services through the 'back door', by cultivating 'connections'. According to a rhyming jingle by the artist Vladimir Mayakovsky, a citizen was ideally set up if they had 'a fiancée in an industrial trust, a godparent in GUM (Moscow's leading department store), and a brother in a commissariat' (*nevesta v treste, kum v GUM, brat v narkomat*).[35]

The Arts and Utopia

In the preceding section, Bolshevik policies in the spheres of healthcare and education were characterized as designs for a 'welfare state', since that idea provides a familiar benchmark against which we can judge their progress. It also accurately represents the ethos of much policy-making. Yet from the viewpoint of Marxist theory, the idea of a welfare state would have seemed a quite inappropriate benchmark, since Bolshevik ambitions went far beyond the idea of a state that protected and promoted the social welfare of its citizens. For them concrete reforms were but steps along a path that was to lead to a radically new form of society based on far-reaching collectivism and equality. Yet it would be wide of the mark to describe the Bolshevik leadership during NEP as being inspired by utopianism: indeed compared with the utopian highpoint of 1920, their sights had been substantially lowered. For sections of the population however—mainly artists, intellectuals, and urban youth—the NEP years offered a space in which a plethora of utopian visions could be elaborated and pursued. A paradox of NEP was that the 'retreat' forced on the Bolsheviks by civil war devastation and economic backwardness and the apparent turn towards pragmatic gradualism was compensated for by bold imaginings and anticipations of the communist future.

The Marxist tradition had generally eschewed the attempt to outline what the future communist society would look like. In the *Communist Manifesto*, it is true, the young Marx and Engels had given qualified approval to the 'practical proposals' of their utopian predecessors, such as Henri de Saint-Simon, Charles Fourier, or Robert Owen, proposals they listed as: 'the abolition of the distinction between town and country, of the family, of the carrying on of industries for the account of private individuals, and of the wage system; the proclamation of social harmony, the conversion of the functions of the state into a mere superintendence of production'.[36] These 'proposals' never ceased to galvanize the conception of communist society held by Marx and Engels, but in their mature work they contrasted their own 'scientific' conception of socialism with that of the utopian socialists, insisting that the latter took no account of stages of historical development or of class struggle as the motive-force of historical change. The Bolsheviks inherited this aversion to utopian speculation, seeing it as antipathetic to their understanding of socialism as something that must be worked out by humanity in accordance with the laws of history, rather than some idealized blueprint.

Yet a utopian vision necessarily sustained revolutionaries in the tsarist period, however hard-nosed they liked to appear.[37] Lenin was deeply influenced by the non-Marxist utopianism of Nikolai Chernyshevskii, whose *What is to Be Done?* (1863) envisioned a community, symbolized in the novel by a crystal palace, united around work, comradeship, and rational egotism. After 1905 a neo-positivist current emerged in the Bolshevik faction that elaborated ideas of god-building and proletarian culture and that imagined the proletariat forging a biologically, intellectually, and socially perfect humanity. Its key exponent was Aleksandr Bogdanov, who penned two sci-fi novels about a communist society on the planet Mars (*Red Star*, published in 1908, and *Engineer Menni*, published in 1913). In the society of the future science has conquered nature through nuclear propulsion, blood transfusion, unisexuality, and, rather worrisomely, through atomic fall-out. Very different in tone was the most famous dystopia of this period, Evgenii Zamiatin's *We*, completed in 1919–20, in which the state imposes conformity on all its citizens, regulating their lives through science, and demanding absolute loyalty.[38] Lenin disliked all such fantasies, yet was not immune himself to utopian flights of fancy. In *State and Revolution*, completed while he was in hiding in Finland in August and September 1917, he set out a vision of communist society in which the police and standing army would be abolished, all officials elected, and administration simplified to the point that a cook or housekeeper could learn to run public affairs (this latter an echo of Saint-Simon's expectation that 'the government of men' would be replaced by 'the administration of things').[39]

The October Revolution generated an efflorescence of radical experimentation in the arts that was unsurpassed anywhere else in the world.[40] It was symbolized in Kazimir Malevich's 'Black Square', Vladimir Tatlin's 'Monument to the Third International', Vsevolod Meyerhold's biomechanical drama, the 'transrational' poetry of Velimir Khlebnikov, the strident verses of Vladimir Mayakovsky, and the experiments of Nikolai Roslavets in forging a new tonal system in music.[41] The avant-garde, which had emerged around 1908, was driven by a desire to destroy old aesthetic norms and convinced that art had the power to transform 'life', which it identified with the utopian possibilities opened up by the Revolution. Many of its representatives, such as Malevich, Aleksandr Rodchenko, Tatlin, and Wassily Kandinsky in the visual arts, gained positions of influence within new Soviet institutions. Though fired by fierce aesthetic conflict, the avant-garde was loosely leftist in political sympathies and iconoclastic in spirit, though the Futurist call to 'Throw Pushkin, Dostoevsky, Tolstoy etc. overboard from the ship of modernity' should probably be taken with a large pinch of salt. Nevertheless all saw the revolutionization of artistic practice as part of the larger project of changing the role of art in society. Mayakovsky buttonholed the masses with his declamatory, staccato verse, as in his poem of 1920:

Onward!
Drive your elbows into ribs like iron spikes,
Crash your fists into the jaws of the elegant charity
gentlemen tightly buttoned into frockcoats![42]

Theatre was supreme among the arts during the civil war, even though most theatre professionals initially perceived the seizure of power as a threat to their artistic autonomy. The principal concern of the Bolsheviks was to give impetus to the drive to democratize the theatre, but though the composition of theatre audiences became more plebeian, the repertoire and production values of the majority of theatres changed barely at all. This was a source of irritation both to Proletkul't and, especially, to the theatrical avant-garde. Meyerhold's production of Mayakovsky's *Mystery-Bouffe*, staged to mark the first anniversary of the October Revolution, met with incomprehension owing to its hybrid of futurism, apocalypticism, circus acrobatics, and folk humour. Meyerhold's system of 'biomechanics', in some ways analogous to the vogue for the 'scientific organization of labour', sought to purge acting of psychological motivation by removing superfluous motion, gesture, and expression from the actor's technique. His efforts to unleash a 'Theatrical October', however, were blocked by the Commissar of Enlightenment, Lunacharskii, who insisted on the value of preserving traditional theatre and the classical repertoire. Nevertheless he defended the principle of creative freedom for different approaches, including the avant-garde, and did not share Lenin's intolerance of 'absurd and perverted' avant-garde art (Figure 7.2).

With NEP, architecture, the novel, and cinema came into their own. Constructivism was the one movement in the visual arts born directly out of the October Revolution. In seeking to fuse the artistic and technological aspects of production, the Constructivists sought to create an environment in which the new socialist person could flourish by remaking the fabric of everyday life along rational collectivist lines. Tatlin urged citizens to 'Declare war on chests of drawers and sideboards', arguing that 'a new everyday life requires new objects...It is for this reason that I show such interest in

Figure 7.2 Liubov' Popova, 'Jug on a table'.

organic form as a point of departure for the creation of new objects'. Tatlin's own monument to the Third International, though pre-dating Constructivism, exemplified this ethos, comprising an immense tower consisting of a stack of three glass geometric volumes, encased in a double conical spiral of iron that thrust up at an acute angle (Figure 7.3). Constructivist interest in the properties of materials and in industrial design had a huge influence on the modern movement in architecture, photography, commercial advertising, home furnishings, fabrics, and cinema. In print graphics, for instance, it produced a geometric style with sharp angles for dynamism and circles for stability, often featuring scraps of photographic imagery or declamatory text.

Figure 7.3 Vladimir Tatlin and assistant in front of a model of his Monument to the Third International, 1919.

It was probably in literature that the 1920s saw the most creative ferment.[43] Poets such as Aleksandr Blok, Sergei Esenin, and Andrei Belyi identified with the 'spiritual maximalism' of the Revolution, denouncing petty-bourgeois philistinism and celebrating the destructive energies of the peasantry. Somewhat in this spirit was what many consider to be the first 'Soviet' novel, Boris Pil'niak's *Naked Year* (1922), set amid the chaos of civil war. This depicted the Revolution as a vengeful, Asiatic force stripping off the veneer of civilization. Other writers such as Konstantin Fedin, Mikhail Zoshchenko, and Viacheslav Ivanov hailed the Revolution as a liberation of the fantastic imagination, but came under fire for being 'ideologically empty' from those, such as the Proletkul'tist Smithy group, who rejected anything that smacked of art for art's sake, lauding instead collectivism, labour, and the cult of the machine. As the memory of the civil war faded, writing began to become less partisan, more reflective of the uncertainties of NEP society. Noteworthy was the efflorescence of satire in the tragicomic work of Zoshchenko, whose subject matter was the petty absurdity of daily Soviet life and whose language parodied the speech of semi-literate proletarians. A humanistic, apolitical aesthetic also began to gain ground, evident in the poetry of Mandelstam and Akhmatova, who sought to cultivate lyricism and a language of precision, clarity, and restraint. It was in reaction to this—and, more fundamentally, to the unsettling eddies of NEP—that in 1928 the Association of Proletarian Writers demanded that literature should obey a 'social command'. This aesthetic, which saw fiction as having little value except as a sociological document, chimed with the tastes of newly literate readers who craved for positive, unambiguous characters, a secure narrative, and moral certainties. In the realm of literary theory, scholars such as Viktor Shkovskii, Boris Eikhenbaum, and Vladimir Propp created the formalist school, which stressed the formal qualities of the text, such as structure, rhythm, and technical use of language, rather than content.

The cinema, too, blossomed, generating stylistic diversity, innovation, and theoretical advance, with Soviet studios making 514 films between 1925 and 1929.[44] Classics of world cinema were produced by directors such as Sergei Eisenstein, Dziga Vertov, Vsevolod Pudovkin, and Aleksandr Dovzhenko, some of whom had cut their teeth making propaganda 'shorts' during the civil war and many of whom were influenced by Constructivism. As in other artistic fields there was sharp debate: in cinema it concerned the virtues of documentary as opposed to feature film, of propaganda as opposed to entertainment. The Factory of Eccentric Actors looked to American jazz, dance, and technology for inspiration and its iconoclastic film of Gogol's *Overcoat* sought through the concept of 'impeded form' to stimulate the visual awareness of the audience by juxtaposing unexpected images. This principle of montage was central to the very different aesthetic of the Cine-Eye group, based around the film director Dziga Vertov, which proclaimed: 'No illusion! Down with the actor and scenery!' Perhaps the most masterly exponent of montage was Sergei Eisenstein, whose revolutionary trilogy (*Strike, Battleship Potemkin, October*), with its mythic presentation of the masses as hero, was characterized by visual daring and operatic style. With the brashness typical of the avant-garde, he proclaimed: 'By "film" I understand tendentiousness and nothing else.' Yet most of this cinema was not popular with the public nor with party leaders. Even Eisenstein's films, though politically impeccable, were greeted lukewarmly by officialdom, because of their experimental editing, shooting, and mise-en-scène. The cinema-going public preferred Mary Pickford and Douglas Fairbanks, and no less than 85 per cent of movies screened were imports, mainly from the USA. The revival of commercial mass culture that took place with NEP left the leadership in no doubt that the public preferred escapist fiction, light music, comedy, and variety acts to avant-garde art or political propaganda. Official concern that art should become more accessible to workers and peasants was one reason why in the second half of the 1920s the regime came to look with increasing favour on the many artists who had continued, in spite of the Revolution, to work within broadly realist and figurative genres.

The end of the civil war saw no letting up in the persecution of intellectual dissent. In August 1921 the execution of Petrograd poet Nikolai Gumilëv, arrested in the sweep against a putatively counter-revolutionary group led by geography professor Tagantsev, marked a watershed in the state's relations with intellectuals. In June 1922 various independent journals were shut down, including an academic journal, *The Economist (Ekonomist)*, which had a tiny circulation, but which Lenin described as 'the organ of contemporary serf-owners who cover themselves in the mantle of science and democracy'. In that year the Politburo discussed the deportation of 'wavering' intellectuals no fewer than thirty times, eventually deciding to expel about 200 intellectuals (plus their family members) in August. They included the historians A. A. Kizevetter and A. V. Florovskii, and the religious philosophers N. A. Berdiaev and S. L. Frank.[45] Nevertheless, on the whole, the 1920s were a decade in which a degree of pluralism was tolerated in education, the arts, and the sciences, even if the authorities steadily tightened their ideological grip.

NEP saw a revival of the civil society that had flourished after 1905. In 1928 there were still 4,480 public organizations in existence, according to an incomplete list for the RSFSR, embracing everything from scientific, to antiquarian, to sporting organizations. However, of 368 All-Union organizations that applied for formal recognition, the OGPU turned down no fewer than 261 on the grounds that they might threaten public order, encourage nationalist dissension, or promote mysticism. The Vegetarian Society, for instance, was refused recognition 'for political considerations'.[46] With NEP private publishing houses were licensed once again. They published a wide variety of books, although their share of the total output of books was small and declining. In 1922 the ominously named Main Directorate for the Protection of State Secrets in the Press (Glavlit) was set up, charged with censoring domestic and imported printed works, manuscripts, and photos. In the tradition of the tsarist censor, it drew up lists of banned works. In April 1925 it even forbade the press to publish information on suicides or cases of insanity connected to unemployment or hunger.[47] A parallel agency was created in 1923 to monitor the content of plays, films, concerts, phonograph records, and other public performances. The Chief Committee for Repertoire in 1926 banned the staging of plays in the countryside that criticized Soviet policy, presented a positive view of religion, celebrated the traditional rural way of life, or that featured monks (even as marginal characters). By July 1924, it had banned 216 foreign films because of the 'threat to the ideological education of workers and peasants in our country', including Fritz Lang's *Dr Mabuse.*[48] Moreover, many films that were allowed were deemed not to be suitable for a 'worker-peasant' audience. This was a much stricter censorship than had appertained after the 1905 Revolution. One senses that the Bolsheviks were not motivated simply by ideological rectitude but by a fear that alien cultural forces threatened to engulf them.

In 1922 the universities lost most of their autonomy—in spite of a strike by academics in Moscow and elsewhere—although the Academy of Sciences, remarkably, maintained its autonomy until 1929, when it was purged of 'counter-revolutionaries'.[49] In 1921 an Institute of Red Professors was formed to train cadres to take over the universities, and the State

Academic Council began rather tentatively to weed out 'theologians, mystics, and representatives of extreme idealism' from institutions of higher education. In principle, historical materialism and the history of the Bolshevik party were made compulsory subjects for all students but lack of teachers and textbooks meant that this remained a dead letter. Natural sciences were left alone, and by the mid-1920s scientific research claimed a higher proportion of GDP in Russia than in most western countries. Economics saw genuinely innovative thinking on Marxist lines by Nikolai Kondrat'ev, Eugen Varga, Evgenii Slutskii, Preobrazhenskii, and Bukharin. Within philosophy 'dialecticians' argued that dialectics was a universal science embracing nature and society, while 'mechanicists' argued that philosophy had no place in scientific enquiry. History, although not subject to direct party interference, was dominated by the Marxist Mikhail Pokrovskii, who explained Russia's development exclusively in terms of class struggle and modes of production.

Higher education suffered from under-funding throughout the 1920s. The Bolsheviks were committed to opening up higher education to workers and poor peasants, and in 1919 set up workers' faculties to provide crash courses to enable workers and poor peasants to enrol on degree programmes. Some 43,000 students graduated from these during the 1920s—not a high number. Universities were overcrowded and conditions appalling, with many students permanently hungry and sick. The number of graduates increased from 136,000 in 1913 to 233,000 in 1928, and women significantly increased their representation.[50] In June 1922 communist cells in the universities were ordered to weed out students from non-proletarian backgrounds ('the grandfather of such and such was a landowner'). In 1924 18,000 students were purged, many of them accused of being supporters of Trotsky. Academically able middle-class students who, unlike the students from the workers' faculties, had to pay fees, resented being excluded on non-academic grounds. By 1925 the world's first instance of affirmative action in higher education had not been unsuccessful, since workers and peasants comprised 43 per cent of the universities' student body. At the same time, it had led to a fall in academic standards, so that in 1925 academic criteria for selection were reintroduced. Nevertheless, two years later 55 per cent of all students were repeating a year. In spite of the substantial change in the social composition of the student body, Bukharin could complain to the Thirteenth Party Congress in 1924 that: 'Very little of higher education has been won to us.'

During the 1920s the position of the intelligentsia remained ambiguous.[51] The state needed teachers, scientists, planners, managers, doctors, and engineers and so it encouraged the educated to put their expertise to the service of socialism. From the mid-1920s, salaries began to rise and material privileges accrued. As against that, the regime continued to fear the intelligentsia as a competing elite with pretensions to moral authority, one likely to impede its efforts to establish ideological hegemony. The longer-term aim was to replace the 'bourgeois' intelligentsia with a new 'proletarian' one that would be loyal to the Soviet state. However, progress towards that goal was slow and some consider that it was to accelerate progress that in 1928 a 'Cultural Revolution'—in upper case—was launched.[52] This saw zealous exponents of proletarian principles attack exponents of more tolerant or pluralistic positions in various intellectual and cultural fields. Between 1928 and 1931 hard-liners shoved out moderates, denounced avant-garde experimentalism, and drastically limited the range of approved styles in art, music, architecture, film, and all academic disciplines. Nevertheless the extraordinary fact is that despite its travails, which would worsen massively during the 1930s, the intelligentsia retained a distinct social identity, partly through informal networks, personal ties, and institutional loyalties and partly through adherence to the nineteenth-century ideal of raising the cultural level of the common people.

The 1920s was thus an era of unbounded artistic diversity and creativity, yet it saw the party steadily step up its direction of artistic developments. Through censorship, control of funding—especially in relation to expensive ventures such as film—and through direct intervention, the party increased its control of the arts and literature. Convinced of the power of art to shape human consciousness, it was not prepared to leave the direction of intellectual and cultural life to the spontaneous whims of the individual artist or to the commercial vagaries of the market. In addition, party leaders were bothered by the gap between the avant-garde and popular taste and by the fact that the propaganda potential of the arts was undercut by artists' fondness for formal innovation and abstraction. Stalin, a great aficionado of the cinema, described film in 1924 as 'the most important means of mass agitation'. Yet most of the films that have entered into cinema history were difficult for popular audiences to appreciate. Increasingly, the avant-garde's ethos of permanent revolution was at odds with the party's concern for political stability. That said, the exercise of party control was never secure or efficient at this time, and at the end of our period the issue of what should constitute an appropriate art for a socialist society erupted in fierce disputation.

Family and Gender Relations

The Bolsheviks came to power with a radical programme for the liberation of women and the radical transformation of the family.[53] Their reforming zeal was evidenced in the comprehensive Code on Marriage, the Family, and Guardianship, ratified in October 1918, which equalized women's legal status with men's, removed marriage from the hands of the Church, allowed a married couple to choose either the husband's or wife's surname, allowed both spouses to retain the right to their own property and earnings, granted children born outside wedlock the same rights as those born to married couples, and, not least, made divorce available at the request of either party. Under the old regime the Church had granted divorce in only the rarest of circumstances involving adultery, abandonment, sexual incapacity, or penal exile, although between 1884 and 1914, 30,000 to 40,000 wives managed to persuade the imperial chancellery to allow them to separate from their husbands.[54]

In Bolshevik ideology the key to woman's liberation lay in taking her out of the confines of the family, where she was subordinate to her husband and oppressed by the drudgery of childcare and housework, and bringing her into the sphere of wage work. There she would gain economic independence and develop class consciousness. For this to happen, however, it was recognized that the state would need to take over the tasks of childcare and housework, described by Lenin as 'the most unproductive, the most savage and the most arduous work a woman can do'. During the first years of the Revolution, official propaganda summoned women to set aside their responsibilities to husbands and children and to become fighters on behalf of oppressed humanity. Efrosiniia Marakulina, a peasant who became an instructor in Viatka province, was hailed as an archetypal 'new woman': 'She forgot her family, her children, the household. With enthusiasm she threw herself into the new business of enlightening her dark, downtrodden sisters.'[55] Aron Zalkind, a 'psychoneurologist', deprecated 'weak, fragile femininity', the result of 'thousands of years of women's enslavement', and urged working-class women 'physiologically to become more like men'.[56] Yet those who aspired to become 'new women' were few in number. By and large, the social and economic chaos of the civil war meant that women's energies were concentrated on the struggle for survival. Their lack of interest in the drama of revolution reinforced the traditional image of the woman as *baba*, as 'dark' and 'backward', and in thrall to her husband and priest.

It was to shake lower-class women out of their apathy that a Women's Department was established by the party in 1919, headed by Inessa Armand and Alexandra Kollontai.[57] Historically, the Bolsheviks had mistrusted separate organization of women, since they believed it smacked of 'bourgeois' feminism and threatened to bring division into the ranks of the proletariat. Yet they had been the first Russian socialist party to seek to organize working women. Much of the credit for this went to Kollontai, who had been one of the few to rally to Lenin's view of the First World War, although after she became a leader of the Workers' Opposition she found herself the object of his spleen. The Women's Department believed that working women could be liberated only if they joined forces with working men, but they insisted that women's 'backwardness' could only be overcome if they were mobilized around issues of direct interest to them, such as literacy classes, crèches, collective dining rooms, or consumer cooperatives. During the 1920s women's issues figured low on the priorities of the party leadership, and the Department was permanently under-funded and heavily dependent on volunteers. Yet it undertook a range of campaigns, centred on conferences of women delegates, against wage and hiring discrimination, sexual harassment, layoffs of women, alcoholism, and wife-battering. In 1926–7, 620,000 women across the USSR attended delegate conferences held by the Department. In far-away Irkutsk on 1 March 1927 the inter-union conference of working women passed a resolution declaring that 'it is necessary to fight for the liberation of women and to struggle against men'; while in equally far away Barnaul a women's conference described relations between men and women workers as 'abnormal'. No doubt Moscow looked askance at this feminist deviation in Siberia.

In the newly formed republics of Central Asia feminism was mobilized as part of a cultural revolution (Figure 7.4). Up to 1926 attacks on Muslim clerics as 'class oppressors' and on landlords who controlled land and water

Figure 7.4 A demonstration for women's liberation in Baku, Azerbaijan, c.1925.

rights had been only partially effective. Thus in 1927 party leaders in Tashkent decided, partly at the urging of enthusiastic Zhenotdel activists, to focus on attacking 'feudal-patriarchal relics'.[58] In that year an aggressive campaign was launched against bride price, polygamy, female segregation, and seclusion, aimed at breaking the power of mullahs and village and clan elders. On 8 March 1927, International Women's Day, 10,000 women threw off the head-to-toe veils of horsehair and cotton which women over the age of 9 or 10 were required to wear in the presence of unrelated men. Their menfolk protested that the Bolsheviks were 'turning women into harlots' and more than 800 women died in honour crimes. Moscow seized on this 'heavy-handed bungling', and it became an indirect reason why the Women's Department was shut down in 1930. However, there is little doubt that Moscow countenanced the initiative of local party leaders, especially in Uzbekistan, to launch a broad offensive against Islam, although one centred on religious schools and the property belonging to religious endowments (*waqf*).[59]

The Bolsheviks showed far less interest in challenging male gender roles.[60] They rejected the patriarchal notion that men had a God-given right to rule over women by virtue of their assumed superior physical strength and wisdom—'rooting out the "old master right of the man"', as Lenin put it—and during the 1920s the trade unions and the Women's Department attacked practices associated with patriarchal authority, such as wife-beating, drunkenness, and the physical abuse of children. Yet fundamentally the Revolution reconfigured rather than unseated the dominant masculine norm. As we have seen, a fraternal model substituted for a patriarchal model of masculinity. In the party, Cheka, and Red Army, young men fought for the Revolution as brothers, united in comradeship and commitment to struggle. This was not just a matter of the civil war promoting an aggressive, 'macho' style, symbolized in the gun-toting, leather-jacketed 'commissar' or Cheka operative. Revolutionary fraternity ran deep in the new political culture, reflected in priority of the public over the private, the military front over the home front, production over reproduction. There was little space for women in the fighting band of brothers, and female identities continued largely to be defined by the family and motherhood. The dominance of a masculine norm was subliminally conveyed in pictorial representations of Revolution, where totemic workers, peasants, or Red Army soldiers were men, and where women occupied a secondary role as helpers.[61] In spite of the discourse of women's emancipation, male party leaders continued to take for granted certain assumptions about the complementary roles of the sexes, associating men with the public, women with the private, and even perpetuating a nineteenth-century tendency to idealize the female sex as morally superior to men, especially because of their maternal role. In the course of the 1920s, gender was one of the first areas in which a 'return of the repressed' became apparent, as the fraternal model of masculinity gave way to a more patriarchal one, even as the discourse of women's emancipation continued to reverberate.

Initially, many Bolsheviks believed that the family, as an institution based on private property, would be abolished under Communism, with the state taking responsibility for the education and care of children and for domestic labour. Yet the battering that the family received between 1918 and 1922 came about more as a result of socio-economic disintegration than of ideological attack. Under the assault of war, flight, hunger, and disease, spouses separated, children were cast adrift, and casual sexual relationships flourished. Legislation made it easier for men to divorce their spouses and the numerical imbalance between the sexes made it easier still for men to take up with new partners. As a result, the economic position of many women, left to support families without the assistance of menfolk, worsened. For poor, vulnerable single mothers, the stability of the patriarchal family was preferable to abandonment. Moreover, the ideological attack on the family fomented rumours, especially among the elderly and the religious, that the Bolsheviks were out to 'nationalize' women, share wives, or snatch children from their cradles.

Partly in response to the devastation caused by war, the marriage rate recovered rapidly during the 1920s, so that by 1926 it was over a third higher than in 1913. High female unemployment meant that there was a growing trend for the husband to be the family breadwinner. At the same time, cuts in state subsidies led to the closure of the public dining halls, crèches, and communal laundries that had been a feature of War Communism, leaving women once again responsible for looking after children, cooking, cleaning, and sewing. A time-budget survey of seventy-six working-class families in 1922 showed that women only managed six hours and forty-four minutes of sleep, compared with eight hours for men.[62] The plight of abandoned women and children, unemployment, and women's family responsibilities shaped responses to the nationwide debate led to the new Family Code promulgated in 1926. This simplified divorce procedure, but introduced stricter rules on alimony, making men rather than the state responsible for the maintenance of children; it also established joint ownership of property acquired during marriage. To some extent, it compromised with popular assumptions about the mutual responsibilities of family members, but it was also in tune with an emerging consensus among legal experts that the family would have to serve as the basic institution of social welfare for the time being since the state lacked resources for a full-blown welfare system. It also chimed with rising concern that glaring social problems such as illegitimacy, abandoned children, hooliganism, and juvenile crime were linked to the breakdown of the family.

If the 1920s saw conventional assumptions about the family and marriage increasingly influence official thinking, it would be wrong to assume that the Revolution had had no impact on popular attitudes and practice. Within less than a decade European Russia had the highest divorce rate in the world, divorce being widespread even in rural communities. A woman in Kemerovo informed the village soviet: 'For ten years I could see no way out and feared to sin. But now it is permissible, thanks to the decree issued by our dear Il'ich. A woman can release herself from her kulak husband and live freely.'[63] Such women, of course, were a minority, but they dramatized the fact that the traditional way of life was under strain. Moreover, if marriage was as popular as ever, the age of marriage was rising in both town and countryside; and although church marriage continued to be the norm in the countryside, less than a third of marriages in Moscow were accompanied by a church ceremony by 1925.

From a nadir in 1922, the birth rate grew exceptionally fast, but the 1920s also saw the long-term trend towards a fall in fertility gather pace. This was mainly evident in the towns, but as levels of female education and employment rose, and as the age of marriage was delayed, there was an overall decline in fertility. In 1920 Russia became the first country in the world to legalize abortion, a measure motivated by concern that in the prevailing conditions society could not support children properly, rather than by recognition of a woman's right choose whether or not to have a child. Indeed most Bolsheviks took it for granted that it was a woman's duty to fulfil her role as mother. Even Kollontai believed that 'childbirth is a social obligation'. Nevertheless by the late 1920s, the number of abortions in Russian cities already surpassed the number of births and the typical woman seeking an abortion was not the unmarried or unemployed young woman envisaged in the 1920 decree, but a married woman with at least one child, who was equally likely to be a housewife or a wage earner.

In the maelstrom of civil war traditional sexual taboos had been swept aside. Surveys of students in the 1920s purported to show that around a half of women and nearly two-thirds of men had had casual sex, and that as many as 85 per cent believed that sex was a matter of physiological need. Some in the Komsomol were convinced that love was a 'bourgeois' phenomenon, condemned to wither away. Few party leaders, however, saw 'sexual revolution' as an element in the wider social revolution. Kollontai demanded 'freedom for winged Eros', liberated from the trammels of private property, the subjugation of women, and moral hypocrisy. She championed women's right to autonomy and fulfilment in personal relations rather than 'free love', but she became notorious for a statement in which she had likened the sexual act to 'quenching hunger or thirst'. Her views were quite untypical of mainstream Bolshevik thinking. Lenin, in particular, deplored the 'hypertrophy in sexual matters' and advocated sublimation through 'healthy sport, swimming, racing, walking, bodily exercises of every kind and many-sided intellectual interests'. As early as 1922 Bukharin, speaking at the Komsomol Congress, called for an end to 'anarchy in the realm of conduct', and henceforward exhortations to channel sexual energy into socialist construction came thick and fast. A consensus emerged which repudiated the extremes of 'asceticism' and promiscuity, but on the grounds of science rather than morality.[64] Zalkind, for example, upheld elements in the radical critique of 'bourgeois' sexual relations, condemning 'intimism'—the inward orientation of two people romantically in love—yet insisting that the 'proletariat at the stage of socialist accumulation is a thrifty, niggardly class and it is not in its interests to allow creative energy to seep into sexual channels'. Such thinking, coloured by contemporary interest in eugenics, put sexuality at the heart of a strategy of social engineering designed to enhance the reproductive and productive capacity of the new society. Such thinking lay behind the decriminalization of sodomy, since homosexuality under the influence of German sexology was now seen as a medical condition rather than as a sin or crime. As the 1920s progressed, official thinking was increasingly animated by anxiety about sexual disorder.[65] By 1929, for example, 'hardened' prostitutes, once seen as social victims, had begun to be sent to labour camps for wilfully refusing to play a productive part in collective life. The increasing emphasis on the danger of sexual anarchy reflected Bolshevik fears that their orderly, rational project risked being overwhelmed by the libidinal energies of the body and the elemental forces of nature.

Youth: A Wavering Vanguard

In Soviet Russia young people made up a majority of society: in 1926 under-20s accounted for just over half the rural population.[66] The Bolsheviks looked on children as the generation that would make the socialist future and concentrated scarce resources on their welfare and education. The Women's Department and other agencies launched campaigns to improve the quality of childcare and to discourage practices such as corporal punishment. New limitations on child labour, combined with the lengthening of schooling, delayed entry into adulthood. The rapid decline in infant mortality during the 1920s and the decline in family size may also have served to increase the emotional investment of parents in their children. In late-imperial Russia the idea of childhood as a time of innocence had taken root, and the Bolsheviks built upon the optimism implicit in this idealization.[67] Building on international progressive thinking in pedagogy and public health, they saw the kindergarten as a substitute for the family, an institution in which the values of the new society could be instilled in pre-school children. Later in the 1920s, as responsibility for childcare reverted to the family, the emphasis of pedagogy shifted to training the child, albeit still with a strong emphasis on ensuring that the experience of kindergarten was a happy one.[68] The Bolsheviks believed that children belonged first and foremost to society, although there was no consensus as to where the line should be drawn between parental and state responsibilities. The legal expert A. Goikhbarg, a key author of the Marriage Code, besought parents to reject 'their narrow and irrational love for their children' and opined that the state would 'provide vastly better results than the private, individual, unscientific and irrational approach of individually "loving" but ignorant parents'.[69] But his was a minority view. Since the government did not have resources to take on the upbringing of children, parents continued to shoulder most of the responsibility. In theory, however, their right to do so was conditional on their performing their duties in accordance with the values of the Revolution. 'If fathers persistently try to turn their children into narrow little property owners or mystics, then . . . children have the ethical right to forsake them.' Crucially, children were urged to re-educate their parents in the values of the new society: in 1928 thousands took to the streets bearing slogans: 'Against our drunken fathers', 'We demand sobriety of our parents'.

In 1922 the Young Pioneers was formed to organize sports, excursions, and summer camps for children aged 10 to 16. By 1926 it had over 2 million members, 46 per cent of them female, including nearly 300,000 in the Oktiabriata, which catered for 8- to 11-year-olds (later 7- to 9-year-olds). With its motto of 'Always prepared', its oath, flags, and drill, it was redolent of the Boy Scouts, which had had between 30,000 and 50,000 members in 1917 but which had been banned for being 'imperialistic'.[70] Every Pioneer swore an initiation oath: 'I will firmly uphold the cause of the working class in its struggle for the liberation of the workers and peasants throughout the world.' The organization's jaunty, march-like song proclaimed: 'Let the bonfires soar | Blue nights! | We are Pioneers | the children of workers | The era is near | of bright years | The motto of the Pioneers is | Be prepared'. Yet clearly not all Pioneers had such high-minded ideals.[71] In 1929 Shura Klimova, a 14-year-old girl from Barnaul, wrote to the journal *Pioneer*, outlining her wish to become a film star: 'I always look good in photographs...and I would like to be known throughout the world and be the finest film star in our Soviet Union.' The journal was inundated with letters, most of them seeking to put her back on the 'right path'. She was taunted by her classmates, who slipped notes to her during lessons, saying 'Dear Millionairess, please give 15,000 rubles to our school' or 'Esteemed Mary Pickford, when shall we see your first movie?' When her father took her out of school and found her a job at a railway station, Shura wrote once again to the journal, this time in outrage: 'He forgot one thing—to ask me first!'[72] That the plucky Shura may have been more typical of Soviet children than the zealous Pioneers who condemned her 'conceit and aristocratic ways' is suggested by that fact that surveys of schoolchildren showed that only 2 per cent wished to become Communists when they grew up.

One of the most appalling problems facing the Bolsheviks was the terrifying number of orphaned and abandoned children who lived on city

Figure 7.5 Jewish orphans in Ukraine, c.1922.

streets, in railway stations, and in cellars, and who survived by begging, peddling, or stealing (see Figure 7.5).[73] The problem had emerged before the First World War, but escalated massively with war, Revolution, and famine. By 1922 at least 7 million children, over three-quarters of them boys, had been abandoned by or lost contact with their parents. They formed a distinct subculture with their gangs, hierarchies, turf, codes, rituals, and slang. Heroic efforts were made to settle them in children's homes and colonies, and from 1923 in experimental labour communes based on 'self-government'. Most of these were inspired by a child-centred approach to rehabilitation, but the most famous of the communes, that of the Ukrainian ex-schoolteacher Anton Makarenko, rejected this in favour of group-imposed discipline and military drill. By the late 1920s, the number of abandoned children had been reduced to around 200,000, although conditions in children's homes remained grim. The huge number of children living on the streets was a major cause of the rise in juvenile crime, which continued to be treated leniently until the 1930s, when a full-scale reversal of official attitudes took place, with leading jurists denouncing the 'putrid view that children should not be punished'.[74]

By 1925 1.5 million young people were Komsomol members, yet this represented less than 6 per cent of eligible youth. In the early 1920s the Komsomol concentrated on organizing and inspiring urban youth, but in the mid-1920s increasing efforts were made to organize rural youth, with the initiative taken by demobilized soldiers. By 1926 nearly 60 per cent of members were peasants.[75] Whereas heroism, sacrifice, and combativeness had been lauded during the civil war, 'smartness, discipline, training, and self-organization' became the watchwords of NEP.[76] Some young men bemoaned the turn away from civil war romanticism and proved unwilling to knuckle down to the tasks of economic and cultural development. The proportion of young women in the Komsomol rose to about one-fifth by the mid-1920s—higher than in the party—but young men predominated, since they had higher levels of literacy, often had experience of army service and seasonal work, and were generally less tied down by family obligations. Campaigns were waged against the more egregious expressions of male chauvinism—treating female recruits as sexual objects, setting them to such tasks as cleaning and sewing—but little was done to address the fact that many young women felt alienated by the politicized and increasingly bureaucratic culture of the Komsomol. By 1926 the organization was willing to sponsor the dances it had once deplored, but its routines of meetings, speeches, political education, and demonstrations alienated men and women alike. One consequence was that although by the late 1920s the Komsomol had twice the membership of the All-Union Communist Party, turnover of membership was high. Nevertheless the young were increasingly at odds with their parents over such matters as church attendance or church marriage, fired by adolescent rebellion and zealous advocacy of the new Soviet rituals. For their part, traditionally minded parents deplored the effect of the Komsomol on their offspring: 'Kol'ka has stuck up a picture of Lenin in place of the icon and now goes to rallies, carrying banners and singing scurrilous songs.'[77]

Official rhetoric cast youth in the role of revolutionary vanguard, yet much anxiety was expressed about the waning of revolutionary fervour among young people.[78] In 1923 the student newspaper at Petrograd University claimed that only 10 per cent of students 'actively' supported the Revolution; that 60 per cent were 'non-party'; 15 per cent to 20 per cent 'clearly anti-Soviet'; and 10 per cent totally apathetic. This reflected difficulties young people faced, including unemployment, homelessness, and payment of tuition fees, as well as a wider public unease that the Revolution was losing its way. In his preface to a volume of essays on the 'new way-of-life', a Bolshevik pundit, A. Slepkov, contrasted the 'healthy, energetic, cultured social activists' to the 'petty-bourgeois mongrels and those who suffer from moral and ideological rickets'.[79] These 'petty-bourgeois mongrels' were exemplified in the figure of the hooligan, who caused something of a moral panic in the mid-1920s. The causes of the real or imagined increase in hooliganism were unclear, feeding fears that the social body was becoming diseased. Other social phenomena that provoked soul-searching among idealists included young women with red lipstick, bobbed hair, and high heels and young men with tight double-breasted jackets and Oxford trousers, their dress and demeanour connoting bourgeois decadence. One 'forsaken worker' wrote: 'Wherever you look, posters and notices display themselves announcing some "masked ball", some "dance" or other such entertainment.... Seize the time while your soul is still impressionable...before your thoughts become decrepit, before need cuts off your wings. Go to lectures, to the theatre, to museums, where you will develop yourselves.'[80] Even more troubling was the 'epidemic' of suicides that followed that of the poet Sergei Esenin in December 1925, which was construed as evidence that young people were falling prey to an unhealthy introspection. Finally, there were those youngsters who, in disillusionment with a 'sinful world' and in search of absolute values, turned to religious denominations such as Baptists, Adventists, and Evangelicals, whose advocacy of chastity, temperance, politeness, smart dress, and abstention from swearing provided them with a moral compass.

Propaganda and Popular Culture

For the Bolsheviks the word 'propaganda' lacked any negative connotation.[81] Possessed, as they believed they were, of the knowledge required to create a qualitatively better society, they had no compunction in using the full panoply of state power to disseminate their ideas and values and to discredit those of their enemies, seeking to mould the thinking, emotions, and behaviour of the populace at large. The Bolsheviks did not conceive of propaganda as brainwashing, but as 'political enlightenment', education designed to raise political awareness, overcome ignorance, and to produce fighting, thinking citizens. The party had historically distinguished between 'propaganda', which Plekhanov had defined as presenting many ideas to a few, and 'agitation', which he defined as presenting a few ideas to the many. In 1920 the Central Committee of the RKP(b) set up a department of 'agitprop', and party committees at all levels were soon required to set up similar departments. However, the Chief Political Enlightenment Committee—which was actually a state body under the Commissariat of Education—had overall responsibility for coordinating propaganda through its provincial and local subsections. It sent out instructions to local departments, organized special campaigns, and put on training courses for propagandists. At local level there might be scores of agitprop groups, attached not only to party organs but also to soviets, factory committees, and trade unions. The new Soviet holidays were the peak time for agitprop activity. Around sixteen in number, some completely new, such as the anniversary of Lenin's death on 21 January or the Day of the Paris Commune on 18 March, others appropriations of traditional holidays, such as St John's day, which became Electrification Day, these holidays saw agitprop organizations take to the streets in carnivalesque mode.[82]

Agitprop was underfunded and poorly coordinated, yet the Bolsheviks were creative in the methods they used to disseminate official ideology and promote particular campaigns. The bedrock of agitprop was oral communication in the form of meetings, speeches, and debates; this was supplemented by visual propaganda in the form of posters, cartoons, slides, newsreels, exhibitions, and cinema; and, as the literacy drive advanced, by popular newspapers (many stuck to walls in public spaces), leaflets, brochures, and information bulletins. Agitprop organs made clever and innovative use of theatrical forms. The 'living newspaper'—a genre in which 'Blue Blouse' agit-groups specialized—acted out the current news through collective declamation, satirical rhyming couplets (*chastushki*), jokes, songs, and dance. In the Red Army, Komsomol, trade unions, and other organizations, mock trials were staged, designed to expose wrongdoing. In the Red Army, for example, a member of the collective might be put on trial by his fellows for desertion, banditry, or indiscipline, prompting debate about and judgement of his culpability. As a form of amateur dramatics, these seem to have been popular, although later they lost much of their spontaneity and became more like shaming rituals.[83] In the cities the trade unions ran a well-organized system of workers' clubs, which by 1927 had 7 million members, and which held lectures and debates, had their own libraries, and hosted theatrical performances, film showings, and concerts.

One way to assess the effectiveness of propaganda—that is, its success in shaping the ideas and social values of the population—is to look at changes in the Russian language. The Revolution had an enormous impact on everyday speech. Words that had been in common use, such as 'official' (*chinovnik*) or 'policeman' (*gorodovoi*), disappeared, while a flood of new words appeared, which referred to the emerging realities of Soviet life—words such as 'comrade' (*tovarishch*), Cheka, or *ispolkom*, a soviet executive committee—many of them foreign in origin, such as *proletariat*. Other words underwent a change of meaning, such as 'citizen' (*grazhdanin*), which now took on a pejorative tone, since it was used of someone who was not a 'comrade'. Many hitherto unusual verbs became widely used: to 'link up' (*sviazat'*), to 'deepen' (*uglubit'*), to sharpen (*zaostrit'*). And military metaphors suffused official discourse, so that talk of 'fronts', 'struggles', and 'mobilizations' abounded.[84]

Language in general became more formulaic—evident in the use of slogans, fixed expressions, and stereotyped metaphors. The significance of this should not be minimized, since language, especially when it is articulated with social practices and political institutions, shapes the way we perceive the social world. There is evidence, for example, that peasants quickly learned to discuss village society in terms of the class categories approved by the regime, a good tactic if one wished to make claims on the state, justify oneself, or discredit one's fellows.[85] Because Soviet usages of language were rooted in the experiences of daily life—in work, school, residents' committee, or army unit—they were unavoidable. For those who identified with the socialist project, mastery of the language of power was vital. The earnest efforts of worker correspondents and village correspondents—those tasked with reporting to the press on events in their milieux—to master the Soviet lexicon were touching, sometimes comical. 'We youth awakening from eternal hibernation and apathy, forming influence in our blood, brightly reflecting the good progresses and initiatives, step by step however slowly (are) moving away from old and rotten throw-backs and branches.' The strange words and locutions of official propaganda had an almost magical power for those said to be 'half-schooled'.

Propaganda set out to discredit and invalidate customary frames of reference, such as religious discourse, and to set the boundaries of what was politically thinkable. Yet this was not easily achieved. The evidence suggests that official propaganda had only a limited effect, for within popular culture different discourses—religious, folkloric, populist, dialectal—were well entrenched and these continued to shape orientations to the social world, often in ways that conflicted with official ideology. The young literary theorist Mikhail Bakhtin became attuned in the 1920s to the interactions and tensions between different orders of discourse, and alert to the importance of social context in determining uses of speech, and this shaped his groundbreaking theories of language in the 1930s.[86] Members of the Komsomol, for example, were the most eager section of the population to master the new Soviet lexicon, yet many older party members were shocked at the way their conversations were saturated with the slang of the urban slums, village colloquialisms, and criminal argot.[87] Criminal argot, in particular was fashionable, with phrases such as a 'little lady chekist' (*chekushka*) for a revolver; 'bullfinch' (*snegir'*) for a militiaman; and 'pigeon' (*golub'*) for a thief.[88] One party official wrote deprecatingly:

> The sharp Komsomol in perfect command of such 'literary' turns of phrase as 'smack you in the gob'...is considered by companionable comrades to be entirely ideologically reliable, evidently of proletarian origin...Comrades, who consider it more cultivated or polite to address others as *vy* [the polite form of 'you'], in certain circumstances are accused by Komsomol members of coming from a socially alien background or, at least, of not having broken with the remnants of a bourgeois education.[89]

All of this reminds us that official propaganda did not operate in a vacuum: that it had to contend with a robust popular culture, in which different discourses coexisted and contended. Popular culture, for example, delighted in puncturing the pretensions of the powerful through folk tales, carnivalesque celebrations, jokes, and songs. An article in *Pravda* complained: 'In editorial boards and clubs, in buses and mess halls, in theatres and taverns, in the army and at meetings—everywhere the *anekdot* (anecdote) reigns supreme and, more to the point, the bawdy, spicy anecdote.' A typical anecdote, or humorous story, was one inspired by a report that Lenin had suggested compensating the loss of revenue from alcohol by developing a cosmetics industry. Satirizing the typical institutions and practices of Soviet power, the anecdote told of how the government intended to introduce compulsory labour service in the lipstick industry; create a Main Administration for Lipstick and Soviet Power; inaugurate a Communist Lipstick Week; and commission Iurii Steklov, the editor of *Izvestiia*, to write an editorial denouncing 'the anti-lipstick policy of the counter-revolution'. Every major government initiative, such as the introduction of the new currency in 1924, would spur a wave of jokes. According to one, a priest watched with bewilderment as a peasant took the new Soviet money and made the sign of the cross with it. 'Why are you making the sign of the cross?' he asked. 'That is Soviet money.' 'Indeed it is Soviet money', the peasant replied, 'but the silver it contains, Father, belongs to the Church.' A further source of black humour lay in the endless acronyms that Soviet power spawned: VKP(b), the All-Union Communist Party (Bolshevik), the official name of the party from 1925, was said to stand for *vtoroe krepostnoe pravo*, the 'second serfdom'; while VChK, the All-Russian Cheka, was said to stand for *vsiakomu cheloveku kaput*, that is, 'everyone is done for'.[90]

A further reminder of the robustness of popular culture and its partial impermeability to official propaganda can be seen in the fact that rumour was rife in these years and a matter of serious concern to the authorities. The political police carefully monitored rumours, partly in order to evaluate the popular mood and partly to monitor the activities of enemies of the regime. Rumour is often an expression of social anxiety and of a shared conviction that information is scarce and that it is dangerous not to know what is going on. Sharing stories with others helped to assuage worry and disgruntlement and to build social solidarity. By far the most common rumour in the NEP years concerned the impending outbreak of war, which usually took the form of stories that Britain or Poland was about to invade. In Kargopol' county in Vologda in March 1923 the GPU reported:

> There is a rumour spreading through the county that a war has begun with Poland and the great majority of peasants welcome it. They say that it will stop the predatory policy of Soviet power, and that the Poles will hang and drown the communists in rivers. Soon, they say, we will overthrow and wipe the cursed Bolsheviks and their hated regime from the face of the earth, and we will be liberated from the yoke of the Yids, which is unleashing persecution on the Orthodox Church and closing churches.[91]

Most rumours were not so patently hostile to the regime, yet people showed little trust in the official media so were ever ready to put their own interpretation on some unusual event. In 1925 the visit to Kursk of V. M. Molotov, secretary of the Central Committee, inspired talk in the city about the 'bad relations with western states, especially America'. 'Our government is painfully worn down, and it is worried that things in the USSR are now so bad. It is visiting the localities to cajole the peasants in case America bashes it on the head. It is saying, "You *muzhiki* mustn't let us down."'[92]

Some of the rumours of war were of a supernatural type. In the Urals in February 1927 tales of fiery pillars in the sky were taken to be portents of a war with Germany.[93] This reminds us that idioms and practices of a religious, magical, or folkloric type were still very much alive in popular culture and were used by ordinary people to impose meaning on the dislocating changes that were overwhelming their lives. Many rumours, for example, were apocalyptic in character, an interpretation of signs of the times which suggested that the Bolshevik regime was the Antichrist that the Bible says will precede the Second Coming of Christ. The Book of Revelation speaks of the mark of the Beast; and in Russian the word for 'mark' and the word for 'press' (*pechat'*) are the same. So when a 'Day of the Soviet Press' was instituted in 1922 it evoked considerable alarm.[94] Similarly, the five-pointed red star, symbol of the Soviet Union and in actuality a variant of a masonic symbol, was seen as the symbol of the Antichrist. Stories circulated that confirmed the linkage between the regime and the Antichrist: fifteen matchsticks would make the name LENIN as well as the number 666, the number of the Beast; moreover, if one ascribed numbers to the different letters that make up the word *Kommunizm*, using a special occult scheme, they too totalled 666.[95] The fact that such apparently trivial stories were collected by the political police attests to the fact that the authorities felt far from secure.

Cultural Revolution

Aleksandr Bogdanov, author of the aforementioned sci-fi novels, had been the only serious competitor to Lenin for leadership of the Bolshevik faction after 1905.[96] Yet his ideas were distinctive in many respects. He believed that the working class must advance to socialism along three paths—the political, economic, and cultural—and socialism entailed the creation of a 'proletarian culture' that would supersede the bourgeois culture of the past. A week before the October seizure of power in 1917 a conference of proletarian organizations of culture and enlightenment met and showed itself to be influenced by Bogdanov's ideas. Its resolution explained:

> The proletarian movement for culture and enlightenment must be permeated by a militant socialist spirit, its aim is to arm the working class with knowledge, organise its artistic feeling so as to succeed in its titanic struggle for a new social system. The conference proposes that in science, as in art, the proletariat must display autonomous creativity, but to do this it must master the whole cultural legacy of the past and present. The proletariat willingly accepts the cooperation of socialist and even non-party intellectuals in cultural and educational affairs, but it considers that a critical attitude is necessary towards the fruits of the old culture, which it apprehends not as a pupil, but as a creator summoned to erect bright new buildings out of old stones.[97]

During the civil war a Proletkul't movement blossomed, which sponsored a vast array of literary, artistic, theatrical, musical, scientific, and sporting activities that involved millions of people doing these things for themselves. The movement was diverse and eclectic, but was loosely divided between those concerned with disseminating the 'rudimentary blessings of culture' among the broad masses and those concerned with training a worker elite to forge a radically new proletarian culture. Neither Lenin nor Lunarcharskii, the Commissar of Enlightenment and brother-in-law of Bogdanov, had much enthusiasm for this concept of proletarian culture, seeing it as slighting the culture of the past; they argued the paramount task was one of raising the cultural level of the masses to the point where they could appropriate humanity's cultural heritage. At the end of 1920, a combination of financial difficulties and internal wrangles, combined with Lenin's animus and the party's increasing intolerance of autonomous organizations, led to Proletkul't being subordinated to the Commissariat of Enlightenment.

In 1921, following victory on the military and political fronts, Lenin stole Bogdanov's thunder by declaring that 'culture' was now the 'third front' of revolutionary activity. In his last writings, he outlined a conception of 'cultural revolution' as a prerequisite for Russia's transition to socialism. Compared with that of Bogdanov, his conception was rather modest and did not differ radically from the project of the nineteenth-century intelligentsia to raise the cultural level of the people. In a society steeped in 'Asiatic' backwardness, Lenin argued, the propagation of literacy, solid work habits, and the application of science and technology were vital to socialist construction.[98] 'Culturedness' could embrace anything from punctuality, clean fingernails, and having a basic knowledge of biology, to carrying out one's trade-union duties efficiently. Its antithesis, 'lack of culture', was an equally capacious notion, encompassing anything from poor personal hygiene, drunkenness, or ignorance of Marxism, to going to church. Its multifarious connotations were neatly captured in a notice pinned on the wharf in Samara: 'Do not throw rubbish about, do not strike a match near the oil pumps, do not spit sunflower seeds, and do not swear or use bad language.'[99] 'Culturedness' had a purposeful character and was synonymous with striving to live according to the requirements and values of the emerging socialist order. Other Bolshevik leaders supported a more grandiose conception of cultural revolution: Bukharin averred that it meant nothing less than a 'revolution in human characteristics, in habits, feelings and desires, in way-of-life and culture'. In this radical conception of cultural revolution, the aim was nothing less than the creation of a 'new Soviet person' through the total transformation of daily life.

Figure 7.6 Kazakh peasants learn to read.

In Bolshevik eyes literacy was the precondition for full and active participation in socialist society, and they invested much energy and imagination into bringing the written word to the people (see Figure 7.6).[100] Between 1920 and 1928, 8.2 million attended literacy school, of whom 70 per cent completed the course. The danger of illiteracy was illustrated in a widely circulated poster that depicted a blindfolded peasant in bast shoes approaching the edge of a cliff with hands outstretched. Initially, resources were concentrated on the Red Army, where soldiers had little choice but to attend literacy classes, but demobilization, combined with the swingeing cuts in public expenditure, led to a dispersal of energies. By 1926–7 there were just over 16,000 reading rooms in the countryside, equivalent to between two and five per township, which provided peasants with books and newspapers. They proved popular.[101] The one in Enangskoe settlement in Vologda had 4,315 books and, in addition, it arranged study circles, exhibitions, performances, and film shows. The head of the reading hut, who was always a party member in receipt of the same low salary as a village schoolteacher, was expected to promote government campaigns, including the cult of Lenin. In villages where the party did not have the resources to set up reading huts, it created 'red corners'. Surveys of the activities of the reading huts showed that readers preferred fiction to political and scientific material, and periodically there were campaigns to remove 'trash' from the libraries. This sometimes led to excesses, as when the Bol'shaia Ken'shinskaia village reading room in Penza threw out the novels of Dostoevsky.[102]

The 1926 census showed that 51 per cent of the population was literate, compared with 23 per cent in 1897. This was an impressive result, yet it concealed some disquieting anomalies. Whereas more than three-quarters of the urban population over the age of 9 were literate, only 45 per cent of the rural population were. And whereas two-thirds of men could read, only 37 per cent of women could. Moreover, in the Central Asian republics, such as Turkmenistan, 97 per cent of the population was illiterate. The educational level of those who went through the crash literacy programmes was, obviously, not very high. When sixty-four soldiers were asked in 1923 to read an article in *Pravda* about the assassination of the Soviet ambassador, Vatslav Vorovskii, in Lausanne, none could explain the title: 'The Impertinence of Killers'.[103] Yet the campaign to liquidate illiteracy awoke a thirst for knowledge on the part of newly literate readers. A poor peasant sent a letter to the *Peasant Newspaper*: 'Send me a list of books published on the following subjects because I am interested in everything: chemistry, science, technology, the planets, the sun, the earth, the planet Mars, world maps, books on aviation, the number of planes we possess, the number of enemies the Socialist Republic has, books on comets, stars, water, the earth and sky.'[104]

As children of the Enlightenment, who had embraced a militant nineteenth-century materialism, the Bolsheviks believed in disseminating science and rationality to bring about liberation from religion and superstition and to enhance human autonomy. They sought to inculcate a materialist worldview through schools, health propaganda, the promotion of modern agricultural practices, and anti-religious propaganda. In 1923 the Twelfth Congress of the RKP(b) stated that 'systematic work must be done to create in the new generation a serious urge to master science and technology'.[105] In 1926, the programme for workers' anti-religious circles explained: 'Natural phenomena have a law-governed character and are independent of the desires of man. As human society studies the laws of nature, it subordinates natural phenomena to its will.'[106] Through lectures, exhibitions, pamphlets, and primary schools, different agencies set about explaining phenomena such as thunder and lightning, germs and basic hygiene, electricity, and the internal combustion engine. For the more curious, popular books and pamphlets were published on a gamut of topics from astronomy, evolution, biology, and geography to agronomy.

In the mid-1920s a vigorous debate got under way about the transformation of daily life along socialist lines.[107] This centred on the fraught issue of the relationship of the personal to the political, (already touched on above in the section on the family and gender). One of the most radical aspirations generated by the Revolution was the desire to live collectively, to share things in common. Students were in the forefront of this movement to live the 'new way of life', sharing accommodation and domestic labour and generally seeking to overcome individualism; but during the 1920s such communes spread beyond student groups. By the time of the First Five-Year Plan, young workers were engaged in forming 'production communes' which engaged in shock work and socialist competition in an effort to revolutionize the culture of the workplace.[108] Experimental urban planners dreamed of new forms of housing and patterns of urban spatial organization, using concrete and steel, with form following function. The architect Mosei Ginzburg construed the communal house as a 'social condenser', designed to 'encourage dynamic coexistence of activities and to generate through their interference unprecedented events'.[109] The architect N. S. Kuz'min, intent on achieving the 'scientific organization of daily life', designed a super-commune for 5,140 miners in Anzhero-Sudzhensk.[110] Much of this utopian imagining remained confined to the drawing board, but the 1920s saw enthusiasm for the idea of the 'commune' reach its apogee. In the countryside there were a couple of thousand agrarian communes by the end of the civil war. Most were very small, but some such as the Novorepinskaia commune in Samara grew to embrace 8,500 members and 77,200 hectares. These communes owned land, livestock, and equipment in common and shared the surplus equally, according to the number of 'eaters' rather than labourers in a household. Such communes were more traditional in their inspiration than the residential and workplace communes of the cities, often inspired by religious rather than Marxist values, especially among non-Orthodox Christian denominations and disciples of Tolstoy.[111]

At a time when official policies seemed to benefit 'class enemies', progress to socialism was seen as peculiarly dependent on individual behaviour in the private sphere. As Krupskaia told the Komsomol Congress in 1924: 'We must strive to bind our private life to the struggle for and construction of communism. Earlier it was perhaps not clear to us that the division between private life and public life sooner or later leads to the betrayal of communism.' From this perspective, aspects of daily life as various as dress, hygiene, personal morality, leisure, and use of language took on political significance. Was it acceptable for a Communist to swear? The answer was clearly no, since swearing was a symbol of the moral degradation of the common people.[112] Soviet factories manufactured lipstick and Soviet publishing houses put out fashion magazines, but was wearing lipstick or reading about western fashion compatible with socialism? Most participants said no, for wearing makeup or fashionable clothes implied an individualist concern with looking good that was not compatible with collectivist values. Yet the Bolsheviks never eschewed 'bourgeois' values in their entirety. The cultured Soviet citizen was expected to be punctual, efficient, orderly, and neat in appearance; but too keen an interest in good manners, nice clothes, or tidy hair laid one open to the charge of being petty-bourgeois or 'philistine'.

The project to bring about a cultural revolution met deepest resistance in respect of the key rites of passage of birth, marriage, and death. Since the rituals that marked these were all religious, the regime encouraged people to undergo civil registration of births, weddings and funerals. In the cities there was a rather rapid move away from getting married in church. In Moscow—not typical, of course—by 1928 only 11.8 per cent of marriages were in church.[113] Nevertheless in the countryside a church wedding was a focus of community solidarity and rural Communists were often censured for getting married in church. Sometimes an attempt was made to graft the symbols of the new society on to the rituals of the old. 'A Communist gets married in a village. All the wedding procession goes to church. In front is the red flag with the inscription: 'Workers of the World, Unite!' Next come the icons. Then comes the bridegroom with a red sash on his chest.' The move away from baptising one's children was much slower. By 1928 the percentage of children in Moscow who were baptised had fallen to 57.8 per cent, though again the percentage was much higher outside the capital. Efforts to create an alternative to baptism centred on a ritual of 'Octobering', which was only ever popular among a tiny minority. In January 1924, for example, a meeting of the Kremenchug woodturners' union organized a 'red baptism' of a girl who was given the name 'Ninel' (Lenin spelt backwards) in a ceremony that began with an exaltation of 'conscience' and 'reason' against the 'absurd religious rituals which befog and oppress the working class', and which culminated with the child being given a badge inscribed 'Study, steel yourself, struggle and unite'. Even to Communists and Komsomol members, however, such rituals were not especially attractive. More attractive was giving a revolutionary name to one's offspring, instead of a Christian name. Names such as 'Spark', 'Rebel', 'Electricity' bespoke modernity and revolutionary fervour.[114]

Least popular of all were official attempts to promote 'civil funerals'. In Moscow in 1928 65.7 per cent of people still opted for a church funeral, and in the countryside this was almost universal. Indeed as late as the 1950s, fewer than half of all Soviet funerals were secular. The abandonment of traditional rituals of mourning and commemoration threatened to leave the community impoverished and the bereaved deprived of customary ways of coping with grief.[115] Civic funerals, moreover, struck a blow at any idea that the deceased might be destined for a life beyond the grave. Even less popular was cremation which was promoted as a clean, economical way of death, but no more than a handful of crematoria were actually built. All of these life-cycle transitions were marked by ancient religious rituals with deep cultural and emotional resonance, and the Bolsheviks struggled to find secular substitutes for them. The ersatz socialist rituals reflected the lack in official ideology of a sense of existential drama and transcendence. Peasants missed the mystery, joy, and ebullience of ritual, the dancing at weddings, the plates of food for the dead.

Yet change was under way in the countryside and the younger generation responded rather positively to 'cultural revolution' as it was construed in the NEP years. Seeing the traditional way of life as superannuated, many young peasants looked to the cities and yearned to become 'cultured': 'Dressed in a cultured fashion I went to the cinema. I really wanted to visit the Park of Culture and Rest but I didn't have enough money.' By 1928 over 12 per cent of letters to the *Peasant Newspaper* concerned issues of 'civilization' and the 'backwardness' of peasant life. Typically such letters began: 'I am a dark peasant'; 'I write to you from a god-forsaken place'; 'Lying on a dark stove, I am thinking...' A peasant in Samylovo in Kostroma province in November 1927 described his location thus: 'Far away from Moscow, the heart of the republic...in the thick forests and ravines of our abandoned and poverty-stricken village'.[116] Such peasants were gripped by a desire to 'acquire political development and to understand the world', 'to have literature and leadership', 'to have an education and to destroy all the nonsense that has been drummed into our heads'. They feared that otherwise they would become surplus to requirements in the new order. Even the millions who did not respond to the Soviet project with any warmth internalized its categories of 'cultured' and 'backward', 'revolutionary' and 'reactionary'.

NEP saw a steady rise in censorship, in curbs on intellectuals, and in outright suppression of cultural activity of which the state disapproved. Nevertheless 'cultural revolution' as practised in these years saw groups and individuals take spontaneous initiatives and make their own experiments in living a socialist way of life. And many state-sponsored initiatives—in literacy, the popularization of science, revolutionizing daily life—evoked a positive response in the population, mainly among the younger generation. Undoubtedly, a 'totalitarian' potential existed within the project of cultural revolution, yet we have seen that society retained sufficient autonomy in these years to resist the efforts of the state to impose its designs. It was only with the First Five-Year Plan that a more sweeping conception of 'cultural revolution' took hold, one that entailed an onslaught on religion and an attack under the banner of proletarian principles on cultural pluralism, academic hierarchies, and all forms of intellectual activity deemed to be 'bourgeois'.

The Attack on Religion

Some contemporary ethnographers argued that the immense socio-economic disruption and psychological strains engendered by the Revolution revitalized 'archaic' elements in popular culture that had been undergoing erosion since the nineteenth century.[117] In July 1924 reports from drought-stricken provinces noted a 'marked revival of religious sentiment'. In the Don oblast' there were rumours that Elijah the Prophet had appeared to some peasant children and in the village of Gibblovka in Podol'sk a priest encouraged the digging up of corpses to which villagers then prayed for rain.[118] In a village near Nadezhdinsk in the Urals Ivan Timofeevich Taushankov, who had served in the tsarist army and then joined the Red Army, helped set up a party cell and a reading room in his native village. His wife, who was unhappy at his joining the party, had their child secretly baptised and insisted on keeping the household icons on display. In a report of 1929 Ivan despaired of his fellow villagers, many of whom, to judge by their surnames, were his relatives:

> Here the priests are hard at work and nothing is heard of the party or of anti-religious work. You hear only about wizards, and of how someone has injured a cow or cut off the tail of a heifer or shorn a sheep or infected the vegetables with clubroot…Last Lent our peasants held a carnival for ten days. After the celebrations, Comrade Maksim Prokof'evich Taushankov, chairman of the village soviet, called a meeting of all men and women, old and young, and when everyone had arrived he suggested to the owner of the building, V. G. Taushankov, that he light the icon lamp and put candles in front of the icons, and then he gave a report about how wizards have been

> organizing thefts of milk and proposed that everyone pray and then curse all living things within their homes. It turned out that there were two old women who did not come to the meeting and now everyone reckons they are the witches since there have been no more incidents.[119]

Until 1917 the Orthodox clergy had guarded against forms of popular religiosity that they considered excessive or superstitious. With the fracturing of the hierarchy, popular religiosity flourished uncontrolled. At the time of the seizure of Church valuables in 1922—on which more below—a wave of discoveries of self-renewing icons occurred. One such discovery in Chembarskii county in Tambov province was described by a member of the county committee of the Bolshevik party: 'On 12 February (1922) I personally saw the renewed icon of Jesus. The local people say that the icon was shabby but that in three to four hours it became covered with gold. Citizen Nikolai Demin, to whom the icon belongs, is 26 to 27 years of age. He insists the icon renewed itself. This is what everyone believes.' The reappearance of drought in 1924 engendered a new wave of icon renewals in the black-earth provinces of southern Russia. In Tambov at least 1,000 renewals were reported in the course of the year, and there were similar numbers in the provinces of Orël and Voronezh.[120] The authorities were foxed by this phenomenon, reaching for an explanation in terms of social stress, nefarious counter-revolutionary activity, or amateur psychology. The provincial food-supply committee spoke of a 'mass psychosis among the dark peasant masses caused by the drought and partial harvest failure'. The provincial party committee added that the 'mass religious psychosis' was being whipped up by the 'surreptitious agitation of priest, nuns, and others'.

Such phenomena may be understood as an assertion of faith at a time when the Church was under assault from the regime and when the Church itself had succumbed to schism (encouraged by the political police). In February 1922 against the background of the famine in the Volga region the Bolsheviks ordered the Church to give up ecclesiastical treasures to aid famine victims. The previous year Patriarch Tikhon had urged people to donate articles to the starving but had exempted sacramental vessels. In March in Shuia, a textile town to the north-east of Moscow, police and soldiers seized such vessels, provoking a sharp clash in which four members of the laity were killed and ten injured (see Figure 7.7). In private Lenin made no pretence of the fact that the seizures were intended to strike a blow against the authority of the Church. He ordered that the Shuia 'insurrectionists' be put on trial, and that it culminate in the 'shooting of a very large number of the most influential and dangerous of Black Hundreds'. A show trial ensued which resulted in the execution of eight priests, two laymen and a laywoman, and the imprisonment of twenty-five others. In Petrograd, where popular agitation against the seizures had an antisemitic coloration, Metropolitan Veniamin and three others were also tried and executed. It is reckoned that between 1922 and 1923 the seizure of Church valuables provoked 1,414 clashes.[121]

In May 1922 a group of radical priests, known as Renovationists, came out in support of Soviet power and forced the abdication of the

Figure 7.7 The seizure of church valuables, 1922.

'counter-revolutionary' Tikhon, whom the Bolsheviks had placed under house arrest.[122] The Renovationists called a Church council the following year, which endorsed a series of reforms that had long been under discussion, including the replacement of Church Slavonic with vernacular Russian, the adoption of the Gregorian calendar, and greater participation by the laity in services and diocesan administration. By 1925 two-thirds of parishes had formally affiliated to the Renovationists, not without the covert assistance of the OGPU, which actively undermined support for Tikhon. Yet the reforms were not popular with the laity, who disliked attempts to cut the number of feast days and impose a calendar that did not fit the time-honoured rhythm of the seasons, since their faith was intimately bound up with the feast days of local saints and the marking of fasts.[123] In June 1923 the Bolsheviks withdrew support from the Renovationists after Tikhon pledged loyalty to the regime. While many of the faithful questioned the Patriarch's action, they were pleased to see the Renovationists get their comeuppance. By the late 1920s the Renovationists had been routed, but following the death of Tikhon in April 1925, the Church was rent by other schisms, partly deepened when his successor, Metropolitan Sergei, swore fealty to the Soviet system in May 1927. From the mid-1920s, recognizing that the Church was not going to buckle under pressure, the regime moderated its policy, putting the accent on anti-religious propaganda rather than frontal attack.

Official policy towards Protestant denominations and indigenous cults such as Old Believers, who had separated from the Orthodox Church in 1666—all of which were referred to indiscriminately as 'sectarians'—was more conciliatory, since they had been subject to discrimination under tsarism and their emphasis on hard work, sobriety, strict moral standards, and community were thought to be conducive to the formation of model agricultural communes.[124] There are no reliable figures on the number of Old Believers, although some put the figure as high as 20 million, and the number of Protestant and indigenous sects is estimated at anything between 6 and 10 million members. In late 1928 in Vyborg district, the heart of proletarian Leningrad, at least 12,000 people attended sectarian services, of whom over one-fifth were workers. The sects were allowed to publish journals, hold conferences, and organize charities and cooperatives. Yet even in the early 1920s the GPU kept a strict eye on them, and from April 1926, official policy became more restrictive.

The mid-1920s were also the moment when policy towards Islam hardened, with mullahs depicted in propaganda as obscurantist and oppressive. The 1922–3 constitutions of the republics in Central Asia and the Caucasus had allowed considerable scope for the practice of Islam, including the practice of sharia law, but the number of Islamic schools was steadily reduced so that by 1926 only 969 existed in the 13,650 districts in the Volga–Urals region where there was a mosque.[125] From 1926, a more frontal assault on Islamic institutions got under way. In respect of Judaism, too, the regime initially acted cautiously, fearing to fan popular antisemitism. In Petrograd the number of synagogues and prayer-houses actually increased to seventeen. However, the Jewish sections of the party militantly counterposed Yiddish and secular culture to Hebrew religious culture and in the mid-1920s the GPU began closing down synagogues and religious schools, and hounding rabbis. In sum, as the policy towards the Orthodox Church briefly eased, that towards other faiths hardened.

From the campaign to seize Church valuables in 1922 through to the all-out onslaught on religion that accompanied the Cultural Revolution, the majority view in the party leadership was that the battle against religion would be a long-term affair that would mainly centre on propaganda and education.[126] In 1922 Emelian Iaroslavskii (1878–1943), a strong supporter of Stalin, founded a weekly newspaper, *The Godless* (*Bezbozhnik*), to propagate atheism among the masses (the journal briefly adopted a calendar that counted the years from 1917 as year zero). In 1925 he founded the League of Militant Godless to oppose anti-religious zealots in the Komsomol, known as 'priest-eaters', who revelled in offending believers by lampooning the feasts of Christmas and Easter, burning icons and books, or turning pigs loose in church. By contrast, the League favoured propaganda, including public debate with believers on such topics as whether the world was created in six days. Clergy inveighed against the militants in the anti-religious movement as 'debauchers and libertines' and, to some extent, villagers were able to keep atheistic propaganda out of the classroom since they paid for the upkeep of the schools. By 1930 the League claimed over 2 million members, but the figure is deceptive since the organization was badly run and internally divided. It is true that religious observance started to decline, especially in the cities, where religious commitment became a matter of personal conviction rather than of communal custom, but this was due more to urbanization, schooling, army service, and the general climate of secularism than to the anti-religious campaign.

One of the ironies of these years is that despite a vehement campaign to discredit and destroy all forms of religion, the Stalin faction reinscribed certain elements of popular religiosity into official political culture. The cult of Lenin was the most obvious example.[127] During his lifetime Lenin had been adulated but had not been the object of a cult of personality. Following his death, however, the Stalin group quite consciously sought to establish its legitimacy by sanctifying the dead leader. During the civil war the Bolsheviks had waged a campaign to expose the popular belief that saints' bodies did not decompose, yet Lenin's body was now embalmed like that of some latter-day pharaoh and placed in a mausoleum that instantly became a shrine. In October 1923, the Politburo, conscious that Lenin's days were numbered, discussed funeral arrangements. It is alleged that Stalin explained that 'certain comrades in the provinces' were greatly concerned about these arrangements:

> They say that Lenin is a Russian and ought to be buried in accordance with this fact. For example, they are categorically opposed to the cremation, the incineration of Lenin's body. In their opinion, cremation does not at all conform to the Russian conception of love and veneration of the deceased. It could even appear to be an insult to his memory. Russians have always thought of cremation, annihilation, the scattering of the remains as the last judgement on those who have been executed. Certain comrades believe that contemporary science offers the possibility, by means of embalming, of preserving the body of the deceased for a long time.[128]

This desire to preserve the leader's body physically was consonant with the Orthodox belief in the inseparability of body and soul. In addition, much of the discourse following Lenin's death stressed his immortality—'Lenin is with us always and everywhere'—and the fact that he was the physical embodiment, the 'incarnation' (*voploshchenie*), of the Revolution: terms that resonated with Christian meaning.

The NEP years highlighted the vast disparity between ideal and reality. Utopian imagining flourished, visible in the hopes placed in electrification, the 'scientific organization of labour', and the transformation of everyday life. Yet the 'retreat' on the economic front was a constant reminder of the backwardness and vulnerability of the nascent Soviet state. The return of the market, the revival of 'bourgeois' social groups, international isolation, fears of war, the increasing gap between the Soviet Union and the capitalist states, all engendered anxiety that the country was moving away from socialism. Despite the continuing idealism and energy of the regime, the tendency, especially as represented by the rising Stalin faction, was to clamp down. NEP society can by no stretch of the imagination be described as 'liberal' yet it was more pluralistic than the brutally conformist society that was to be inaugurated in 1928 with Stalin's 'Great Break'.

Epilogue: The 'Great Break', 1928–1931

In November 1928 Stalin declared that the Soviet Union must 'catch up and surpass' the capitalist countries; otherwise, 'they will destroy us'. The previous month the Five-Year Plan (1928–32) had been formally inaugurated, the first example in history of a government seeking to transform an entire economy and society through planned action by the state. Under this and the Second Five-Year Plan (1933–7) the Soviet Union became a major, self-sufficient military and economic power, achieving a substantial increase in industrial output and an extraordinarily high level of investment. The First Five-Year Plan was accompanied by a political rhetoric replete with military metaphors, with appeals to storming and target-busting, and with calls to workers to show heroism and revolutionary optimism. 'There are no fortresses the Bolsheviks cannot storm', Stalin declared. Yet the reality was very far from being a planned economy and a workers' state. Planners were under constant pressure to raise targets, with party officials believing that objective constraints could be overcome by feats of human will, and the result was a wasteful 'command' economy in which enterprise directors were forced to circumvent official supply channels to fulfil their plan targets. A minority of workers believed that the socialism promised in 1917 was now being realized, and these enthusiastically supported the campaign to fulfil and over-fulfil the plan. Yet investment in industry was achieved at the expense of real wages and most workers suffered as working conditions deteriorated severely. The majority, rather than engaging in feats of target-busting, responded by going absent, by changing jobs, by drunkenness, and by indiscipline. Trade unions lost an effective right to defend workers and the new enterprise bosses, many of them former workers, revelled in the crude display of their authority (as Lazar Kaganovich said, 'the earth should tremble when the director walks around the plant').

The other key element in the 'Great Break' was the violent collectivization of agriculture, which 'solved' the problem of low grain marketing that had dogged the regime since its inception. Peasants were herded into collective farms, several million 'kulaks' were expropriated and deported, and the traditional structures of village life and traditional patterns of farming were destroyed. The onslaught provoked intense peasant resistance: in 1930 there were 13,754 peasant uprisings. One result of the turmoil unleashed by the regime was a massive famine in 1932–3. Eventually, the regime was forced to compromise, allowing private plots and a limited collective farm market alongside collectivized agriculture, but by 1936 peasant society had been drastically restructured and drastically demoralized. Without any right to a passport, the peasants were reduced to something like the condition of the peasant estate in the late nineteenth century. Millions moved from countryside to the tens of thousands of construction sites, creating what Moshe Lewin called a 'quicksand society', in which social structures came under intense strain.

Urban and some rural youth—more educated, less care-worn, more enthusiastic, more assimilated to Soviet values than their parents—provided a cohort of supporters for 'socialist construction'. Many struggled to better their educational qualifications, to read improving literature, to acquire the perquisites of 'culturedness'. Children repudiated parents, spouses repudiated one another in an attempt to free themselves from the stigma of alien class status. Komsomol and young party members became involved in driving out 'social aliens' from their midst. 'Bourgeois' specialists were also kicked out. During the 'Cultural Revolution', there was an intense drive to create a proletarian intelligentsia and the zealous advocates of 'proletarian' principles were allowed to assault the proponents of more pluralistic positions. By 1931 the Cultural Revolution was over and by the mid-1930s there was evidence of a certain 'embourgeoisement' of party cadres, who sought to emulate in their dress, home furnishings, language, and deportment a style that was considered 'cultured'.

The 'Great Break' saw the consolidation of Stalin's autocratic rule exercised through the party and secret police. There was a resurgence of elements of traditional political culture (Stalin as father of his people, Stalin as the 'good tsar' surrounded by evil boyars). The OGPU expanded and refined its operations through dekulakization and mass deportations. Dissent within the party was almost completely expunged. The purge, with its probing for deviations in the biography of the party member and exaltation of confession ('recognizing one's errors'), entrenched itself. There was a pervasive psychology of conspiracy, an obsession with secrecy and the unmasking of hidden enemies. Ordinary people were beholden to officialdom, rendered passive, even infantilized by state power—the state would look after their every need, make up their minds for them. At the same time they were constantly exhorted to act in the name of socialism. Despite the escalating repression, people continued to complain and write petitions and denunciations to the authorities. Sheila Fitzpatrick suggests that popular attitudes to the regime fell mainly in the range between passive acceptance and cautious hostility, but attitudes were contradictory and inconsistent.[129] There was endemic fear and fatalism, yet many learned, in Stephen Kotkin's phrase, to 'speak Bolshevik', to use the official ideology for their own ends.[130] In more subliminal ways, their subjection to constant bombardment by slogans and images of a glorious future convinced millions that they were engaged in building socialism, even though the daily reality was a struggle to survive.

Robert Tucker characterized the 'Great Break' as a 'revolution from above'.[131] At first sight, this is a curious designation, since the transformations were instigated by the state itself—rather than being facilitated by a crisis of state power—indeed they led to a massive strengthening of state power. Moreover, in key respects the 'Great Break' brought down the curtain on many of the radical impulses set in train in 1917—in the sphere of family, law, and the transformation of daily life—although it was certainly not lacking in radical ambition, nor indeed in an element of utopianism. Yet insofar as the impact of crash industrialization and forced collectivization on society is concerned, the 'Great Break' fully merits the term 'revolution', since it changed the economy, social relations, and cultural patterns far more profoundly than the October Revolution had done.

CONCLUSION

The Russian Revolution brought about massive political and social change. A 300-year-old dynasty was destroyed and a one-party state, inspired by Marxism-Leninism, installed. A dynastic empire was replaced by a federation of soviet socialist republics. Key sectors of the economy ceased to be in private ownership and passed into the hands of the state, to be run by a complex bureaucracy of commissariats, trusts, and syndicates. The nascent industrial and commercial bourgeoisie vanished with a speed and irreversibility that was not matched in subsequent socialist revolutions, and the class of gentry landowners which had been the principal, although never completely reliable, social support of the autocracy was swept away with equal speed in a spontaneous peasant revolution. The Orthodox Church, another pillar of the old regime, was one of the few institutions to survive, but was institutionally undermined and its political and social influence drastically reduced. The counter-revolution, which emanated principally from the officer class of the tsarist army, was decisively defeated in a bitter civil war, although the new Soviet state continued to face external enemies at least as threatening as those faced by its tsarist predecessor. The intelligentsia and professional middle classes survived but were no longer the moral challenge to the state that they had been under the old regime. By contrast, the working class, which had been the most militant force opposing the autocracy, became in theory the new ruling class in the socialist state, even as it gradually lost much of its former fighting spirit. The liberal and socialist parties that had established a rather tenuous existence after 1905 were neutralized by the Bolsheviks who quickly consolidated power through a centralized party-state, an army, and a political police. The civil society that had grown apace after 1905 withered, but society and culture under NEP remained resilient and capable of thwarting the more intrusive penetration by the state. A youthful population that emerged out of demographic collapse began to reject the inherited culture of the patriarchal village, family, and Church.

Looked at from a different angle, one notes striking continuities between the tsarist and Soviet states. As the Bolshevik regime began to stabilize, the deeper structuring forces of Russian history began to reassert themselves: those of geography (huge distances, scattered populations, inadequate communications), climate (the vulnerability of agriculture to severe winters and drought), geopolitics (the difficulty of defending frontiers and the costs of maintaining an army over such a huge area), the constraints of the market and the paucity of capital, the ingrained patterns of a religious and patriarchal peasant culture, and the traditions of bureaucratic government. The Bolsheviks, who had so resoundingly rejected Russia's heritage in favour of proletarian internationalism, found that the greater the distance they travelled from October, the more they were hemmed in by these deep structuring forces. They did not become wholly captive to those forces, nor did revolutionary energies exhaust themselves, as Stalin's 'revolution from above' demonstrated, but in many areas the more utopian ideals of the early years were gradually abandoned and a new synthesis of revolutionary and traditional culture crystallized. This came about in part as hopes for international revolution faded and as the Bolsheviks adapted to the domestic economic, social, and cultural environment and to the international state system. It came about, too, because the Bolsheviks were transformed from a party of insurrection into a party of state-builders.

This book has tried to offer an analysis that links human agency and the power of ideas to the deeper structuring forces of geopolitics, empire, economy, and culture. There was nothing preordained about the collapse of the tsarist autocracy nor even of the Provisional Government. The autocracy was not a decrepit and immobile regime blind to the changes that were taking place around it. From the 1860s, with the emancipation of the serfs and the reforms of Alexander II, and with urgency from the 1890s, the autocracy struggled to keep abreast militarily and economically of the major European powers by industrializing the country, creating a network of modern communications, and modernizing its armed forces, all the while striving to maintain social stability. Time, however, was not on its side, since the major industrial powers—Germany, the USA, Britain, and France—were expanding their geopolitical and economic might and threatening to reduce Russia to a third-rate power. And as this backward society underwent rapid modernization, new social and political forces were unleashed that undermined domestic order and challenged the legitimacy of the autocracy. Industrialization, urbanization, and rural to urban migration produced embryonic social classes—notably, industrial workers, a modern business class, and the professional middle classes—all of which fitted uncomfortably into a traditional system of social estates dominated by the nobility. The autocracy was thus far from being a stable regime, as the 1905 Revolution was dramatically to prove. In that year, its survival was largely due to the lack of synchronization of the different challenges it faced. The brief but strained 'union of all working people, of all the vital forces of the people, of all fair-minded intellectuals' that appeared in 1905 nevertheless exerted intense pressure on the regime to concede civil and political rights.[1] In the October Manifesto Nicholas II was forced to make not insignificant political concessions, although initially these did little to quell the intense revolutionary turmoil. The 'Stolypin coup' of June 1907, however, signalled that the regime had triumphed over the forces that would overthrow it. In this context the third duma settlement provided a framework by which the regime could have pushed through a programme of modernization in a less tempestuous fashion. But this was not to be: the prospect was blocked essentially by the actions of one man, Nicholas himself, who would not countenance any diminution of his authority as autocrat. This did not make another revolution inevitable. Despite political stasis, a civil society expanded in the years up to the First World War and the case can be made that although society remained deeply unstable, Russia was moving away from revolution, as the countryside quietened down, as industrial output picked up, and as Russia's armed forces were strengthened. The international environment, however, was what was most menacing to the regime, and it was the outbreak of war in 1914 that doomed its chances of survival.

The record of the autocracy in dealing with the demands of total war was not as dismal as contemporaries believed, but the human costs of war were hideous, and the social and economic disruption it caused was massive, especially in the western provinces. Crucially, war placed huge demands on a backward economy that could only be met at the expense of the living standards of the civilian population, and this widened the gulf between privileged elites and the common people. The continuing political stalemate between duma and government ultimately persuaded even the high-ranking generals and politicians that Nicholas II must go. The last quarter of a century of the Romanov dynasty, then, was ultimately a story of a modernizing regime overtaken by domestic and international forces that it had in part itself inspired but that took on a magnitude that overwhelmed it. But it is also a story of a tsar whose refusal to adapt to the new social and political realities of the regime he headed doomed that regime to extinction.

The soaring hopes released by the February Revolution were soon dashed. The failure to establish democratic government may have been determined by the autocratic traditions of Russia and the weakness of the social forces that are conventionally assumed to have had an interest in democratic government, but we should not forget that in spring 1917 there was widespread enthusiasm for 'freedom'. The problem was that soldiers, workers, and peasants understood this as entailing real economic power to the people and this heavily 'socialized' conception of democracy was in tension with the liberal conception of civil and political rights tied to the defence of private property. In the absence of progress towards the solution of their pressing socio-economic problems of land, food shortages, and the threat to jobs, the popular classes quickly became disillusioned with the new order. What doomed the prospects for democracy, however, was the decision of the Provisional Government to continue the war. There was nothing preordained about this. For the liberal politicians who took power, the continuation of the war was a matter of honour, of standing by the commitments to the Allies in the hope that they would help democratic Russia to consolidate once victory had been secured. This was the view shared by the most capable of the moderate socialists, Kerensky, who pushed for a new military offensive. The moderate socialist leadership of the Petrograd Soviet in fact could have taken power in March had they so wished, for they enjoyed the support of a majority of the country. Tsereteli at this time crafted a rather sophisticated peace policy that a government based on the Petrograd Soviet could have promoted by dealing directly with the Allied governments rather than via the international socialist movement. The Allies would doubtless have rejected this proposal to suspend hostilities on the Eastern Front, but 'revolutionary defencism' was in tune with the policy of peace without victory that Woodrow Wilson had favoured prior to the entry of the USA into the war in spring 1917. If a moderate socialist government had followed the logic of this policy and simply declared that the army would engage only in defensive operations, Germany certainly would not have objected, and it remains doubtful that the Allies would have been in a position to intervene quickly to uphold the Eastern Front. In the event of a suspension of hostilities, some progress, difficult and slow to be sure, could have been made in tackling the fundamental issues of land and the economic crisis, and a Constituent Assembly could have been speedily summoned. Such counterfactual speculation will annoy some readers, but it serves a heuristic function of opening up for consideration issues that are normally assumed to be closed. And it reminds us of the extent to which the rapid shift to the left in politics was due to the policies of the moderate socialists. They refused to take power because they believed that the 'bourgeoisie' was destined to rule and they chose to acquiesce in the Allied demand for an offensive in June, despite knowledge of the intense popular desire for release from a punishing and futile war. It was this willingness to continue the war rather than to press the logic of revolutionary defencism that was the basic reason for the failure of democracy in 1917. Ironically, following the Kornilov rebellion, a majority of moderate socialists did come round to the view that the coalition with the 'bourgeoisie' was unworkable—something their bourgeois allies, the Kadets, had never doubted—and took up demands for a speedy end to the war, the transfer of land to the land committees, and the immediate summoning of the Constituent Assembly. If these demands had been raised by the Petrograd Soviet in spring it might have made all the difference. As it was, the decision to continue the war focused the otherwise disparate grievances of the lower classes, polarizing society in a way that undermined prospects for parliamentary-type politics.

The Bolsheviks had entered the public arena during the 1905 Revolution, already fierce critics of the moderate socialist orientation towards the liberal opposition. But they had been pushed to the side-lines during the Years of Reaction and then again by the war. Upon his return to Russia in April 1917, after a decade-long absence, Lenin's brilliant political instincts, in particular his deep mistrust of Russian liberals and his passionate belief that the war signalled a global crisis of capitalism, helped him size up the various political forces in a trenchant and perspicacious fashion. Against the leaders of his own party, he insisted that there must be implacable opposition to the imperialist war and to the new government of 'capitalists and landowners'. He recognized the deep unpopularity of the war and the likelihood that the masses would turn against the Provisional Government once its inability or unwillingness to tackle their grievances became apparent. However, it was not until the threat of counter-revolution loomed in the shape of General Kornilov that the masses rallied around the Bolshevik slogans of 'Bread, peace, and land' and 'All power to the soviets'. In the soviets support for the Bolsheviks—and their Left SR, Menshevik Internationalist, and anarchist allies—soared, not least because soviet power was understood as involving the decentralization of power to the masses themselves. The Bolshevik party proved effective not because of its disciplined character, but because its activists, armed with slogans and a newspaper, campaigned relentlessly in the soviets, factory committees, trade unions, and soldiers' committees.

The vision that the Bolsheviks upheld in October was one of a socialist society rooted in soviet power, workers' control, abolition of the standing army, and far-reaching democratic rights, leading in the longer term to an international workers' revolution, the complete abolition of capitalism, and the reduction of the powers of the state to ones of simple administration. However, the exigencies of fighting a bitter civil war and of coping with an unprecedented collapse of social and economic life quickly sobered up the new Soviet government. Rival socialist parties, civil liberties, and the abolition of the death penalty were early casualties of Bolshevik determination to hold on to power. The idea of the working class as the agent of socialist revolution gave way gradually to the idea of the party and the Red Army as the guarantors of the workers' state. Within the party itself this culture of authoritarianism soon made itself felt. M. S. Ol'minskii, initiator of the commission to study the history of the Bolshevik party (Istpart), told the Ninth Party Conference in September 1920 that Old Bolsheviks understood that the sacrifice of democracy was dictated by the emergency of war, 'but many of our comrades understand the destruction of all democracy as the last word in communism, as real communism'. Bukharin could declare without embarrassment that 'proletarian compulsion, beginning with executions and ending with obligatory labour service, are methods of forging communist humanity out of the human material left by the capitalist epoch'. The idea that workers' revolution would be carried into Europe via soviets gave way to the idea that the Bolshevik revolution would be carried abroad via the Red Army. Bukharin talked of 'red intervention'; and Radek averred, 'we were always for revolutionary war...the bayonet is an essential necessity for introducing communism'. Once the civil war was over, there would be no going back to the vision of 1917. With NEP, the idea of workers' power at the level of the factory gave way to the desperate drive to raise labour productivity and the priority became one of building a modern, industrial state through short-term sacrifices by the peasantry and the working class. Before Lenin's death, socialist revolution had been redefined as the party-state mobilizing the country's human and material resources to overcome economic, social, and cultural backwardness as rapidly as possible.

With NEP and the impending 'revolution from above' inaugurated by Stalin, it is worth reflecting further on the comparison between the tsarist and Bolshevik states, for the developmental state of the Bolsheviks had certain features in common with its tsarist precursor. First, under both systems the state itself played the principal role in economic development, although the tsarist government took on this task because the indigenous forces promoting capitalism were weak, whereas the Bolsheviks took it on willingly in the name of socialism. And like their tsarist predecessor, the Bolsheviks could only build an industrial economy through extracting resources from the populace, which meant overwhelmingly the peasantry. The Bolshevik state also played a role in crafting the social structure of the new society, granting privileges to some groups and discriminating against others, in a way that had parallels in the imperial state crafting the system of social estates. The Bolshevik state was probably stronger than its tsarist predecessor, since notwithstanding the collapse of governmental authority during the civil war, it began in the course of NEP to penetrate local society to an unprecedented if still imperfect extent and to eliminate all sources of opposition. Yet in many respects, too, it remained a 'weak' state. Its capacity to extract the resources from the peasantry that it required for industrialization remained limited and rural government remained weak. If a strong state is one that can rely on a smoothly functioning bureaucracy and routine methods of government, then the resort to campaigns, 'storming', and to plenipotentiary rule by local satraps and their clients highlights the weaknesses of the Bolshevik state.[2]

One of the most unexpected outcomes of the Revolution was that the Bolsheviks would manage to reunite most of the territory that had once constituted the tsarist empire. In stark contrast, the First World War brought about the complete downfall of its Austro-Hungarian, Ottoman, and German rivals. This leads some historians to construe the Soviet empire as simply a slightly modified version of the dynastic empire of the tsars. Yet Lenin had been at pains to insist that when dealing with non-Russian peoples the Bolsheviks should avoid the Great Russian chauvinism he believed had been the hallmark of tsarist imperialism. Some of his closest comrades, often themselves from non-Russian backgrounds, did not share his sensitivity. And after Stalin's rise to power, elements of Russian ethnic dominance—such as their over-representation in senior political positions, the assumption of a Russian civilizing mission, the assumption that sedentary agriculture was superior to pastoralism—did reassert themselves. Even so, if this made the Soviet Union an empire—and this is a concept that is hard to define—it was a very different empire from its tsarist predecessor.[3] Apart from the obvious difference that it was rooted in communist ideology and based on a command economy, the Soviet Union formally offered universal citizenship to all its inhabitants, regardless of ethnicity. And it institutionalized nationality both as a principle of territorial organization and as a defining feature of individual identity. By contrast, the tsarist empire, though multi-ethnic and multi-confessional, fought shy of institutionalizing nationality. Paradoxically, the Soviet Union engaged in vigorous nation-building so that national identity came to hold sway over religious, tribal, or kin-based identities, even as it claimed to transcend the national principle in favour of the class principle and of proletarian internationalism.

A major theme of recent research has been the ubiquity of violence in the Russian Revolution, a topic discussed in Chapter 4. The group of US historians sometimes called the 'modernity school' has stressed the centrality of violence to Bolshevik state-building, which it sees as reliant on practices of categorization, information gathering, policing, incarceration, and deportation that were common to other inter-war European states, but writ large in the Soviet case.[4] They see the First World War as a watershed that led to a massive expansion and militarization of practices designed to shape the 'social body'. The use of terms such as 'annihilation' or 'extermination' by the Bolsheviks is seen as an expression of 'excisionary' violence; that is, violence designed to remove specific groups perceived to be socially harmful or politically dangerous from the social body. It is seen as adumbrating the violence of the totalitarian regimes of the inter-war period which saw society, in the words of Zygmunt Bauman, 'as an object of designing, cultivating and weed-poisoning'.[5] This perspective offers insight into some aspects of the civil war, but it is much more relevant to the violence of Stalinism. Indeed, as argued in Chapter 4, surveying the civil war as a whole, one is struck by the extent to which fighting was rather traditional, all sides preferring close combat and the mobility provided by cavalry and relying on sabres and rifles, rather than aerial bombardment and poison gas.

The ubiquity of violence of all kinds in the civil war has been revealed by the opening of archives. Popular support was not irrelevant to the ultimate success of the Reds: workers had no wish to see a White victory, and when peasants were faced with that prospect of a White victory, they generally rallied to the Reds, in spite of their fierce opposition to the policies of food requisitioning, conscription, and the pursuit of deserters. Nevertheless, the extent to which the new regime relied on violence is now much clearer than it once was. Classic theorists of totalitarianism never doubted the central role played by violence, especially the Red Terror, in bringing the Soviet regime into existence, but they tended to see violence as a product of ideology, as an expression of class hatred. Recent work brings out the great number of perpetrators of violence—from the Red Army, the Cheka, and food detachments, through to the White armies and their attendant warlords, through to insurgent ethnicities, peasants, Greens, and bandits—and highlights the variety of functions that it played and the range of meanings it could communicate. Violence was not only used by contenders for power to crush opponents and seek to establish a monopoly of force; it was used by peasant communities to protect themselves against outsiders or to uphold moral economies (as when crowds beat up hapless 'speculators').[6] It was used, too, by ordinary people against other ordinary people, manifest in low-level actions such as raids on neighbouring communities for food, fodder, horses, or booty, and use of bloodshed to settle ancient scores.[7] Violence was not only instrumental, it was also a way of bolstering social identities and of creating bonds of solidarity, as with *otomany* in Ukraine, and also a way of creating and dramatizing differences of power, of sending messages to potential adversaries, and of warding off threats.[8]

In fact, purely in relation to the 1920s (Stalinism in the 1930s was a different matter), it is not obvious that Soviet society *was* more violent than its tsarist predecessor. Historians often fail to convey how ingrained violence was in late-imperial Russia, evinced in colonial conquest, police repression, counter-insurgency, terrorism by left and right, and anti-Jewish pogroms, extending, too, into more everyday forms of violence, such as practices of *samosud* ('self-judgement'), meted out by peasant communities on those who transgressed their norms,[9] to the flogging of prisoners, to beatings in the workplace, child abuse, and wife-beating. At least some of these violent practices diminished under the Soviet regime. Any judgement on this matter, however, depends on how violence—a notoriously slippery and easily expandable concept—is defined. For the Bolsheviks, the institutionalized inequalities and injustices of the old order—poverty, malnutrition, exploitation at work, susceptibility to cold, damp, and disease—were what was fundamental. Not everyone would accept that these are best understood under the rubric of what would later be called 'institutionalized violence', but insofar as these phenomena (so much woven into the fabric of daily life that they were taken for granted) caused bodily suffering and privation there is a case for categorizing them as violence. And in both the 1905 and 1917 Revolutions the liberal and socialist opposition construed poverty and exploitation as affronts to the innate dignity of the human person. The Bolshevik Revolution certainly did not remove poverty and exploitation: indeed it would be decades before the material conditions of life in general surpassed those of the tsarist regime. But we should pause before accepting the view that the Russian Revolution initiated a cycle of escalating violence that inevitably culminated in the gulag.

The Bolsheviks promised that the Revolution would elevate working people to the status of a ruling class. This never came about. Even with respect to basic working and living conditions, the Revolution brought about only limited improvements. Peasants certainly achieved their historic demand that land pass into the hands of those who worked it, but rural living standards had scarcely begun to reach pre-war levels when violent collectivization was unleashed, and they would not improve until the 1960s. For workers, the picture was more mixed. Following the spectacular collapse of industry during the civil war, workers did experience some improvements compared with the pre-revolutionary situation, especially in respect of working hours and labour rights, although much less so in terms of wages. The eight-hour working day, which had been a key demand of the 1905 Revolution, was achieved within days of the October seizure of power. This was symbolically important, but the Bolshevik government was not actually the first government to institute it on a state-wide scale: in February 1917 the Mexican government had incorporated an eight-hour day into its constitution (although it did not become operational until 1931). And in Western Europe the First World War hastened the legalization of the eight-hour day, with Germany instituting it as a consequence of the November Revolution in 1918 and France in April 1919. In addition, there was significant improvement in health care and education in the 1920s, although this was not matched in housing.

* * *

This book has explained the evolution of the Bolshevik regime with particular regard to the historical circumstances of war and economic backwardness that shaped it, whereas many historians in recent decades have emphasized the culpability of the Bolsheviks themselves, pointing to the role of their ideas and actions in bringing about Stalinism. One of the most trenchant interpretations of the history of the Soviet Union has been that of Martin Malia, who argued that the Soviet Union was an 'ideocracy' whose development was driven by the millenarian vision of a total transformation of man and society. He contended that tyranny was the inevitable outcome of the Bolshevik determination to abolish private property, profit, and the market, since it necessarily entailed the suppression of civil society and individual autonomy. Many other historians ascribe similar determinacy to ideology, although they differ in respect of the elements of Marxism-Leninism they see as logically entailing totalitarianism. Some agree with Malia that its seeds lay in the abolition of the market and private property, others see them as lying in the concept of a dictatorship of the proletariat, or in the belief in class struggle as the motor of history, or in the conviction that Marxism provided 'scientific' knowledge of the laws of history, or in the belief that human nature could be transformed through revolution, or in the Bolshevik rejection of morality as a constraint on action, or in the Leninist model of the vanguard party. Doubtless some, and perhaps all, of these elements in Marxism-Leninism played a part in facilitating Stalin's tyranny. There is no doubt that beliefs mattered to the Bolsheviks. That they believed they were realizing the Marxist vision is indisputable, and it is impossible to understand their vast ambition, their astounding energy, and their ruthless determination without taking seriously the ideology that inspired them. Ideology, moreover, could work negatively, by blinkering their vision. In 1905, for example, the labour movement had talked of 'human rights', yet this disappeared after the language of class became hegemonic in 1917. The Bolsheviks simply did not believe in abstract rights, and one consequence was that it left Soviet citizens bereft of a language in which they could seek redress against the arbitrary actions of the state. Yet we should also remember that Marxism-Leninism was a bundle of very diverse ideas and values. And the fierce battles that raged within the party during the civil war testify to the coexistence of different understandings of socialism. Moreover, the emancipatory impulses within Bolshevism are easily overlooked. In 1917 it was its promise to abolish inequality and exploitation, its rejection of the war as imperialist, its belief in the equality of people regardless of class, race, or gender, its promise to dismantle the bureaucratic state and place power in the hands of local soviets that made it appealing to millions of people across the globe.

The foregoing account has highlighted the ways in which the legacy of the First World War, the desperate struggles to win the civil war, to feed the towns, and to deal with the ravages of famine and disease, or the requirement to deal with the consequences of international pariah status severely constrained the Bolsheviks' scope for action. By looking at the weight of the tsarist past, moreover, I have suggested that the Bolsheviks found themselves facing many of the same problems and pressures—the need rapidly to industrialize, to modernize agriculture, to build defence capacity—that had faced their tsarist predecessors. Of course, they interpreted the circumstances they faced in terms that were different from those used by Witte or Stolypin, and consequently devised different policies to overcome them. But objectively, the tasks of modernization that they faced—set by the competitive pressures of the international state system and by the uneven development of capitalism—were the same. Historians writing from a position of sympathy for the Bolsheviks often suggest that their course of action was determined by implacable circumstances that it was beyond their power to overcome. Certainly, the constraints within which they operated were very real, but at each turning point the Bolsheviks made choices. And in seeking to understand why the Revolution evolved in the woeful direction it did, we have to recognize that alternative courses of action might have been taken. In this respect, ideology mattered crucially, setting the frame within which choices were made. But it did not determine the course of action that would be taken. It could not tell the Bolsheviks what the optimal strategy for industrialization should be in the 1920s or how to deal with more immediate (but just as critical) short-term problems, such as whether or not to sign the Treaty of Brest-Litovsk.

Moreover, many factors, other than those connected to ideology or circumstances, shaped the course of the Revolution. One thinks of the crucial role played by political leadership in 1917: the personal and intellectual qualities of Lenin that disposed squabbling comrades to accept his authority. One thinks also of the role played by contingency in shaping historical outcomes: the fact that Lenin died at the age of 53, at a point when he recognized the dangerous sides of Stalin's personality (a man he had done much to promote) but was in no position to block his former protégé's rise to preeminence. One thinks, too, of the role of simple accident: Trotsky gave the example of V. N. L'vov, the garrulous Procurator of the Holy Synod, who unwittingly tipped off Kerensky to the fact that Kornilov was planning changes to the Prime Minister's cabinet, thereby setting the Prime Minister against the man with whom he had been planning a form of military dictatorship.[10] Or, again, one thinks of the role played by unintended consequences. Against the background of the Kronstadt rebellion, the Tenth Party Congress instituted a temporary ban on factions within the Bolshevik party. The charge of 'factionalism' would provide Stalin with a big stick with which to beat the opposition.

This brings us, finally, to the question of the relationship of Leninism to Stalinism. It is beyond question that there was much in Leninist theory and practice that adumbrated Stalinism. Lenin was the architect of the party's monopoly on power; it was he who subordinated the soviets and trade unions to the party; he who would not tolerate those who thought differently; he who dismantled many civil and political freedoms; he who crushed the socialist opposition. At the height of the civil war Lenin even went so far as to suggest that the will of the proletariat 'may sometimes be carried out by a dictator'. In other words, Lenin must bear considerable responsibility for the institutions and culture that allowed Stalin to come to power. Crucially, he bequeathed a structure of power that favoured a single leader, and this made the ideas and capacities of the leader of far more consequence than in a democratic polity. What this logically entails—though it is often overlooked by those who see Stalinism as arising seamlessly out of Leninism—is that if Bukharin or Trotsky had become general secretary the horrors of Stalinism would not have come to pass, although economic backwardness and international isolation would still have critically constrained their room for manoeuvre. A good example of the extraordinary power of the leader of a Leninist-type party is Deng Xiaoping who, from the end of the 1970s, broke utterly with Maoism, and moved China from a command economy to a market economy and from a totalitarian to an at least partially open society, albeit under strict one-party rule. We may, of course, doubt whether Bukharin's vision of socialism at a snail's pace could have narrowed the economic and military gap between the Soviet Union and the capitalist powers, notwithstanding the instability of global capitalism that ensued with the Great Depression. And we may be equally sceptical that Trotsky could have furthered the revolution in the advanced capitalist countries that he saw as necessary for the ultimate victory of socialism in Russia. Nevertheless we can be confident that although the left shared Stalin's determination to smash the fetters of socio-economic and cultural backwardness, it would not have unleashed anything like the violent collectivization or Great Terror that soon ensued. In the last analysis, Stalin exploited to the full the role of leader, which had developed into a centrepiece of the Leninist model of democratic centralism, playing his cards skilfully, and understanding the potential of a totalitarian party-state to bring about the root-and-branch transformation of the economy and society. As a person, moreover, Stalin did not scruple at the human cost.

If continuities between Leninism and Stalinism were real, the 'revolution from above' also introduced real *dis*-continuity, wreaking havoc upon Soviet society. In bringing about what he called the 'Great Break', Stalin believed he was advancing the cause of socialism, yet whether Lenin would have recognized the regime he brought into being as socialist is very doubtful. Stalin presided over the consolidation of a new ruling elite, the restoration of economic and social hierarchies, the reconfiguration of patriarchal authority, the resurgence of a certain Russian chauvinism, the rejection of artistic experimentation in favour of a stifling conformism, the snuffing out of virtually all the progressive experiments in social welfare and new ways of living of the 1920s. Crucially, although the institutions of rule did not change, personal dictatorship, the unrestrained use of force, the cult of power, paranoia about encirclement and internal wreckers, and spiralling of terror across an entire society, all served to underline the difference between Stalinism and Leninism. To some extent, Stalinism represented the resurgence of elements in Russia's political culture. This is a leitmotif of the work of Richard Pipes, who emphasizes the enduring influence of tsarism as a patrimonial regime in which the tsar's absolute and unconstrained authority derived from his ownership of the country's resources, including the lives of his subjects. In addition, Pipes argues that the Russian peasantry lacked a sense of civic responsibility, was politically passive, and supportive of autocracy. It is not difficult to see these things at work in the political culture of Stalinism. Of course, the Revolution released a flood of change that destabilized cultural norms and practices, but, as Moshe Lewin pointed out, the 'contamination effect' of tradition is often greater, the quicker customary patterns are broken. So that notwithstanding cultural revolution, one also sees a kind of 'return of the repressed'. At the same time, and contra Pipes, we need to be cautious about interpreting Russia's political culture as a monolithic system. A culture is a contested field in which different norms and practices compete, so that the Russian peasantry could be disposed both to acquiesce in autocracy and to rise up against the social order, depending on context. We should also be cautious about seeing traditional political culture as a causal factor in the rise of

Stalinism. Culture is best seen as a context that often shapes political outcomes negatively rather than positively by, for example, furnishing few resources to counter the resurgence of autocratic forms of rule. Yet those caveats made, the similarity between tsarism and Stalinism cannot be gainsaid, manifest above all in the primacy of the state over society and the individual, in the absence of civil institutions mediating between people and government, in the highly personalized relationship of the people to authority, in the highly centralized system of government, and in the lack of legal restraints on power.

* * *

In 1859 in the preface to *A Contribution to the Critique of Political Economy*, Karl Marx wrote:

> No social order is ever destroyed before all the productive forces for which it is sufficient have been developed, and new superior relations of production never replace older ones before the material conditions for their existence have matured within the framework of the old society. Mankind thus inevitably sets itself only such tasks as it is able to solve, since closer examination will always show that the problem itself arises only when the material conditions for its solution are already present or at least in the course of formation.

The Bolsheviks believed that the First World War was evidence that capitalism was in terminal crisis, that it had exhausted its potential to develop the productive capacity of humanity any further, and that the conditions for socialism now existed in embryo. While one can admire their determination to break from the futility and carnage of the First World War, their assessment of the significance of the war was way off the mark. Leaders of the Second International, whom Lenin held in contempt because of their capitulation to nationalism in 1914, had regularly warned of not confusing revolution that emerges from war with socialist revolution. The French socialist leader Jean Jaurès, who was assassinated at the end of July 1914 just as he was about to attend a conference of the Second International to try to persuade it not to support war, had warned in the shadow of the Balkan wars that: 'If the social revolution emerges from this chaos instead of coming about as the supreme expression of progress, as a higher act of reason, justice, and wisdom, it will be part of this universal mental crisis, an excess of the contagious fury brought about by the suffering and violence of war.'[11] A similar sentiment had been expressed a decade earlier by Karl Kautsky, leader of the German Social Democrats: 'Revolution which arises from war is a sign of the weakness of the revolutionary class, and often the cause of further weakness because of the sacrifice it brings with it, as well as by the moral and intellectual degradation to which war gives rise.' In the event the Bolsheviks ignored these warnings and the order they brought into being bore the birthmarks of the 'contagious fury' begotten by the First World War.

The Bolsheviks never doubted that a decadent capitalist system would collapse sooner rather than later (indeed this view was still held by Soviet leaders into the 1960s). A hundred years on, with the Soviet Union defunct for more than a quarter of a century—that is, more than a third of the length of time that it actually existed—it is clear that the Russian Revolution did not come into existence because of the terminal crisis of capitalism. Like the socialist regimes it helped bring into being after the Second World War, the Soviet Union proved capable of generating extensive growth in industrial production and of building up a defence sector, but much less capable of competing with capitalism once the latter shifted towards more intensive forms of production and towards 'consumer capitalism'. In this respect the record of the Chinese Communists in promoting their country to the rank of a leading economic and political world power was far more impressive than that of the regime on which it broadly modelled itself. Indeed as the twenty-first century advances, it may come to seem that the Chinese Revolution was *the* great revolution of the twentieth century, deeper in its mobilization of society, more ambitious in its projects, more far-reaching in its achievements, and probably more enduring than its Soviet counterpart. Yet in the end the Chinese Communists achieved historically unprecedented economic growth by emulating capitalism, by putting in place a system of investment-led and export-led growth, and by privatizing state assets and stimulating private enterprise. Through the twentieth century, capitalism displayed immense dynamism and innovation, permitting the raising of the standard of living of millions of people even as it concentrated immense wealth in a few hands and created new forms of alienation. This is not intended as a paean to capitalism. Indeed as we move through the twenty-first century the compulsion of capitalism to accumulate is fast reaching a point where it imperils the very existence of the planet. The point is simply that the primary significance of 1917 for the history of the twentieth century no longer seems to lie in its challenge to capitalism so much as in the fact that it brought into being a state capable of making an immense contribution to the defeat of fascism and later of posing a threat (both real and imagined) to the geopolitical primacy of the USA in the Cold War. Still, in the future the ambition of its challenge to capitalism may once again inspire.

For contemporaries the significance of 1917 lay in the promise to put the working class into power and to put an end to inequality and exploitation. A century on, that does not appear to be its lasting significance. What stand out as being of greater significance are elements of the social revolution that the Bolsheviks would have considered secondary to proletarian emancipation: commitments to such causes as anti-colonialism, women's rights, experiments in law, welfare, and education, or new concepts of urban planning and architecture. The Bolsheviks cannot claim exclusive credit for putting the struggle against colonialism on the political agenda of the twentieth century. There had been a rising tide of humanitarian critique of colonial abuses, and the Social Democrats in Germany had spoken out against German policy in Southwest Africa back in 1906. Moreover, in the year that the First Congress of the Comintern convened (1919), the Pan-African Congress also met for the first time, to articulate a liberal as opposed to a socialist critique of colonial abuses and to call for home rule for African peoples. But it was the Comintern that popularized militant anti-imperialism and served as a training ground for many who would become leaders of national-liberation struggles in the post-war era. Where else but in a Comintern congress in 1924 could the young Ho Chi Minh denounce the brutal treatment of African labour? Similarly, without minimizing the imperial dimension of the Soviet

Union, the Bolshevik programme of nation-building, with its commitment to affirmative action and empowerment programmes for ethnic minorities, looks forward to much that took place in the West only from the 1960s. Likewise, judged against the standards of the time, many of the policies of the Women's Department aimed at the liberation of women from patriarchy also anticipate the demands of the women's movement in the West from the late 1960s.

The Russian Revolution of 1917 ended in tyranny. Yet it raised fundamental questions about how justice, equality, and freedom can be reconciled which have not gone away. Its answers were flawed, but it opened up certain progressive possibilities that the dismal record of Stalinism and Maoism should not blind us to. In a world that is saturated by the mass media, it becomes ever harder to think rigorously and critically about the principles on which our society is organized and about the direction in which humanity is going. Everything conspires to make us acquiesce in the world as it is, to discourage belief that it can be organized in a more just and rational fashion. Yet that is what the Bolsheviks tried to do. Their revolution wrought calamity on a scale commensurate with the transformation in the human condition that they sought to achieve. And a hundred years on, it is easier to appreciate the illusions under which they laboured than the ideals that inspired them. Yet we shall not understand the Russian Revolution unless we see that for all their many faults, the Bolsheviks were fired by outrage at the exploitation that lay at the heart of capitalism and at the raging nationalism that had led Europe into the carnage of the First World War. Nor will we understand the *year* 1917 if we do not make an imaginative effort to recapture the hope, idealism, heroism, anger, fear, and despair that motivated it: the burning desire for peace, the deep resentment of a social order riven between the haves and the have-nots, anger at the injustices that ran through Russian society. That is why millions across the world, who could not anticipate the horrors to come, embraced the 1917 Revolution as a chance to create a new world of justice, equality, and freedom.

NOTES

Introduction

1. François Furet, *Interpreting the French Revolution* (Cambridge: Cambridge University Press, 1981), 1.
2. Arno Mayer, *The Furies: Violence and Terror in the French and Russian Revolutions* (Princeton, NJ: Princeton University Press, 2001), 3.
3. Compare Simon Schama on the French Revolution: 'In some depressing unavoidable sense, violence *was* the revolution.' Simon Schama, *Citizens: A Chronicle of the French Revolution* (London: Viking, 1989), xv.

Chapter 1

1. Orlando Figes, *A People's Tragedy: The Russian Revolution, 1891–1924* (London: Jonathan Cape, 1996).
2. V. O. Kliuchevsky, *A History of Russia*, vol. 1 (London: J. M. Dent, 1911), 2.
3. D. C. B. Lieven, *Towards the Flame: Empire, War and the End of Tsarist Russia* (London: Allen Lane, 2015), 9.
4. Cited in Paul Kennedy, *Rise and Fall of the Great Powers* (New York: Random House, 1987), 177.
5. Lieven, *Towards the Flame*, 85.
6. <http://demoscope.ru/weekly/ssp/rus_lan_97.php>.
7. Jane Burbank and Mark von Hagen (eds), *Russian Empire: Space, People, Power, 1700–1930* (Bloomington: Indiana University Press, 2007); John W. Slocum, 'Who, and When, Were the *Inorodtsy*? The Evolution of the Category of "Aliens" in Imperial Russia', *Russian Review*, 57:2 (1998), 173–90.
8. Theodore Weeks, *Nation and State in Late Imperial Russia: Nationalism and Russification on the Western Frontier, 1863–1914* (DeKalb: Northern Illinois University Press, 1996); Alexei Miller, 'The Empire and Nation in the Imagination of Russian Nationalism', in A. Miller and A. J. Rieber (eds), *Imperial Rule* (Budapest: Central European University Press, 2004), 9–22.
9. Robert D. Crews, *For Prophet and Tsar: Islam and Empire in Russia and Central Asia* (Cambridge, MA: Harvard University Press, 2006).
10. Paul Werth, *At the Margins of Orthodoxy: Mission, Governance, and Confessional Politics in Russia's Volga-Kama Region, 1827–1905* (Ithaca, NY: Cornell University Press, 2002).
11. Alexander Morrison, *Russian Rule in Samarkand, 1868–1910: A Comparison with British India* (New York: Oxford University Press, 2008).

12. Robert Geraci, *Window on the East: National and Imperial Identities in Late-Imperial Russia* (Ithaca, NY: Cornell University Press, 2001).
13. Charles Steinwedel, 'To Make a Difference: The Category of Ethnicity in Late Imperial Russian Politics, 1861–1917', in D. L. Hoffmann and Yanni Kotsonis (eds), *Russian Modernity: Politics, Knowledge, Practices* (Basingstoke: Macmillan, 2000), 67–86.
14. Andreas Kappeler, *The Russian Empire: A Multiethnic History* (Harlow: Pearson, 2001); Willard Sunderland, 'The Ministry of Asiatic Russia: The Colonial Office That Never Was But Might Have Been', *Slavic Review*, 60:1 (2010), 120–50.
15. Geoffrey Hosking, *Russia: People and Empire* (London: Fontana, 1998).
16. Miller, 'The Empire and Nation', 9–22.
17. Dominic Lieven, *Nicholas II: Emperor of All the Russias* (New Haven, CT: Yale University Press, 1989).
18. <http://www.angelfire.com/pa/ImperialRussian/royalty/russia/rfl.html>.
19. Abraham Ascher, *The Revolution of 1905, vol. 2: Authority Restored* (Stanford, CA: Stanford University Press, 1992), 222.
20. Richard Pipes, *Russia under the Old Regime* (New York: Penguin, 1977).
21. Peter Waldron, 'States of Emergency: Autocracy and Extraordinary Legislation, 1881–1917', *Revolutionary Russia*, 8:1 (1995), 1–25.
22. Waldron, 'States of Emergency', 24.
23. Neil Weissman, 'Regular Police in Tsarist Russia, 1900–1914', *Russian Review*, 44:1 (1985), 45–68 (49).
24. Jonathan W. Daly, *The Watchful State: Security Police and Opposition in Russia, 1906–1917* (DeKalb: Northern Illinois University Press, 2004), 5–6. Daly, incidentally, gives a higher figure—100,000—than Weissman for the number of police of all kinds in 1900.
25. Figes, *People's Tragedy*, 46.
26. T. Emmons and W. S. Vucinich (eds), *The Zemstvo in Russia: An Experiment in Local Self-Government* (Cambridge: Cambridge University Press, 1982), 215.
27. Hans Rogger, *Russia in the Age of Modernisation and Revolution, 1881–1917* (London: Longman, 1983), 72.
28. J. S. Curtiss, *The Russian Church and the Soviet State* (Boston: Little, Brown, 1953), 10.
29. Gregory L. Freeze, 'Handmaiden of the State? The Orthodox Church in Imperial Russia Reconsidered', *Journal of Ecclesiastical History*, 36 (1985), 82–102.
30. Simon Dixon, 'The Orthodox Church and the Workers of St Petersburg, 1880–1914', in Hugh McLeod, *European Religion in the Age of Great Cities, 1830–1930* (London: Routledge, 1995), 119–41.
31. Vera Shevzov, *Russian Orthodoxy on the Eve of Revolution* (Oxford: Oxford University Press, 2004).
32. A. K. Baiburin, 'Poliarnosti v rituale (tverdoe i miagkoe)', *Poliarnost' v kul'ture: Almanakh 'Kanun'* 2 (1996), 157–65.
33. Vera Shevzov, 'Chapels and the Ecclesial World of Pre-revolutionary Peasants', *Slavic Review*, 55:3 (1996), 585–613.
34. Chris J. Chulos, *Converging Worlds: Religion and Community in Peasant Russia, 1861–1917* (DeKalb: Northern Illinois University Press, 2003), 159.

35. J. S. Curtiss, *Church and State in Russia: the Last Years of the Empire*, (New York: Columbia University Press, 1965), 118.
36. David G. Rowley, '"Redeemer Empire": Russian Millenarianism', *American Historical Review*, 104 (1999), 1582–602.
37. James H. Billington, *The Icon and the Axe: An Interpretive History of Russian Culture* (New York: Vintage Books, 1970), 514.
38. Nadieszda Kizenko, *A Prodigal Saint: Father John Kronstadt and the Russian People* (University Park, PA: Pennsylvania State University Press, 2000), 271.
39. Sergei Fomin (comp.), *Rossiia pered vtorym prishestviem: prorochestva russkikh sviatykh* (Moscow: Sviato-Troitskaia Sergieva Lavra, 1993). This is a compendium of prophecies of doom about the fate of Russia by saints, monks, nuns, priests, theologians, and a sprinking of lay writers, including Dostoevsky, V. V. Rozanov, and Lev Tikhomirov.
40. David Moon, *The Russian Peasantry, 1600–1930* (London: Longman, 1999).
41. Richard G. Robbins, *Famine in Russia, 1891–1892: The Imperial Government Responds to a Crisis* (New York: Columbia University Press, 1975).
42. R. W. Davies, Mark Harrison, and S. G. Wheatcroft (eds), *The Economic Transformation of the Soviet Union, 1913–1945* (Cambridge: Cambridge University Press, 1994), 59.
43. Stephan Merl, 'Socio-economic Differentiation of the Peasantry', in R. W. Davies (ed.), *From Tsarism to the New Economic Policy* (Basingstoke: Macmillan, 1990), 52.
44. A. G. Rashin, *Naselenie Rossii za sto let* (Moscow: Gos. Statisticheskoe Izd-vo, 1956), 198–9.
45. Davies et al. (eds), *Economic Transformation*, 59; David L. Ransel, 'Mothering, Medicine, and Infant Mortality in Russia: Some Comparisons', Kennan Institute Occasional Papers, 1990, <https://www.wilsoncenter.org/sites/default/files/op236_mothering_medicine_ransel_1990.pdf>.
46. Christine D. Worobec, *Family and Community in the Post-Emancipation Period* (Princeton, NJ: Princeton University Press, 1991), 175.
47. P. N. Zyrianov, 'Pozemel'nye otnosheniia v russkoi krest'ianskoi obshchine vo vtoroi polovine XIX—nachale XX veka', in D. F. Aiatskov (ed.), *Sobstvennost' na zemliu v Rossii: istoriia i sovremennost'* (Moscow: ROSSPEN, 2002), 154. Some sources put the number of peasant households in European Russia at 9.2 million.
48. Worobec, *Family*, 25.
49. Moon, *Russian Peasantry*, 172.
50. Barbara Alpern Engel, *Between the Fields and the City: Women, Work and Family in Russia, 1861–1914* (Cambridge: Cambridge University Press, 1994); E. Kingston-Mann and T. Mixter, 'Introduction', in Esther Kingston-Mann and Timothy R. Mixter (eds), *Peasant Economy, Culture and Politics in European Russia, 1800–1921* (Princeton, NJ: Princeton University Press, 1991), 14–15.
51. *Naselenie Rossii v XX veke: istoricheskie ocherki*, vol. 1: *1900–1939gg.* (Moscow: ROSSPEN, 2000), 57.
52. Worobec, *Family*, 64; Barbara A. Engel, *Women in Russia, 1700–2000* (Cambridge: Cambridge University Press, 2004), 90; B. M. Firsov and I. G. Kiseleva (eds), *Byt*

velikorusskikh krest'ian-zemlepashtsev: opisanie materialov Etnograficheskogo biuro Kniazia V. N. Tenisheva: na primere Vladimirskoi gubernii (St Petersburg: Izd-vo Evropeiskogo doma, 1993), 262.

53. Worobec, *Family*, 177.
54. Mandakina Arora, 'Boundaries, Transgressions, Limits: Peasant Women and Gender Roles in Tver' Province, 1861–1914', PhD Duke University, 1995, 44–50.
55. *Naselenie Rossii*, 48.
56. Stephen G. Wheatcroft, 'Crises and the Condition of the Peasantry in Late Imperial Russia', in Kingston-Mann and Mixter (eds), *Peasant Economy, Culture and Politics of European Russia.*
57. David Moon, 'Russia's Rural Economy, 1800–1930', *Kritika: Explorations in Russian and Eurasian History*, 1:4 (2000), 679–90.
58. Paul R. Gregory, *Before Command: An Economic History of Russia from Emancipation to the First Five-Year Plan* (Princeton, NJ: Princeton University Press, 1994); Boris Mironov, *Blagosostoianie naseleniia i revoliutsii v imperskoi Rossii, XVII—nachalo XX veka* (Moscow: Novyi Khronograf, 2010).
59. Boris Mironov and Brian A'Hearn, 'Russian Living Standards under the Tsars: Anthropometric Evidence from the Volga', *Journal of Economic History*, 68:3 (2008), 900–29.
60. J. Y. Simms, 'The Crisis of Russian Agriculture at the End of the Nineteenth Century: A Different View', *Slavic Review*, 36:3 (1977), 377–98; Eberhard Müller, 'Der Beitrag der Bauern zur Industrialisierung Russlands, 1885–1930', *Jahrbücher für Geschichte Osteuropas*, 27:2 (1979), 199–204.
61. Wheatcroft, 'Crises and the Condition of the Peasantry', 138, 141, 151.
62. Judith Pallot, *Land Reform in Russia, 1906–1917: Peasant Responses to Stolypin's Project of Rural Transformation* (Oxford: Clarendon Press, 1999), 95.
63. Pallot, *Land Reform*, 97.
64. Yanni Kotsonis, *Making Peasants Backward: Agricultural Cooperatives and the Agrarian Question in Russia, 1861–1914* (London: Macmillan, 1999), 57.
65. Rogger, *Russia in the Age of Modernisation*, 81. Zhurov suggests that nationally between one-fifth and one-quarter of households were wealthy at the beginning of the twentieth century. Iu. V. Zhurov, 'Zazhitovchnoe krest'ianstvo Rossii v gody revoliutsii, grazhdanskoi voiny i interventsii (1917–1920 gody)', in *Zazhitochnoe krest'ianstvo Rossii v istoricheskoi retrospektive (zemlevladenie, zemlepol'zovanie, proizvodstvo, mentalitet), XXVII sessiia simpoziuma po agrarnoi istorii Vostochnoi Evropy* (Moscow: RAN, 2000), 147–54.
66. Teodor Shanin, *The Awkward Class: Political Sociology of Peasantry in a Developing Society, 1910–1925* (Oxford: Clarendon Press, 1972).
67. I. L. Koval'chenko, 'Stolypinskaia agrarnaia reforma (mify i real'nost)', *Istoriia SSR*, 2 (1991), 68–9.
68. L. V. Razumov, *Rassloenie krest'ianstva Tsentral'no-Promyshlennogo Raiona v kontse XIX–nachale XX veka* (Moscow: RAN, 1996).
69. 'Letter from Semyon Martynov, a peasant from Orël, August 1917', in Mark Steinberg, *Voices of Revolution* (translations by Marian Schwartz) (New Haven, CT: Yale University Press, 2001), 242.

70. John Channon, 'The Landowners', in Robert Service (ed.), *Society and Politics in the Russian Revolution* (Basingstoke: Macmillan, 1992), 120.
71. Rogger, *Russia in the Age of Modernisation*, 89 (85).
72. Worobec, *Family*, 31.
73. Arcadius Kahan, *Russian Economic History: The Nineteenth Century* (Chicago: Chicago University Press, 1989), 190.
74. Gregory Guroff and S. Frederick Starr, 'A Note on Urban Literacy in Russia, 1890–1914', *Jahrbücher für Geschichte Osteuropas*, 19:4 (1971), 520–31 (523–4).
75. V. P. Leikina-Svirskaia, *Russkaia intelligentsiia v 1900–1917 godakh* (Moscow: Mysl', 1981), 7.
76. Barbara E. Clements, *History of Women in Russia: From the Earliest Times to the Present* (Bloomington: Indiana University Press, 2012), 130.
77. Engel, *Women in Russia*, 92; A. G. Rashin, *Formirovanie rabochego klassa Rossii* (Moscow, 1958), 595.
78. Patrick L. Alston, *Education and the State in Tsarist Russia* (Stanford, CA: Stanford University Press, 1969), 248.
79. Ben Eklof, *Russian Peasant Schools: Officialdom, Village Culture, and Popular Pedagogy, 1861–1914* (Berkeley: University of California, 1986), 90.
80. James C. McClelland, *Autocrats and Academics: Education, Culture and Society in Tsarist Russia* (Chicago: University of Chicago Press, 1979), 44.
81. Eklof, *Russian Peasant Schools*, 89.
82. E. M. Balashov, *Shkola v rossiiskom obshchestve 1917–1927gg. Stanovlenie 'novogo cheloveka'* (St Petersburg: Dmitrii Bulanin, 2003), 42; Scott J. Seregny, 'Teachers, Politics and the Peasant Community in Russia, 1895–1918', in Stephen White et al. (eds), *School and Society in Tsarist and Soviet Russia* (Basingstoke: Macmillan, 1993), 121–48.
83. Balashov, *Shkola*, 12.
84. Peter Gatrell, *The Tsarist Economy, 1850–1917* (London: Batsford, 1986).
85. Peter Gatrell, 'Poor Russia, Poor Show: Mobilizing a Backward Economy', in Stephen Broadberry and Mark Harrison (eds), *The Economics of World War I* (Cambridge: Cambridge University Press, 2005), 235–75 (238).
86. Gatrell, 'Poor Russia', 237.
87. Rogger, *Russia in the Age of Modernisation*, 126; *Naselenie Rossii v XX veke*, vol. 1, 26.
88. Catherine Evtuhov, *Portrait of a Russian Province. Economy, Society, and Civilization in Nineteenth-Century Nizhnii Novgorod* (Pittsburgh: University of Pittsburgh Press, 2011).
89. S. N. Semanov, *Peterburgskie rabochie nakanune pervoi russkoi revoliutsii* (Moscow: Nauka, 1966), 152.
90. S. A. Smith, *Red Petrograd: Revolution in the Factories* (Cambridge: Cambridge University Press, 1983), 13.
91. Thomas C. Owen, *Capitalism and Politics in Russia: A Social History of the Moscow Merchants, 1855–1905* (Cambridge: Cambridge University Press, 1981).
92. A. J. Rieber, *Merchants and Entrepreneurs in Imperial Russia* (Chapel Hill: University of North Carolina Press, 1982).

93. Susan P. McCaffray, *The Politics of Industrialization in Tsarist Russia: The Association of Southern Coal and Steel Producers, 1874–1914* (DeKalb: Northern Illinois University Press, 1996).
94. Figes, *People's Tragedy*, 113.
95. 'Prokhorovtsy kuptsy', <http://www.russianfamily.ru/p/prokhorovi.html>.
96. N. A. Ivanova and V. P. Zheltova, *Soslovno-klassovaia struktura Rossii v kontse XIX–nachale XX veka* (Moscow: Nauka, 2004), 224.
97. Gregory L. Freeze, 'The Soslovie (estate) Paradigm and Russian Social History', *American Historical Review*, 91:1 (1986), 11–36; Elise Kimerling Wirtschafter, *Social Identity in Imperial Russia* (DeKalb: Northern Illinois University Press, 1997).
98. Ivanova and Zheltova, *Soslovno-klassovaia struktura Rossii*, 90–1; Alison K. Smith, *For the Common Good and their Own Well-Being: Social Estates in Imperial Russia* (New York: Oxford University Press, 2015), 150.
99. *Rabochii klass Rossii ot zarozhdeniia do nachala XXv.* (Moscow: RAN, 1989), 273.
100. Rashin, *Formirovanie*, 172.
101. O. I. Shkaratan, *Problemy sotsial'noi struktury rabochego klass a SSSR* (Moscow: Mysl', 1970), 192.
102. L. D. Trotsky, *The History of the Russian Revolution*, <https://www.marxists.org/archive/trotsky/1930/hrr/apdx1.htm>.
103. Shkaratan, *Problemy*, 146; E. E. Kruze, *Peterburgskie rabochie v 1912–14 godakh* (Leningrad: Izd-vo Akademii Nauk SSSR, 1961), 76.
104. Peter Gatrell, *Russia's First World War: A Social and Economic History* (London: Pearson, 2005), 72.
105. Kahan, *Russian Economic History*, 172.
106. Joseph Conrad, *Under Western Eyes* (New York: Harper, 1911), 292.
107. Edith W. Clowes, Samuel D. Kassow, and James L. West (eds), *Between Tsar and People: Educated Society and the Quest for Public Identity in Late Imperial Russia* (Princeton, NJ: Princeton University Press, 1991).
108. Franco Venturi, *Roots of Revolution: A History of the Populist and Socialist Movements in 19th Century Russia* (Chicago: Chicago University Press, 1960).
109. Samuel H. Baron, *Plekhanov: The Father of Russian Marxism* (London: Routledge, 1963).
110. Robert J. Service, *Lenin a Political Life*, (3 vols), vol. 1: *The Strengths of Contradiction* (Basingstoke: Macmillan, 1985), 138–40.
111. Quoted in Robert J. Service, *Lenin: A Biography* (Basingstoke: Macmillan, 2000), 98.
112. Lenin gave no less weight to theoretical reflection than Marx. His fifty-five volumes of *Collected Works* contain 24,000 documents.
113. Israel Getzler, *Martov: A Political Biography of a Russian Social Democrat* (Cambridge: Cambridge University Press, 1967), 21.
114. V. I. Lenin, 'To the Rural Poor' (1903), <https://www.marxists.org/archive/lenin/works/1903/rp/>.
115. Allan K. Wildman, *The Making of a Workers' Revolution: Russian Social Democracy, 1891–1903* (Chicago: University of Chicago Press, 1967).

116. Oliver Radkey, *The Agrarian Foes of Bolshevism: Promise and Default of the Russian Socialist Revolutionaries, February to October 1917* (New York: Columbia University Press, 1958); Maureen Perrie, *The Agrarian Policy of the Russian Socialist-Revolutionary Party from its Origins through the Revolution of 1905–07* (Cambridge: Cambridge University Press, 1976).
117. Shmuel Galai, *The Liberation Movement in Russia, 1900–1905* (Cambridge: Cambridge University Press, 1973).
118. Abraham Ascher; *The Revolution of 1905*, vol. 1: *Russia in Disarray* (Stanford, CA: Stanford University Press, 1988).
119. Gerald D. Surh, *1905 in St Petersburg: Labor, Society and Revolution* (Stanford, CA: Stanford University Press, 1989).
120. Ascher, *Revolution of 1905*, vol. 1, 136–42.
121. <https://en.wikipedia.org/wiki/Łódź_insurrection>.
122. Mark Steinberg, *Moral Communities: The Culture of Class Relations in the Russian Printing Industry, 1867–1907* (Berkeley: University of California Press, 1992), 174–6.
123. A. P. Korelin and S. V. Tiutukin, *Pervaia revoliutisiia v Rossii: vzgliad cherez stoletie* (Moscow: Pamiatniki istoricheskoi mysli, 2005), 544; Rosa Luxemburg, 'The Mass Strike' (1906), <https://www.marxists.org/archive/luxemburg/1906/mass-strike>.
124. <http://sandinist.livejournal.com/29592.html>.
125. Ascher, *Revolution of 1905*, vol. 1, ch. 8; Beryl Williams, '1905: The View from the Provinces', in Jonathan D. Smele and Anthony Haywood (eds), *The Russian Revolution of 1905: Centenary Perspectives* (Abingdon: Routledge, 2005), 34–54.
126. Laura Engelstein, *Moscow 1905: Working-Class Organization and Political Conflict* (Stanford, CA: Stanford University Press, 1982), 220.
127. Ascher, *Revolution of 1905*, vol. 2, 22.
128. John Bushnell, *Mutiny amid Repression: Russian Soldiers in the Revolution of 1905–1906* (Bloomington: Indian a University Press, 1985), 76.
129. Shane O'Rourke, 'The Don Cossacks during the 1905 Revolution: The Revolt of Ust-Medvedevskaia Stanitsa', *Russian Review*, 57 (Oct. 1998), 583–98 (594).
130. Ascher, *Revolution of 1905*, vol. 1, 267.
131. Elvira M. Wilbur, 'Peasant Poverty in Theory and Practice: A View from Russia's "Impoverished Center" at the End of the Nineteenth Century', in Kingston-Mann and Mixter (eds), *Peasant Economy, Culture and Politics of European Russia*, 101–27.
132. Ascher, *Revolution of 1905*, vol. 1, 162; James D. White, 'The 1905 Revolution in Russia's Baltic Provinces', in Smele and Haywood (eds), *The Russian Revolution of 1905*, 55–78.
133. Maureen Perrie, 'The Russian Peasant Movement of 1905–1907: Its Social Composition and Revolutionary Significance', *Past and Present*, 57 (1972).
134. Robert Edelman, *Proletarian Peasants: The Revolution of 1905 in Russia's Southwest* (Ithaca, NY: Cornell University Press, 1987).
135. Barbara Alpern Engel, 'Men, Women and the Languages of Russian Peasant Resistance', in Stephen Frank and Mark Steinberg (eds), *Cultures in Flux: Lower-Class Values,*

Practices and Resistance in Late Imperial Russia (Princeton, NJ: Princeton University Press, 1994), 41–5.

136. Scott J. Seregny, 'A Different Type of Peasant Movement: The Peasant Unions in the Russian Revolution of 1905', *Slavic Review*, 47:1 (Spring 1988), 51–67 (53).
137. O. G. Bukovets, *Sotsial'nye konflikty i krest'ianskaia mental'nost' v rossiiskoi imperii nachala XX veka: novye materially, metody, rezul'taty* (Moscow: Mosgorarkhiv, 1996), 141, 147.
138. Andrew Verner, 'Discursive Strategies in the 1905 Revolution: Peasant Petitions from Vladimir Province', *Russian Review*, 54:1 (1995), 65–90 (75).
139. Ascher, *Revolution of 1905*, vol. 2, 121.
140. Carter Ellwood, *Russian Social Democracy in the Underground: A Study of the RSDRP in the Ukraine, 1907–1914* (Amsterdam: International Institute for Social History, 1974).
141. Stephen F. Jones, *Socialism in Georgian Colors: The European Road to Social Democracy, 1883–1917* (Cambridge, MA: Harvard University Press, 2005), ch. 7.
142. Toivo U. Ruan, 'The Revolution of 1905 in the Baltic Provinces and Finland', *Slavic Review*, 43:3 (1984), 453–67.
143. Crews, *For Prophet and Tsar*, 1.
144. Adeeb Khalid, *The Politics of Muslim Cultural Reform: Jadidism in Central Asia* (Berkeley: University of California Press, 1998).
145. Jeff Sahadeo, *Russian Colonial Society in Tashkent, 1865–1923* (Bloomington: Indiana University Press, 2007).

Chapter 2

1. Abraham Ascher, *P. A. Stolypin: The Search for Stability in Late Imperial Russia* (Stanford, CA: Stanford University Press, 2001).
2. Terence Emmons, *The Formation of Political Parties and the First National Elections in Russia* (Cambridge, MA: Harvard University Press, 1983).
3. Geoffrey A. Hosking, *The Russian Constitutional Experiment: Government and Duma, 1907–1914* (Cambridge: Cambridge University Press, 1973).
4. George Gilbert, *The Radical Right in Imperial Russia* (London: Routledge, 2015).
5. More than 26,000 people were executed, exiled, or imprisoned for political offences between 1907 and 1909: Peter Waldron, *Between Two Revolutions: Stolypin and the Politics of Renewal in Russia* (London: UCL Press, 1998), 63.
6. Anna Geifman, *Thou Shalt Kill: Revolutionary Terrorism in Russia, 1894–1917* (Princeton, NJ: Princeton University Press, 1995).
7. Linda H. Edmondson, *Feminism in Russia, 1900–17* (London: Heinemann, 1984); Rochelle Goldberg Ruthchild, *Equality and Revolution: Women's Rights in the Russian Empire, 1905–1917* (Pittsburgh: University of Pittsburgh Press, 2010).
8. Susan Morrissey, 'Subjects and Citizens, 1905–1917', in Simon Dixon (ed.), *The Oxford Handbook of Modern Russian History* (Oxford: Oxford Handbooks Online, 2013).
9. Eric Lohr, 'The Ideal Citizen and Real Subject in Late Imperial Russia', *Kritika: Explorations in Russian and Eurasian History*, 7:2 (2006), 173–94.

10. Joseph Bradley, *Voluntary Associations in Tsarist Russia: Science, Patriotism, and Civil Society* (Cambridge, MA: Harvard University Press, 2009).
11. There are two excellent introductions to the debate on where Russia was going after 1905: R. B. McKean, *Between the Revolutions: Russia, 1905 to 1917* (London: The Historical Association, 1998); Ian D. Thatcher, *Late Imperial Russia: Problems and Prospects: Essays in Honour of R. B. McKean* (Manchester: Manchester University Press, 2005).
12. Hosking, *Constitutional Experiment*; Waldron, *Between Two Revolutions*.
13. Joshua A. Sanborn, *Drafting the Russian Nation: Military Conscription, Total War, and Mass Politics, 1905–1925* (DeKalb: Northern Illinois University Press, 2003).
14. D. C. B. Lieven, *Towards the Flame: Empire, War and the End of Tsarist Russia* (London: Allen Lane, 2015), 176, 180.
15. Peter Gatrell, *Government, Industry, and Rearmament in Russia, 1900–1914* (Cambridge: Cambridge University Press, 1994), 152–5.
16. David Stevenson, *Armaments and the Coming of War: Europe, 1904–1914* (Oxford: Oxford University Press, 1996), 7. 'Only Russia could keep up with [Germany] and that inefficiently.' Alan J. P. Taylor, *The Struggle for Mastery in Europe, 1848–1918* (Oxford: Oxford University Press, 1954), xxviii.
17. Melissa K. Stockdale, *Paul Miliukov and the Quest for a Liberal Russia, 1889–1918* (Ithaca, NY: Cornell University Press, 1996), 186–8.
18. Waldron, *Between Two Revolutions*, 171–3.
19. Hosking, *Constitutional Experiment*, 106.
20. Laura Engelstein, *The Keys to Happiness: Sex and the Search for Modernity in Fin-de-Siècle Russia* (Ithaca, NY: Cornell University Press, 1992).
21. Clowes, Kassow, and, West (eds), *Between Tsar and People*.
22. McClelland, *Autocrats*, 52.
23. Jeffrey Brooks, *When Russia Learned to Read* (Princeton, NJ: Princeton University Press, 1985).
24. Louise McReynolds, *News under Russia's Old Regime: The Development of a Mass-Circulation Press* (Princeton, NJ: Princeton University Press, 1991), 225.
25. McReynolds, *News*, 237, 234.
26. James von Geldern and Louise McReynolds, *Entertaining Tsarist Russia: Tales, Songs, Plays, Movies, Jokes, Ads, and Images from Russian Urban Life, 1779–1917* (Bloomington: Indiana University Press, 1998), xx.
27. Cited in Engel, *Between the Fields and the City*, 155.
28. Wayne Dowler, *Russia in 1913* (DeKalb: Northern Illinois University Press, 2010), 112.
29. R. E. Zelnik (trans. and ed.), *A Radical Worker in Tsarist Russia* (Stanford, CA: Stanford University Press, 1986), 71.
30. D. N. Zhbankov, *Bab'ia storona: statistiko-etnograficheskii ocherk* (Kostroma, 1891), 27.
31. See the photographs in Christine Ruane, *The Empire's New Clothes: A History of the Russian Fashion Industry, 1700–1917* (New Haven, CT: Yale University Press, 2009), 197, 202.
32. Ascher, *Revolution of 1905*, vol. 2, 134.
33. O. S. Porshneva, *Mentalitet i sotsial'noe povedenie rabochikh, krest'ian i soldat Rossii v period pervoi mirovoi voiny (1914-mart 1918g)* (Ekaterinburg: UrO RAN, 2000), 146.

34. Heather Hogan, *Forging Revolution: Metalworkers, Managers, and the State in St Petersburg, 1890–1914* (Bloomington: Indiana University Press, 1993), 161–74.
35. Tim McDaniel, *Autocracy, Capitalism, and Revolution in Russia* (Berkeley: University of California Press, 1988).
36. Leopold H. Haimson and Ronald Petrusha, 'Two Strike Waves in Imperial Russia, 1905–1907, 1912–1914', in Leopold H. Haimson and Charles Tilly, *Strikes, Wars and Revolutions in an International Perspective* (Cambridge: Cambridge Uuniversity Press, 1989), 101–66 (125).
37. A. P. Korelin and S. V. Tiutukin, *Pervaia revoliutisiia v Rossii: vzgliad cherez stoletie* (Moscow: Pamiatniki istoricheskoi mysli, 2005), 536.
38. N. D. Postnikov, *Territorial'noe razmeshchenie i chislennost' politicheskikh partii Rossii (1907–fevral' 1917)* (Moscow: IIU MGOU, 2015).
39. Postnikov, *Territorial'noe razmeshchenie*, 56.
40. Postnikov, *Territorial'noe razmeshchenie*, 56; Michael S. Melancon, *Stormy Petrels: The Socialist Revolutionaries in Russia's Labor Organizations, 1905–1914* (Pittsburgh: University of Pittsburgh Centre for Russian and East European Studies, 1988).
41. Konstantin N. Morozov, 'Partiia sotsialistov-revoliutsionnerov vo vremia i posle revoliutsii 1905–1907 gg.', *Cahiers du monde russe*, 48:2 (2007), 301–30.
42. Postnikov, *Territorial'noe razmeshchenie*, 56.
43. Reginald E. Zelnik (ed.), *Workers and Intelligentsia in Late Imperial Russia: Realities, Representations, Reflections* (Berkeley: International and Area Studies, University of California at Berkeley, 1999).
44. A. Buzinov, *Za Nevskoi Zastavoi* (Moscow: Gosudarstvennoe Iz-vo, 1930), 29.
45. Michael Melancon, *The Lena Goldfields Massacre and the Crisis of the Late Tsarist State* (College Station: Texas A&M University Press, 2006), 116.
46. Haimson and Petrusha, 'Two Strike Waves in Imperial Russia', 107.
47. Hogan, *Forging Revolution*, 161.
48. F. A. Gaida, 'Politicheskaia obstanovka v Rossii nakanune Pervoi mirovoi voiny v otsenke gosudarstvennykh deiatelei i liderov partii', *Rossiiskaia istoriia*, 6 (2011), 123–35; Jonathan W. Daly, *The Watchful State: Security Police and Opposition in Russia, 1906–1917* (DeKalb: Northern Illinois University Press, 2004), 147.
49. Victoria E. Bonnell, *Roots of Rebellion: Workers' Politics and Organizations in St Petersburg and Moscow, 1900–1914* (Berkeley: University of California Press, 1983).
50. *Shestoi s"ezd RSDLP (bol'shevikov): Avgust 1917 goda. Protokoly* (Moscow, 1958), 47.
51. D. A. Loeber (ed.), *Ruling Communist Parties and their Status under Law* (Dordrecht: Martinus Nijhoff, 1986), 63. Not all historians are persuaded that the Bolsheviks were taking over leadership of the labour movement: see R. B. McKean, *St Petersburg Between the Revolutions: Workers and Revolutionaries, June, 1907–February 1917* (London: Yale University Press, 1990).
52. Postnikov, *Territorial'noe razmeshchenie*, 56.
53. Patricia Herlihy, *The Alcoholic Empire: Vodka and Politics in Late Imperial Russia* (Oxford: Oxford University Press, 2002), 145.
54. V. B. Aksenov, '"Sukhoi zakon" 1914 goda: ot pridvornoi intrigi do revoliutsii', *Rossiiskaia istoriia*, 4 (2011), 126–39.

55. For a view that individual and collective actors recoiled from taking decisive action in the political and social crisis on the eve of the war, for fear that they would be overwhelmed by an accelerating process of social polarization, see Leopold H. Haimson, '"The Problem of Political and Social Stability in Urban Russia on the Eve of War" Revisited', *Slavic Review*, 59:4 (2000), 848–75.
56. Dowler, *Russia in 1913*, 279.
57. Gilbert, *Radical Right*, ch. 6.
58. *Rossiia 1913 god: statistiko-dokumental'nyi spravochnik* (St Petersburg: BLITs, 1995), 413–14.
59. William C. Fuller, *Civil–Military Conflict in Imperial Russia, 1881–1914* (Princeton, NJ: Princeton University Press, 1985), 257.
60. Mark D. Steinberg, *Petersburg: Fin de Siècle* (New Haven: Yale University Press, 2011), 244.
61. Gatrell, *Government, Industry, and Rearmament*.
62. <http://www2.stetson.edu/~psteeves/classes/durnovo.html>.
63. Norman Stone, *The Eastern Front, 1914–1917* (London: Penguin, 1998).
64. Mark Mazower, *Dark Continent: Europe's Twentieth Century* (London: Allen Lane, 1998), ix; David Stevenson, *1914–1918: The History of the First World War* (London: Penguin, 2005), xix.
65. G. F. Krivosheev (ed.), *Rossiia i SSSR v voinakh XX veka: poteri vooruzhyennykh sil. Statisticheskoe issledovanie* (Moscow: OLMA, 2001).
66. Boris Kolonitskii, *Tragicheskaia erotika: obrazy, imperatorskoi sem'i v gody Pervoi mirovoi voiny* (Moscow: NLO, 2010), 73.
67. Joshua Sanborn, *Imperial Apocalypse: The Great War and the Destruction of the Russian Empire* (Oxford: Oxford University Press, 2014), 29.
68. Cited in Peter Gatrell, 'Tsarist Russia at War: The View from Above, 1914–February 1917', *Journal of Modern History*, 87:3 (2015), 668–700 (689).
69. David R. Stone, *The Russian Army in the Great War: The Eastern Front, 1914–1917* (Lawrence: University Press of Kansas, 2015), 48; Eric Lohr, *Nationalizing the Russian Empire: The Campaign Against Enemy Aliens during the First World War* (Cambridge, MA: Harvard University Press, 2003), 136.
70. Peter Gatrell, *A Whole Empire Walking: Refugees in Russia during World War One* (Bloomington: Indiana University Press, 1999), 3.
71. Tomas Balkelis, 'Demobilization and Remobilization of German and Lithuanian Paramilitaries after the First World War', *Journal of Contemporary History*, 50:1 (2015), 38–57 (38).
72. Donald Bloxham, *The Great Game of Genocide: Imperialism, Nationalism and the Destruction of the Ottoman Armenians* (Oxford: Oxford University Press, 2005).
73. Edward J. Erickson, *Ottoman Army Effectiveness in World War One* (London: Routledge, 2007), 1.
74. A. B. Astashov, *Russkii front v 1914-nachale 1917 goda: voennyi opyt i sovremennost'* (Moscow: Novyi Khronograf, 2014), 19, 23.
75. P. P. Shcherbinin, 'Women's Mobilization for War (Russian Empire)', *International Encyclopedia of the First World War*, <http://encyclopedia.1914-1918-online.net/article/womens_mobilization_for_war_russian_empire>.

76. Stone, *Russian Army*, 4.
77. Stone, *Russian Army*, ch. 7.
78. Edward D. Sokol, *The Revolt of 1916 in Russian Central Asia* (Baltimore: Johns Hopkins Press, 1954). Gene Huskey refers to an 'unknown genocide', in which 100,000 to 120,000 out of 780,000 Kyrghyz were slaughtered: Gene Huskey, 'Kyrgyzstan: The Politics of Demographic and Economic Frustration', in Ian Bremmer and Ray Taras (eds), (Cambridge: Cambridge University Press, 1997), 400.
79. Astashov, *Russkii front*, 116, 160.
80. William G. Rosenberg, 'Reading Soldiers' Moods: Russian Military Censorship and the Configuration of Feeling in World War I', *American Historical Review*, 119:3 (2014), 714–40 (716).
81. A. B. Astashov and P. A. Simmons, *Pis'ma s voiny 1914–1917* (Moscow: Novyi khronograf, 2015), 128.
82. Joshua Sanborn, 'The Mobilization of 1914 and the Question of the Russian Nation', *Slavic Review*, 59:2 (2000), 267–89; S. A. Smith, 'Citizenship and the Russian Nation during World War I: A Comment', *Slavic Review*, 59:2 (2000), 316–29.
83. Astashov, *Russkii front*, 133–4, 179–87.
84. Quoted in A. B. Astashov, 'Russkii krest'ianin na frontakh Pervoi mirovoi voiny', *Otechestvennaia istoriia*, 2 (2003), 72–86 (75); Karen Petrone, *The Great War in Russian Memory* (Bloomington: Indiana University Press, 2011), 91.
85. Mark von Hagen, 'The Entangled Front in the First World War', in Eric Lohr et al. (eds), *The Empire and Nationalism at War* (Bloomington, IN: Slavica, 2014), 9–48 (36); Sanborn, *Imperial Apocalypse*, 130.
86. Igor V. Narskii, 'The Frontline Experience of Russian Soldiers in 1914–16', *Russian Studies in History*, 51:4 (2013), 31–49.
87. Astashov, *Russkii front*, 224, 279–300.
88. Krivosheev (ed.), *Rossiia*, table 52.
89. Dietrich Beyrau, 'Brutalization Revisited: The Case of Russia', *Journal of Contemporary History*, 50:1 (2015), 15–37 (18).
90. Krivosheev (ed.), *Rossiia*, table 56.
91. Kolonitskii, *Tragicheskaia erotika*, 396.
92. Hubertus Jahn, *Patriotic Culture in Russia during World War I* (Ithaca, NY: Cornell University Press, 1995).
93. Lohr, *Nationalizing the Russian Empire*.
94. Jahn, *Patriotic Culture*.
95. Gatrell, *Russia's First World War*, 42–3.
96. E. N. Burdzhalov, *Russia's Second Revolution: The February 1917 Uprising in Petrograd*, trans. and ed. Donald J. Raleigh (Bloomington: Indiana University Press, 1987), 60.
97. Porshneva, *Mentalitet*, 191.
98. Lewis Siegelbaum, *The Politics of Industrial Mobilization in Russia, 1914–1917: A Study of the War Industries Committees* (Basingstoke: Macmillan, 1983), 165.
99. David R. Jones, 'Imperial Russia's Forces at War', in A. R. Millett and W. Murray (eds), *Military Effectiveness*, vol. 1: *The First World War* (Boston: Unwyn Hyman, 1988), 249–328 (260).

100. Gatrell, *Russia's First World War*, 45.
101. Andrei Markevich and Mark Harrison, 'Great War, Civil War, and Recovery: Russia's National Income, 1913–1928', *Journal of Economic History*, 71:3 (2011), 672–703.
102. Gatrell, 'Tsarist Russia at War', 693.
103. Jones, 'Imperial Russia's Forces', 271.
104. Gatrell, *Russia's First World War*, 126.
105. Gatrell, *Russia's First World War*, 136.
106. Jones, 'Imperial Russia's Forces', 260.
107. Gatrell, 'Poor Russia', 247.
108. Yanni Kotsonis, *States of Obligation: Taxes and Citizenship in the Russian Empire and Early Soviet Republic* (Toronto: University of Toronto Press, 2014).
109. Steven G. Marks, 'War Finance (Russian Empire)', <http://encyclopedia.1914-1918-online.net/article/war_finance_russian_empire>.
110. Marks, 'War Finance'.
111. M. D. Karpachev, 'Krizis prodovol'stvennogo snabzheniia v gody pervoi mirovoi voiny (po materialam Voronezhskoi gubernii)', *Rossiiskaia istoriiia*, 3 (2011), 66–81 (67).
112. M. V. Os'kin, 'Prodovol'stvennaia politika Rossii nakanune fevral'ia 1917 god; poisk vykhoda iz krizisa', *Rossiiskaia istoriia*, 3 (2001), 53–66 (55).
113. S. G. Wheatcroft, 'Agriculture', in Davies (ed.), *From Tsarism*, 93.
114. I. I. Krott, 'Sel'skoe khoziaistvo zapadnoi Sibiri, 1914–17gg.', *Voprosy istorii*, 11 (2011), 103–18.
115. N. F. Ivantsova, *Zapadno-sibirskoe krest'ianstvo v 1917—pervoi polovine 1918gg.* (Moscow: Prometei, 1993), 71, 75.
116. Mark Baker, 'Rampaging Soldatki, Cowering Police, Bazaar Riots and Moral Economy: The Social Impact of the Great War in Kharkiv Province', *Canadian-American Slavic Studies*, 35: 2–3 (2001), 137–55 (141).
117. D. V. Kovalev, *Agrarnye preobrazovaniia i krest'ianstvo stolichnogo regiona v pervoi chetverti XX veka* (Moscow: Moskovskii pedagogicheskiki gos. Universitet, 2004), 123.
118. Peter Waldron, The End of Imperial Russia, 1855–1917 (Basingstoke: Palgrave, 1997) 155. Tiutukhin states that there were about 800 rural disturbances between July 1914 and March 1917. S. V. Tiutukhin, 'Pervaia mirovaia voina i revoliutsionnyi protsess v Rossii', in V. L. Mal'kov (ed.), *Pervaia mirovaia voina: prolog XX veka* (Moscow: Nauka, 1998), 236–49 (245).
119. Shkaratan, *Problemy*, 219.
120. Porshneva, *Mentalitet*, 165.
121. Porshneva, *Mentalitet*, 201.
122. A. S. Sidorov (ed.), *Revoliutsionnoe dvizhenie posle sverzheniia samoderzhaviia (27 fevralia–14 aprelia 1917g.)* (Moscow: RAN, 1957), 421.
123. Iu. I. Kir'ianov, 'Massovye vystupleniia na pochve dogorovizny v Rossii (1914–fevral' 1917g.', *Otechestvennaia istoriia*, 3 (1993), 3–18 (4).
124. Kir'ianov, 'Massovye', 8.
125. Barbara Alpern Engel, 'Not by Bread Alone: Subsistence Riots in Russia during World War One', *Journal of Modern History*, 69 (1997), 696–721.

126. Engel, *Women in Russia*, 133.
127. Iu. I. Kir'ianov, *Sotsial'no-politicheskii protest rabochikh Rossii v gody Pervoi mirovoi voiny. Iiul' 1914–fevral' 1917 gg.* (Moscow: RAN, 2005).
128. Porshneva, *Mentalitet*, 202.
129. Iu. I. Korablev (ed.), *Rabochee dvizhenie v Petrograde v 1912–1917gg.* (Leningrad: Lenizdat, 1958), 484.
130. Shkaratan, *Problemy*, 198, 210.
131. McKean, *St Petersburg*, 394.
132. Kir'ianov, *Sotsial'no-politicheskii protest*, 185.
133. Michael Melancon, *The Socialist Revolutionaries and the Russian Anti-War Movement, 1914–1917* (Columbus, OH: Ohio State University Press, 1990), 113–14.
134. S. V. Tiutukhin, *Men'shevizm: stranitsy istorii* (Moscow: ROSSPEN, 2002), 307.
135. Roger W. Pethybridge, *Witnesses to the Russian Revolution* (London: Allen Unwin, 1964), 76, 78.

Chapter 3

1. Tsuyoshi Hasegawa, *The February Revolution: Petrograd 1917* (Seattle: University of Washington Press, 1981).
2. Cited Figes, *People's Tragedy*, 323.
3. A. B. Nikolaev, *Revoliutsiia i vlast': IV Gosudarstvennaia duma 27 fevralia–3 marta 1917 goda* (St Petersburg: Izd-vo RGPU, 2005).
4. Pethybridge, *Witnesses*, 76, 78, 119–20.
5. Orlando Figes and Boris Kolonitskii, *Interpreting the Russian Revolution: The Language and Symbols of 1917* (New Haven, CT: Yale University Press, 1999), ch. 1; Pavel G. Rogoznyi, 'The Russian Orthodox Church during the First World War and Revolutionary Turmoil, 1914–1921', in Murray Frame et al. (eds), *Russian Culture in War and Revolution, 1914–22*, 1 (Bloomington, IN: Slavica, 2014), 349–76.
6. Nadezhda Krupskaya, *Reminiscences of Lenin*, <https://www.marxists.org/archive/krupskaya/works/rol/rol22.htm>.
7. I. L. Arkhipov, 'Obshchestvennaia psikhologiia petrogradskikh obyvatelei v 1917 godu', *Voprosy istorii*, 7 (1994), 49–58 (52).
8. Rex Wade, *The Russian Revolution, 1917* (Cambridge: Cambridge University Press, 2000), ch. 3.
9. V. I. Startsev, *Vnutrenniaia politika vremennogo pravitel'stva pervogo sostava* (Leningrad: Nauka, 1980), 116.
10. William G. Rosenberg, *Liberals in the Russian Revolution: The Constitutional Democratic Party, 1917–1921* (Princeton, NJ: Princeton University Press, 1974).
11. Starstev, *Vnutrenniaia politika*, 208–45. I am indebted to Ian Thatcher for this point.
12. Ziva Galili y Garcia, *The Menshevik Leaders in the Russian Revolution: Social Realities and Political Strategies* (Princeton, NJ: Princeton University Press, 1989).
13. William G. Rosenberg, 'Social Mediation and State Construction(s) in Revolutionary Russia', *Social History*, 19:2 (1994), 168–88.

14. For the Soviet proclamation see Alfred Golder (ed.), *Documents of Russian History, 1914–1917* (New York: The Century Co., 1927), 325–6.
15. Rex A. Wade, *The Russian Search for Peace: February to October 1917* (Stanford, CA: Stanford University Press, 1969).
16. Starstev, *Vnutrenniaia politika*, 204.
17. G. A. Gerasimenko, *Pervy akt narodovlastiia v Rossii: obshchestvennye ispolnitel'nye komitety 1917g.* (Moscow: Nika, 1992), 82.
18. Gerasimenko, *Pervy akt*, 106.
19. William G. Rosenberg, 'The Russian Municipal Duma Elections of 1917', *Soviet Studies*, 21:2 (1969), 131–63, 157.
20. Nikolai N. Smirnov, 'The Soviets', in Edward Acton et al. (eds), *Critical Companion to the Russian Revolution, 1914–1921* (London: Arnold, 1997), 429–37 (432).
21. Smirnov, 'Soviets', 434.
22. V. I. Lenin, *State and Revolution*, <https://www.marxists.org/archive/lenin/works/1917/staterev>.
23. A. F. Zhukov, *Ideino-politicheskii krakh eserovskogo maksimalizma* (Leningrad: Izd-vo Leningradskogo universiteta, 1979), 49.
24. Leopold H. Haimson et al. (eds), *Men'sheviki v 1917 godu* (3 vols), vol. 2 (Moscow: Progress-Akademiia, 1995), 48–9.
25. Michael Melancon, 'The Socialist Revolutionary Party, 1917–1920', in Acton et al. (eds), *Critical Companion to the Russian Revolution*, 281–90; Kh. M. Astrakhan, *Bol'sheviki i ikh politicheskie protivniki v 1917g.* (Leningrad: Leninizdat, 1973), 233.
26. Christopher Read, *Lenin: A Revolutionary Life* (Abingdon: Routledge, 2005).
27. N. N. Sukhanov, *The Russian Revolution 1917: A Personal Record*, ed. Joel Carmichael (Princeton, NJ: Princeton University Press, 1983), 272–3.
28. Angelica Balabanoff, *Impressions of Lenin* (Ann Arbor: University of Michigan Press, 1964), 2.
29. A. N. Potresov, *Izbrannoe* (Moscow: Mosgosarkhiv, 2002), 284.
30. Robert Service, *Lenin: A Political Life* (3 vols), vol. 2: *Worlds in Collision* (Basingstoke: Macmillan, 1991).
31. Neil Harding, *Lenin's Political Thought: Theory and Practice in the Democratic and Socialist Revolutions* (Chicago: Haymarket, 2009), 59–70.
32. V. I. Lenin, 'The Tasks of the Proletariat in the Present Revolution', <https://www.marxists.org/archive/lenin/works/1917/apr/04.htm>.
33. Robert Service, *The Bolshevik Party in Revolution: A Study in Organizational Change* (Basingstoke: Macmillan, 1979).
34. V. I. Miller, 'K voprosu o sravnitel'noi chislennosti partii bol'shevikov i men'shevikov v 1917g.', *Voprosy istorii KPSS*, 12 (1988), 109–18.
35. There are no biographies in English of Zinoviev and Kamenev. However, the following entries are good: <http://spartacus-educational.com/RUSzinoviev.htm>; <http://spartacus-educational.com/RUSkamenev.htm>. See, too, Catherine Merridale, 'The Making of a Moderate Bolshevik: An Introduction to L. B. Kamenev's Political Biography', in Julian Cooper, Maureen Perrie, and E. A. Rees (eds), *Soviet History, 1917–1953: Essays in Honour of R. W. Davies* (Basingstoke: Macmillan, 1995), 22–41.

36. Ian D. Thatcher, *Trotsky* (London: Routledge, 2003); Isaac Deutscher, *The Prophet Armed: Trotsky, 1879–1921* (London: Oxford University Press, 1954).
37. Ian D. Thatcher, 'The St Petersburg/Petrograd Mezhraionka, 1913–1917: The Rise and Fall of a Russian Social Democratic Workers' Party Unity Faction', *Slavonic and East European Review*, 87: 2 (2009), 284–321.
38. *Shestoi s"ezd RSDRP (bol'shevikov) avgust 1917 goda: Protokoly*, 20, 23.
39. Christopher Read, *From Tsar to Soviets: The Russian People and their Revolution, 1917–21* (London: UCL Press, 1996), chs 4–6; Allan Wildman, *The End of the Russian Imperial Army*, vol. 1 (Princeton, NJ: Princeton University Press, 1980).
40. Evan Mawdsley, *The Russian Revolution and the Baltic Fleet: War and Politics, February 1917–April 1918* (Basingstoke: Macmillan, 1978).
41. <https://www.marxists.org/history/ussr/government/1917/03/01.htm>.
42. *Pravda*, 21, 30 Mar. 1917.
43. Startsev, *Vnutrenniaia politika*.
44. 'Vserossiiskaia konferentsiia frontovykh i tylovykh voennykh organizatsii RSDRP(b)', *Politicheskie deiateli Rossii 1917. Biograficheskii slovar'* (Moscow: Bol'shaia rossiiskaia entsiklopediia, 1993).
45. K. A. Tarasov, 'Chislennost' voennoi organizatsii bol'shevikov nakanune oktiabria 1917 goda', *Trudy Karel'skoi nauchnogo tsentra RAN*, 3 (2014), 146–8.
46. David Mandel, *The Petrograd Workers and the Fall of the Old Regime* (Basingstoke: Macmillan, 1983); David Mandel, *The Petrograd Workers and the Soviet Seizure of Power* (Basingstoke: Macmillan, 1984); Diane Koenker, *Moscow Workers and the 1917 Revolution* (Princeton, NJ: Princeton University Press, 1981).
47. Smith, *Red Petrograd*.
48. Figes, *People's Tragedy*, ch. 10.
49. *Izvestiia*, 96, 20 June 1917.
50. Wildman, *End of the Russian Imperial Army*.
51. Richard Pipes, *The Russian Revolution: 1899–1919* (New York: Knopf, 1990), 770; Alexander Rabinowitch, *Prelude to Revolution: The Petrograd Bolsheviks and the July 1917 Uprising* (Bloomington: Indiana University Press, 1968).
52. Rabinowitch, *Prelude*, 173.
53. Sukhanov, *The Russian Revolution*, 446.
54. O. N. Znamenskii, *Iiul'skii krizis 1917 goda* (Moscow: Nauka, 1964), 124.
55. Orlando Figes, *Peasant Russia, Civil War: The Volga Countryside in Revolution, 1917–1921* (Oxford: Clarendon Press, 1989); John Channon, 'The Peasantry in the Revolutions of 1917', in E. R. Frankel et al. (eds), *Revolution in Russia: Reassessments of 1917* (Cambridge: Cambridge University Press, 1992), 105–30.
56. Graeme J. Gill, *Peasants and Government in the Russian Revolution* (Basingstoke: Macmillan, 1979), 46–63, 75–88.
57. J. L. H. Keep, *The Russian Revolution: A Study in Mass Mobilization* (New York: Norton, 1976), 179.
58. Keep, *Russian Revolution*, 160.
59. Channon, 'The Landowners', in Service (ed.), *Society and Politics in the Russian Revolution*, 120–46.

60. Aaron B. Retish, *Russia's Peasants in Revolution and Civil War: Citizenship, Identity, and the Creation of the Soviet State, 1914–1922* (Cambridge: Cambridge University Press, 2008); John Channon, 'The Bolsheviks and the Peasantry: The Land Question during the First Eight Months of Soviet Rule', *Slavonic and East European Review*, 66:4 (1988), 593–624.
61. V. V. Kabanov, *Krest'ianskaia obshchina i kooperatsiia Rossii XX veka* (Moscow: RAN, 1997), 81.
62. Ronald G. Suny, 'Nationalism and Class in the Russian Revolution: A Comparative Discussion', in Frankel et al. (eds), *Revolution in Russia*, 219–46; Ronald G. Suny, *The Revenge of the Past: Nationalism, Revolution and the Collapse of the Soviet Union* (Stanford, CA: Stanford University Press, 1993), ch. 2.
63. Mark von Hagen, 'The Great War and the Mobilization of Ethnicity in the Russian Empire', in B. R. Rubin and Jack Snyder (eds), *Post-Soviet Political Order: Conflict and State Building* (London: Routledge, 1998), 34–57.
64. John Reshetar, *The Ukrainian Revolution, 1917–1920* (Princeton, NJ: Princeton University Press, 1952); Bohdan Krawchenko, *Social Change and National Consciousness in Twentieth-Century Ukraine* (Basingstoke: Macmillan, 1985), ch. 1.
65. Steven L. Guthier, 'The Popular Base of Ukrainian Nationalism in 1917', *Slavic Review*, 38:1 (1979).
66. David G. Kirby, *Finland in the Twentieth Century* (London: Hurst, 1979), 46; Anthony F. Upton, *The Finnish Revolution, 1917–1918* (Minneapolis: University of Minnesota Press, 1980), ch. 6.
67. Ronald G. Suny, *The Making of the Georgian Nation* (Bloomington: Indiana University Press, 1988), ch. 9.
68. Tadeusz Świętochowski, *Russian Azerbaijan, 1905–1920: The Shaping of National Identity in a Muslim Community* (Cambridge: Cambridge University Press, 1985), ch. 4.
69. Boris I. Kolonitskii, 'Antibourgeois Propaganda and Anti-"Burzhui" Consciousness in 1917', *Russian Review*, 53 (1994), 183–96 (187–8).
70. Donald J. Raleigh, *Revolution on the Volga: 1917 in Saratov* (Ithaca, NY: Cornell University Press, 1986).
71. T. A. Abrosimova, 'Sotsialisticheskaia ideeia v massovom soznanii 1917g.', in *Anatomiia revoliutsii. 1917 god v Rossii: massy, partii, vlast'* (St Petersburg: Glagol', 1994), 176–87 (177).
72. Steinberg, *Voices*, 17.
73. Michael C. Hickey, 'The Rise and Fall of Smolensk's Moderate Socialists: The Politics of Class and the Rhetoric of Crisis in 1917', in Donald J. Raleigh (ed.), *Provincial Landscapes: Local Dimensions of Soviet Power, 1917–53* (Pittsburgh: University of Pittsburgh Press, 2001), 14–35.
74. Kolonitskii, 'Antibourgeois Propaganda', 190, 191.
75. Kolonitskii, 'Antibourgeois Propaganda', 189.
76. Figes and Kolonitskii, *Interpreting*, 154.
77. A. Ia. Livshin and I. B. Orlov, 'Revolutsiia i spravedlivost': posleoktiabr'skie "pis'ma vo vlast'", in *1917 god v sud'bakh Rossii i mira: Oktiabr'skaia revoliutsiia* (Moscow: RAN, 1998), 254, 255, 259.
78. Howard White, 'The Urban Middle Classes', in Service (ed.), *Society and Politics in the Russian Revolution*, 64–85.

79. *Bor'ba za massy v trekh revoliutsiiakh v Rossii: proletariat i srednie gorodskie sloi* (Moscow: Mysl', 1981), 19.
80. O. N. Znamenskii, *Intelligentsiia nakanune velikogo oktiabria (fevral'-oktiabr' 1917g.)* (Leningrad: Nauka, 1988), 8–9.
81. *Bor'ba za massy*, 169.
82. Michael C. Hickey, *Competing Voices from the Russian Revolution* (Santa Barbara, CA: ABC-CLIO, 2011), 387.
83. Michael Hickey, 'Discourses of Public Identity and Liberalism in the February Revolution: Smolensk, Spring 1917', *Russian Review*, 55:4 (1996), 615–37 (620); V. V. Kanishchev, '"Melkoburzhuaznaia kontrrevoliutsiia": soprotivlenie gorodskikh srednikh sloev stanovleniiu "diktatury proletariata" (oktiab'r 1917–avgust 1918g.)', in *1917 god v sud'bakh Rossii i mira*, 174–87.
84. Stockdale, *Paul Miliukov*, 258.
85. *Revoliutsionnoe dvizhenie v avguste 1917g. (razgrom Kornilovskogo miatezha)* (Moscow: Izd-vo AN SSSR, 1959), 407.
86. V. F. Shishkin, *Velikii oktiabr' i proletarskii moral'* (Moscow: Mysl', 1976), 57.
87. Steinberg, *Voices*, 113.
88. O. Ryvkin, '"Detskie gody" Komsomola', *Molodaia gvardiia*, 7–8 (1923), 239–53 (244); Krupskaya, 'Reminiscences of Lenin'.
89. Ruthchild, *Equality and Revolution*, 227.
90. Engel, *Women in Russia*, 135; Ruthchild, *Equality*, 231.
91. Jane McDermid and Anna Hillyard, *Women and Work in Russia, 1880–1930* (Harlow: Longman, 1998), 167.
92. Engel, *Women in Russia*, 141.
93. Sarah Badcock, 'Women, Protest, and Revolution: Soldiers' Wives in Russia during 1917', *International Review of Social History*, 49 (2004), 47–70.
94. Steinberg, *Voices*, 98.
95. D. P. Koenker and W. G. Rosenberg, *Strikes and Revolution in Russia, 1917* (Princeton, NJ: Princeton University Press, 1989), 314.
96. Smith, *Red Petrograd*, 193.
97. Z. Lilina, *Soldaty tyla: zhenskii trud vo vremia i posle voiny* (Perm': Izd-vo Petrogradskogo Soveta, 1918), 8.
98. L. G. Protasov, *Vserossiiskoe uchreditel'noe sobranie: istoriia rozhdeniia i gibeli* (Moscow: ROSSPEN, 1997), 233.
99. Beate Fieseler, 'The Making of Russian Female Social Democrats, 1890–1917', *International Review of Social History*, 34 (1989), 193–226.
100. Marks, 'War Finance (Russian Empire)'.
101. Koenker and Rosenberg, *Strikes*, 68–72.
102. Tsuyoshi Hasegawa, 'Crime, Police, and Mob Justice during the Russian Revolutions of 1917', in Rex A. Wade (ed.), *Revolutionary Russia: New Approaches* (London: Routledge, 2004), 46–72 (50–1).
103. Sarah Badcock, *Politics and the People in Revolutionary Russia* (Cambridge: Cambridge University Press, 2007), 157.

104. Hickey, *Competing Voices*, 339–40.
105. Kh. M. Astrakhan, *Bol'sheviki i ikh politicheskie protivniki v 1917 godu* (Leningrad: Lenizdat, 1973), 187.
106. V. I. Startsev, *Krakh Kerenshchiny* (Leningrad: Nauka, 1982), 94–138.
107. Sukhanov, *The Russian Revolution*, 529.
108. Mandel, *The Petrograd Workers and the Soviet Seizure of Power*, 254.
109. Alexander Rabinowitch, *The Bolsheviks Come to Power: The Revolution of 1917 in Petrograd* (Chicago: Haymarket, 2004); Marc Ferro, *October 1917: A Social History of the Russian Revolution* (London: Routledge and Kegan Paul, 1980).
110. James D. White, 'Lenin, Trotskii, and the Arts of Insurrection: The Congress of Soviets of the Northern Region, 11–17 October', *Slavonic and East European Review*, 77:1 (1999), 117–39.

Chapter 4

1. Thomas H. Rigby, *Lenin's Government: Sovnarkom 1917–1922* (Cambridge: Cambridge University Press, 1979); Alexander Rabinowitch, *The Bolsheviks in Power: The First Year of Soviet Rule in Petrograd* (Bloomington: Indiana University Press, 2007).
2. Lutz Häfner, *Die Partei der Linken Sozialrevolutionäre: In der Russischen Revolution von 1917–1918* (Cologne: Böhlau, 1994).
3. <http://www.hist.msu.ru/ER/Etext/DEKRET/index.html>.
4. *Moskovskii Voenno-Revoliutsionnyi komitet, oktiabr'-noiabr' 1917 goda* (Moscow: Moskovskii rabochii, 1968), 182–3.
5. *Velikii oktiabr' i zashchita ego zavoevanii: pobeda sotsialisticheskoi revoliutsii* (Moscow: Nauka, 1987), 197.
6. Protasov, *Vserossiiskoe uchreditel'noe sobranie*.
7. N. S. Lar'kov, 'Sibirskii Oktiabr' i marginaly', in *Iz istorii revoliutsii v Rossii*, vol. 1 (Tomsk: Tomskii gos. Universitet, 1996), 169–75; A. V. Dobrovol'skii, 'Partiia sotsialistov-revoliutsionerov vo vlasti i v oppozitsii, 1917–1923 gody' (avtoreferat dissertatsii) (Novosibirsk, 2004), ch. 2, section 3.
8. S. V. Iarov, *Gorozhanin kak politik: revoliutsiia, voennyi kommunizm i NEP glazami petrogradtsev* (St Petersburg: Dmitrii Bulanin, 1999), 20.
9. Protasov, *Vserossiiskoe uchreditel'noe sobranie*, 320.
10. Mark von Hagen, *War in a European Borderland: Occupations and Occupation Plans in Galicia and Ukraine, 1914–1918* (Seattle: University of Washington Press, 2007).
11. Risto Alapuro, *State and Revolution in Finland* (Berkeley: University of California Press, 1988), 177.
12. Adam Tooze, *The Deluge: The Great War and the Remaking of Global Order* (New York: Viking, 2014), xxxix.
13. N. S. Lar'kov, *Nachalo grazhdanskoi voiny v Sibiri: armiia i bor'ba za vlast'* (Tomsk: Tomskii gos. Universitet, 1995), 36.
14. State Archive of Perm' Oblast', ГАПО ф. Р-359, оп.1, д.2, л.77.

15. E. G. Gimpel'son, *Formirovanie sovetskoi politicheskoi systemy, 1917–1923gg.* (Moscow: Nauka, 1995), 26.
16. Vladimir N. Brovkin, *The Mensheviks after October: Socialist Opposition and the Rise of the Bolshevik Dictatorship* (Ithaca, NY: Cornell University Press, 1987), 134.
17. V. A. Koklov, 'Men'sheviki na vyborakh v gorodskie sovety tsentral'noi Rossii vesnoi 1918g', in *Men'sheviki i men'shevizm: sbornik statei* (Moscow: Izd-vo Tip. Novosti 1998), 44–68, (51).
18. Koklov, 'Men'sheviki', in *Men'sheviki i men'shevizm*, 49.
19. A. F. Zhukov, *Ideino-politicheskii krakh eserovskogo maksimalizma* (Leningrad: Izd-vo Leningradskogo universiteta, 1979), 124.
20. Gimpel'son, *Formirovanie*, 42.
21. <http://www.hist.msu.ru/ER/Etext/DEKRET/18-06-14.htm>.
22. The following section draws on: Jonathan D. Smele, *The 'Russian' Civil Wars, 1916–1926* (London: Hurst, 2016); Evan Mawdsley, *The Russian Civil War* (New York: Pegasus, 2005); W. Bruce Lincoln, *Red Victory: A History of the Russian Civil War* (New York: Simon and Schuster, 1989).
23. Krivosheev (ed.), *Rossiia i SSSR v voinakh XX veka.*
24. *Naselenie Rossii v XX veke*, vol. 1, 148.
25. Joshua Sanborn, 'The Genesis of Russian Warlordism: Violence and Governance during the First World War and the Civil War', *Contemporary European History*, 19 (2010), 195–213.
26. Geoffrey Swain, *Russia's Civil War* (2nd edn) (Stroud: History Press, 2008).
27. P. N. Vrangel', *Zapiski (noiabr' 1916–noiabr 1920)* (2 vols), vol. 1 (Moscow: Kosmos, 1991), 100.
28. Peter Kenez, *Civil War in South Russia, 1918: The First Year of the Volunteer Army* (Berkeley: University of California Press, 1971).
29. Mark von Hagen, *Soldiers in the Proletarian Dictatorship: The Red Army and the Soviet Socialist State, 1917–1930* (Ithaca, NY: Cornell University Press, 1990); Francesco Benvenuti, *The Bolsheviks and the Red Army, 1918–1922* (Cambridge: Cambridge University Press, 1988).
30. V. Ia. Grosul, 'Krasnye generaly grazhdanskoi voiny', *Rossiiskaia istoriia*, 4 (2011), 139–54.
31. A. Lunacharskii, 'Revolutionary Silhouettes' (1923), <https://www.marxists.org/archive/lunachar/works/silhouet/trotsky.htm>.
32. Eduard Dune, *Notes of a Red Guard*, trans. and ed. Diane P. Koenker and S. A. Smith (Urbana: University of Illinois Press, 1993).
33. Richard Pipes, *The Russian Revolution* (New York: Knopf, 1990), 770.
34. Dobrovol'skii, 'Partiia sotsialistov-revoliutsionerov', ch. 4, section 2.
35. Yanni Kotsonis, 'Arkhangel'sk, 1918: Regionalism and Populism in the Russian Civil War', *Russian Review*, 51:4 (1992), 526–44; Liudmila G. Novikova, 'Northerners into Whites: Popular Participation in the Counter-Revolution in Arkhangel'sk Province, Summer–Autumn 1918', *Europe-Asia Studies*, 60:2 (2008), 277–93.
36. A. G. Kavtaradze, *Voennye spetsialisty na sluzhbe Respubliki sovetov 1917–1920gg.* (Moscow: Nauka, 1988).

37. G. A. Trukan, *Put' k totalitarizmu, 1917–1929gg.* (Moscow: Nauka, 1994), 61.
38. S. Karpenko, 'The White Dictatorships': Bureaucracy in the South of Russia: Social Structure, Living Conditions, and Performance (1918–1920)', *Soviet and Post-Soviet Review*, 37:1 (2010), 84–96.
39. Peter Kenez, *Civil War in South Russia, 1919–1920: The Defeat of the Whites* (Berkeley: University of California Press, 1977), 88–93, 282.
40. Orlando Figes, 'The Red Army and Mass Mobilization during the Russian Civil War', *Past and Present*, 129 (1990), 168–211; Sanborn, *Drafting the Russian Nation*.
41. Kavtaradze, *Voennye spetsialisty*, 175–8.
42. Norman G. O. Pereira, *White Siberia: The Politics of Civil War* (Montreal: McGill-Queen's University Press, 1996).
43. Jonathan D. Smele, *Historical Dictionary of the 'Russian' Civil Wars, 1916–1926* (2 vols) (Lanham, MD: Rowman and Littlefield, 2015), 1303.
44. Figes, *People's Tragedy*, 699.
45. Victoria E. Bonnell, *Iconography of Power: Soviet Political Posters under Lenin and Stalin* (Berkeley: University of California Press, 1999), 5.
46. Richard Pipes, *The Formation of the Soviet Union: Communism and Nationalism, 1917–1923* (Cambridge, MA: Harvard University Press, 1954); Jeremy Smith, *The Bolsheviks and the National Question, 1917–1923* (New York: St Martin's, 1999).
47. *Izvestiia*, 11, 16 Jan. 1918, 3; *Izvestiia*, 12, 17 Jan. 1918, 2.
48. Alfred E. Senn, *The Emergence of Modern Lithuania* (New York: Columbia University Press, 1959).
49. O. V. Budnitskii, *Rossiiskie evrei mezhdu krasnymi i belymi (1917–1920)* (Moscow: ROSSPEN, 2006), 275–6; Oleg Budnitskii, 'Shots in the Back: On the Origin of the Anti-Jewish Pogroms of 1918–1921', in E. M Avrutin and H. Murav (eds), *Jews in the East European Borderlands* (Boston: Academic Studies Press, 2012), 187–210.
50. <http://www.orenport.ru/docs/82/futor/index.html>.
51. Peter Holquist, *Making War, Forging Revolution: Russia's Continuum of Crisis, 1914–1921* (Cambridge, MA: Harvard University Press, 2002).
52. Adeeb Khalid, 'Nationalizing the Revolution in Central Asia: The Transformation of Jadidism, 1917–1920', in Ronald G. Suny and Terry Martin (eds), *A State of Nations: Empire and Nation-Making in the Age of Lenin and Stalin* (Oxford: Oxford University Press, 2001), 145–64.
53. Marco Buttino, *La Rivoluzione capovolta: L'Asia centrale tra il crollo dell'impero Zarista e la formazione dell'URSS* (Naples: L'ancora del Mediterraneo, 2003).
54. Daniel E. Schafer, 'Local Politics and the Birth of the Republic of Bashkortostan, 1919–1920', in Suny and Martin (eds), *A State of Nations*, 165–90.
55. M. A. Persits, 'Vostochnye internatsionalisty v Rossii i nekotorye voprosy natsional'no-osvoboditel'nogo dvizheniia (1918–iul' 1920)', *Komintern i Vostok: bor'ba za leninskuiu strategiiu i taktiku v natsional'no-osvoboditel'nom dvizhenii* (Moscow: Nauka, 1969), 53–109 (96).
56. 'Biuro Sekretariata TsK RKP (iiun'1923g.)', in *Tainy natsional'noi politiki TsK RKP: stenograficheskii otchet sekretnogo IV soveshchaniia TsK RKP 1923g.* (Moscow: INSAN, 1992), 74; <http://historystudies.org/2012/07/landa-r-g-mirsaid-sultan-galiev/>.

57. James Ryan, *Lenin's Terror: The Ideological Origins of Early Soviet State Violence* (London: Routledge, 2012).
58. Latsis, 'Pravda of krasnom terrore', *Izvestiia*, 26, 6 Feb. 1920, 1.
59. Michael Melancon, 'Revolutionary Culture in the Early Soviet Republic: Communist Executive Committees versus the Cheka', *Jahrbücher für Geschichte Osteuropas*, 57:1 (2009), 1–22 (9).
60. George Leggett, *The Cheka: Lenin's Political Police: The All-Russian Extraordinary Commission for Combatting Counter-Revolution and Sabotage, 1917–1922* (Oxford: Clarendon Press, 1981), 467.
61. The use of torture by the Cheka was hinted at in the press. See the complaint by a party member who had fallen into the clutches of the Cheka in Moscow. *Izvestiia*, 18, 26 Jan. 1919, 2.
62. I. N. Kamardin, 'Rabochii protest v Povolzh'e v 1919–1920gg'. <http://www.istprof.atlabs.ru/2306.html>.
63. <http://www.astrakhan.ru/history/read/87/>; <http://mybiblioteka.su/1-68247.html>.
64. A. G. Tepliakov, 'Chekisty Kryma v nachale 1920-kh gg', *Voprosy istorii*, 11, Nov. 2015, 139–45.
65. <https://ru.wikipedia.org/wiki/Муравьёв,_Михаил_Артемьевич>.
66. Dietrich Beyrau, 'Brutalization Revisited: The Case of Russia', *Journal of Contemporary History*, 50:1 (2015), 15–37.
67. Martin Conway and Robert Gerwarth, 'Revolution and Counter-Revolution', in Donald Bloxham and Robert Gerwarth (eds), *Political Violence in Twentieth-Century Europe* (Cambridge: Cambridge University Press, 2011), 140–76 (141). Stathis Kalyvas, *The Logic of Violence in Civil War* (Cambridge University Press, 2006), 365–87.
68. Hoffmann and Kotsonis (eds), *Russian Modernity*; Peter Holquist, 'Violent Russia, Deadly Marxism? Russia in the Epoch of Violence, 1905–21', *Kritika*, 4:3 (2003), 627–52.
69. Holquist, *Making War*, ch. 6.
70. Cited in Mawdsley, *Russian Civil War*, 67.
71. Smele, *Historical Dictionary*, 138–41, 1142–3, 92. I am grateful to Erik Landis for drawing my attention to Marat Khairulin, 'Boi za Kazan' (avgust–sentiabr' 1918g.). Khronika deistvii aviatsii', <http://www.retroplan.ru/encyclopaedia.html?sobi2Task=sobi2Details&sobi2Id=764>.
72. Vladimir N. Brovkin, *Behind the Front Lines of the Civil War: Political Parties and Social Movements in Russia, 1918–1922* (Princeton, NJ: Princeton University Press, 1994).
73. Scott B. Smith, *Captives of Revolution: The Socialist Revolutionaries and the Bolshevik Dictatorship, 1918–1923* (Pittsburgh: University of Pittsburgh Press, 2011).
74. Z. Galili and A. Nenarokov (eds), *Men'sheviki v 1918 godu* (Moscow: ROSSPEN, 1999).
75. D. B. Pavlov, *Bol'shevistskaia diktatura protiv sotsialistov i anarkhistov 1917—seredina 1950-kh godov* (Moscow: ROSSPEN, 1999), 63.
76. Brovkin, *Behind the Front Lines*, 268.
77. Gimpel'son, *Formirovanie*, 78.
78. *Sovetskaia derevnia glazami VChK-OGPU*, vol. 1:, *1918–22: Dokumenty i materialy* (Moscow: ROSSPEN, 1998), 32.

79. A. I. Chernykh, *Stanovlenie Rossii Sovetskoi: 20-e gody v zerkale sotsiologii* (Moscow: Pamiatniki Istoricheskoi Mysli, 1998), 262; Richard Sakwa, *Soviet Communists in Power: A Study of Moscow during the Civil War, 1918–21* (New York: St Martin's, 1988).
80. State Archive of Perm' Oblast', ГАПО ф. 201, оп.1, д.11, л.7.
81. Robert V. Daniels, *The Conscience of the Revolution: Communist Opposition in Soviet Russia* (Cambridge, MA: Harvard University Press, 1960).
82. James Harris, 'Stalin as General Secretary: The Appointments Process and the Nature of Stalin's Power', in Sarah Davies and James Harris (eds), *Stalin: A New History* (Cambridge: Cambridge University Press, 2005), 66.
83. G. Gimpel'son, *Sovetskie upravlentsy, 1917–1920gg.* (Moscow: RAN, 1998), 167.
84. I. S. Rat'kovskii and M. V. Khodiakov, *Istoriia sovetskoi Rossii* (St Petersburg: Lan', 1999), 54.
85. S. A. Pavliuchenkov, *Voennyi kommunizm v Rossii: vlast' i massy* (Moscow: RKT-Istoriia, 1997), 189.
86. I. V. Pavlova, *Stalinizm: Stanovlenie mekhanizma vlasti* (Novosibirsk: Sibirskii khronograf, 1993), 50.
87. Gimpel'son, *Sovetskie upravlentsy*, 203.
88. Bertram D. Wolfe, *Strange Communists I Have Known* (London: George Allen and Unwin, 1966), 88.
89. Balabanoff, *Impressions of Lenin*, 102–3.
90. <https://www.marxists.org/archive/kautsky/1919/terrcomm/ch08b.htm#s6>.
91. <https://www.marxists.org/archive/trotsky/1920/terrcomm/ch02.htm>.
92. Service, *Lenin: A Biography*, 299; V. I. Lenin, 'Second All-Russian Congress of Miners', 23 Jan. 1921, <https://www.marxists.org/archive/lenin/works/1921/jan/23.htm>.

Chapter 5

1. Diane Koenker, William Rosenberg, and Ronald Suny (eds), *Party, State and Society in the Russian Civil War* (Bloomington: Indiana University Press, 1989).
2. <http://statehistory.ru/1439/Finansovaya-politika-Sovetskoy-Rossii-v-1917-1921-gg>.
3. Mauricio Borrero, *Hungry Moscow: Scarcity and Urban Society in the Russian Civil War, 1917–1920* (New York: Peter Lang, 2003).
4. A. A. Il'iukhov, *Zhizn' v epokhu peremen: material'noe polozhenie gorodskikh zhitelei v gody revoliutsii i grazhdanskoi voiny* (Moscow: ROSSPEN, 2007), 36.
5. Viktor Shklovskii, *A Sentimental Journey* (Ithaca, NY: Cornell University Press, 1984), 175.
6. Il'iukhov, *Zhizn'*, 169–70.
7. Il'iukhov, *Zhizn'*, 83.
8. Il'iukhov, *Zhizn'*, 178–9.
9. Cited in Il'iukhov, *Zhizn'*, 168.
10. Silvana Malle, *The Economic Organization of War Communism 1918–1921* (Cambridge: Cambridge University Press, 1985).
11. V. I. Lenin, *The Impending Catastrophe and How to Combat It*, <https://www.marxists.org/archive/lenin/works/1917/ichtci/>.

12. Smith, *Red Petrograd*, 224.
13. Ronald Kowalski, *The Bolshevik Party in Conflict: The Left Communist Opposition of 1918* (Basingstoke: Macmillan, 1991).
14. <http://histerl.ru/sovetskie_soyz/obrazovanie/promyshlennost.htm>.
15. Thomas F. Remington, *Building Socialism in Bolshevik Russia: Ideology and Industrial Organization, 1917–1921* (Pittsburgh: University of Pittsburgh Press, 1984).
16. The following is based on Lars T. Lih, *Bread and Authority in Russia, 1914–1921* (Berkeley: University of California Press, 1990); V. V. Kabanov, *Krest'ianskoe khoziaistvo v usloviiakh 'Voennogo Kommunizma'* (Moscow: Nauka, 1988).
17. S. V. Iarov, *Krest'ianin kak politik. Krest'ianstvo Severo-Zapada Rossii v 1918–1919gg. Politicheskoe myshlenie i massovyi protest* (St Petersburg: RAN, 1999), 25.
18. Iarov, *Krest'ianin kak politik*, 23.
19. Kabanov, *Krest'ianskoe khoziaistvo*, 181.
20. Mary McAuley, *Bread and Justice: State and Society in Petrograd, 1917–1922* (Oxford: Clarendon Press, 1991).
21. Il'iukhov, *Zhizn'*, 186.
22. V. I. Lenin, 'Declaration of the Rights of the Working and Exploited People', <https://www.marxists.org/archive/lenin/works/1918/jan/03.htm>.
23. Il'iukhov, *Zhizn'*, 47.
24. Steven G. Marks, 'The Russian Experience of Money, 1914–1924', in Frame et al. (eds), *Russian Culture in War and Revolution*, 121–50 (136).
25. G. E. Kornilov, 'Formirovanie sistemy prodovol'stvennoi bezopasnosti naseleniia Rossii v pervoi polovine XX veka', *Rossiiskaia istoriia*, 3 (2011), 91–101 (95).
26. L. Futorianskii and V. Labuzov, *Is istorii Orenburgskogo kraia v period vosstanovleniia, 1921–27gg.* (Orenburg: Orenburgskii gos. universitet, 1998), 16.
27. H. H. Fisher, *The Famine in Soviet Russia, 1919–23* (Stanford, CA: Stanford University Press, 1927), 292–3.
28. Peter H. Juviler, *Revolutionary Law and Order: Politics and Social Change in the USSR* (New York: Free Press, 1976), 18.
29. *Zemlia*, 17 June 1917, 1; *Krasnaia gazeta*, 15 March 1918, 2.
30. *Moskovskii Voenno-Revoliutsionnyi komitet, oktiabr'-noiabr' 1917 goda* (Moscow: Moskovskii rabochii, 1968), 48.
31. V. V. Nikulin, 'Spetsifika gosudarstvenno-pravovoi politiki v period grazhdanskoi voiny v sovetskoi Rossii', *Genesis: istoricheskie issledovaniia*, 4 (2013), <http://e-notabene.ru/hr/article_324.html>.
32. A. L. Litvin, *Krasnyi terror i belyi terror, 1918–22gg.* (Kazan': Tatarskoe gazetno-zhurnal'noe izd-vo, 1995), 27.
33. <http://www.hist.msu.ru/ER/Etext/DEKRET/o_sude1.htm>.
34. Matthew Rendle, 'Revolutionary Tribunals and the Origins of Terror in Early Soviet Russia', *Historical Research*, 84:226 (2011), 693–721.
35. Peter H. Solomon, *Soviet Criminal Justice under Stalin* (Cambridge: Cambridge University Press 1996), 22.
36. Nikulin, 'Spetsifika', <http://e-notabene.ru/hr/article_324.html>.

37. *Moskovskii Komsomolets*, 13 July 1996, 8.
38. *Golos naroda: pis'ma i otkliki riadovykh sovetskikh grazhdan o sobytiiakh 1918–1932gg.* (Moscow: ROSSPEN, 1998), 86.
39. I. I. Reshchikov, *Kaluzhskaia derevnia v 1923g.* (Kaluga: n.p., 1925).
40. William B. Husband, *Revolution in the Factory: The Birth of the Soviet Textile Industry, 1917–20* (Oxford: Oxford University Press, 1990), 94.
41. V. V. Kanishchev, 'Prisposoblenie radi vyzhivaniia: meshchanskoe bytie epokhi "Voennogo kommunizma"', in P. V. Volobuev (ed.), *Revoliutsiia i chelovek: byt, nravy, povedenie, moral'* (Moscow: RAN, 1997).
42. T. M. Smirnova, '"Byvshie". Shtrikhi k sotsial'noi politike sovetskoi vlasti', *Otechestvennaia istoriia*, 2 (2000), 37–48.
43. James C. McClelland, 'The Professoriate in the Russian Civil War', in Koenker, Rosenberg, and Suny (eds), *Party, State and Society*, 243–65; Jane Burbank, 'The Intelligentsia', in Acton et al. (eds), *Critical Companion to the Russian Revolution*, 515–28.
44. A. T. Grechaninov, *Moia zhizn'* (New York: Novyi Zhurnal, 1954).
45. Mikhail Beizer, *Evrei Leningrada, 1917–1939: Natsional'naia zhizn' i sovetizatsiia* (Moscow: Mosty kul'tury, 1999), 73.
46. Christopher Read, *Culture and Power in Revolutionary Russia: The Intelligentsia and the Transition from Tsarism to Communism* (Basingstoke: Macmillan, 1990), 69.
47. Isabel A. Tirado, *Young Guard! The Communist Youth League, Petrograd, 1917–1920* (New York: Greenwood Press, 1988), 177.
48. V. I. Lenin, 'The Tasks of the Youth Leagues', <https://www.marxists.org/archive/lenin/works/1920/oct/02.htm>.
49. Anne E. Gorsuch, *Youth in Revolutionary Russia: Enthusiasts, Bohemians and Delinquents* (Bloomington: Indiana University Press, 2000), 42.
50. *Iunyi Proletarii*, 16, 25 Nov. 1919, 5.
51. M. I. Odintsov, *Rossiiskaia tserkov' v gody revoliutsii, 1917–1918: sbornik* (Moscow: Krutitskoe patriarshee podvor'e, 1995).
52. *Izvestiia*, 186, 30 Aug. 1918.
53. Curtiss, *The Russian Church*, 83–4.
54. M. G. Nechaev, *Tserkov' na Urale v period velikikh potriasasenii: 1917–1922* (Perm': Ural'skii gos. universitet, 2004), 204.
55. Dmitrii Sokolov, 'Russkaia Pravoslavnaia Tserkov' v period gonenii (1917–1937gg.)', <http://www.rusk.ru/st.php?idar=112187.>.
56. Tver' Documentation Centre for Modern History: Тверской центр документации новейшей истории, ф.1, оп.1, д.119, лл.21–2.
57. S. G. Strumilin, 'Obshchii obzor Severnoi oblasti', *Materialy po statistike truda Severnoi oblasti*, vol. 1 (Petrograd, 1918), 18–19.
58. Diane P. Koenker, 'Urbanization and Deurbanization in the Russian Revolution', in Koenker, Rosenberg, and Suny (eds), *Party, State and Society*, 81–104.
59. V. Iu. Cherniaev et al. (eds.), *Piterskie rabochie i 'diktatura proletariata', oktiabr' 1917–1929: ekonomicheskie konflikty, politicheskii protest* (St Petersburg: BLITS, 2000), 13.

60. Sheila Fitzpatrick, *The Cultural Front: Power and Culture in Revolutionary Russia* (Ithaca, NY: Cornell University Press, 1992), 26.
61. Jonathan Aves, *Workers against Lenin: Labour Protest and the Bolshevik Dictatorship* (London and New York: Tauris, 1996), 57.
62. David Priestland, *Stalinism and the Politics of Mobilization* (Oxford: Oxford University Press, 2007), ch. 1.
63. D. O. Churakov, *Revoliutsiia, gosudarstvo, rabochii protest: formy, dinamika i priroda massovykh vystuplenii rabochikh v sovetskoi Rossii, 1917–1918gg.* (Moscow: Rossiiskaia politicheskaia entsiklopediia, 2004).
64. V. A. Koklov, 'Men'sheviki na vyborakh v gorodskie sovety tsentral'noi Rossii vesnoi 1918g', in *Men'sheviki i men'shevizm: sbornik statei* (Moscow: Izd-vo Tip. Novosti, 1998), 52.
65. Iarov, *Gorozhanin kak politik*, 24; Brovkin, *Behind the Front Lines*, 161.
66. Pavliuchenkov, *Voennyi kommunizm v Rossii*, 146.
67. Jon Smele, *Civil War in Siberia: the Anti-Bolshevik Government of Admiral Kolchak, 1918–1920* (Cambridge: Cambridge University Press, 1996), 337, 609.
68. Stephen Wheatcroft, 'Soviet Statistics of Nutrition and Mortality during Times of Famine', *Cahiers du monde russe*, 38:4 (1997), 529; Pavliuchenkov, *Voennyi kommunizm v Rossii*, 146.
69. B. N. Kazantsev, 'Materialy gosudarstvennykh, partiinykh i profsoiuznykh organov o vystupleniiakh rabochikh na predpriiatiakh Sovetskoi Rossii v 1918–28gg.', in Iu. I. Kir'ianov, W. Rosenberg, and A. N. Sakharov (eds), *Trudovye konflikty v sovetskoi Rossii 1918–1929gg.* (Moscow: Editorial URSS, 1998), 38–66 (48).
70. Iarov, *Gorozhanin kak politik*, 49.
71. Pavliuchenkov, *Voennyi kommunizm*, 157.
72. Cherniaev et al. (eds), *Piterskie rabochie*, 177–83; *Krasnaia gazeta*, 15 March 1919, 2.
73. Cherniaev et al. (eds), *Piterskie rabochie*, 18.
74. Aves, *Workers against Lenin*, 24.
75. Cherniaev et al. (eds), *Piterskie rabochie*, 274.
76. A. Vyshinskii, 'Uroki odnoi konferentsii', *Pravda*, 8 Feb. 1921, 1; Simon Pirani, *The Russian Revolution in Retreat, 1920–23: Soviet Workers and the New Economic Policy* (London: Routledge, 2008).
77. The following draws on Erik Landis, *Bandits and Partisans: The Antonov Movement in the Russian Civil War* (Pittsburgh: University of Pittsburgh Press, 2008).
78. V. V. Kondrashin, *Krest'ianskaia vandeia v Povolzh'e 1918-21gg.* (Moscow: Ianus-K, 2001), 40.
79. Pavliuchenkov, *Voennyi kommunizm*, 129.
80. I. V. Shvedov and V. S. Kobzov, 'Revoliutsionnye komitety Urala v gody grazhdanskoi voiny (istoriko-pravovoi aspekt)', *Problemy pravy*, 5:43 (2013), 199–205 (202).
81. Iarov, *Krest'ianin kak politik*, 62.
82. Landis, *Bandits*, 316.
83. <http://www.tstu.ru/win/kultur/other/antonov/pril1.htm>.
84. V. V. Moskovkin, 'Vosstanie krest'ian v Zapadnoi Sibiri v 1921 godu',*Voprosy Istorii*, 6 (1998), 46–64. For a fierce critique of this, see Vladimir I. Shishkin, 'Zapadno-Sibirskii

miatezh 1921 goda: dostizheniia i iskazheniia rossiiskoi istoriografii', *Acta Slavica Iaponica*, 17 (2000), 100–29.

85. Pavliuchenkov, *Voennyi kommunizm*, 136.
86. Paul Avrich, *Kronstadt, 1921* (Princeton, NJ: Princeton University Press, 1970); Israel Getzler, *Kronstadt, 1917–1921: The Fate of Soviet Democracy* (Cambridge: Cambridge University Press, 1983).
87. V. P. Naumov and A. A. Kosakovskii (eds), *Kronshtadt 1921: Dokumenty* (Moscow: Rossiia XX vek, 1997), 60.
88. See Russian Wikipedia entry for Дело Таганцева.
89. Barbara C. Allen, *Alexander Shlyapnikov, 1885–1938: Life of an Old Bolshevik* (Leiden: Brill, 2015), 245.
90. Gimpel'son, *Formirovanie*, 193.
91. Gimpel'son, *Sovetskie upravlentsy*, 171.
92. E. A. Sikorskii, 'Sovetskaia sistema politicheskogo kontrolia nad naseleniem v 1918–1920 godakh', *Voprosy Istorii*, 5 (1998), 91–100 (98).

Chapter 6

1. The great work on the history of these years is E. H. Carr's fourteen-volume *A History of Soviet Russia*, which covers the period from 1917 to 1929. It falls into four parts: *The Bolshevik Revolution, 1917–23* (3 vols, 1950–3); *The Interregnum, 1923–1924* (1954); *Socialism in One Country, 1924–26* (4 vols, 1958–63); *Foundations of a Planned Economy, 1926–1929* (6 vols, 1969–78, the first two co-authored with R. W. Davies).
2. V. P. Danilov, 'Vvedenie', *Kak lomali NEP: Stenogrammy plenumov TsK VKP(b), 1928–1929gg.*, 5 vols (Moscow: Materik, 2000), vol. 1, 5–13 (6).
3. Mark Harrison, 'Prices in the Politburo 1927: Market Equilibrium versus the Use of Force', in Paul R. Gregory and Norman Naimark (eds), *The Lost Politburo Transcripts* (New Haven, CT: Yale University Press, 2008), 224–46.
4. V.I. Lenin, 'On Cooperation', <https://www.marxists.org/archive/lenin/works/1923/jan/06.htm>.
5. Moshe Lewin, *The Making of the Soviet System* (London: Methuen, 1985).
6. Pirani, *Russian Revolution in Retreat.*
7. L. N. Liutov, *Obrechennaia reforma: promyshlennost' Rossii v epokhu NEPa* (Ul'ianovsk: Ul'ianovskii gos. universitet, 2002), 17.
8. Danilov, 'Vvedenie', 6.
9. Mark Harrison, 'The Peasantry and Industrialization', in Davies (ed.), *From Tsarism*, 110.
10. Wheatcroft, 'Agriculture', in Davies (ed.), *From Tsarism*, 98.
11. Harrison, 'The Peasantry', 113.
12. Harrison, 'The Peasantry', 110.
13. E. H. Carr and R. W. Davies, *Foundations of a Planned Economy, 1926–1929*, vol. 1 (London: Macmillan, 1969), 971.
14. Danilov, 'Vvedenie', 9.

15. *Tragediia sovetskoi derevni. Kollektivizatsiia i raskulachivanie. Dokumentyi i materialy*, vol. 1 (Moscow: Rossiiskaia Polit. Entsiklopediia, 1999), 37–8; James Hughes, *Stalin, Siberia and the Crisis of the New Economic Policy* (Cambridge: Cambridge University Press, 1991), 126–33.
16. V. P. Danilov and O. V. Khlevniuk, 'Aprel'skii plenum 1928g.', in *Kak lomali NEP: Stenogrammy plenumov TsK VKP(b), 1928–1929gg.*, 5 vols (Moscow: Materik, 2000), vol. 1, 15–33 (29).
17. V. P. Danilov, *Rural Russia under the New Regime* (Bloomington: Indiana University Press, 1988), 269.
18. Danilov, *Rural Russia*, 171.
19. James W. Heinzen, *Inventing a Soviet Countryside: State Power and the Transformation of Rural Russia, 1917–1929* (Pittsburgh: University of Pittsburgh Press, 2004).
20. Roger Pethybridge, *The Social Prelude to Stalinism* (Basingstoke: London, 1974), 226.
21. K. B. Litvak, 'Zhizn' krest'ianina 20-kh godov: sovremennye mify i istoricheskie realii', in *NEP: Priobreteniia i poteri* (Moscow: Nauka, 1994), 186–202.
22. R. W. Davies, 'Introduction', in Davies (ed.), *From Tsarism*, 13.
23. Davies, 'Introduction', in Davies (ed.), *From Tsarism*, 5.
24. M. M. Gorinov, 'Sovetskaia istoriia 1920–30-kh godov: ot mifov k real'nosti', in *Istoricheskie issledovaniia v Rossii: Tendentsii poslednikh let* (Moscow: AIRO-XX, 1996).
25. Mark Harrison, 'National Income', in and Davies et al. (eds), *Economic Transformation*, 38–56, 42.
26. Lewis Siegelbaum, *Soviet State and Society between Revolutions, 1918–29* (Cambridge: Cambridge University Press, 1992), 110.
27. Cited in Steve Smith, 'Taylorism Rules OK? Bolshevism, Taylorism and the Technical Intelligentsia: The Soviet Union, 1917–41', *Radical Science Journal*, 13 (1983), 3–27; Mark R. Beissinger, *Scientific Management, Socialist Discipline and Soviet Power* (London: I. B. Tauris, 1988).
28. Diane P. Koenker, 'Factory Tales: Narratives of Industrial Relations in the Transition to NEP', *Russian Review*, 55:3 (1996), 384–411 (386).
29. *Golos naroda*, 214.
30. Olga Velikanova, *Popular Perceptions of Soviet Politics in the 1920s* (Basingstoke: Palgrave, 2013), 13.
31. Chris Ward, *Russia's Cotton Workers and the New Economic Policy: Shop-Floor Culture and State Policy, 1921–29* (Cambridge: Cambridge University Press, 1990).
32. Davies (ed.), *From Tsarism*, 186.
33. Siegelbaum, *Soviet State*, 204.
34. L. S. Gaponenko, *Vedushchaia rol' rabochego klassa v rekonstruktsii promyshlennosti SSSR* (Moscow: Akademiia obshchestvennykh nauk, 1973), 88.
35. J. D. Barber and R. W. Davies, 'Employment and Industrial Labour', in Davies et al. (eds), *Economic Transformation*, 81–105 (84).
36. Daniel Orlovsky, 'The Hidden Class: White-Collar Workers in the Soviet 1920s', in Lewis H. Siegelbaum and Ronald G. Suny (eds), *Making Workers Soviet: Power, Class and Identity* (Ithaca, NY: Cornell University Press, 1994), 220–52 (228).

37. Shkaratan, *Problemy*, 269.
38. Siegelbaum, *Soviet State*, 136.
39. Wendy Goldman, *Women at the Gates: Gender and Industry in Stalin's Russia* (Cambridge: Cambridge University Press, 2002), 12.
40. Barber and Davies, 'Employment', in Davies et al. (eds), *Economic Transformation*, 84.
41. Siegelbaum, *Soviet State*, 205.
42. Diane P. Koenker, 'Men against Women on the Shop Floor in Early Soviet Russia: Gender and Class in the Socialist Workplace', *American Historical Review*, 100:5 (1995), 1438–64 (1458).
43. Rebecca Spagnolo, 'Serving the Household, Asserting the Self: Urban Domestic Servant Activism, 1900–1917', in Christine D. Worobec (ed.), *The Human Tradition in Imperial Russia* (Lanham, MD: Rowman & Littlefield, 2009), 141–54 (143).
44. Rebecca Spagnolo, 'Service, Space and the Urban Domestic in 1920s Russia', in Christina Kiaer and Eric Naiman (eds), *Everyday Life in Early Soviet Russia: Taking the Revolution Inside* (Bloomington: Indiana University Press, 2006), 230–55.
45. Liutov, *Obrechennaia reforma*, 106.
46. Siegelbaum, *Soviet State*, 203.
47. Andrew Pospielovsky, 'Strikes during the NEP', *Revolutionary Russia*, 10:1 (1997), 1–34 (16).
48. Kir'ianov, Rosenberg, and Sakharov (eds), *Trudovye konflikty*, 23.
49. Liutov, *Obrechennaia reforma*, 124.
50. A. Iu. Livshin, *Obshchestvennye nastroeniia v Sovetskoi Rossii, 1917–1929gg.* (Moscow: Universitetskii gumanitarnyi litsei, 2004); L. N. Liutov, 'Nastroeniia rabochikh provintsii v gody nepa', *Rossiiskaia istoriia*, 4 (2007), 65–74.
51. Vladimir Brovkin, *Russia after Lenin: Politics, Culture and Society* (London: Routledge, 1998), 186.
52. Gimpel'son, *Formirovanie*, 168.
53. Liutov, *Obrechennaia reforma*, 133.
54. V. P. Vilkova (ed.), *VKP(b): vnutripartiinaia bor'ba v dvadtsatye gody: dokumenty i materialy, 1923g.* (Moscow: ROSSPEN, 2004).
55. <https://www.marxists.org/history/ussr/government/party-congress/10th/16.htm>.
56. Gimpel'son, *Formirovanie*, 177.
57. Moshe Lewin, *Lenin's Last Struggle* (London: Faber, 1969).
58. For an interesting interpretation of the inner-party conflict that sees it as rooted in an underlying difference between 'revivalist' and 'technicist' types of Bolshevism, see Priestland, *Stalinism*, ch. 2.
59. Richard B. Day, *Leon Trotsky and the Politics of Economic Isolation* (Cambridge: Cambridge University Press, 1973).
60. Stephen F. Cohen, *Bukharin and the Bolshevik Revolution: A Political Biography, 1888–1938* (New York: Knopf, 1973).
61. David R. Stone, *Hammer and Rifle: The Militarization of the Soviet Union 1926–1933* (Lawrence: University of Kansas Press, 2000).
62. G. L. Olekh, *Krovnye uzy: RKP(b) i ChK/GPU v pervoi polovine 1920-x godov: mekhanizm vzaimootnoshenii* (Novosibirsk: NGAVT 1999), 92–3.

63. Stephen Kotkin, *Stalin: Paradoxes of Power, 1878–1928* (London: Penguin, 2015), 432.
64. Harris, 'Stalin as General Secretary, in Davies and Harris (eds), *Stalin: A New History*, 63–82 (69).
65. Excellent biographies of Stalin include Robert Service, *Stalin: A Biography* (Basingstoke: Macmillan, 2004); Oleg V. Khlevniuk, *Stalin: New Biography of a Dictator* (New Haven, CT: Yale University Press, 2015).
66. I. V. Stalin, 'The October Revolution and the Tactics of the Russian Communists', <https://www.marxists.org/reference/archive/stalin/works/1924/12.htm>.
67. James Harris, 'Stalin and Stalinism', *The Oxford Handbook of Modern Russian History*, Oxford Handbooks Online,1–21 (6).
68. Alfred J. Rieber, 'Stalin as Georgian: The Formative Years', in Davies and Harris (eds), *Stalin: A New History*, 18–44.
69. E. A. Rees, *Political Thought from Machiavelli to Stalin* (Basingstoke: Palgrave, 2004), 222.
70. 'Stalin i krizis proletarskoi diktatury', <http://scepsis.net/library/id_941.html>.
71. R. W. Davies, *The Industrialization of Soviet Russia*, vol. 3: *The Soviet Economy in Turmoil* (Basingstoke: Palgrave, 1929), xxiii.
72. Heinzen says 70,000 were employed in the Commissariat of Agriculture by the end of the decade. Heinzen, *Inventing*, 2.
73. Michael Voslenskii, *Nomenklatura: The Soviet Ruling Class* (New York: Doubleday, 1984); Harris, 'Stalin as General Secretary', 69.
74. Shkaratan, *Problemy*, 272.
75. *Golos Naroda*, 199.
76. Graeme Gill, *Origins of the Stalinist Political System* (Cambridge: Cambridge University Press, 1990), 118.
77. Sheila Fitzpatrick, *Education and Social Mobility in the Soviet Union, 1921–1934* (Cambridge: Cambridge University Press, 1979).
78. E. A. Wood, *The Baba and the Comrade: Gender and Politics in Revolutionary Russia* (Bloomington: Indiana University Press, 1997).
79. Wendy Z. Goldman, *Women, the State and Revolution: Soviet Family Policy and Social Life, 1917–1936* (Cambridge: Cambridge University Press, 1993), 111.
80. Olekh, *Krovnye uzy*, 90.
81. *Golos naroda*, 152.
82. Nikita Petrov, 'Les Transformations du personnel des organes de sécurité soviétiques, 1922–1953', *Cahiers du monde russe*, 22:2 (2001), 375–96 (376).
83. S. A. Krasil'nikov, *Na izlomakh sotsial'noi struktury: marginaly v poslerevoliutsionnom rossiiskom obshchestve (1917—konets 1930-kh godov)* (Novosibirsk: NGU, 1998), table 4.
84. V. K. Vinogradov, 'Ob osobennostiakh informatsionnykh materialov OGPU kak istochnik po istorii sovetskogo obshchestva', in *'Sovershenno sekretno': Liubianka-Stalinu o polozhenii v strane (1922–1934)*, vol. 1, part 1: 1922–23 (Moscow: RAN, 2001), 31–76
85. Roger Pethybridge, *One Step Backwards, Two Steps Forward: Soviet Society and Politics in the New Economic Policy* (Oxford: Oxford University Press, 1990).
86. Solomon, *Soviet Criminal Justice*.

87. Neil B. Weissman, 'Local Power in the 1920s: Police and Administrative Reform', in Theodore Taranovski (ed.), *Reform in Modern Russian History* (Washington, DC: Woodrow Wilson Center and Cambridge University Press, 1995), 265–89.
88. Neil Weissman, 'Policing the NEP Countryside', in Sheila Fitzpatrick, A. Rabinowitch, and R. Stites (eds), *Russia in the Era of NEP* (Bloomington: Indiana University Press, 1991), 174–91 (177); R. S. Mulukaev and N. N. Kartashov, *Militsiia Rossii (1917–1993gg.)* (Orël: Oka, 1995), 43.
89. Joan Neuberger, *Hooliganism: Crime, Culture and Power in St Petersburg, 1900–1914* (Berkeley: University of California Press, 1993).
90. Tracy McDonald, *Face to the Village: The Riazan Countryside under Soviet Rule, 1921–1930* (Toronto: University of Toronto Press, 2011), 90.
91. David A. Newman, 'Criminal Strategies and Institutional Concerns in the Soviet Legal System: An Analysis of Criminal Appeals in Moscow Province, 1921–28', Ph.D. dissertation, UCLA (2013), 183.
92. Priestland, *Stalinism*, 150.
93. Velikanova, *Popular Perceptions*, 138.
94. T. V. Pankova-Kozochkina, 'Rabotniki sel'skikh sovetov 1902-kh godov: nomenklaturnye podkhody bol'shevikov i sotsial'nye trebovaniia krest'ianstva (na materialakh Iuga Rossii)', *Rossiiskaia istoriia*, 6 (2011), 136–46.
95. *Golos naroda*, 215.
96. Olga A. Narkiewicz, *The Making of the Soviet State Apparatus* (Manchester: Manchester University Press, 1970), 61.
97. I. N. Il'ina, *Obshchestvennye organizatsii Rossii v 1920-e gody* (Moscow: RAN, 2000), 72.
98. A. A. Kurënyshev, *Vserossiiskii krest'anskii soiuz, 1905–1930* (Moscow: AIRO-XX, 2004).
99. Velikanova, *Popular Perceptions*, 158.
100. McDonald, *Face to the Village*, 104–5.
101. Diane P. Koenker and Ronald D.Bachman (eds), *Revelations from the Russian Archives: Documents in English Translation* (Washington, DC: Library of Congress, 1997), 38.
102. Gill, *Origins*, 113.
103. M. Ia. Fenomenov, *Sovremennaia derevnia. Opyt kraevedcheskogo obsledovaniia odnoi derevni*, vol. 2 (Leningrad: Goz. izd-vo, 1925), 39.
104. Litvak, "Zhizn' krest'ianina', 194.
105. D. Kh. Ibragimova, *NEP i perestroika: massovoe soznanie sel'skogo naseleniia v usloviiakh perekhoda k rynku* (Moscow: Pamiatniki istoricheskoi mysli, 1997).
106. Litvak, 'Zhizn' krest'ianina', 194.
107. Tooze, *Deluge*, 11.
108. Alexander Vatlin and S. A. Smith, 'The Comintern', *Oxford Handbook of the History of Communism* (Oxford: Oxford University Press, 2014), ch. 10.
109. John Riddell (ed.), *To See the Dawn: Baku, 1920—First Congress of the Peoples of the East* (New York: Pathfinder, 1993), 45.
110. Riddell, *To See the Dawn*, 70.

111. H. G. Wells, *Russia in the Shadows* (New York: Doran, 1921), 96.
112. Stephen White, 'Communism and the East: The Baku Congress, 1920', *Slavic Review*, 33:3 (1974), 492–514 (501).
113. Riddell, *To See the Dawn*, 204–7.
114. E. H. Carr, *The Bolshevik Revolution*, vol. 2 (London: Macmillan 1952), 265.
115. S. A. Smith, *A Road is Made: Communism in Shanghai, 1920–1927* (Honolulu: University of Hawaii Press, 2000).
116. Jon Jacobson, *When the Soviet Union Entered World Politics* (Berkeley, CA: University of California Press, 1994), 50.
117. Velikanova, *Popular Perceptions*, ch. 1.
118. Lewin, *Lenin's Last Struggle*, ch. 4.
119. Francine Hirsch, *Empire of Nations: Ethnographic Knowledge and the Making of the Soviet Union* (Ithaca, NY: Cornell University, 2005), 229, 331.
120. Terry Martin, *The Affirmative Action Empire: Nations and Nationalism in the Soviet Union, 1923–1939* (Ithaca, NY: Cornell University Press, 2001).
121. Yuri Slezkine, 'The USSR as a Communal Apartment, or How a Socialist State Promoted Ethnic Particularism', *Slavic Review*, 53:2 (1994), 415.
122. Michael G. Smith, *Language and Power in the Creation of the USSR, 1917–1953* (Berlin: Mouton de Gruyter, 1998), 125, 134.

Chapter 7

1. On aspects of society and culture in NEP Russia see the two collections of essays: Fitzpatrick, Rabinowitch, and Stites (eds), *Russia in the Era of NEP*; Abbot Gleason, Peter Kenez, and Richard Stites (eds), *Bolshevik Culture: Experiment and Order in the Russian Revolution* (Bloomington: Indiana University Press, 1985).
2. Sheila Fitzpatrick, 'Ascribing Class: The Construction of Soviet Identity in Soviet Russia', in S. Fitzpatrick (ed.), *Stalinism: New Directions* (London: Routledge, 1999), 20–46.
3. *Naselenie Rossii v XX veke*, vol. 1, 149.
4. Shanin, *Awkward Class*.
5. Danilov, *Rural Russia*, 275.
6. Merl, 'Socio-economic Differentiation of the Peasantry', in Davies (ed.), *From Tsarism*, 47–65.
7. Moshe Lewin, *Russian Peasants and Soviet Power* (London: Allen and Unwin, 1968).
8. I. I. Klimin, *Rossiiskoe krest'ianstvo v gody novoi ekonomicheskoi politiki (1921–1927), chast' pervaia* (St Petersburg: Izd-do Politekhnicheskogo universiteta, 2007), 208.
9. *Golos naroda*, 152.
10. Alan M. Ball, *Russia's Last Capitalists: The Nepmen, 1921–1929* (Berkeley: University of California Press, 1987).
11. Daniel T. Orlovsky, 'The Antibureaucratic Campaign of the 1920s' in Taranovski (ed.), *Reform*, 290–315.
12. Krasil'nikov, *Na izlomakh sotsial'noi struktury*, table 1.

13. V. I. Tikhonov, V. S. Tiazhel'nikova, and I. F. Iushin, *Lishenie izbiratel'nykh prav v Moskve v 1920–1930-e gody* (Moscow: Mosgorarkhiv, 1998), 132.
14. Hoffman and Kotsonis (eds), *Russian Modernity*.
15. Susan Gross Solomon and John F. Hutchinson (eds), *Health and Society in Revolutionary Russia* (Bloomington: Indiana University Press, 1990).
16. A. Iu. Rozhkov, *V krugu sverstnikov: Zhiznennyi mir molodogo cheloveka v sovetskoi Rossii 1920-kh godov* (Krasnodar: OIPTs, 2002).
17. Neil B. Weissman, 'Origins of Soviet Health Administration: Narkomzdrav, 1918–1928', in Solomon and Hutchinson (eds), *Health and Society*, 97–120.
18. Neil Weissman, 'Prohibition and Alcohol Control in the USSR: The 1920s Campaign against Illegal Spirits', *Soviet Studies*, 38:3 (1986), 349–68.
19. James Riordan *Sport in Soviet Society: Development of Sport and Physical Education in Russia and the USSR* (Cambridge: Cambridge University Press, 1977).
20. Robert Edelman, *Serious Fun: A History of Spectator Sports in the USSR* (Oxford: Oxford University Press, 1993), 46.
21. *Smena*, 21 Aug. 1925, 5.
22. Larry E. Holmes, *The Kremlin and the Schoolhouse* (Bloomington: Indiana University Press, 1991).
23. Fitzpatrick, *Education and Social Mobility*, ch. 1.
24. For contrasting evaluations of experimentalism: V. L. Soskin, *Obshchee obrazovanie v sovetskoi Rossii: pervoe desiatiletie, chast' 2, 1923–1927gg.* (Novosibirsk: Novosibirskii gos. universitet, 1999); Balashov, *Shkola*.
25. William Partlett, 'Breaching Cultural Worlds with the Village School: Educational Visions, Local Initiative, and Rural Experience at S. T. Shatskii's Kaluga School System 1919–32', *Slavonic and East European Review*, 82:4 (2004), 847–85 (859).
26. Holmes, *The Kremlin*, 94.
27. Shkaratan, *Problemy*, 289.
28. Gimpel'son, *Sovetskie upravlentsy*; Chernykh, *Stanovlenie Rossii sovetskoi*.
29. E. O. Kabo, *Ocherki rabochego byta* (Moscow: Iz-do VTsSPS, 1926), 175.
30. Il'iukhov, *Zhizn'*, 151.
31. William J. Chase, *Workers, Society and the Soviet State: Labor and Life in Moscow, 1918–1929* (Urbana: University of Illinois Press, 1987), 185.
32. Gimpel'son, *Sovetskie upravlentsy*, 205.
33. Andrei Platonov, *Chevengur*, trans. Anthony Olcott (Ann Arbor, MI: Ardis, 1978), 135.
34. Victor Serge, *Memoirs of a Revolutionary* (Oxford: Oxford University Press, 1963), 198.
35. Vladimir Mayakovsky, 'Vziatochniki', <http://www.stihi-rus.ru/1/Mayakovskiy/7.htm>.
36. Karl Marx and Friedrich Engels, 'Communist Manifesto' (1848), <https://www.marxists.org/archive/marx/works/download/pdf/Manifesto.pdf>.
37. Richard Stites, *Revolutionary Dreams: Utopian Vision and Experimental Life in the Russian Revolution* (New York: Oxford University Press, 1989); Catriona Kelly and David Shepherd, *Russian Cultural Studies: An Introduction* (Oxford: Oxford University Press, 1998).

38. Alexander Bogdanov, *Red Star: The First Bolshevik Utopia*, trans. Charles Rougle (Bloomington: Indiana University Press, 1984); J. A. E. Curtis, *The Englishman from Lebedian: A Life of Evgeny Zamiatin* (Boston: Academic Studies Press, 2013).
39. Lenin, *State and Revolution*.
40. J. Bowlt and O. Matich (eds), *Laboratory of Dreams: The Russian Avant-Garde and Cultural Experiment* (Stanford, CA: Stanford University Press, 1996).
41. *The Great Utopia: The Russian and Soviet Avant-Garde, 1917–1932* (New York: Guggenheim Museum, 1992).
42. Mayakovsky, '150 million', in René Fülöp-Miller, *The Mind and Face of Bolshevism* (New York: Harper Torchbooks, 1965), 159.
43. E. A. Dobrenko and Marina Balina (eds), *The Cambridge Companion to 20th-Century Russian Literature* (Cambridge: Cambridge University Press, 2011); Robert A. Maguire, *Red Virgin Soil: Soviet Literature in the 1920s* (Princeton, NJ: Princeton University Press, 1968).
44. Richard Taylor, *The Politics of the Soviet Cinema, 1917–1929* (Cambridge: Cambridge University Press, 1979); Peter Kenez, *Cinema and Soviet Society, 1917–1953* (Cambridge: Cambridge University Press, 1992).
45. Lesley Chamberlain, *Lenin's Private War: The Voyage of the Philosophy Steamer and the Exile of the Intelligentsia* (London: St Martin's Press, 2007).
46. Il'ina, *Obshchestvennye organizatsii Rossii*, 32, 74.
47. T. M. Goriaeva (ed.), *Istoriia sovetskoi politicheskoi tsenzury: dokumenty i kommentarii* (Moscow: ROSSPEN, 1997), 444.
48. Goriaeva, *Istoriia*, 277, 430–2.
49. Michael David-Fox, *Revolution of the Mind: Higher Learning among the Bolsheviks, 1918–1929* (Ithaca, NY: Cornell University Press, 1997).
50. R. W. Davies and Maureen Perrie, 'Social Context', in Davies (ed.), *From Tsarism*, 36.
51. Christopher Read, *Culture and Power in Revolutionary Russia* (New York: St Martin's Press, 1990); Fitzpatrick, *The Cultural Front*.
52. Sheila Fitzpatrick, *Cultural Revolution in Russia, 1928–1931* (Bloomington: Indiana University Press, 1978).
53. Goldman, *Women, the State and Revolution*.
54. Barbara A. Engel, *Breaking the Ties that Bind: The Politics of Marital Strife in Late Imperial Russia* (Ithaca, NY: Cornell University Press, 2011), 6.
55. K. N. Samoilova, *Rabotnitsy v Rossiiskoi revoliutsii* (Petrograd: Gosizdat, 1920), 3.
56. Chernykh, *Stanovlenie Rossii sovetskoi*, 179.
57. Beatrice Farnsworth, *Aleksandra Kollontai: Socialism, Feminism and the Bolshevik Revolution* (Stanford, CA: Stanford University Press, 1980); Barbara E. Clements, *Bolshevik Feminist: The Life of Aleksandra Kollontai* (Bloomington: Indiana University Press, 1979).
58. Douglas Northrup, *Veiled Empire: Gender and Power in Stalinist Central Asia* (Ithaca, NY: Cornell University Press, 2004); Marianne Kamp, *The New Woman of Uzbekistan* (Seattle: Washington University Press, 2006), 162–78. Shoshana Keller, *To Moscow, Not Mecca: The Soviet Campaign against Islam in Central Asia, 1917–1941* (Westport, CT: Praeger, 2001).

59. Beatrice Penati, 'On the Local Origins of the Soviet Attack on the "Religious" Waqf in the Uzbek SSR (1927)', *Acta Slavonica Iaponica*, 36 (2015), 39–72.
60. Karen Petrone, 'Masculinity and Heroism in Imperial and Soviet Military-Patriotic Cultures', in B. E. Clements, Rebecca Friedman, and Dan Healey (eds), *Russian Masculinities in History and Culture* (Basingstoke: Palgrave, 2002), 172–93.
61. Victoria E. Bonnell, 'The Representation of Women in Early Soviet Political Art', *Russian Review*, 50 (1991), 267–88.
62. S. G. Strumilin, 'Biudzhet vremeni rabochikh v 1923–24gg.', in S. G. Strumilin, *Problemy ekonomiki truda* (Moscow: Nauka, 1982).
63. *Golos naroda*, 157.
64. Frances Bernstein, *The Dictatorship of Sex: Gender, Health, and Enlightenment in Revolutionary Russia, 1918–1931* (DeKalb: Northern Illinois University Press, 2007).
65. Eric Naiman, *Sex in Public: The Incarnation of Early Soviet Ideology* (Princeton, NJ: Princeton University Press, 1997), 92.
66. A. E. Gorsuch, *Youth in Revolutionary Russia* (Bloomington: Indiana University Press, 2000).
67. Catriona Kelly, *Children's World: Growing up in Russia, 1890–1991* (New Haven, CT: Yale University Press, 2007).
68. Lisa A. Kirschenbaum, *Small Comrades: Revolutionizing Childhood in Soviet Russia, 1917–1932* (London: RoutledgeFalmer, 2001).
69. Goldman, *Women, the State and Revolution*, 9.
70. Matthias Neumann, *The Communist Youth League and the Transformation of the Soviet Union* (London: Routledge, 2011), 3.
71. See Russian Wikipedia entry for: Взвейтесь кострами, синие ночи.
72. 'Kem ia khochu byt' *Pioner* 2 (1929).
73. Alan M. Ball, *And Now my Soul Is Hardened: Abandoned Children in Soviet Russia, 1918–1930* (London: University of California Press, 1994).
74. Goldman, *Women, the State and Revolution*, 326.
75. Neumann, *Communist Youth League*, 7; Isabel A. Tirado, 'The Revolution, Young Peasants, and the Komsomol's Anti-Religious Campaigns (1920–1928)', *Canadian-American Slavic Studies*, 26:1–3 (1999), 97–117 (97).
76. A. Zalkind, 'Kul'turnyi rost sovetskogo molodniaka', *Molodoi Bol'shevik*, 19–20 (1927).
77. Tirado, 'The Revolution', 105.
78. Gorsuch, *Youth in Revolutionary Russia*.
79. Vladimir Slepkov, 'Komsomol'skii zhargon i Komsomol'skii "obychai"', in A. Slepkov (ed.), *Byt i molodezh*, (2nd edn) (Moscow, 1926), 46–7.
80. *Krasnaia gazeta*, 19 Mar. 1918, 4.
81. Peter Kenez, *The Birth of the Propaganda State: Soviet Methods of Mass Mobilization, 1917–1929* (Cambridge: Cambridge University Press, 1985), 7.
82. State Archive of the Russian Federation: ГАРФ, ф.А-2313 оп. 4 д. 139, l. 47.
83. Elizabeth Wood, *Performing Justice: Agitation Trials in Early Soviet Russia* (Ithaca, NY: Cornell University Press, 2005).
84. Michael S. Gorham, *Speaking in Soviet Tongues: Language Culture and the Politics of Voice in Revolutionary Russia* (DeKalb: Northern Illinois University Press, 2003).

85. Figes, *Peasant Russia, Civil War.*
86. M. M. Bakhtin, *The Dialogic Imagination*, ed. Michael Holquist (Austin: University of Texas Press, 1981).
87. K. Selishchev, *Lazyk revoliutstonnoi epokhi: iz nabluzhdenii nad russkim iazykom poslednykh let, 1917–26* (Moscow, 1928).
88. Smith, *Language and Power*, 113.
89. Slepkov, 'Komsomol'sku zhargon', 46–7.
90. Aleksandr Rozhkov, 'Pochemu kuritsa povesilas': Narodnye ostroslovtsy o zhizni v "bol'shevizii"', *Rodina*, 10 (1999), 60–4.
91. G. F. Dobronozhenko, *VChK-OGPU o politicheskh nastroeniiakh severnogo krest'ianstva 1921–27 godov* (Syktyvkar: Syktyvkarskii gos. Universitet, 1995), 54.
92. A. V. Golubev, 'Sovetskoe obshchestvo i "voennye trevogi" 1920-kh godov', *Otechestvennaia istoriia*, 1 (2008), 36–58 (38).
93. Golubev, 'Sovetskoe obshchestvo', 50.
94. 'And he causeth all, both small and great, rich and poor, free and bond, to receive a mark in their right hand, or in their foreheads: and that no man might buy or sell, save he that had the mark, or the name of the beast, or the number of his name.' Revelation 13:16–17.
95. F. M. Putintsev, *Kulatskoe svetoprestavlenie* (Moscow: Bezbozbnik, 1930), 13, 25.
96. Zenovia A. Sochor, *Revolution and Culture: The Bogdanov–Lenin Controversy* (Ithaca, NY: Cornell University Press, 1988).
97. *Oktiabr'skaia revoliutsiia i fabzavkomy* (The October Revolution and the Factory Committees), (2 vols), vol. 2, ed. S. A. Smith (Millwood, NY: Kraus International Publications, 1983), 89.
98. Michael David-Fox, 'What is Cultural Revolution?', *Russian Review*, 58 (Apr. 1999), 181–201.
99. Ella Winter, *Red Virtue: Human Relationships in the New Russia* (London: Gollancz, 1933), 35.
100. Charles E. Clark, *Uprooting Otherness: The Literacy Campaign in NEP-Era Russia* (Selinsgrove, PA: Susquehanna University Press, 2000).
101. Charles E. Clark, 'Uprooting Otherness: Bolshevik Attempts to Refashion Rural Russia via the Reading Rooms of the 1920s', *Canadian Slavonic Papers*, 38:3–4 (1996), 305–29 (320).
102. N. Rosnitskii, *Litso derevni. Po materialam obsledovaniia 28 volostei i 32,730 krest'ianskikh khoziaistv Penzenskoi gubernii* (Leningrad: Gos. Izd-vo, 1926), 103.
103. Régine Robin, 'Popular Literature of the 1920s: Russian Peasants as Readers', in Fitzpatrick, Rabinowitch, and Stites (eds), *Russia in the Era of NEP*, 253–67, (256).
104. Robin, 'Popular Literature', 261.
105. Gorsuch, *Youth in Revolutionary Russia*, 19.
106. *Antireligioznik*, 10 (1926), 53.
107. N. B. Lebina, *Povsednevnaia zhizn' sovetskogo goroda: normy i anomalii: 1920–1930 gody* (St Petersburg: Neva, 1999), ch. 2, part 3.
108. Andy Willimott, *Living the Revolution: Urban Communes & Soviet Socialism, 1917–1932* (Oxford: Oxford University Press, 2016).

109. Hugh D. Hudson, *Blueprints and Blood: The Stalinization of Soviet Architecture, 1917–37* (Princeton: Princeton University Press, 1994).
110. Anatole Kopp, *Town and Revolution: Soviet Architecture and City Planning, 1917–1935* (London: Thames and Hudson, 1970).
111. Eric Aunoble, *Le Communisme tout de suite! Le mouvement des communes en Ukraine soviétique (1919–20)* (Paris: Les Nuits rouges, 2008).
112. S. A. Smith, 'The Social Meanings of Swearing: Workers and Bad Language in Late-Imperial and Early-Soviet Russia', *Past and Present*, 160 (1998), 167–202.
113. This and the statistics on baptisms and funerals are taken from N. S. Burmistrov, 'Religioznye obriady pri rozhdeniiakh, smertiakh, brakakh po statistichekim dannym administrativnykh otdelov Mossoveta', *Antireligioznik*, 6 (1929), 89–94.
114. *Golos naroda*, 170–2.
115. Catherine Merridale, *Night of Stone: Death and Memory in Russia* (London: Granta, 2000).
116. N. N. Kozlova, *Gorizonty povsednevnosti sovetskoi epokhi. Golosa iz khora* (Moscow: RAN, 1996), 128; Litvak, 'Zhizn' krest'ianina', 194.
117. V. P. Buldakov, *Krasnaia smuta: Priroda I posledstviia revoliutsionnogo nasiliia* (Moscow: ROSSPEN, 1997).
118. Koenker and Bachman (eds), *Revelations from the Russian Archives*, 456–8.
119. State Archive of the Russian Federation: ГАРФ, ф.Р-5407, оп.2, д.177, л.22.
120. <http://www.grad-kirsanov.ru/article.php?id=orthodox.11>.
121. N. A. Krivova, 'The Events in Shuia: A Turning Point in the Assault on the Church', *Russian Studies in History*, 46:2 (2007), 8–38.
122. Edward E. Roslof, *Red Priests: Renovationism, Russian Orthodoxy, and Revolution, 1905–1946* (Bloomington: Indiana University Press, 2002).
123. Gregory Freeze, 'Counter-Reformation in Russian Orthodoxy: Popular Response to Religious Innovation, 1922–1925', *Slavic Review*, 54:2 (1995), 305–39.
124. A. Iu. Minakov, 'Sektanty i revoliutsiia', < http://dl.biblion.realin.ru/text/14_Disk_EPDS_-_vse_seminarskie_konspekty/Uchebnye_materialy_1/sekt_novosibirsk/Documents/sekt_revol.html>.
125. Mustafa Tuna, *Imperial Russia's Muslims: Islam, Empire, and European Modernity, 1788–1914* (Cambridge: Cambridge University Press, 2015), 237.
126. Daniel Peris, *Storming the Heavens: The Soviet League of the Militant Godless* (Ithaca, NY: Cornell University Press, 1998).
127. Nina Tumarkin, *Lenin Lives! The Lenin Cult in Soviet Russia* (Cambridge, MA: Harvard University Press, 1983).
128. N. Valentinov, *Novaia ekonomicheskaia politika i krizis partii posle smerti Lenina* (Stanford, CA: Stanford University Press, 1971), 91.
129. Sheila Fitzpatrick, *Everyday Stalinism: Ordinary Life in Extraordinary Times: Soviet Russia in the 1930s* (Oxford: Oxford University Press, 1999), 224–5.
130. Stephen Kotkin, *Magnetic Mountain: Stalinism as a Civilization* (Berkeley: University of California Press, 1997), 198–237.
131. Robert C. Tucker, *Stalin in Power: The Revolution from Above, 1928–1941* (New York: W. W. Norton, 1990).

Conclusion

1. The phrase was Lenin's. See V. I. Lenin, 'Our Tasks and the Soviet of Workers' Deputies', 2–4 Nov. 1905, in *Lenin Collected Works* (Moscow: Progress, 1965), 10. 17–28.
2. Lynne Viola, 'Collectivization in the Soviet Union: Specificities and Modalities', in Constantin Iordachi and Arnd Bauerkämper (eds), *The Collectivization of Agriculture in Communist Eastern Europe: Comparison and Entanglements* (Budapest: Central European University Press, 2014), 49–78 (64–5).
3. Ronald Suny suggests that empire is 'a composite state in which the centre dominates the periphery to the latter's disadvantage'. Ronald G. Suny, 'Ambiguous Categories: States, Empires and Nations', *Post-Soviet Affairs*, 11:2 (1995), 185–96 (187).
4. Peter Holquist, 'Violent Russia'.
5. Zygmunt Bauman, *Modernity and the Holocaust* (Cambridge: Polity, 1989), 13; David L. Hoffmann, *Cultivating the Masses: Modern State Practices and Soviet Socialism, 1914–1939* (Ithaca, NY: Cornell University Press, 2011).
6. Landis, *Bandits*.
7. Liudmila G. Novikova, 'Russia's Red Revolutionary and White Terror: A Provincial Perspective', *Europe-Asia Studies*, 65:9 (2013), 1755–70.
8. Felix Schnell, *Räume des Schreckens: Gewalt und Gruppenmilitanz in der Ukraine, 1905–1933* (Hamburg: Hamburger Edition, 2012); Stefan Plaggenborg, 'Gewalt und Militanz in Sowjetrußland 1917–1930', *Jahrbucher fur Geschichte Osteuropas*, 44 (1996), 409–30.
9. Stephen P. Frank, *Crime, Cultural Conflict, and Justice in Rural Russia, 1856–1914* (Berkeley: University of California Press, 1999), 245–8.
10. Trotsky, *History of the Russian Revolution*, vol. 2, ch. 32.
11. 'L'Odeur de ce charnier', 25 Nov. 1912, *La Dépêche de Toulouse*, in Jean-Pierre Roux (ed.), *Jean Jaurès: Rallumer tous les soleils* (Paris: Omnibus, 2006), 880.

PICTURE CREDITS

Sovfoto/UIG/age footstock: **7.2**, **7.3**; akg-images/ullstein bild: **5.2**; GL Archive/Alamy Stock Photo: **3.3**; Ian Dagnall Computing/Alamy Stock Photo: **4.3**; Pictorial Press Ltd/Alamy Stock Photo: **6.1**; World History Archives/Alamy Stock Photo: **3.1**; The Art Archive/Private Collection/CCI: **4.1**; Tallandier/Bridgeman Images: **7.7**; Süddeutsche Zeitung Photo/Mary Evans Picture Library: **7.1**; Bettmann/Getty Images: **1.2**; Heritage Images/Getty Images: **1.1**; Laski Diffusion/Newsmakers/Getty Images: **1.3**; Tow/Slava Katamidze Collection/Getty Images: **4.2**; ullstein bild/Getty Images: **1.4**; Walter Gircke/ullstein bild/Getty Images: **7.4**; Universal History Archive/UIG via Getty Images: **7.5**; The Graduate Institute of International and Development Papers, Geneva - Boris Souvarine Papers: **3.2**; RIA Novosti/TopFoto: **5.1**, **7.6**

INDEX